"Eloquent, learned, driven by deep conviction of the truth of Scripture and passion for its beauty, these sermons display the virtues associated with great preaching of the past, yet the style is fresh and wholly contemporary. This volume is the fruit of a life dedicated to biblical preaching. Rutledge calls for 'a complete overhaul of preaching,' and — what is much more — she shows us how to proceed with that work."

— **ELLEN F. DAVIS**
Duke Divinity School

"Fleming Rutledge is wonderfully lucid and engaging, robust and thoughtful. Her readings of the Old Testament nourish and challenge both heart and mind in today's world."

— **WALTER MOBERLY**
Durham University

"In her sermons Fleming Rutledge hits just the right chords of challenge, biblical fidelity, and graciousness. I love her style and her overall approach, and there is much to be learned from her specific applications."

— **PHILIP YANCEY**
author of *What Good Is God?*

# And God Spoke to Abraham

## PREACHING FROM
## THE OLD TESTAMENT

### Fleming Rutledge

WILLIAM B. EERDMANS PUBLISHING COMPANY

GRAND RAPIDS, MICHIGAN / CAMBRIDGE, U.K.

Published 2011 by

Wm. B. Eerdmans Publishing Co.

2140 Oak Industrial Drive N.E., Grand Rapids, Michigan 49505 /

P.O. Box 163, Cambridge CB3 9PU U.K.

Printed in the United States of America

17  16  15  14  13  12  11      7  6  5  4  3  2  1

**Library of Congress Cataloging-in-Publication Data**

Rutledge, Fleming.

And God spoke to Abraham: preaching from the Old Testament / Fleming Rutledge.

p.      cm.

ISBN 978-0-8028-6606-6 (pbk.: alk. paper)

1. Bible. O.T. — Sermons.

2. Episcopal Church — Sermons.

3. Sermons, American — 21st century.

4. Sermons, American — 20th century.   I. Title.

BS1151.55.R88   2011

221.6 — dc23

2011027516

www.eerdmans.com

*Dedicated to the members of*
*the Wednesday Morning Women's Bible Study*
*at Grace Church in New York*

*1981-1995*

# Contents

## Contents

# Contents

## Contents

# Contents

# Acknowledgments

There are many in biblical scholarship to whom I owe a profound and lasting debt of gratitude. Chief among them are two men whom I met in seminary, though not in life: Brevard Childs and Gerhard von Rad. These two were *biblical theologians* of the highest order, and the work of Childs in rethinking the church's interpretation of the biblical canon will be remembered as one of the most significant theological contributions to the preaching and teaching of Scripture in the past hundred years.[1] Going back farther, I will never forget the powerful effect that Bernhard Anderson's first edition of *Understanding the Old Testament* had upon me when I was in college. John Bright's *History of Israel* was even more formative for me in later years. From my seminary days I thankfully name my late professors Samuel Terrien, for his theology of the *deus absconditus* (the God who hides himself), and Edmund Steimle, who in teaching homiletics insisted upon full commitment to preaching the Old Testament. More recently, two mentors in the field of Old Testament who have helped me personally are my friends Patrick Miller and Ellen Davis, both of whom have encouraged me tremendously in the publication of this book.

When I assembled this collection, I discovered that my thoughts were continually of the congregations to whom these sermons were preached —

---

1. As Christopher Seitz has recently noted, Childs's influence is presently declining in the world of the academic guilds. I am, however, convinced that *sub specie aeternitatis* his contributions have been of incomparable benefit to the church.

especially those where I have been privileged to spend extended time. I am particularly thankful to have spent fourteen years in the pulpit of Grace Church in New York, where many of these sermons were heard with an enthusiasm that says more about the depth of that congregation's commitment than it does about the skills of the preacher. Indeed, without that commitment this book would not exist, because I had long since lost many of the sermons. Two members of Grace Church, Richard Scalera and Margaret Lee, spent countless hours finding them and getting them into shape for the publisher. Words can't sufficiently express my gratitude to these two tireless servants of the Word and of God's people.

I am also thankful for the opportunity to preach many sermons at Christ Church in Sheffield, Massachusetts, during the rectorship of my dear friend Susan Crampton. The present rector in Sheffield, Annie Ryder, performed a great service to me in publishing this book by performing the taxing labor of proofreading all 436 pages of it, and I am deeply indebted to her.[2]

It would be difficult to name all of the other churches of various denominations where I have preached, because there are so many, but my appreciation for them is profound.[3] It is a great privilege to be invited as a guest preacher, and I have particularly fond memories of the parishioners who have received me as a guest in their homes on these occasions.

All of my books have been published by Eerdmans, and I am grateful, as always, to the house for its consistent quality. Mary Hietbrink has been my editor twice, and I appreciate her patience, good spirit, and good humor as much as I do her thoroughness. Willem Mineur has done all my dust jackets, and he is not only a first-rate designer but a joy to work with. My friend Roger VanHarn did double duty by reading about sixty-five sermons and deciding which ones to leave out, a service that readers will doubtless appreciate!

There are three people whom I want to acknowledge in a special way. My sister Betsy McColl, who loves the gospel message as much as anyone I know, has scrutinized a good many of these sermons with her gimlet eye and has often suggested that I add more explanatory footnotes. Sometimes I obeyed her and sometimes not. For instance, where I referred to "our great-

2. This parish is now distinguished for being a successfully conjoined Episcopal-Lutheran congregation under Annie Ryder's leadership.
3. At St. John's in Salisbury, Connecticut, I was privileged to preach almost every Sunday for a year (from 1996 to 1997). Most of those sermons have been published in previous collections.

est poet," she urged me to "remember the math majors" and identify William Shakespeare! Seriously, there is no one who has encouraged me more, not only by reading sermons but, more important, by her loyalty to the one, holy, catholic, and apostolic church and her wholehearted commitment to the faith of the God of Abraham, Isaac, and Jacob. She and I together give thanks for the many devout Christians who were our family relatives and ancestors. A bronze plaque dedicated to them in Christ Church, Charlottesville, says, "These kept the faith." May it be so of our descendants as well.

My husband, Dick, it should be said a hundred times, has not merely encouraged me; his unflagging support has made it all possible. With him, also, I share the indissoluble bond of faith and hope. His devotion to the well-being of the Church of Christ and its Sunday worship has been a constant of his life for decades. His commitment to the increase of the knowledge of the Lord, especially among men (who, in our time, are greatly outnumbered by women in the pews) has been an inspiration to many.

The third person is Pennie Curry, a formidably gifted and assiduous student of the Bible in her own right, and the most devoted friend to Dick and me, and to our family, that could possibly be imagined. She is among the fifty-odd members of the Wednesday Morning Women's Bible Study at Grace Church, 1981-1985, to whom this book is dedicated. At one point, the oldest member of the group was eighty-six and the youngest was twenty-one — and a similar range of ages continued throughout the fourteen years that I was privileged to be with them. Because it was New York City, some of the women had full-time jobs (including those in the performing arts), yet were on flexible schedules that permitted a morning commitment. Several were mothers of young children. Not all were Episcopalians — there were Catholics, Lutherans, nondenominational evangelicals, and others, including uncommitted seekers. The central core was made up of a group of older women who served, in some cases, almost as surrogate mothers to the younger ones. It was a miraculous coming together in the Spirit, and I count it as one of the most significant experiences of my life.

*Rye Brook, New York*
*July 2010*

# *Introduction*

## The Unique Significance of the Old Testament

Even as a very small child, I was mesmerized by the Old Testament. My grandmother and my aunt, who lived only three blocks away, read it to me constantly, always from the King James Version.[1] I particularly remember some of the Psalms; the "hart panting after the water-brooks" was a favorite image. Most of all, the stories with their unforgettable characters — Joseph, Moses, Ruth, Elijah, Samuel, Esther, Daniel — bored their way into my consciousness. As I have grown older, I find that my love for the Old Testament has only increased, with depth and breadth added as I have pondered the prophets and the Wisdom literature in addition to the Pentateuch, the histories, and the Psalms that I learned as a child. The Old Testament, with its undergirding revelation of the power of the Word of God, has strongly

---

1. We are constantly told that the King James Version is impossible for modern people to understand, or irrecoverably archaic and alien. "We don't talk like that anymore," a clergyman said to me not long ago, dismissing a suggestion that it be retained in worship on occasion. Yet as far as I know, no one is seriously proposing modernizing the language of Shakespeare (though nothing would surprise me). Until very recently, the KJV was exclusively used in African-American churches, and a great many African-Americans did indeed "talk like that." It was only a few years ago that I myself heard a black person say, "They know not what they do." She was not quoting the Lord directly; she was using his words *contextually* to explain her own attitude of forgiveness. If she had said, "They don't know what they're doing," it would have become simply a personal statement without dominical authority or biblical resonance.

directed the course of my more recent preaching. As I have been called upon more frequently to teach younger preachers, it has become more clear to me than ever that the church cannot teach homiletics at all without the revelatory Old Testament declaration *Thus says the Lord.*

## The Operating System

It is true to say that we can't understand the New Testament without the Old, but that is an inadequate account of its importance. I have heard the Old Testament described as the operating system for the New Testament, and that seems to me to be the very best way of conveying its unique, indispensable significance. The Second Testament simply will not work without its engine; it is "powered on" by it. Without the primary declaration *And God said . . . ,* the New Testament is disconnected from its source. Without the calling of Israel, the story of Jesus has no context. Without the Law and the Prophets set in motion by the God who speaks, the New Testament is a house with no foundation, a plant with no roots, a pump with no well.

It is perhaps obvious that the Epistle to the Hebrews is incomprehensible without the Torah, and that Revelation draws deeply from the Old Testament at almost every point, but even more striking is the way that Paul's epistles are grounded in a particularly profound and radical reading of the only Scriptures that Paul knew or needed — a fact about his letters that is insufficiently emphasized. Moreover, it should be noted that in the first decades of the Christian church, "the Scriptures" meant the Hebrew Scriptures, and it is clear that the evangelists, preachers, and converts in those early days felt no need to look elsewhere for an explanation of what had happened in Jesus of Nazareth.[2]

## The Theology of the Old Testament

The indispensability of the Old Testament does not cancel out the problem of its interpretation within the Christian church. The way its text works in

---

2. Within a few decades, to be sure, the need arose for a written scripture about the life of Jesus, as the introduction to Luke's Gospel indicates. But this does not obviate the point that the Hebrew Scriptures provided the earliest Christians with a full theological background and explanation for understanding what had happened to them.

Christian preaching is fraught with controversy. The urgency of rethinking the church's attitude toward the Scriptures that we read in common with the Jews cannot be overstated. Since the murder of six million Jews in the heart of Christian Europe, we can never again read the Hebrew Scriptures in the same way. At every turn it is imperative that we remember that *the Torah constituted the Jewish community*. We cannot simply appropriate the Old Testament for the church and interpret it Christologically without giving thought and care to what we are doing.

The complementary factor here is that the church is committed to her Lord Jesus Christ.[3] This commitment requires us to read the Old Testament in light of the New. Indeed, it is impossible for a confessing Christian to do otherwise. One can make a strenuous intellectual effort, in good faith, to read and expound the Hebrew Scriptures as though one were not a Christian, and perhaps succeed in this for a while, but in the long term this would mean either abandoning the Christian confession altogether, or presenting ourselves in a false, sentimental way as though we ourselves were Jews. The challenge for Christian interpretation is to acknowledge and celebrate the unique power of the Old Testament in shaping the apostolic faith and the destiny of the church's Lord.

Thus far we have established two things: that the Old Testament is indispensable for the New, and that it is not only possible but vital to preach from the Old Testament for the way it drives the New. But it is also important to teach the Old Testament *for its own sake*. "The scandal of particularity" has been a familiar catch-phrase for many years, but it is still useful, highlighting as it does the unique *historical* features of the biblical story, with its continual references to identifiable, locatable people, places, and events. This particularity, it must be noted, refers *not only* to the historical claims made for Jesus of Nazareth *but also* to the election, within history, of the Jewish people.[4] Respect for the integrity of Jewish heritage is therefore a major reason for allowing the Old Testament to speak with power from pulpit and lectern.

Reverence for the story of Israel in light of the past hundred years is

---

3. I use "her" for the church advisedly, remembering not only the New Testament image of the "Bride of Christ" but also the imagery of the Old Testament prophets (especially Hosea, Jeremiah, and Ezekiel) who repeatedly portray the fugitive Israelites as those whom God shaped into a people and "married" in the desert.

4. I regret that there is no sermon in this collection on the book of Esther. The place of this book in the canon of Scripture guarantees the importance of the physical survival of the Jews within the plan of God, and it warns us to guard against an exclusively spiritualized concept of the chosen people.

not, however, the only compelling reason for a deep commitment to the entirety of the Old Testament. An even more compelling reason is a *theological one: the church's need for a comprehensive view of who God is.* Thus we must read the New Testament in light of the Old.[5]

In Romans 3:2-4, the apostle Paul calls on the only scripture that he knows — namely, what we call the Old Testament — in order to speak authoritatively of his theme, the righteousness *(dikaiosune)* of God (Rom. 1:17). Paul quotes Psalm 51: "Let God be true though every man be false, as it is written, 'that God may be justified *[dikaiosune]* in his words.'" Paul wishes to guard against a possible misunderstanding of the new community's relationship to "the oracles of God" entrusted to the Jews (Rom. 1:2). He sees no need to redefine the righteousness of God as he has received it from the Scriptures; instead, he identifies it with the climactic, decisive action of God in Christ. This is a particularly striking example of the way that the earliest Christians embraced the theological continuity between the God of Israel and the Triune God revealed in Jesus Christ. We may also see it in the first chapter of the Epistle to the Hebrews, where the writer links the speaking of God through the Old Testament prophets to his speaking through his Son "in these last days" as though that continuity were a foregone conclusion.[6] A third example is the Prologue of the Gospel of John, which is linked in a very obvious and intentional way to Genesis 1, as if to fasten the two creative acts of the Word together permanently, each interpreting the other.

These New Testament examples are only a handful from a virtually endless series of illustrations that can be given. For the Christians of the first century, it was self-evident that "the scriptures" were the "living and active" Word of God (Heb. 4:12). It was only later that a distinction began to

5. "God's word to Israel is the first-order inheritance for those adopted in Christ, the fully sufficient and necessary broker of God's very self to Israel and the world. Whatever authority the New Testament will in time come to possess is no rival to such a view, but is based on it, without which its corollary claim to be scripture, alongside that first scripture, is groundless." See Christopher Seitz, *Word Without End* (Grand Rapids: Wm. B. Eerdmans, 1998), p. 50.

6. A caveat belongs here. The word *continuity* should not be over-interpreted. I mean it to signify that the God of the Old and New Testaments is the same God. The letters of Paul show something more. The Apostle preaches that God in Christ has constituted an entirely new world order where the righteousness *(dikaiosune)* of God abolishes the old order in which religious human beings (of every persuasion) contrive to stand on their own spiritual achievements. In that sense, *dis*continuity is the word. The point for the study and proclamation of the Old Testament is that Paul found this gospel prefigured in the Old Testament text — as shown, for instance, in his repeated invocation of the figure of Abraham.

[ 4 ]

be made by some between the Testaments, with Marcion (d. A.D. 160) as the most extreme example. One of Paul's most radical disciples, he proposed a drastic renunciation of the Old Testament and its Law. (It has been said of Marcion that he understood Paul so well that he misunderstood him.) He was perhaps the first to articulate the supposed distinction between the "wrathful Jewish God" of the Old Testament and the loving God of Jesus Christ.[7] The teaching of Marcion was decisively repudiated by the orthodox church in A.D. 144, but the insidious tendency to reject or downgrade the Old Testament on the grounds of its inferiority is with us still.

### The Necessity of the Old Testament for Knowing God

This is an urgent matter because of several trends in the churches of our time:

- There is a trend toward a "Jesus *kerygma*"[8] that focuses almost exclusively on the person and teachings of Jesus, distilled from the narratives of the Gospels when they are stripped of their Christology (as if that could actually be done). More to the point here, the "Jesus *kerygma*" neglects the God of Israel, with whom Jesus lived in intimate communion and whom he called his Father.
- There is a corresponding ignorance in our congregations not only of the content of the Old Testament, but also of the prodigious God whom it sets forth. More concretely, there are intrinsic, inalienable features of God in the Old Testament which we would not be able to extract from the New Testament taken by itself. Some of the most important of these are the following:
  - the *aseity* (being-from-himself) of God
  - the concept of the performative Word of God
  - the righteousness of God as both noun and verb
  - the election of Israel

7. This contrast, all too frequently drawn, requires not only the ignoring of large parts of the Old Testament but also a willful disregard of the many passages of judgment in the words of Jesus.

8. *Kerygma,* in Greek, means "announcement" or "proclamation." It is used as a technical term for the preaching of the church, particularly the New Testament church. More to the point, it can be used to denote the message of the gospel, or *evanggelion* (good news), as distinguished from didactic instruction. Instruction can and should be undertaken by preachers, but always in the context of and guided by the *kerygma.*

– God's "jealousy" and the nonexistence of other gods
– the identity of God as Lawgiver

The sermons in this collection take up many of these themes as they appear in Old Testament texts. The importance of this attention given to the Old Testament can hardly be exaggerated, because in spite of the greatly increased attention being given — as a result of the Holocaust — to our relationship with the Jews, our familiarity with the God who chose the Jews to be his people has not increased. Indeed, it is remarkable how many Christians continue, unthinkingly, to speak of "the God of the Old Testament" as though this supposedly wrathful and judgmental God had been supplanted by an endlessly tolerant and indulgent Jesus. This ill-informed attitude is not exactly anti-Semitic, but it can be called into the service of anti-Semitism.

It is remarkable how much has changed within the mainline churches in recent years. During the first decade of my ministry, parishioners frequently told me that they were uncomfortable with my frequent evocation of the name of Jesus. Among Episcopalians, this was considered suspiciously *déclassé;* only backwoods, tent-revival evangelists called upon "*Jee*-sus." I never hear that complaint anymore. On the contrary, the "Jesus *kerygma*" now dominates the scene. The complaints I hear now are likely to be based on objections to the *Christology* of the New Testament, now considered in many circles to be a discredited layer of interpretation that needs to be peeled back. More to the point in the present context, however, "Jesus" has been disassociated from the concrete and specific God revealed in the Old Testament, so that *theo*logy (*theos* — God) takes a back seat to various *anthropo*logically centered messages. This lends itself well to the current fashion for a greatly reduced "historical" conception of Jesus as Mediterranean Jewish peasant, Galilean sage, shaman, rabbi, "axial" spiritual genius, ethical teacher, incendiary zealot, and so forth — with ample attention given to his Jewish milieu but very little accorded to the One who "keeping watch over Israel neither slumbers nor sleeps" (Ps. 121:4).

These reflections were jump-started when, recently, a thoughtful man in a congregation where I had preached several sermons commented that I seemed to speak more often of God than of Jesus. Recognizing that his observation was true, I pondered this for several months, wondering whether it was owing to the fact that I had been concentrating on the Old Testament, or reacting against the "Jesus *kerygma*," or something more complicated. Then I came across something that was written about John Calvin. When Calvin speaks of "God," he always means the Three-Personed, Trinitarian God, the Father of our Lord Jesus Christ, and no other God. That was the clue I was looking for.

Since then, the more I have preached from the Old Testament, the less necessary it has become to refer explicitly to God the Son in every sermon. We have had too restricted a sense of the revelation of the Triune God found in the Law and the Prophets. If the God of Abraham, Isaac, and Jacob is truly the Father of our Lord Jesus Christ, then the witness of the entire Scripture is a seamless garment. No change within God occurred in the intertestamental period; there is no break in the revelation of God's self, as though there had been an alteration in God.[9]

This commitment to both Testaments — the entire canon of Scripture — is not to suggest that we should not listen to the individual biblical voices in their distinct form. The variety in the Old Testament — from the narratives of the patriarchs to the court history of 1-2 Samuel to the poetry of the Song of Songs to the contentions of Amos and beyond — could hardly be overstated. I hope that the attention given in these sermons to these varying voices will help to demonstrate some of the ways in which these multivocal messages can be heard in all their diversity while still proclaiming univocally, "Hear, O Israel, the Lord our God, the Lord is One."[10]

Brevard Childs sums up the argument:

> What binds the testaments indissolubly together is their witness to the selfsame divine reality . . . which undergirds both collections, and cannot be contained within the domesticating categories of "religion." Scripture . . . points beyond itself to the reality of God. The ability to render this reality is to enter the "strange new world of the Bible" [which tells] the entrance of God's word into our world of time and space.[11]

9. Again, I do not mean to suggest that nothing radical occurred with the incarnation of the Son. The passages in Matthew 5 ("it was said to the men of old . . . but I say to you") point to the way in which Christ has become "the end of the Law" (Rom. 10:4). "God has done what the Law, weakened by the flesh, could not do: sending his own Son in the likeness of sinful flesh and for sin, he condemned sin in the flesh, in order that the just requirement of the law might be fulfilled in us who walk not according to the flesh but according to the Spirit" (Rom. 8:3-4). The relation of humanity to God under the law has been entirely overhauled by the new rule of faith in Christ, whose righteousness rectifies (justifies — same root, *dikaiosune*) the believer. The point to note in this context is that *the God who is doing this is the same God who gave the Law and called the prophets.*

10. Deuteronomy 6:4 — the Jewish confession of faith, called the *Shema.*

11. Brevard Childs, *Biblical Theology of the Old and New Testaments* (Minneapolis: Fortress Press, 1993), p. 721. The phrase "the strange new world of the Bible" is taken from Karl Barth's fa-

### The Theme of the Divine Agency

It is sometimes said, rather fatuously, that a preacher has one basic sermon that he or she preaches over and over. I've always thought that was insulting not only to preachers but also to the inexhaustible riches of the Scriptures. It is true, however, that there are some biblical themes that predominate, and thus there is necessarily some repetition. The theme of the divine agency, so often overlooked or misunderstood, is certainly a principal motif in these sermons, as it is an omnipresent presupposition in the Bible.

Much preaching today is *anthropo*logical rather than *theo*logical. In an anthropological sermon, the acting subject is the human being with his hopes, needs, wishes, and religious longings, rather than the God who moves in on human beings whether they have spiritual inclinations or not. In an anthropological sermon, the central appeal is made to the human decision. More and more, the central theological divide in the churches has to do with this matter of the acting subject: is it us, or is it God? When John Donne wrote the sonnet "Batter My Heart, Three-Person'd God," he was aligning himself with Augustine, Luther, and Calvin, who wrote so powerfully of the imprisonment of the human will and its need for deliverance from outside itself. This is the biblical diagnosis of the human predicament, and there is no antidote to it from within the world, which, as the baptismal service used to say, is the realm of sin, the flesh, and the devil.[12]

When the sermons in this book are taken as a whole, it should become clear that the Old Testament is being read in a particular way. This is, of course, inevitable; it would be disingenuous to pretend that any reading of the Old Testament could be context-free. Nevertheless, it is possible to argue that some interpretations are more governed *by the text itself* than are others. When an interpreter assumes that the thoughts expressed by the biblical writers are their own thoughts in disguise, she can believe that if she chooses, but it is dishonest to put this idea forward as though it was faithful to the intention of the Bible itself. In other words, if we interpret "Thus says the Lord" to mean "This is what an ancient storyteller *thought* that God said, or ought to have said," then we have entirely lost the biblical

mous essay by that name. I am particularly grateful for Childs's commentary on Exodus and his more recent book, *The Struggle to Understand Isaiah as Christian Scripture.* Childs was committed to helping preachers to declare the Old Testament message according to a rule of faith.

12. The older service included this response by the sponsors: "I will, God being my helper." The newer service, removing the verb *to be*, weakens this to "I will, with God's help." In both cases, however, the intention is to affirm the impotence of the human will without God's intervention.

text's sense of itself. The reader does not have to *believe* the testimony of the Bible in order to recognize the claims intrinsic to it. The writers of the Old Testament did not write a story of "man's search for God." What they wrote was, emphatically, *God's search for us.* Throughout the Bible, God is overwhelmingly the subject of the verbs, not the object of humanity's religious longings.

The subject of the verbs in a sermon, therefore, should largely be God. God is not lying back on a cloud waiting to see if we will straighten ourselves out. Behold, God is "coming forth out of his place" (Isa. 26:21). These collected sermons, therefore, even with their manifest deficiencies, are a witness to God not as the object of our journeys but as the acting subject directing them. This is the God of the Old Testament and the New.

### Fear and Love

John Donne, who I would argue was the greatest preacher ever in the English language, delivered a sermon on Psalm 34:11: "Come, ye children, hearken unto me; I will teach you the fear of the Lord." In nineteenth-century America, it was still commonly said that children needed to be taught the fear of the Lord; I personally remember hearing this as recently as the 1940s. In this generation, however, it is very difficult to recover this sense of the fear of the Lord, since "fear" has taken on a wholly negative connotation in regard to God. Instead, young people today crave fear in the form of horror movies, which are widely marketed to them. Biblical fear, of course, has little in common with terror of this sort. Donne shows that "true" fear is distinguished from "false" fear: "he that fears God fears nothing else." The true fear of God is closely linked with love.

In his sermon "The Fear of the Lord," preached in 1624, Donne quotes Augustine: "There is the slightest difference between the testaments, fear and love" *(Brevissima differentia testamentorium, timor et amor).* This would seem to be an impeccable patristic source for the notion that we have just rejected — namely, that the fearsome Old Testament God is to be rejected in favor of the loving Father of Jesus. This is not what Augustine intended, however, and Donne in his spellbinding sermon (which must have taken at least forty-five minutes to deliver) shows what the relation of the Testaments truly is. He "shows" in the fashion of the dictum "Don't *tell* me; *show* me!" Donne's special gift in "showing" was to weave the biblical text in and out of his own text so that one is scarcely distinguishable from the other.[13] When he has finished, the text is fixed in your mind permanently.

Here is the ending of Donne's "The Fear of the Lord":

[As Augustine wrote] the Old Testament is a Testament of fear, the New of love; yet in this they grow all one, that we determine the Old Testament in the New, and that we prove the New Testament by the Old. . . . So the two Testaments grow one Bible; so in these two affections, if there were not a jealousy, a fear of losing God, we could not love him; nor can we fear to lose him, except [unless] we do love him . . . for this fear is inchoative love, and this love is consummative fear. The love of God begins in fear, and the fear of God ends in love; and that love can never end, for God is love.[14]

## Problems Associated with the Old Testament Today

### *What to Call It?*

There is considerable disagreement about how we are to refer to the Old Testament, especially in Christian worship. In mainline Protestant churches, it is quite common now to hear "the Hebrew Scriptures" used to introduce the first reading. This raises serious questions about Christian appropriation of the Jewish Tanakh with insufficient respect for the variations. I refer especially to the way the books are arranged in the Tanakh, which is significantly different from the arrangement in the Christian Old Testament, wherein the messianic prophecies from Malachi — evoking the return of Elijah — dramatically conclude the canonical collection. When the "Writings," which form the third and final section of the Tanakh, are moved to the center as they are in the Christian Old Testament, a quite different impression is given. Closing the canon with the prophetic books points forward to the Day of the Lord and an eschatological hope in a way that the Writings do not.

Some are using the terms "First Testament" and "Second Testament,"

---

13. Sadly, many people have difficulty reading Donne today. For various cultural reasons, our ability to follow a complex sentence is profoundly reduced.

14. Donne's sermon is found in Ellen F. Davis's anthology titled *Imagination Shaped: Old Testament Preaching in the Anglican Tradition* (Valley Forge, Pa.: Trinity Press International, 1995), pp. 95-113.

which avoids the difficulty with "Hebrew Scriptures." However, the larger question has to do with the way in which the Christian community expresses its desire to avoid offending Jews. We are living in a time when the church's outreach to Jews coincides with ever-increasing ignorance of the content of the actual Hebrew legacy. The well-meant intention of the Revised Common Lectionary to redress this problem by assigning larger portions of the Old Testament to be read in worship has met with limited success, in my observation. In the mainline church environment of today, it is much easier to find information about Celtic spirituality, labyrinth-walking, Jungian dream interpretation, the latest findings of the Jesus seminar, and other such eclectic topics than it is to find in-depth teaching about the Old Testament.

In any case, I have consulted several leading Old Testament scholars from our major seminaries, and they have unanimously expressed preference, sometimes in emphatic terms, for the traditional Christian term "Old Testament." I am therefore continuing to use it with confidence.


### Problems Posed by the Lectionary

In recent years, the mainline churches have become increasingly dependent on a common lectionary for worship and preaching on Sundays.[15] An Old Testament text is always indicated, and yet sermons on Old Testament texts have become increasingly infrequent. Many preachers, especially in my own Episcopal denomination, routinely base their Sunday sermons on a passage from the Synoptic Gospels; some have even assumed that it is a rule! In an age when biblical illiteracy is widespread even in the church, the Old Testament has fallen into the background and, in some poorly informed circles, has even become suspect. This may or may not be the result of lectionary use, but it has happened concurrently with its widespread adoption.[16]

There is a running discussion among preachers about choosing sermon texts. Some are wedded to the Sunday lectionary, while others find it re-

15. The Revised Common Lectionary is in widespread use in the mainline churches at present.

16. In the Episcopal Church there are three readings — one from the Old Testament, one from the Epistles, and one from a Gospel — plus a Psalm every Sunday. This has led Episcopalians to boast that they hear more Scripture than any other denomination. The downside of this is that there is less time for homiletical exposition of the texts, and that it is not possible to attend closely to more than one or at most two texts at a time. Too much can be too little.

stricting.[17] I preached exclusively from the common lectionary for the first twenty-five years of my preaching career and found it enriching in many ways, especially as it contributed to a sense of the liturgical year.[18] Another great virtue of the lectionary is that it sometimes forces the preacher to come to terms with passages that would not have been chosen otherwise. Conversely, it is often noted that it forbids the systematic exposition of one book at a time, a practice that has distinguished some of the greatest preachers of history. Admittedly, it is possible, using the lectionary, to do a series of sermons on a few books, although one is restricted to the times and seasons that the lectionary dictates — the dog days of summer may not be the best time for a series on Romans, for instance, though I have participated in such a series more than once. There is no opportunity in the lectionaries currently in use to preach through any Old Testament book.

Another serious problem presented by the lectionary is that of the omissions. Those who chose the passages have signaled by their omissions a particular attitude toward Scripture. In innumerable cases, difficult passages have been skipped over, elided, or ignored. A sign of our times is that these portions are frequently related to the subject of judgment, one that our present culture wishes to avoid. Even those who would prefer not to preach on, or hear about, this theme have begun to notice that its absence says something about our culture of permissiveness. Perhaps that is one reason that some preachers look forward not only to Advent, but to the Sundays just before Advent, when the theme of judgment has managed to survive in the appointed texts.

The Revised Common Lectionary has presented preachers with yet another problem, doubtless unanticipated. Whereas the older lectionary featured Old Testament passages that spoke to the Gospel reading, the Old Testament readings are now likely to be independent of the others. Since the Old Testament lessons are frequently long and attention-getting, the effect is unsettling. It feels strange to hear the entire story of Naboth's vineyard (for instance) read on Sunday morning, followed by a Psalm and two New Testament readings and a sermon on the Gospel reading. It shows no respect for the Old Testament passage when it is left unexpounded.

The most serious problem with the lectionary is the lack of context.

17. If one was preaching from the Daily Office lectionary, a much more comprehensive survey of Scripture would be required.

18. I am speaking here of the Episcopal Church Book of Common Prayer lectionary, which was shared by several other denominations until the Revised Common Lectionary overtook it in popularity.

When everyone is reading from a printed sheet, no one is learning where in the Bible the passage is located, or how it is linked to what comes before it and after it. A whole generation of churchgoers is being raised with no sense of actually handling the Bible, of finding the passage and reading it in its sequence. The large Bibles on the lecterns are sitting unused, their pages gathering dust; some have been removed altogether. The wonderful sight of the reader mounting up to the lectern and turning the pages to find the place is seldom seen today in Episcopal churches; the readers come up with flimsy little pieces of paper which for the most part will be left in the pew or thrown away.

The lectionary has certain advantages, but concentration on one book at a time, in its total context, encourages biblical literacy more than shifting every week from one to another.[19] Because of the crucial need to provide context, seriousness, and continuity in biblical proclamation, a preacher is blessed when he or she has a steady pulpit from which to preach on most Sundays. When one is preaching every Lord's Day to the same congregation, one can take one's time to expound a whole book. One of the preachers I most admire has recently preached all the way through Ecclesiastes and Jonah, to very eager congregations. Moreover, the hearers were expected to follow along in a copy of the actual Bible, rather than from a printed excerpt.[20] This sort of expository preaching is not a model for everyone in every place, but surely it should be considered; the present lectionary-based system is not improving the knowledge and understanding of the Bible among Christians.

## The Sermons and How to Read Them

This collection is offered to illustrate one preacher's encounter with the Old Testament over a period of thirty-five years (1975-2010) in a variety of settings. I am well aware that sermon collections can be faulted on a number of accounts. This one can be criticized for various reasons: there is too

19. Perhaps the numerous preachers who almost always preach from the Synoptic Gospels are working partly from the need for continuity in the exposition of one book at a time. This, however, does not solve the problem of the neglect of the Old Testament, the Epistles, and to some extent John's Gospel as well.

20. It is sad to relate that the placement of Bibles in the pews of certain Episcopal churches has been strenuously resisted by some members, and in some cases has caused serious breaches in the congregation. The appearance of the Bible in the pew seems, for some people, to signal a move to the religious right.

much emphasis on some texts and not enough on others; some books of the Old Testament are represented far more than others; the quality of the sermons is uneven. I plead guilty to all of these. I hope I am not mistaken, however, in thinking that this particular collection will have some value as an example and an encouragement. I would like to offer whatever help I can to preachers who are struggling through their vocation, listening in season and out of season to the way that the various voices of the Bible speak directly of God to the present situation in the present moment.

There are many different types of sermons in this collection, and I hope that readers will understand that they operate in different contexts and will not judge them according to a single standard. Most of them were originally delivered in parish churches, but others were heard by congregations of a more specialized type. Thus, the ones that were addressed to ordained clergy can be somewhat more like addresses or lectures than sermons. A sermon delivered in a local congregation is quite different from one which was delivered as a keynote for a conference. Some of the sermons are focused on the thorough exposition of particular Old Testament texts; others range more widely through many passages.

There are a few conspicuous repetitions in the sermons, which I have not tried to remove. When preaching over a period of many years on certain passages, as for instance the Abraham saga, there are inevitably some themes that will reappear. For this reason, I urge the general reader to read selectively rather than simply front-to-back. The preacher seeking help, however, might want to read all the sermons from a given text or book. In such a case I ask for indulgence concerning the repetitions.

### The Dispute about Sermon Introductions

More to the point, many of these sermons can be faulted for being insufficiently expository, and that would be a fair criticism. If I had my preaching life to live over again, perhaps I would do it differently. However, I was trained very early (by the great Lutheran preacher Edmund Steimle) to use the first minutes of the sermon for reeling in the congregation by calling up the text into the contemporary setting. This, of course, takes time away from strict exposition. Karl Barth adamantly opposed introductions in sermons, for this and other reasons. He thought the Scripture as Word of God was paramount and should not be put in second place even for a moment. He was right about that. Rightly or wrongly, however, I have never really departed from the method I was taught. It still seems to me that the narrative arc of a sermon is what sustains the attention of the hearers, so that one can *begin* with the contemporary situation, then focus on the text in some detail before finally allowing the text to speak precisely *into* the contemporary situation.

### *Topical or Universal? The Afterlife of the Printed Sermon*

To a collection of her father's Old Testament sermons, Ursula von Rad contributed a foreword. In it, she explains that the sermons

> . . . quite unmistakably bear the marks of oral address . . . the text [of the collected sermons] can be understood only in terms of the specific situation in which it was written. It is related throughout to a very particular group of hearers and partners in dialogue.

Von Rad's daughter thus acknowledges the very particular nature of the expository biblical sermon as oral address in a specific, unrepeatable setting. She is correct. And yet I have cherished her father's book more than almost any other book of sermons I possess.[21] I do not equate my sermons with von Rad's, but my love for his, even though I do not share their particular context, encourages me to think that mine might be of some use in spite of the way they have been detached from their original time and place.

It is true that printed sermons are second-order proclamation. They are written (if they are written) for the ear, not the eye. And yet over the years I have profited more than I can say from the written sermons of some of the great preachers of the past. I have all of Charles Spurgeon in my laptop. I have a full set of twelve volumes of the sermons of Alexander McLaren and have mined them all. John Calvin's sermons on Job still live today. I picked up a little paperback of sermons on Elijah by F. W. Krummacher, a nineteenth-century preacher whose work influenced me in a very direct way in the sermon "The Little Church in the Wilderness." I have returned again and again to the Old Testament sermons of von Rad.[22]

21. Gerhard von Rad, *Biblical Interpretations in Preaching,* trans. John E. Steely (Nashville: Abingdon Press, 1977).

22. I also recommend von Rad's *God's Work in Israel* (Nashville: Abingdon Press, 1980). This is a collection of lectures, but very helpful for preaching. Although von Rad's *Heilsgeschichte* approach to the Old Testament is no longer considered adequate, his heart for communicating the story of God could hardly be surpassed.

Some of the sermons in this collection are more topical than others. In some cases where current events called for a specific response, this topicality might be seen as a disadvantage. However, the preacher seeking help may find it useful to see examples of the text speaking to every sort of situation, sometimes even in crisis. Instead of changing or eliminating these topical references, I have footnoted them when I, or my helpful editors, thought it was necessary.

## The Arrangement of the Sermons

The sermons are arranged in the order of their texts' placement in the canon of Scripture. The intent of this volume is to be helpful to preachers, and to laypeople who seek assistance with a particular passage. Therefore, the table of contents can be used to find sermons from many of the Old Testament books in their traditional order.

## Sermons with More Than One Text

Frequently the sermons have been based on more than one text. In such cases, I have listed the most important text — the one that controls the sermon — first in the table of contents. If there is another important text, it is listed second. Often there are other texts that play secondary roles: they are not listed.

A very few of the sermons have significant New Testament content. I made a decision in this small number of cases that the Old Testament text played a sufficiently important role to be included here.

## Where the Sermons Were Preached

The earlier sermons (1975-1995) were mostly preached in parish churches. After 1995, I became a peripatetic preacher. Some of the more recent sermons were delivered within my own Episcopal denomination, but many more were addressed to Presbyterian or Methodist congregations, and more still in various seminaries and theological colleges in the United States, Canada, and the United Kingdom. If there are local references in the sermon, I have identified the location. More often, however, I have not done so, hoping for the sermon to have a more general application.

## Sermon Length

Most, though not all, of the sermons collected here would require twenty minutes or more to deliver, and a few as much as thirty minutes. Many of them are from Grace Church in New York, where the congregation in the eighties and nineties was accustomed to long sermons and expected them. Sermons preached on Wednesday night at Grace Church (many of which are included here) were well attended by young adults — artists and professionals in their twenties and thirties who looked forward to the challenging sermons. In the Episcopal Church of the twenty-first century, twenty-minute sermons are increasingly rare. Many of the sermons in this book, however, were delivered in Presbyterian and Methodist pulpits, where greater length is still the custom. Others were given in seminaries and theological colleges, where greater length was expected. One or two sermons have been lengthened specifically for this book, in order to include longer quotations; I have indicated that in the footnotes. In book form, however, none of them should be too long to be read in a single sitting — and that is a chief value of a sermon collection for today's busy but seriously committed Christian.

## The Footnotes

Often I have put material into sermons and then found that I had to take it out to make the sermon shorter. A lot of this material found its way into the footnotes so that I could avoid losing it altogether. I have put a lot of effort into footnoting all the quotations, but in a very few cases, unfortunately, I have lost the references.

## Who Are These Sermons For?

I have two groups in mind: preachers and their hearers. I hope that this collection will provide inspiration and encouragement for pastors who have, perhaps, been wary of preaching from the Old Testament or simply have not made a commitment to it. As for laypeople, many have told me that they find sermon collections helpful because they can read just one, in a brief time, as a devotional as well as an educational exercise. Some of the more recent sermons are more scholarly than others because they were delivered to congregations of clergy and/or seminarians. I have always noted where this is the case.

### *A Note to Preachers*

Some of the sermons are based exclusively on one Old Testament text, whereas others are a combination of two or more. A few are not strictly expository, and I am hesitant to include them, but I hope they will nevertheless serve as examples of conscientious commitment to the living power of the Word even when no one passage governs them. I offer this collection, then, in all its variety, because the way that the Old Testament and the New speak to each other is part of the essence of our faith grounded in the revelation of God to the Hebrew people.

Here is a sample of the way in which I have used (and, I devoutly hope, been used by) various Old Testament texts:

- Some of the sermons that dig deeply into a single Old Testament passage are these:
  – The three sermons from the Elijah cycle
  – The four sermons on Isaiah 28
  – "The Bloody Passageway"
  – "Entertaining Angels Unawares"
  – "The Radical Freedom of God"
- Some of the sermons that range through various Old Testament passages are these:
  – "The Terrors of Grace"
  – "The God of Hurricanes"
  – "Whose Righteousness?"
  – "'Spirituality' or Holy Spirit?"
  – "Patriotism and Prophets"
- Sermons with a significant New Testament component are these:
  – "The Man in the Bed"
  – "Nothing More True"
  – "To Know the Living God" (which directly addresses the relation of the Old Testament to the New)

### *Biblical Translations*

Most of the passages quoted are from the Revised Standard Version. Others used occasionally include the New Revised Standard Version and the King James (Authorized) Version. In the 2010 book *Pen of Iron,* Robert Alter joins the long line of writers who lament the loss of the common language that English-speaking peoples possessed when the KJV was the only translation in common usage. I have used it from time to time, hoping that its grandeur and power will not be completely lost.

## The Role of the Listener

### *Learning to Read the Bible with an Open Heart*

In her book *Imagination Shaped,* Ellen F. Davis quotes John Henry Newman:

> I consider . . . that it is not reason that is against us, but imagination. The mind, after having, to the utter neglect of the Gospels, lived in science, experiences, on coming back to Scripture, an utter strangeness in what it reads.

Davis calls preachers to a vocation of reshaping the imagination of hearers so that they learn once again the language of that "utterly strange" world. She beckons us to a lifetime of thinking in "fundamentally new ways about the presence and power of God." By "new" she does not mean modern rationalism, but the shaping of the imagination so that hearers may enter "the strange new world of the Bible."[23] She gives an example of a sermon in which the miracle of the loaves and fishes becomes a moral lesson about the importance of sharing. This sort of rationalization is characteristic of the post-Enlightenment mind but utterly foreign to the biblical mind. The preacher who pedantically explains that the "Reed Sea" was actually very shallow and subject to tidal fluctuations has completely missed the message. Davis summons the preacher to invite the congregation "to contemplate the multiplication of the loaves and fishes or the parting of the Red Sea *without translating away the wonder.*"[24] Whether I have succeeded in that or not, I do not know; but I have taken heart from her reminder that literal-mindedness is the enemy of biblical interpretation.

It used to be commonly said that a passage or poem was learned "by heart." This lovely phrase suggests something of what the preacher at-

23. Again, this is the frequently cited title of an early essay by Karl Barth.
24. Davis, *Imagination Shaped,* p. 251.

tempts to do when expounding a passage. It is not the same thing as "speaking from the heart" — which preachers are often enjoined to do. Preaching from the *biblical* heart is quite the opposite from declaring the *preacher's* heart, for sermon preparation requires the preacher to set aside his own needs, opinions, and preferences, and allow himself to be reshaped in accordance with the "strange new world" in which God reveals the true nature of reality.

The preacher is not explaining, rationalizing, demythologizing, or deconstructing. Nor is she setting forth "prophetic" truths — a great temptation today in mainline pulpits. Davis follows Charles Rice in suggesting that preaching today needs to be less "heroic" and more "ironic." "Heroic" preaching means that the preacher takes on a degree of self-importance and moral certainty.[25] In such preaching (often erroneously referred to as "prophetic"), the preacher identifies herself closely with the message in a way that will make some hearers feel excluded. "Ironic" preaching, on the other hand, suggests a stance in which the preacher accepts ambiguity and an uncertain future, trusting in the providence of God alone. In "ironic" sermons, it will be clear that the preacher struggles with the same temptations as the hearers.[26] This means that passages will be interpreted from the "heart" with all the vulnerability and uncertainty that suggests, rather than being attached to a political agenda (as in the mainlines) or a declaration of "biblical principles" (as in the evangelical churches). This stance of "heart," which Davis links with imagination, is akin to Keats's concept of "negative capability."[27] It is not in the least sentimental or evasive, but addresses the core of human existence. In so doing, the preacher seeks to listen to the text as a hearer among hearers, so that in the transmission she is simply a channel for the Word, not an authority over it.

---

25. The historian István Deák describes a bad sermon: "a sense of self-righteousness, disdain for different opinions." See *Essays on Hitler's Europe* (Lincoln: University of Nebraska Press, 2001), p. 103.

26. Early in my ministry I delivered a sermon on a particular issue that was disturbing to the congregation. It must have had all the unfortunate traits of "heroic" preaching, because afterwards one of the lay leaders said, "You're way ahead of the rest of us." He did not mean it as a compliment. I never forgot that. May God deliver the preacher from sounding as if she is "way ahead" of the congregation.

27. ". . . negative capability, that is when man is capable of being in uncertainties, mysteries, doubts, without any irritable reaching after fact and reason." Keats, quoted in Aileen Ward, *John Keats: The Making of a Poet* (New York: Viking, 1963), p. 161.

## Introduction

### *Preacher and Hearers Together*

As has already been pointed out, many of these sermons were single-shot offerings, delivered at conferences and convocations where the congregation and the preacher come together for a day or a weekend and then never see one another again. These occasions are often designed specifically for the edification of seminary students and parish clergy who are seeking to become better preachers. Generally speaking, however, these are not the best settings for sermons, because biblical preaching uses the language of relationship. It is engendered from the Word of the God who is love. I once heard about a wise older preacher correcting a young pastor who said, "I love to preach!" The older man said, "It is far more important to love the people among whom you preach."

The best setting for preaching, therefore, is the local congregation where people can be loved and cared for in their daily struggles and perplexities. In this setting as no other, the preacher can become practiced in the language of love from the pulpit. It is an urgent, at-risk language; it expects a response, so rejection is always a real possibility. What we must guard against is being rejected for the wrong reasons. It is not the pastor's imperfect love that is being set forth, but God's inexhaustible *agape;* not the preacher's opinions about an issue, but God's call from his Word; not the speaker's agenda, but the story of God's providence. On the occasions when the text speaks of God's judgment, the challenge for the preacher is twofold: he must not flinch from the subject set before him in the text, and he must show that he himself is under the judgment of which it speaks. This stance of the preacher is best worked out in the daily grind. When the pastor is known to her people not so much as one who calls others to the Word as one who herself lives under the Word, then the potency of the preaching has an exponential range. The way in which a pastor conducts herself in the sight of her community adds immeasurably to the authenticity of her sermons and the opportunity for faithful hearing. Thus the effectiveness of a sermon will depend not so much upon the exegetical, linguistic, and verbal skills of the preacher as upon his or her knowledge and love of God and his Word.

The priest or minister who is able to preach on most Sundays of the year has a splendid opportunity with regard to the Old Testament. Many weeks can be spent expounding one book, or one section from one book. A passage can be looked at from one point of view one Sunday, and another the next. Episodes from the lives of the local people can be woven into the sermons so that the text can be seen in its direct relationship to them. The more extensively the Scriptures are preached and taught, the more the people who hear them will grow familiar with the world of the Bible and the way it calls our own conception of the world into question. When a congregation is learning to love the Bible in all its complexity and simplicity, the congregation will find itself being changed.

### Biblical Narrative in the Congregation

However, preaching by itself is not enough for thorough submersion in the world of the Bible. From my thirty-five years of experience as an ordained minister and thirty years of deep lay involvement before that, I can testify that if the Bible is not being studied regularly in small groups, the congregation is shut off from much of its power. It is in the small groups that the preaching takes incarnate shape. I have seen this over and over again in many settings, and I have heard many others testify to the same thing. It is a strange characteristic of congregations today that very little attention is being given to this sort of biblical shaping, and few opportunities are offered.[28]

In today's environment, it is not so easy to persuade a group of people that studying the Bible is life-giving. The lay theologian William Stringfellow tells a story that is worth reproducing at length, because it dramatically illustrates the loss of biblical understanding even in high places:

> I recall, a few years ago, serving on a commission of the Episcopal Church charged with articulating the scope of the total ministry of the Church in modern society. The commission [included] a few laity and the rest [were] professional theologians, ecclesiastical authorities and clergy. . . . Toward the end of [the first] meeting, some of those present proposed that it might be an edifying discipline for the group, in its future sessions, to undertake some concentrated study of the Bible.[29] It was suggested that constant recourse to the Bible is as characteristic and significant a practice in the Christian life as the regular . . . celebration of the Eucharist, which was a daily

28. A woman who was in a small Bible-study group for many years called me in desperation when it ended. She couldn't find a similar one anywhere in her city.

29. My educated guess is that "some of those present" equals Stringfellow himself, period.

observance of this commission. Perhaps, it was suggested, Bible study would enlighten the deliberations of the commission. . . .

The proposal was rejected on the grounds, as one Bishop put it, that "most of us have been to seminary and know what the Bible says; the problem now is to apply it to today's world." The bishop's view was seconded (with undue enthusiasm, I thought at the time) by the Dean of one of the Episcopal seminaries as well as by the clergy from national headquarters who had, they explained, a program to design and administer.

The point in mentioning the incident . . . is that the notion implied in the decision not to engage in Bible study is that the Gospel, in its Biblical embodiment, is . . . a static body of knowledge which, once systematically organized, taught, and learned, [is thereafter used] ceremonially, sentimentally, nostalgically, and as a source from which deductions can be made to guide the religious practice and ethical conduct of contemporary Christians.[30]

This assumption — that the Bible is a static body of knowledge like any other — governs much church life today, so much so that churches offer classes in other subjects — if they offer classes at all — as though the Bible has indeed been definitively "taught and learned," and now it is time to study something newer and more useful. What's missing here is the conviction expressed by theologian Douglas Harink, who writes, "The Scriptures have the power not only to direct and guide the community *but also to constitute the world for it.*"[31] This is the crucial conviction that is missing from so many congregations: The living Word is able to bring about a new reality in the community that listens to it.

This way of recommending Bible study is very different from the invitation, so often heard today, to go deeply into ourselves. It is based, rather, on an essentially apocalyptic conviction, arising out of faith in the power of the God who comes to us from outside and beyond ourselves with the gift of his Holy Spirit. Thus the leader of a study group needs to be thoroughly committed to the text itself, rather than to the way the group members "feel" about a given passage. Stringfellow can help us here, too. He tells another memorable story, this time about taking on a group of rowdy inner-

30. William Stringfellow, *Count It All Joy: Reflections on Faith, Doubt, and Temptation* (Grand Rapids: Wm. B. Eerdmans, 1967), pp. 54-55.

31. Douglas Harink, *Paul Among the Postliberals* (Grand Rapids: Brazos Press, 2003), p. 19.

city students for a study of the Epistle to the Romans. He kept them focused with just one question: "What does this say?" Not "What does this say to you?" or "What does this mean in today's world?" or "How is this related to life today?" but simply, *What does this say?*[32] It is surprisingly difficult to maintain a group's attention to that simple question. Practice and discipline are required to keep the focus on the text and not on the immediate issues and needs of the group. Only if the text is allowed to *speak for itself first* does it become clear what it says in the lives of the group members, who may find that their utmost needs are quite different from what they thought when they first began the study. When this happens, the results can be life-changing not only for individuals, but, more important, for the coming into being of a new family called together by adoption and grace.

### About the Children

In the case of Old Testament stories taught to children, we are constantly tempted to moralize them, to make them teach a useful lesson according to our own ideas of what we should be imparting to students.[33] Not only does this domesticate and tame the unruly "strange world of the Bible"; it is also boring for children. A familiar sight in worship services today is Sunday school children corralled up front while an adult asks them questions about what they have learned. The children — with few exceptions — are mute. It's hard to tell whether the questions are at fault or the teaching itself, but in either case, it's clear that the imagination of the children has not been engaged, and consequently the adults also become inured to the idea that the Scriptures are the most exciting thing in the world. The pastors of congregations can help to guide the teaching of children by delivering sermons in the adult congregation which seek to impart a sense of wonder and amazement. Over time, the adults who teach children will pick this up.[34] I have seen this in settings where the preaching was so consistently full of life that the entire congregation, including the children, was reshaped.

---

32. Stringfellow, *Count It All Joy*, pp. 65-72. This is perhaps Stringfellow's best book, and well worth reading for this account alone.

33. Gretchen Wolff Pritchard, author of *Offering the Gospel to Children* and many other books, is a peerless proponent of engaging children in narrative wonder rather than moralizing.

34. The children's program called "Godly Play" has been much admired by lovers of the Scripture.

## Conclusion

The effectiveness of sermons as they are preached can be determined only by the fruits borne in the congregations that hear them. The wind of the Spirit blows where it wills, and that is not for the preacher to know. It is quite likely that some of the less prepossessing sermons in this volume had a greater impact on some listeners than the "big" sermons delivered to large groups.

At any rate — I hope the reader will not think this is prideful — when I went through this collection of sermons one by one over a period of many weeks to prepare them for publication, I had the distinct experience of becoming immersed in the Old Testament's witness to the God whose name is I AM WHO I AM. The power of the accumulated texts seemed to take over from the words I had myself written, even though I was aware of their deficiencies. I have heard of people who have been convicted through their own preaching. To believe in the Word of God is to know that this is possible, because in the final analysis it is not the preacher's work at all that makes a sermon live, but — if God wills — the work of the Spirit.

Robert Wilken, editor of the estimable new series The Church's Bible (Eerdmans), writes this in his Series Preface:

> Early Christian thinkers moved in the world of the Bible, understood its idiom, loved its teaching, and were filled with awe before its mysteries. They believed in the maxim, "Scripture interprets Scripture." They knew something that has largely been forgotten by biblical scholars. . . .[35]

Wilken speaks here to the biblical scholars for whom the series is partly designed, but it is not just biblical scholars who have forgotten the idiom of Scripture. The Bible is virtually unknown to most church members today. A complete overhaul of preaching is needed, and there are two requirements above all:

- A passionate love for the Scriptures and "awe before its mysteries"
- An equally passionate desire to communicate "the world of the Bible and its idiom" to those who do not know it

---

35. Quoted from *Isaiah: Interpreted by Early Christian and Medieval Commentators,* The Church's Bible series, ed. and trans. by Robert Louis Wilken (Grand Rapids: Wm. B. Eerdmans, 2007), p. xi.

How this is to be done in the upcoming generation of people perpetually plugged into the Internet remains to be seen. There are many who are saying that the traditional sermon from the pulpit is dead. Perhaps so. But the power of an amazing story will never die away, and if the Word of God is what the Bible proclaims it to be, it is nothing less than the greatest story ever told.[36]

And so I conclude this introduction with the prayerful hope that the Lord who promised that his Word would not return to him empty will indeed speak through this book, the offering of his unworthy servant:

> For as the rain and the snow come down from heaven, and return not thither but water the earth, making it bring forth and sprout, giving seed to the sower and bread to the eater, so shall my word be that goes forth from my mouth; it shall not return to me empty, but it shall accomplish that which I purpose, and prosper in the thing for which I sent it. (Isa. 55:10-12)

36. In traveling around the country I have seen young people flocking to hear biblical preaching in certain settings. The current phenomenon of the Church of the Redeemer in New York City is one of many examples.

# The Lord Spoke to Abraham

*This sermon was preached in October 2009 at a prominent mainline Protestant church in the South.*

. . . . . . . . . . . . . . . . .

Now the Lord said to Abram, "Go from your country and your kindred and your father's house to the land that I will show you. And I will make of you a great nation, and I will bless you, and make your name great, so that you will be a blessing. I will bless those who bless you, and him who curses you I will curse; and by you all the families of the earth shall bless themselves." So Abram went, as the Lord had told him; and Lot went with him. Abram was seventy-five years old when he departed from Haran. And Abram took Sarai his wife. . . .

(GENESIS 12:1-5)

THERE'S A column in *The Wall Street Journal* every Saturday called "Houses of Worship." The author of last week's column, "Revelation Revised," is Stephen Prothero, a professor of religion at Boston University. Listen carefully to the first two sentences of the professor's article:

Any claim of revelation is preposterous. It presumes that God exists, that God speaks, and that all is not lost when human beings translate that speech into ordinary language.[1]

Now this is a remarkable statement for at least three reasons. *First* of all, it is obviously an in-your-face challenge to classical Christianity. *Second,* it's a perfect definition of biblical revelation — although I'm not sure the author meant it that way. And *third,* it expresses the doubts of a lot of people who sit in pews in mainline churches today. There are people who come to church — some of you are here today — holding various religious views but not really believing that God speaks and certainly not believing that human beings have translated God's speech into ordinary language. There have been people like that in my own family. They supported the church with their attendance and contributions even though they did not really believe in the basic tenets of the Christian faith. The result of this has been a great capitulation on the part of many preachers who don't want to risk alienating significant numbers of their flock.

But not *all* preachers. Will Willimon, who held forth for many years in the pulpit of the Duke Chapel, recently wrote that the Christian faith depends upon three words from the first chapter of Genesis. Can you guess what those three words are?

"And God said . . ."

It's not too strong a statement to say that the entire structure of Christianity stands or falls on that foundation: "And God said . . ." If we believe that, then everything else follows from it.

But "any claim of revelation is preposterous"! And what was it that God said, anyway? "And God said, 'Let there be light,' and there was light." But science has shown us that that couldn't have happened, right? So we fall back on the idea that this is a beautiful myth that arose out of the storytelling imagination of some very gifted and spiritual human beings.

Actually, the creation story *is* a myth, in the sense that a myth is a pictorial way of expressing a fundamental truth — in this case, the truth that God created the world by his Word. That's not what the history-of-religion people have in mind, though. A lot of them, and a lot of biblical scholars also, read and teach Scripture as though it was produced by human initiative out of human religious imagination. A lot of big-name speakers show up regularly at big-name churches to teach that God has evolved out of our

1. *The Wall Street Journal,* October 2.

understanding of God. What sort of god is that? The Old Testament prophets would have said it was an idol. Maybe the atheists are on the right track in thinking that a god projected out of human wishes isn't God at all.

On the other hand, the book of Genesis says that God was there before there was anybody to imagine a God. That's what it says. Look, we don't have to *believe* what Genesis says, but why do we want to make it say something it clearly does not say?

In the mainline churches today, there is a theological problem. Those who think that maybe God not only *exists* but has actually *said* something are often written off as fundamentalists. The opinion-makers miss no opportunity to suggest that it's only the unenlightened people in the "Bible churches" that believe such things. So what are our choices? Do we have to give up believing in a God who speaks in order to be up-to-date?

This morning we have heard a reading that sets the whole Judeo-Christian story in motion. Actually, that's too feeble a way to put it. Listen to what a Jewish scholar says about the story of Abraham leaving home. "It is an event of universal significance, produc[ing] far-reaching consequences for [hu]mankind as a whole, and constituting a major turning-point in human history."[2] How does this uniquely consequential story begin? It begins with these words: "The Lord spoke to Abraham."

The whole Bible is based on the claim that God has spoken. Now the ruling classes in our mainline churches don't generally say outright that this claim is preposterous. That would be going too far. We still read the Bible in church and theoretically hold it in high esteem. But what happens is that we read the Bible *anthropo*logically — the Greek word *anthropos* meaning "humanity," and *theos* meaning "God." The way that we wiggle out of the claim that God speaks is to read the Bible *anthropo*logically instead of *theo*logically.

What does that mean?

Here's an example of a *theo*logical reading. A *theo*logically oriented Old Testament scholar says this about Genesis 12: "[God] is the subject of the first verb at the beginning of the first statement and is thus the subject of the entire subsequent sacred history."[3] *God* is the subject of the verb. In other words, it's not the more or less elevated religious notions of human beings that make biblical history; it's *God* who makes biblical history.

But we don't like this, so we've changed the subject of the verb. The

2. Nahum Sarna, *Genesis* (New York: Schocken Books, 1970), p. 100. This commentary by a Jewish scholar is a joy and a treasure.
3. Gerhard von Rad, *Genesis* (Philadelphia: Westminster Press, 1972), p. 159.

story of Abraham has become an *anthropo*logical story. In today's versions, God no longer speaks. Abraham *thinks* that God speaks. There was a TV series on Genesis a few years ago, and hardly anyone noticed that God was not the subject. Only the very alert and biblically oriented viewers were aware that it was all about the human authors, their religious ideas, their concepts of a God who existed because they had thoughts about him. In a video version of the story of Abraham, when the voice of God speaks, it's actually the voice of the actor who plays the part of Abraham. Do you see what I mean? Without our realizing what was happening, the speaking, acting, procreating God was removed from the story and was replaced by human religious sensibility, or spirituality if you will. Our spirituality becomes the main subject, and God becomes the object.

There will always be those who prefer the story of the human search for God. But that's quite different from the biblical story of the God who came searching for us. The opening chapter in the saga of that search is right here — "God spoke to Abraham."

Now we always want to think that Abraham was chosen because he was a great man of faith: God saw him being faithful and approved of him and chose him. But that's not what happened at all. The biblical account tells us only two things about Abraham and Sarah before God spoke: (1) Abraham was the son of Terah, and (2) Sarah was barren. That's no way to begin a story! This couple is going to become the father and mother of all humanity! We want to know more about them! But this is not a story about a couple. This is a story about the living God.

Let's see if we can get this. We've been talking about "and God said . . ." Well, what did he say? Did he say he was going to send another flood to kill all the ungodly people? Noooo . . . we already heard that one. This is a new chapter. God told Abraham something that sounds very simple but isn't. He said, "Leave home and go to a place that I, God, will show you." Now I'm sure most of you have heard it explained that it was almost inconceivably more difficult for a man of ancient times to leave his roots than it would be for a young man today, when all young people are expected to leave home. For a man of Abraham's time it was nothing short of crazy to set out from home for no economic reason, just because God said so.

But there was a *promise* attached to the command of God:

"I will make of you a great nation, and I will bless you, and make your name great . . . and by you all the families of the earth shall bless themselves." (vv. 2-3)

This isn't primarily a promise to Abraham at all. It's a universal promise, a promise reaching to the ends of the earth and to the end of time as we know it. The offspring of this one man Abraham will be blessed by God, and through those offspring all other families who will ever live will be blessed by God. This is the promise that Abraham lived on for the rest of his life. But isn't this rather odd, to say the least, that an elderly man and an elderly, infertile wife should be promised gazillions of descendants? Have we really thought about this? Why did God choose Abraham for this unique role? Why not someone younger? Someone who already had a child or two? And by the way, remember that after this first call from God, Abraham and Sarah continued to be childless for *decades*. There was absolutely nothing concrete to show for their long, long waiting.

The reason for this is that God is demonstrating the power of his promise. This is not a story about human potential. This is a story about what God did in the life of a man and woman *who had no human potential* — that's the whole point.[4] As they say in the African-American community, this is a story about a God who makes a way out of no way. That is the way the story of redemption begins: with a God who promises to do what is humanly impossible. Only God can do what Paul the apostle said: the God of Abraham "raises the dead and calls into existence the things that do not exist" (Rom. 4:17). God promises that he will make Abraham's name great. It is the power of God and no other power that makes this no-name couple famous over the millennia. They would have been lost in the dust of Mesopotamia for all these thousands of years if God in his majestic purpose had not caused them to be revered today as Father Abraham and Mother Sarah.

Now listen to the rest of Paul's words concerning Abraham:

> He did not weaken in faith when he considered his own body, which was as good as dead because he was about a hundred years old, or when he considered the barrenness of Sarah's womb. . . . He grew strong in his faith as he gave glory to God, fully convinced that God was able to do what he had promised. . . . (Rom. 4:19-21)

*What God had promised.* What is the power of a promise? President Obama has discovered that promises are easy to make but hard to keep. That is the reality that all politicians have to face when the campaigns are

---

4. This insight comes from the work of several scholars, including that of theologian Douglas Harink.

over. Have you had the experience of wanting to promise something and then being unable to do it because you didn't have the ability to follow through? Imagine being able to promise your friend with cancer that she will be healed. Imagine being able to promise a hard-working jobless man that you will definitely be able to find him a good position so that he can support his family. Imagine being able to tell a child with a drug-ridden mother and an absent father in a poverty-stricken neighborhood that he will have a brilliant future. Imagine being able to promise a person with early Alzheimer's that the disease will get better instead of worse. We want to make promises to people, and sometimes we want to make them so much that we do make them, and then we fail because we can't follow through.

This is the reason that it matters so much that God actually speaks. Preposterous it may be, humanly speaking. But here are the words that the church lives by: "God is able to do what he has promised." In spite of all the deconstructionists and the skeptics and the scoffers, there is something about the Word of God in the Bible that eludes them all. There is a mysterious life in the Scriptures that renews God's people generation after generation.

How can this be?

It's because God is real, and he is our God, and he speaks the Word of life, and his Spirit cannot be quenched, and he — God alone — *is able* to keep his promises of blessing and redemption and abundance and righteousness and fullness of joy and eternal life in his presence.

AMEN.

# "Adam, Where Are You?"

*This sermon should be read in tandem with the following one, "Dust to Dust."*

. . . . . . . . . . . . . . . . .

JOHN MILTON begins his epic poem *Paradise Lost* with a prayer to the Holy Spirit. Let us pray:

> Of man's first disobedience, and the fruit
> Of that forbidden tree, whose mortal taste
> Brought Death into the world, and all our woe,
> With loss of Eden, till one greater Man
> Restore us, and regain the blissful Seat,
> Sing, Heavenly Muse. . . .
> Instruct me, for Thou know'st: Thou from the first
> Wast present, and with mighty wings outspread
> Dove-like satst brooding on the vast abyss
> And mad'st it pregnant: what in me is dark
> Illumine, what is low raise and support;
> That to the height of this great argument
> I may assert eternal Providence,
> And justify the ways of God to men.

Is there anybody, anywhere, who thinks that the world is just fine the way it is? Is there anyone who can take a look around and feel satisfied with life? I guess there are such people. "Optimism," said Voltaire's Candide, "is a mania for maintaining that all is well when things are going badly."[1] Robert Browning wrote, "God's in his heaven — all's right with the world."[2] Browning certainly did not entirely believe these sentiments, but the fact that they are his best-known lines probably testifies to the fact that people often prefer to block out the grim realities of life.

The Bible never does this. If the Bible were being written today, it would all be there. The natural disasters would be there — drought in Ethiopia, fires in California, tornadoes in Pennsylvania, cyclones in Bangladesh. The violence would be there — murder in Mamaroneck, rape on the West Side, stun guns in the police precinct. Greed and deceit would be there, both in its low-life, petty-thievery form and in its high-life, corporate form. All the nasty little secrets of the human heart would be there — the adulteries, the jealousies, the deceptions, the compulsions, the failures. And all the irrational, arbitrary, meaningless evil in the world would be there, too — the massacre of innocents, the starving of babies, the extermination of populations. Instead of saying with Dr. Pangloss that this is the best of all possible worlds, the Bible reader might be more likely to protest with Ivan Karamazov that "It's not God that I don't accept — it's the world created by Him I don't and cannot accept."

The Bible begins with "the world created by Him"; chapter 1 ends this way: "and God saw everything that he had made, and behold, it was very good." By chapter 11, at the end of the primeval history, we have seen fratricide, corruption, flood, arrogance, greed, lying, strife, and violence. What happened? What went wrong?

In between Genesis 1 and the rest of the Bible comes Genesis 3. The third chapter of Genesis: How are we to describe it; how can we even begin to do justice to it? This is the undisputed monarch of the world's myths, whether you believe in it or not.

It's generally agreed by all but the most extreme fundamentalist scholars that there should be no simplistic split between myth and history. Many people use the word *myth* to mean simply "something that's not true." But there's a far more serious way of understanding myth. In the words of the noted philosopher Paul Ricoeur, "myth tries to get at the enigma of human

---

1. Voltaire, *Candide*, ch. 19.
2. Robert Browning, "Pippa's Song," in *The Oxford Book of English Verse, 1250-1900.*

existence."[3] C. S. Lewis in the last volume of his space trilogy *(That Hideous Strength)* intends to show that the King Arthur cycle of myths tells what is really true about the destiny of England. Myth, then, rather than being "not really true," means the opposite: myth is charged with a special seriousness and significance.[4]

And so we need to see Adam and Eve not so much as historical individuals, but rather, as primal representatives of humanity. The story of what happened to them is not a past fact having occurred at an identifiable moment in time (unlike the story of Jesus, who "suffered under Pontius Pilate"). Rather, the narrator is speaking of a primeval happening beyond the realm of our experience.[5] The story is told not as propositional truth, not as doctrine, but as a story — as, in fact, all the Bible is a story, not a series of propositions. The myth of Adam and Eve, like other myth, is drama "because what it wants to express is already a drama."[6]

The story of Adam and Eve is the greatest myth ever produced. It is inexhaustible: it has never been fully plumbed, and it has never been explained away. Its greatness is impervious to attack. In a way that has never been successfully challenged, it tells the story of the human race and how it fell from its original state of grace. It is the story of the created order and how it became disorder.

The garden that God planted for man and woman to live in was perfection. It was, in a word, paradise. Maybe we have a hard time understanding what paradise is, since we don't live in it. "Paradise Island," in the Bahamas, may be the closest we can come to it.

However, the biblical paradise, or Garden of Eden, is utterly different from the paradise myths of the nations because it does not depict a bower of sensual delight but, rather, a life of free obedience in the service and in the care of God.[7] This, too, is hard for us to get hold of, since most of us are so far gone from perfect communion with God. Most of the time, I myself can scarcely imagine what it would be like to have intimate fellowship with God. I know only too well that something is drastically wrong. There are aspects of myself that I do not like, and I have bad dreams. My relationships

3. Paul Ricoeur, *The Symbolism of Evil* (New York: Harper & Row, 1967), p. 163.

4. Northrop Frye, *The Great Code* (New York: Harcourt Brace Jovanovich, 1981), p. 33.

5. Claus Westermann, *Creation* (Philadelphia: Fortress Press, 1974), p. 95. (I vigorously disagree with some of Westermann's ideas but find him very helpful in other ways.)

6. Ricoeur, *The Symbolism of Evil*, p. 170.

7. Gerhard von Rad, *Genesis* (Philadelphia: Westminster Press, 1972), pp. 80-81.

with other people do not always — in fact, seldom — seem to be lasting embodiments of real love.

Whatever Paradise may have been like, I know it was not like my life. Maybe that is the only way we know to imagine it, in negatives — in paradise, no labor would be in vain, no thieves would break in and steal, no love would be rejected, no one would come to harm, there would be no discrepancy between my needs and my world.

The myth of Adam and Eve in Paradise tells us that God knows exactly what is good for human beings, even if we do not know. God created (and, in Scripture, only God can create) a habitat that was, among other things, completely human — as opposed to inhuman. An important aspect of this, for example, is the meaning of work in Eden. Adam and Eve were both to work in the garden, "to till it and keep it" (2:15). In God's original plan for the creation, work was an integral part of being human; the difference was that, in Eden, work was always productive and totally rewarding, so that the human being joyfully participated in the results of his or her own labor.[8]

There was only one limitation in the garden. Only one! Think of it! No restrictions whatsoever, except only one. This is a sign to us of the lavish generosity of God which he showered upon his human creatures, like a grandmother who delights in giving pleasure to her grandchild. In fact, think of that grandmother for a moment. She gives the child a huge yard to play in, full of sandboxes and swings and tree houses — the only restriction is that the child must stay in the yard, must not cross the street. You and I, from our adult point of view, understand this prohibition, which is for the child's good — but the child cannot understand it. Perhaps the child loves and trusts his grandmother so much that he will not consider disobeying; on the other hand, perhaps he gets bored with her yard and looks curiously at the sights on the other side of the street, having no idea that his safety is in jeopardy if he crosses. Now suppose that another child suddenly appears and says, "Come on over; there's lots to see over here."

There was only one limitation for Adam and Eve. They were not to eat of the tree of the knowledge of good and evil. *Knowledge,* biblically speaking, means "experience." The first couple were not created to experience evil. They were in a state of innocent ignorance. There is no suggestion in the story that it even occurs to them to eat the fruit from the forbidden tree until suddenly here is this snake. . . .

8. This is eschatologically recapitulated in Isaiah 65:21-23: "My chosen shall long enjoy the work of their hands."

Yes. Suddenly there is a suggestion presented from outside. "Did God say 'You shall not eat of the fruit'?" (3:1). The seeds of doubt are sown. For the first time, the thought occurs: Perhaps the command is unreasonable. Perhaps God, the one giving the command, is not entirely trustworthy. Thus the idea of disobedience is imported into the situation from another sphere. The serpent, representing this other, alien sphere, was in the garden already; this is part of the mystery of evil which the story does not attempt to explain.

Eve is attracted by the serpent's clever arguments. How familiar they are! How many times we have heard them and heeded them! "It won't hurt you; you don't know what you've been missing." Eve thinks it over. She "saw that it was good for food; it was a delight to the eyes; it was to be desired to make one wise." She is far more energetic and imaginative, here, than her husband: she eats the fruit because she is drawn by the snake's clever rhetoric. Adam, on the other hand, just goes compliantly along: "She gave some to her husband, and he ate" (3:6).

The effects are instantaneous: shame and fear. Uneasy self-consciousness comes in where before there had been no thought of self at all. How do I look? What will he think? What will she think? We can't let God see us like this! Quick, get the fig leaves.

"And they heard the sound of the Lord God walking in the garden in the cool of the day, and the man and his wife hid themselves from the presence of the Lord God among the trees of the garden" (3:8).

First, shame; then, fear. The relationship with the creator has been totally disrupted. Until the disobedience, the thought of hiding from God would have been inconceivable; there was no reason, no need to hide. We need to let this sink in; the posture of hiding is pathetic, ludicrous. It would be laughable if it were not so serious — two adults ignominiously crouching in the bushes in their fig leaves. We've all seen scenes in movies where the husband surprises his wife and her lover by coming home early — the lover leaps out of bed stark naked and hides in the closet, or runs out into the yard, not knowing which is worse: being discovered in the act or looking like a fool.

There they are, Adam and Eve — our primal ancestors and representatives, hiding in the bushes, feeling like craven fools and scared almost literally to death — death, which they had not known before. They are no longer innocent, no longer ignorant — now they have experience of evil as well as good. They know now what is on the other side of the street. In a sense they are wiser, yes, but at the cost of unleashing evil upon the entire created order, from the lowest to the highest.

This is our condition. The choices that Adam and Eve had are no longer open to us, as St. Augustine saw long ago. There is no going back. Fear and shame are our chronic symptoms. We are, so to speak, in the bushes for good, hoping that God will not find us, or maybe, if we are really far gone, deciding that there is no God in the first place, in which case we can buy a self-help book to help us get rid of our feelings of guilt and dread.

We are in the bushes. You are in the bushes. Why are you there? Which one of the Commandments have you broken? "Thou shalt have no other gods but me"? "Thou shalt keep holy the Sabbath Day"? "Thou shalt not covet"? "Thou shalt love thy neighbor as thyself"? How do you think we would honestly feel if God really appeared? Sheer, stark terror might be something like it. "Who shall stand when he appeareth?" (Mal. 3:2).

You and I are hiding from God in the bushes. We are so far gone from original righteousness that we don't even realize we are subject to fear and shame because we have neglected his righteous commandments, which are for our good, for our safety, for our happiness. We are hiding wherever we can find the nearest cover — hiding in our offices, hiding in the bottle, hiding in "religion," hiding in busyness, hiding in affluence, hiding in self-deception. And this is what we hear God say: "Adam, where are you?" Fill in your name. Tom, Dick, Harry, Mary, Jane, Ann — where are you?

What is the answer to this question? Clearly not a simple "I'm in the bushes" or "I'm in the bottle" (or the bong). What do you answer? Where are you? Not *who* are you, but *where?* Where are you in relation to God? Where are you in relation to others? Where are you in relation to the person God created you to be? Where are we? In the terms of the story, the way it is told throughout the Bible, there can be only one answer: We are lost. We may not think we are lost; we may have convinced ourselves that we have everything figured out. But when God puts the question to us, our human pretense at knowing all the answers evaporates. And so Adam flounders desperately. He is thinking now only of himself. Before, when Eve was brought to him, he exclaimed ecstatically, "Bone of my bones and flesh of my flesh" (2:23). Now he tries to put as much distance between himself and her as he can, and blames God at the same time — "The woman whom thou gavest to be with me, she gave me the fruit. . . . And I ate" (3:12). And, of course, Eve blames the snake. Thus the loving relationship that God created collapsed into hostile recriminations. As Milton puts it, "Thus they in mutual accusation spent/the fruitless hours, but neither self-condemning/and of their vain contest appeared no end."

"Man's first disobedience": this is what went wrong with the creation.

The breach in creation, the fissure between God's rule and the rule of sin and death, occurred because the human race, including you and me as descendants of Adam and Eve, became rebellious and disobedient to the core — idolatrous, faithless, selfish. There is a distinct suggestion that humanity is not the origin of evil; rather, humanity capitulates to the evil that is already there, and in doing so, "lets hell loose."[9]

What the origin of evil is we cannot say. The Bible is silent. What we can say for certain is that God is in control of it. He puts the snake in its place immediately — on its belly in the dust. As for Adam and Eve, their marital harmony is miserably disrupted: Eve's desire for her husband will result in the multiplication of labor pains, and he will dominate her with previously unintended oppressiveness. Adam's work will no longer be a joy, and it will be an endless labor to make it productive; the ground will produce thorns and thistles. As St. Paul will say in his letter to the Romans, "God gave them over" to their selfish desires, as if to say, "You want you own way instead of mine? You may have it forever — sin and death." And, continues Paul, "the whole creation was subjected to futility" (Rom. 1:24, 26, 28; 8:20) along with them. "Adam, where are you?" Lost, lost — and the world lost, too. The existential despair expressed by so many writers is descriptive of our expulsion from Paradise. This longing for our primal home, our lost Eden, is part of our sense of dislocation, our abandoned condition.

And yet — and yet. This is the God who comes seeking his lost creation. It can't be said often enough: The Bible is not the story of the human search for God; it is the story of the divine search for us. Here it is, right here in the third chapter of Genesis. This is the God who comes to man and woman when we can no longer come to him, when we can only run away and hide. "Adam, where are you?" This is the first thing that happens from God's side. Hardly a minute elapses between the catastrophic fall and the action of God, who comes seeking his lost children. This is the God who clothes Adam and Eve in mercy before sending them out into the now-hostile, now-cruel, newly fallen world.

In *Paradise Lost,* Milton depicts God the Father and God the Son enthroned in heaven, looking down on the earth with Adam and Eve still happy in their "uninterrupted joy" in the garden; marring the picture, however, is the figure of Satan, the fallen angel, thrown down by God from heaven, heading for earth. Knowing what will happen, the Father and the Son together plan the drama of redemption through the self-offering of the

---

9. Karl Barth, *Church Dogmatics* (Edinburgh: T&T Clark, 1956), vol. III/4, p. 450.

Son, who will die on the Cross, the perfectly obedient one, to rewrite the story and make atonement for our disobedience.[10] As they speak, fresh joy fills the heavenly regions, and Milton writes these magnificent words:

> Beyond compare the Son of God was seen
> Most glorious; in him all his Father shone
> Substantially express'd; and in his face
> Divine compassion visibly appear'd,
> Love without end, and without measure grace.

"Adam, where are you?"

Let us pray:

Lord, we are here. Work in us to effect your redemption, work in the world to bring your Kingdom, work to overthrow the demons that are too powerful for us, and work through all things for good according to your most gracious promise. In the name of our Lord and Savior Jesus Christ we pray. Amen.

10. Milton is not perfectly Orthodox here because he makes it seem that the Incarnation was a result of sin, not part of God from the beginning. The rhetorical splendor of Milton, however, is irresistible.

# Dust to Dust

---

*June 1988*                                                        Genesis 3:19

*This sermon should be read as a companion-piece to "Adam, Where Are You?"*

. . . . . . . . . . . . . . . . .

AT THE time of death, the Christian tradition provides for a number of solemn and awe-inspiring moments. Climactic among these are the gestures and words at the graveside. The Book of Common Prayer has these directions:

> While earth is cast upon the coffin, the Celebrant says these words: We commend to Almighty God our brother (or sister), and we commit his body to the ground, earth to earth, ashes to ashes, dust to dust.

When I was a little child, long before I ever had any thoughts of being ordained, I was taught by my tradition-minded family that there were always going to be some undertakers lurking around trying to substitute sand, or even rose petals, for plain old dirt, and that this commercial intrusion upon the old rite was to be resisted at all costs. As an ordained member of the clergy, later, on numerous occasions when I've been conducting an interment, I've hastened to grab a handful of good old dirt from underneath the blanket of green plastic Astroturf before the man in the black suit could come at me with the sand. I've become quite practiced at this, so you can imagine my chagrin at the end of a graveside service last year, when I thought everything was finished and I could let my guard down, and suddenly, here came the undertaker with an armful of roses; presenting each person with a stem, he instructed us all to throw them on the coffin. The clergy have to work overtime these days to reclaim the service from the "funeral directors."[1]

What difference does it make? we may ask. Surely it is much nicer to throw roses than dirt. But like almost everything else in the traditional liturgies of the church, the dirt has a theological significance. The throwing of earth is based on the truth of Holy Scripture, not on human notions of what is upbeat and pleasing. The words "ashes to ashes, dust to dust" are very familiar. People have heard them even if they have never been to a graveside interment. The words are used in a similar way on Ash Wednesday; in churches that impose ashes on the forehead, the officiating priest says, "Dust thou art, and unto dust shalt thou return" (in the newer wording, "Remember that you are dust, and to dust you shall return"). No attempt has been made to prettify this, as far as I know. There was an amusing article in *The New York Times* last Ash Wednesday about Catholics trying to decide whether to "wear" their ashes to the office or not. The *Times* reporter commented that such a tangible reminder of mortality seemed, perhaps, "out of keeping with a culture reputed to be relentlessly cheerful." Notwithstanding, a government official in Washington was quoted as saying that he was going to make that statement. "In a secular world . . . it's a leveler, a reminder that we're going to die." Brian Brown, publicity manager for *Time* magazine, was even more forthright as he declared his intention to go "to the oldest priest in St. Patrick's Cathedral and get the biggest smudge possible so I can walk around the office and remind the yuppies here that the kingdom is not of this earth." With emphatic finality, he stated, "My whole idea is to scare the hell out of the yuppies."[2]

Well, for sure, the reporter and his sources are not so very far off the mark. The saying about "dust to dust" is, indeed, a reminder of our mortal-

---

1. I've noticed that in recent years, at least in some parts of the country, obituaries sometimes say that such-and-such funeral home is "assisting the family," instead of "in charge of arrangements." This is a great improvement. I hasten to add that I have always had excellent relationships with undertakers in the parishes where I have served since 1981 (before that I had a lot to learn). They are eager to cooperate if they know you will continue to recommend them.

2. Peter Steinfels, *The New York Times,* 17 February 1988.

ity, a "leveler" which should "scare the hell out of" *all* of us. It's a good bet, however, that very few, Catholic or Protestant, whether on Ash Wednesday or at a graveside, could identify the source and context of the original quotation. You can, of course; we just heard it read a few moments ago. It's the climax of God's pronouncement to Adam and Eve as they are expelled from the Garden of Eden:

> "In the sweat of your face you shall eat bread till you return to the ground, for out of it you were taken; you are dust, and to dust you shall return."

For the human race, it is the end of the beginning.

The story of Adam and Eve continues to be the most profound prehistoric story ever told. To this day it still stuns even the secular reader into silent respect. Its depths are inexhaustible. We will return to this story again and again as long as there is a race of human beings to read it and tell it.

The dispute about evolution and creation science is a vast irrelevance. The story was never designed to yield its secrets to microscopic postscientific, post-Enlightenment scrutiny. It is, rather, the primordial drama of the way that humanity and the created order got into the state of disorder we are in now. This means that you and I and all the people of this city, nation, and world are brought by the power of matchless storytelling into our closest possible proximity to the disobedience of our first parents. Whoever Adam and Eve *were,* they *are* — us. We are convinced, as we hear the story, that we would have done exactly what they did, for the same reasons, and that we would have hid ourselves afterward, and pretended that we knew nothing about it, and tried to put the blame on someone else, just as they did. We therefore receive God's judgment upon our actions as they did, and we make our "solitary way" (Milton) through this world as they did, utterly vulnerable to sorrow, sickness, futility, pain, and death, protected from the consequences of our disobedience only by the mercy of the creator God, who in spite of everything has continued to protect us from total destruction.

The Paradise that God created for Adam and Eve to live in was exactly what the name suggests — paradise. Everybody has at least some idea of what paradise might be like, and the notion of it being a bower of idyllic beauty, a garden of luxuriant bounty, is common to all cultures. Common also to various ancient mythologies is the idea of a tree of immortality or tree of life, planted in the garden.

The biblical Garden of Eden is different in two ways. In the first place, it does not grow all by itself. It requires tending, stewardship, and work. "The Lord God took the man and put him in the garden of Eden to till it and keep it" (Gen. 2:15). So, from the beginning, humanity was granted the privilege and responsibility of productive labor in the service of God. Implicit in the narrative is the fact that, in Eden, the work was always joyful, always fruitful, always purposeful, and always rewarding. At the end of their workday, Adam and Eve could see the results of what they had accomplished, and they were deeply satisfied, fulfilled, and at peace. There was no sense of discrepancy between who they were and what they did. Work and play were a seamless garment of satisfaction and reward.

But there in the midst of the garden stood this forbidden tree. Here is the second difference between the biblical story and the other ancient narratives about paradise. In those other stories, the fateful tree is the tree of *immortality*. In Genesis, it is very different; the tree of life is pushed to the margin of the story, and the focus becomes "the tree of the knowledge of good and evil." Thus the Bible indicates in the first of a thousand ways that God's nature and concerns are *ethical*. The issue is not living forever, but good and evil; it is not immortality, but morality.[3]

The only thing in the entire garden that was off-limits was the fruit of the tree of the knowledge of good and evil. Everything else was available in lavish, prodigal abundance. We should understand, therefore, that the prohibition was not in the least oppressive. It simply represented the setting of limits by the creator God, as a parent seeks to protect a child from that which would harm him. The tree was not good for Adam and Eve, so God warned them not to touch it. Thus God set before man the serious question of decision and obedience.[4] We are meant to see with utmost clarity that the command of God is good and that — as the Prayer Book puts it — "his service is perfect freedom." It was a life of inexpressible liberty and fulfillment such as we can scarcely imagine, restricted only by the one small prohibition.

Along came the serpent, with tactics of remarkable subtlety. "Did God say . . . ?" This insinuation plants the seed of doubt for the first time. The woman answers more or less innocently, "God said . . . 'You shall not eat of the fruit of the [one] tree . . . lest you die.'" The serpent, again introducing a new note of questioning, says, "You won't die. That's not the reason God

---

3. Nahum M. Sarna, *Understanding Genesis* (New York: Schocken Books, 1970), p. 27.
4. Gerhard von Rad, *Genesis* (Philadelphia: Westminster Press, 1972), p. 80.

forbade the tree. The real reason is that God knows that when you eat of it . . . you will be like God yourself, knowing good and evil" (3:1-5). Then Eve looked at the tree in a way she had never looked at it before. She saw how good the fruit appeared, and she thought how desirable it would be to have knowledge like God himself, and she decided to follow the serpent's suggestion. Thus the good commandment of God was broken by disobedience, and Paradise was lost. From that day forward, work became drudgery, childbearing became painful and dangerous, human relationships became sorrowful, the Garden was shut, and death entered the world in a terrible way that was not part of God's original arrangement.

There is no need to make a great mystery of "the knowledge of good and evil." In Hebrew, "to know" means something like "to experience." God's intention was to protect man from experiencing evil. God himself was to be the judge and determiner of man's life. Man was not supposed to step out of his place and determine his own life. But the serpent's suggestion was the ultimate temptation: "You will be like God." This is the root of all sin — it was then, and it is now. We do not want to let God be God. We want to be God ourselves. We want to determine our own limits. In disobeying him we do not mean to reject him; we just want to have him and our own way as well. Thus it is that we actually attempt to become our own god while at the same time continuing to pay an occasional visit to the real God when it suits us to do so.

Thus the utterance of God to Adam, "Dust thou art, and unto dust shalt thou return," finds its proper context. What is the consequence of the transgression of God's limits? It seemed to offer the promise of an expanded life, but its outcome was the sentence of death. It appeared to hold out the possibility of a higher consciousness, but its result was the unleashing of the power of sin. It purported to be an extension of freedom, but the effect was the enslavement of the human race by newly empowered demonic forces. The only true liberty for man is to be found as he understands himself in relation to the God who is really God. God is the Creator; we are his creatures. God knows what is best for us; our true well-being is found in him alone. As we lift ourselves up against him, so we correspondingly find ourselves more and more estranged from our true selves. Thus, in a mysterious way, the saying that we are dust points us to the good news, because it reorients us to our proper relationship with the creator God, who formed us out of the earth.

You see, in the last analysis, the attempt to "know good and evil" is the most prideful act of all. In the attempt, we think we are declaring ourselves capable of managing the powers of evil. We think we can handle the forbidden fruit; we can control its effects. Did God say, "Thou shalt not steal"? "Thou shalt not covet"? "Thou shalt keep holy the Sabbath day"? "Thou shalt not commit adultery"? Well, yes, he did say that, we reason with ourselves, but he really wasn't telling the truth about what would happen as a result — we won't die, the sky won't fall in, we can handle it, and the fruit is so delightful, and besides, how will we ever really know all about life if we don't grab the brass ring while we have the chance?

In the grabbing, though, a fearful and unforeseen thing happened. In the transgressing of the gracious command of God — in the refusal to recognize that God sets limits for our happiness — all hell broke loose, and humankind discovered that it could not put the genie back in the bottle. There is only One who can keep sin and evil within bounds, and man is not that One. "Dust thou art, O man, and unto dust shalt thou return."

It seems a bit strange, today in June, to hear the story of the Fall. It doesn't seem to fit the sequence of the lectionary particularly well; one might expect it on the first Sunday in Lent, perhaps, but not on an average Sunday in the long season of Pentecost. Dust to dust? It doesn't seem a very cheerful subject for a June morning.

But in fact, as is so often the case with the sterner texts, the bad news is completely enclosed in the good news — in the gospel. The goodness of God emerges in the midst of the catastrophe. Imagine Adam and Eve as they are turned out of the gorgeous, lavishly productive, spiritually nourishing Garden, headed into the inhospitable wastelands for a life of misery, disappointment, deprivation, pain, sorrow, and death. Surely it is a miracle that they survived at all! The man had turned on his wife, blaming her as he begins a life of struggle with the stony soil to eke out a bare subsistence. The woman, now bearing child after child in pain, must labor without ceasing to care for them, feed them, and clothe them with the toil of her hands, yearning in vain for the love and mutuality that is now only a memory of a dream. How could they bear it?

The only possible answer is that God strengthened and cared for them in spite of everything. He did not strike them dead on the spot; he did not utterly abandon them to what they had chosen. In a strange way, the saying preserved by the church, "ashes to ashes, dust to dust," is a signpost on the way to restoration. Low-church Episcopalians don't impose ashes, and I'm not recommending it, but that *Time* magazine man was on to something. Our true Kingdom is not of this earth; God himself is in the process of scaring the hell out of this world, and when Satan is at last overthrown and trampled under the feet of St. Michael the archangel, there will be a new heaven and a new earth, as the final book of the Bible promises — so that we are taken from Genesis to Revelation.

The message this morning is really very simple. God is holy; God is merciful; God is powerful. Because he is holy, he sets limits and establishes boundaries for our good. Because he is merciful, he has not crushed us for our disobedience. Because he is powerful, hell cannot stand against him. The news that *we are dust* is carried behind and before by the proclamation that *God is not dust.* Unlike us, he is the Creator and Redeemer of all that is. In a time and place as far removed from the primordial catastrophe as you and I are, a man who understood better than anybody that Adam and Eve "are us" wrote these words:

> The first man [Adam] was from the earth, a man of dust; the second man [Christ] is from heaven. . . . Just as we have borne the image of the man of dust, we shall also bear the image of the man of heaven. . . .
>
> Lo! I tell you a mystery. We shall not all sleep. . . . For the trumpet will sound, and the dead will be raised imperishable, and we shall be changed. . . . Then shall come to pass the saying that is written: "Death is swallowed up in victory." . . . Thanks be to God, who gives us the victory through our Lord Jesus Christ. (1 Cor. 15:47-57)

AMEN.

# The Bloody Passageway

Genesis 15:1-18

MANY PEOPLE are attracted to anything that is ancient, primitive, primordial. I've always envied a man named John Noble Wilford. He writes articles about archaeology for *The New York Times*. Everybody around him at the paper is writing articles about collapsing banks, Ponzi schemes, drug cartels, suicide bombings, and other features of modern life, while Wilford writes about the tombs of Pharaohs, ancient lost palaces, Neolithic caves, and other cool topics that take us out of the mundane daily round into a realm of adventure and discovery. The sense of being connected with ancient civilizations casts a potent spell. My mother and I once took a trip to the region of France where we were able to see some of the famous cave paintings from the Stone Age. I'll never forget the sensation I had as we stood in the narrow corridors and imagined those remote ancestors, carrying their rudimentary torches into the frightening blackness of the uninhabited caverns in order to draw their beautiful pictures, with greatest difficulty and without live models. I was stunned by the sense of kinship I felt with the prehistoric artists.

Wilford accompanied a group of fossil hunters into the Gobi Desert. He wrote that hunting fossils is "grinding, gritty work," and yet there is a glamour about it for those who have the tenacity to endure it. He describes an evening around a campfire after a day of successful digging. "Away from the fire, [our] voices fade into a night of silences . . . the sky is awash with stars, whole galaxies of them spilling down to the horizon. . . . Fossil prospecting is primordial, hand-and-knee stuff [and] our fire is primordial too. . . . Sitting before the flames, our backs to the enveloping darkness, we are not far removed from the Stone Age hunters. At night they must have sat around fires exulting in the success of the hunt, happy in their survival to hunt another day. It is much the same with us."[1] I can't speak for you, but that account gives me goosebumps.

You are about to hear one of the most remarkable passages in the entire Old Testament, from Genesis 15:[2]

> The word of the Lord came to Abraham in a vision, "Fear not, Abraham, I am your shield; your reward shall be very great." But Abraham said, "O Lord, I continue childless. . . . You have given me no offspring." And behold, the Lord brought him outside and said, "Look toward heaven, and count the stars, if you are able to count them. Your descendants shall be as many as the stars."
>
> And the Lord said to Abraham, "I am the Lord who brought you from Ur of the Chaldeans, to give you this land to possess." But Abraham said, "O Lord, how am I to know that I shall possess it?" And God said, "Bring me a heifer, a goat, a ram, a turtledove, and a pigeon." And Abraham brought him all these, cut them in two, and laid each half over against the other. And when birds of prey came down upon the carcasses, Abraham drove them away.
>
> As the sun was going down, a deep sleep fell on Abraham; and lo, a great dread fell upon him. And when the sun had gone down and it was dark, behold, a smoking fire pot and a flaming torch passed between the pieces. On that day the Lord made a covenant with Abraham, saying, "To your descendants I give this land, from the river of Egypt to the great river, the river Euphrates. . . ."

When I first studied this extraordinary text, it made my hair stand on end in the same way as the trip into the Neolithic caves. In this passage from Genesis, a ceremony is described which is of such great antiquity that one has the sense of going back as far as it is possible to go in biblical history. In this passage, we are in touch with a tradition so old that even the most skeptical interpreters agree that it originated in the time of the patriarchs, two thousand years before Christ. Few portions of the Hebrew scriptures meet

---

1. John Noble Wilford, "Gobi Diary: A Sedimental Journey," *The New York Times,* 10 November 1991.

2. The passage is condensed here for the sake of brevity.

the critical test quite so well as this one; it bears the marks of time immemorial. It carries with it a feeling of awe and mystery which still grips the reader over the millennia.[3]

At the beginning of Genesis 15, we discover Abraham in his tent at night, a very old man with an elderly, barren wife and not a single legitimate child. He has been trekking through the Near East for decades, trusting in a promise for which there was no evidence whatsoever. We can hardly blame Abraham for complaining to God that he was having a hard time trying to believe that he was going to have an heir who would be a blessing to all the nations of the earth. God is patient with Abraham's skepticism; he leads the old man out through the tent flaps into the desert night. Imagine it: "The sky is awash with stars, whole galaxies of them spilling down to the horizon." And God says to Abraham, "Look toward heaven, and count the stars, if you are able. So shall your descendants be."[4]

Now we come to the eerie part of the story. When it is still daylight, God instructs Abraham to bring three animals and two birds. Abraham slaughters them according to the ritual traditions of that primitive time. Then he cuts each of them in half, and lays out the pieces in two rows, one portion of halves over here, the other halves opposite, forming an alley in between. This ritual is said to survive in some form in the Middle East even today. It was the first step in a very ancient covenant-making ceremony.

After the carcasses were laid out, the second step was the two covenant partners passing through the bloody passageway as a sign of solemn commitment to one another. The point of this was that, if either partner violated the terms of the covenant, he was leaving himself open to suffering the fate of the slaughtered animals: "Thus let it be done to me if I ever break the terms of this compact."[5]

Abraham did all the things he was told to do, and then, not knowing what would come next, he waited. Buzzards began to come down to eat the carcasses, and Abraham kept busy driving them away.[6] As evening draws

---

3. E. A. Speiser, *Genesis* (Garden City, N.Y.: Doubleday, 1964), p. 115. Even this methodical, unimaginative commentator is impressed!

4. And, we are told in a verse that reverberates down the ages, "Abraham believed God, and it was reckoned to him as righteousness" (Gen. 15:6). This was one of the passages that shaped the Reformation. The faith evoked by the Word of God is guaranteed by the God who speaks that Word.

5. The same ceremony is clearly referred to in Jeremiah 34:18-19.

6. Gerhard von Rad suggests that the vultures might represent evil powers determined to thwart God's purpose. In that case, Abraham has an important, active role to play. At the crucial

near and darkness begins to fall over the strange scene, the biblical narrator begins to cast his spell with the extraordinary economy, emotional reserve, and narrative skill for which Old Testament storytelling is admired around the world. "As the sun was going down," we read, "a deep sleep fell on Abram, and lo, a dread and great darkness fell upon him." That is all we are told of Abraham's state of mind; the psychological details that interest modern people are omitted. All the emphasis is on the solemnity of the event that is about to occur, the action of God, which causes the human being to feel dread:

> And it came to pass that when the sun had gone down, it was dark. And behold, a smoking fire pot and a flaming torch passed between the pieces. And on that day the Lord made a covenant with Abram, saying, "To your descendants I give this land, from the river of Egypt to the great river, the river Euphrates. . . ."[7]

We should pause for a moment and let the narrative have its way with us before we move to interpretation. We feel something of the awe and dread that Abraham felt as he waited for — he knew not what. We sense the darkness coming on, and we are aware of the spookiness of the dead animals laid out in preparation for some sort of solemn covenant. We feel the impotence of Abraham, a truly aged man with no strength left in his loins, performing yet another task at God's behest but altogether unable to imagine what it might mean or where it might lead. We note that once Abraham has laid out the pieces and driven off the vultures, there is nothing more for him to do without a signal from God. And so Abraham falls into a profound sleep.

Now, recall the purpose of the bloody passageway. If the two partners making the covenant are equals, they will each pass through. That will be a sign from one to the other, both of them, that they intend to keep their cov-

---

point, though, he is insensible. See von Rad, *Genesis* (Philadelphia: Westminster Press, 1972), p. 187.

7. As the historical-critical scholars never tire of pointing out, there are visible seams in the text of Genesis where two different versions of this story have been patched together. That is of interest to textual scholars, but it is not necessary to focus on the seams in order to profit from the theological significance. Von Rad, however, suggests that the two accounts taken together show us how the human partner in the covenant is paradoxically both active and passive. The greater emphasis, however, is on the presence of God giving "a real guarantee," which is established in spite of the "complete passivity of the human partner" (von Rad, *Genesis,* pp. 189-90).

enant or else call down a curse upon themselves. However, if one partner greatly outranks the other, then only the weaker partner would be required to pass through — it begins to sound like a ceremony of initiation, like a Mafia ritual, doesn't it? The suspense in the story is built up with utmost simplicity, but it's palpable; the atmosphere as night falls over the bloody alley is heavy with foreboding. Human activity, human wishing, human willing has come to an end; indeed, the human agent has fallen asleep. The only actor remaining on the stage is God.

And then, in the darkness, Abraham awakens from his premonitory sleep and he sees — what does he see? Behold, a smoking fire pot and a flaming torch move through the aisle of blood.[8] It is the living presence of God.

And in that ceremony, we read, God made a covenant with Abraham. The Creator of the universe has come down into the human story and has bound himself in blood to his mortal creatures. *He* has condescended to *us*. But do you get the amazing revelation here, the missing piece that means everything? God passes through the bloody alley. Abraham does not. Abraham does not do anything. The Lord alone passes through, acting in the role of the weaker party. God has made God's own self the vulnerable partner in the covenant. In this extraordinary event, God attaches himself unconditionally to his fallen human creatures and ratifies his commitment *unilaterally*. God has invoked the bloody curse upon God's own self.

This, indeed, is a story to raise the hairs on our head. There is nothing else like this in the history of religion: the Almighty Lord of the universe enters into a relationship with his chosen human partner *under the conditions of human liability*. Here in the opening pages of the story of salvation, God lays himself open to the full consequences of everything that will come after: the disobedience, the idolatry, the folly, the greed and cruelty, the vanity and selfishness, the pride and deceit that fill the following pages of the Bible. The world had never seen anything in religion like this before. In the ancient world, the gods were arbitrary and capricious. Therefore the *unconditional* nature of the covenant that God made with Abraham sets religion on "a bold, new, independent course."[9] Our inheritance from the Hebrew Bible represents, intellectually and morally, a decisive break with primitive religious thought.

---

8. "Behold" should not be translated "see" or "look." "Behold" (also "lo") in the biblical languages signifies revelation. It is a word of wonder, a word of awe, denoting an event of divine incursion into human affairs.

9. Nahum M. Sarna, *Understanding Genesis* (New York: Schocken Books, 1970), p. 127.

And so you know how the story continues with the birth of Abraham and Sarah's son, Isaac, and how it comes to its appointed culmination two thousand years later, when God keeps his word and takes the bloody curse upon himself. After the people of God have flagrantly disregarded their part in the covenant for thousands of years, God at last steps forward and, on a hill outside Jerusalem, ratifies the covenant for once and for all in the blood of his Son. The fiery presence of Yahweh in the midnight spectacle of the bloody alley becomes the pouring out of the last drop of blood of the Son of God.

Every single one of us here today, no matter how prosperous and glossy we may look, is carrying some sort of baggage. Human life is a bloody affair. If it is not the blood of war and murder, it is the blood of illness and death. If it is not literally blood, it is the burden of disappointment, doubt, anxiety, depression, fear. Some of us hide our inner conflicts more or less successfully behind a polished surface; others are publicly betrayed by the outward and visible signs of inadequacy, decline, failure, disgrace. We must lie down, wrote the poet Yeats, "where all the ladders start/In the foul rag-and-bone shop of the heart."

Here indeed is the link between ourselves and our Stone Age ancestors, between the Hebrews of old and ourselves of today, between yourself and your neighbor in the next pew. Here is the link. We are all terminally afflicted with the human condition, incapable of making or keeping any kind of agreement with a righteous God. Here is the news today: it is precisely to us in our affliction that the Lord comes, blazing his way with galaxies across the sky, trailing clouds of glory, writing his name in fire. He comes to us in our insensibility, in our stupor, in our impotence. He comes without conditions and without requirements. He comes down from heaven into the bloody mess of human history, laying himself open to the worst that we can do, taking the curse of our condition upon himself. He takes it and he carries it all the way.

This is the God of Abraham, Isaac, and Jacob; this is the God and Father of our Lord Jesus Christ. Let him take you by the hand this very day and lead you out where you can see the stars, where the flaming splendor of his appearance dispels your darkness, and above all where he lays himself down in the corridors of death, so that the children of Abraham might, by his blood, attain to the promise of eternal life and a celestial inheritance in the Kingdom that fadeth not away.

AMEN.

# Entertaining Angels Unawares

*July 1983*                                               Genesis 18:1-16

COME BACK for a few moments, deep into the primeval history of humankind. Abraham cannot be understood except against the epic background
of the first eleven chapters of the book of Genesis. These chapters depict
for us a gargantuan, cosmic panorama of creation and fall. One human failure follows upon another — the sin of Adam and Eve, the murder of Abel
by his brother, the wickedness of the whole human race almost completely
destroyed by the Flood, and finally the catastrophe of the Tower of Babel,
where men who wanted to "make a name for themselves" (Gen. 11:4) pre-
sumed too far and were scattered by the Lord God over the face of the
earth.

The old paintings of the Tower of Babel portray the pitiableness of
man in his rebellion — the heavens stretched without limit above, the abandoned tower already beginning to deteriorate, the would-be builders below,
featureless, trapped, and going nowhere, squirming desperately like worms
in a can. At the end of the eleventh chapter of Genesis, this is what we see: a
global landscape of undifferentiated chaos and confusion, estrangement
and hostility, encompassing the entire race of humankind. We must understand that this beginning could very well have been the end. God had given
us our chance, and we had thrown it away. He could very well have left us to

---

This sermon title echoes Hebrews 13:2: "Do not neglect to show hospitality to strangers, for
thereby some have entertained angels unawares."

go slowly mad or blow ourselves up. God was not required to do anything further on our behalf.

But then, quite suddenly and without any advance warning to the reader, a spotlight sweeps across the vast, darkened biblical stage and comes to rest on the solitary figure of Abraham. It is the inaugural moment in the history of redemption.

Abraham! The father of believers, the first patriarch of Israel, our great spiritual ancestor, the heroic progenitor of God's chosen people — and yet, for all that, a figure almost impossibly remote, separated from us by almost four thousand years, far off in the Fertile Crescent of Mesopotamia, a man native to a culture so lost to us that we know it only from digging it out of the ground. Why have the names of generations upon generations of Mesopotamians vanished, while this one name, Abraham, stirs the blood of Jews and Christians to this very day, in spite of his distance from us?

Why Abraham? The answer is given very simply in the first verse of the twelfth chapter: "The Lord spoke to Abraham." Abraham has done nothing whatever to deserve this attention. Abraham is nothing in himself. We are given no information about any achievements or qualities that might distinguish him. Abraham comes to the forefront of the world stage for one reason alone: the Lord spoke to him. This is the first event in the long story of God's free decision to redeem his people, the story that does not come to its completion until A.D. 33 on a hill outside Jerusalem.

"Abraham, [said the Lord], leave your own country, your kinsmen, and your father's house and go to a country that I will show you." (12:1)

Americans are so accustomed to leaving their father's house and going to another place that this command sounds pretty ordinary to us; in fact, we think it's pretty strange if a man *doesn't* leave his father's house. But for a man of Abraham's time, it meant leaving every single thing that gave him his identity. Abraham, leave your ancestors' graves, your grandparents, your land, your friends, your life insurance, and your safe-deposit box, and go to another place far away, unknown to you, a place that I will show you when you get there. God's call to Abraham was a call to abandon every single thing that meant security in this world and to start a new life oriented toward a different kind of security, that which is based on God alone.

God's word came to Abraham in the form of a promise:

"I will make you a great nation, and I will bless you. I will make your name great. . . . And all peoples on earth will be blessed through you." (12:2)

And upon receiving this word from God, we are told, "So Abram went, as the Lord had told him" (12:4). It was a long, long way — many decades — from that first word of God to the end of Abraham's wanderings. Not everything that happened in between can be read out loud in mixed company on Sunday morning. Abraham and his long-suffering wife, Sarah, were flawed people, like all the rest of us. But because they had been chosen by God to be the parents of his people, wonderful things happened to them. In the eighteenth chapter of Genesis, which is our text for today, we find one of the loveliest, most evocative stories about the Lord's mystery and goodness to be found in all the Bible.

Many, many years after God's first call to Abraham, we find the now-elderly patriarch in the land of Canaan with the flocks and herds that he has accumulated, with his various servants and his barren wife, Sarah, settled at a place where there were many trees called terebinths. There was nothing permanent at Mamre then except the altar that Abraham had built for Yahweh. All Abraham's family and retainers lived in tents, befitting their vocation as wanderers under orders from God.

One day Abraham was sitting in the door of his tent during the noon-day siesta. It was a hot, sultry summer day; we can imagine Abraham moving out into the entrance of the tent after lunch in order to catch any passing breezes. Sarah is inside the tent, busying herself with her household duties. Sarah and Abraham have no children. All these years of following the Lord's command — all these years of living on a promise — and no child. How can Abraham be the father of nations without an heir? We can only imagine the doubt, the hopelessness, that he must have felt from time to time. In fact, the idea of the promised child was so preposterous at this late stage in Abraham's life that he seems not to have told Sarah anything about it. Reflecting on the promise, and the impossibility of its ever being fulfilled, Abraham sits drowsily in the doorway of his tent. There is a great stillness, broken only by the faint rustling of the leaves of the terebinths and the buzz of insects. The heat rising from the ground makes everything look hazy and blurred. Abraham is almost asleep. Suddenly, with a start, he pulls himself awake; through the shimmering mirage he sees standing before him three men whom he has never seen before.

Abraham has not been serving the Lord all these years for nothing:

God's law of hospitality is second nature to him by now. He gets hurriedly to his feet and bows low before the strangers. With the elaborate, exquisite courtesy of the Middle East, he urges them to stay and partake of a little water and a morsel of bread — as he modestly refers to it. What actually happens is beautifully described, with an unusual amount of detail (ordinarily the biblical narrators are spare in their descriptions). Abraham arranges a lavish feast for the travelers. It's an enchanting picture — the three guests seated at the table in the shade of the trees while the old man serves them himself, instead of having the servants do it. As a crowning gesture of courtesy, Abraham stands by, respectfully, while they eat, to see if they might want anything.

The solemn dignity of the three strangers is most striking. They eat their enormous meal in silence, while Abraham waits. The atmosphere is still. Suddenly the silence is broken by an unexpected question:

"Where is your wife, Sarah?" (How did they know her name?)

Abraham responded dutifully, "She's there, in the tent."

Then comes the astonishing pronouncement: "[About this time next year] . . . your wife Sarah shall have a son" (18:10). Can you sense the way this announcement is dropped into the midst of the drowsy luncheon like a smooth stone fallen from a great height into perfectly still water? The moment for the fulfillment of the promise, so long delayed, has come. Abraham, dumbstruck, stands rooted to the spot as the realization dawns on him that he has been entertaining God.

Sarah, who has been eavesdropping from inside the tent, has a different reaction. *Sarah laughs.* Sarah snickers. Sarah says to herself in derision, "My husband is a hundred years old, and I'm ninety and barren! Am I going to have sexual pleasure at this stage of my life?"

And the Lord said to Abraham, "Why did Sarah laugh and say 'Will I really have a child, now that I am old?' [God cleaned up Sarah's language a bit.] Is anything too hard for the Lord? At the appointed time next year . . . Sarah will have a son" (18:13-14).

The three men get up to leave, and Abraham walks along with them to see them on their way. Abraham has been walking with God for twenty-five years; but never before has he been granted this level of gracious intimacy, steps matching steps, purpose matching purpose, obedience matching call. In this way, we are told, the Lord visited Abraham and Sarah and brought them both into partnership with him, giving them a great place in his divine plan for all humankind.

It is important for us to understand Sarah's laughter. From a human point of view, it is entirely justified — indeed, almost admirable — for it suggests a good sense of humor and a healthy grasp of reality. Ninety-year-old women don't have children. As Ernst Käsemann has written, "Sarah's laughter is faith's constant companion."[1] It is against the very human accompaniment of Sarah's ribald and mocking laughter that the word of God comes: "Is anything impossible for the Lord?" We hear those words again, thousands of years later, on a Judean road:

> Jesus looked at them [the disciples] and said, "With men it is impossible, but not with God. For God, all things are possible." (Mark 10:27)

Of the three men (or angels) who visited Abraham, which one was the Lord? It is not clear from the text as we have it. At first we just hear of "three men." Then all of a sudden we read, "The Lord said." No doubt the ambiguity is intentional. Some modern commentators say that God was present in all three men, or angels. There is a celebrated icon in a museum in Moscow, painted by Andrei Rublev, which is perhaps the greatest masterpiece of Russian orthodoxy. The painting depicts three beautiful angelic figures, Abraham's visitors, sitting around the table under the trees in a perfect circle, and the name of the icon is — wonder of wonders — *The Holy Trinity*. God the Father, God the Son, and God the Holy Spirit. It is a wonderful and mysterious prefiguration of the Incarnation, when "the Word became flesh and dwelt among us." Some of the ancient commentators were troubled by the thought of the transcendent YHWH taking food just as men do; but can we not see this beautiful story as a foreshadowing of the day when Jesus of Nazareth would take his meals with sinners and, in his risen body, eat fish cooked on a charcoal grill on the beach with those same disciples who, like Abraham and Sarah, had failed to recognize him when he first appeared to them?

Well, we know what happened. A son, Isaac, was indeed born to the old couple, and ultimately the people of Israel would trace their origin to Abraham, just as the Lord had said. However, there came a time when the people would claim to be Abraham's heirs by virtue of blood descent alone: I belong to God because I'm descended from Abraham; I'm an Episcopalian because my parents were Episcopalians; I'm a Christian because I belong to a "Christian" culture. Eventually, there was born into the world another son

---

1. Ernst Käsemann, *Perspectives on Paul* (Philadelphia: Fortress Press, 1969), p. 69.

of aged parents; his name was John, and he stood on the banks of the Jordan River and shouted at the people, "Do not presume to say to yourselves, 'We have Abraham as our father'; for I tell you, God is able to raise up children to Abraham from these stones" (Matt. 3:9). And the One who would come after him stood in the Temple and taught the people that he was the light of the world. The people replied that they did not need any more light, thank you, because "we are descendants of Abraham." And Jesus said, "Truly, I say to you, before Abraham was, I AM" (John 8:39, 58).

A few weeks ago, the *New Yorker* carried a profile of Jean Riboud, who is the chief executive officer of the vast multinational corporation called Schlumberger. Mr. Riboud was quoted in the article as saying that the corporation had to take over the responsibility of providing community, identity, security, and all the other things that had formerly been provided by religion. This statement fascinated me because of its assumption that "religion" was a stage that we have passed through and have now come out on the other side of. Well, there is indeed much truth in the implication that "religion" cannot deliver on its promises. "Religion" cannot deliver because it is projected out of our human wishes, fantasies, fears, and longings.

But the faith of Abraham is not "religion," and it never was. We are talking here about a living God, not some fanciful deity that lives only in human imagination, here today and gone tomorrow. If you asked a Hebrew who his God was, the answer would be "The God of Abraham, Isaac, and Jacob." This is the *real* God, maker of heaven and earth, Lord of the universe, the God who stoops to involve himself with real historical people who have identifiable names and live in identifiable places. This is not an entity in the empyrean with vaguely defined characteristics, but the God who attached himself to a bunch of unlikely characters in a real geographical location. This is the God who entered history and took up residence. This is not "religion." This is the God who is before Abraham and after him, before Jean Riboud and after him.

A few months ago, a young woman I know made an extremely difficult and personally costly ethical decision. I asked her later how she found the strength to do it. I will never forget her answer. She looked at me with a steady, unclouded gaze and said simply and with total conviction, *"Because of the God who lives."*

To each new generation after Abraham, *the God who lives* draws near with the same gifts of faith and hope that he gave to Abraham and Sarah. Which do you want — the apparent security of all the possessions and the status that we have accumulated in this world, or the true security belonging to those who rest in the hand of God? Abraham took the road marked out by the living Lord. It was the beginning of God's salvation for all the world. Now the Lord comes to us once more, in his three-personed splendor and pity and love. It is *his* table now, and *we* are the guests — guests of the Father, and the Son, and the Holy Spirit; and the angels and archangels join their voices to ours. Come with Abraham and Sarah, and find hope for your hopelessness, joy for your sorrow, purpose for your life, and the never-failing guidance of the Lord your God, whose intimate presence may at any moment invade your tent and your table with astonishment and joy.

Amen.

# The Future of God

GRACE CHURCH IN NEW YORK

*The Second Sunday in Lent 1988*                    Genesis 22:1-14

WHAT WOULD it mean to give up the future?

We could think about this from the standpoint of individuals. Why do we fix up our apartments, work toward being promoted, make investments, plan vacations, raise children, buy season tickets? We do these things be-cause we take it for granted that we will have a future. Years ago, when my uncle's wife dropped dead suddenly of an aneurysm, a list was found in her desk drawer of all the people she was planning to invite to a party. I was very young then — only twenty-one — and it was my first close experience of premature death; the fact that the curtain had come down on my youthful, vibrant aunt while she was in the midst of making plans for the immediate future left a taste of ashes in my mouth.

We can also think about the loss of the future from the standpoint of society. Why do we hold elections, build skyscrapers, renovate houses, ap-point judges, pass laws, shore up bridges, attend meetings, pay taxes? None of this would make any sense whatever without a future.

It's been a while since the anti-nuclear movement was at its height. We fool around with the idea of the end of the world as we know it in apocalyp-tic cinematic visions, and we are constantly reminded that ecological disas-ter might be a very real possibility, but the fears of the Cold War period have abated. Perhaps we simply can't bear to think about it very much.

I remember being taken to the top of the World Trade Center in 1984, when my own preoccupation with the nuclear prospect was intense. For some reason, as I looked out at the view, I was seized not by delight, but by horror — I thought of a bomb being dropped on New York and what that would mean.[1] No Statue of Liberty, and no golden door to welcome immigrants. No Broadway, no theatre, no actors. No financial district and no finances. No Fulton Fish Market, no seafood restaurants, no seafood. No Metropolitan Opera, no Central Park, no Yankee Stadium, no Chrysler Building, no Lincoln Center, no Brooklyn Bridge. The Vermeers in the Frick Gallery, the manuscripts in the Morgan Library, the archives of the Historical Society, the records of the Sloan-Kettering researchers, the collections of the Public Library, everything we have in common to bring us joy and give us hope — all gone in ashes, dust, rubble. I was so unnerved by this vision of the loss of the future that weeks later I was still having a crisis of faith. I called up one of my theological mentors and asked him if he could see me and talk to me about it.

During the six-week season of Lent, the Old Testament lessons that are appointed to be read are chosen from among the most powerful in the Bible. They are twenty-megaton passages. In the one that you heard today, from the twenty-second chapter of Genesis, God announces to Abraham that he is going to destroy Abraham's future.

The story of Abraham's journey to sacrifice his son Isaac is well known, but it's necessary to see it in its total context. It's clear from what we call the primeval history in Genesis (chapters 1–11) that the human race has been in a self-destructive downward spiral ever since the disobedience of Adam and Eve. The great inaugural event, the appearance of God to introduce his plan of salvation, occurs at the beginning of chapter 12, and the long journey of Abraham is essentially completed with today's story, ten chapters and forty-odd years later.

The first thing that happens is an event of the Word of God. The Lord says to Abraham, "Leave your country, your people, and your father's house, and go to the land that I will show you" (12:1). This was no small thing to ask. It meant being severed from everything that made a man secure and consequential in those days. It meant abandoning every single anchor to the past and setting out in an unknown direction with nothing to trust except the Word of the Lord.

Abraham's life during the next decades was extremely difficult, for he

---

1. A certain amount of imagination is required of readers here, to project themselves back before 9/11. In the days after 9/11, many turned to a hymn by R. S. Bridges, "All My Hope on God Is Founded," especially these words: "Tower and temple fall to dust/But God's pow'r, hour by hour, is my temple and my tower."

had to live as a nomad in a foreign land, with assorted troubles from neighbors and from the members of his own family. All those years, he and his wife, Sarah, had borne the sorrow of childlessness; many times they were tempted to declare God absurd for having promised them a blessing through their offspring when the two of them, both elderly, had no offspring.

The *context* of the promise of God is all-important. Over and over and over, for a period of twenty-five years, God continued to appear to Abraham and make promises. Imagine believing a promise for twenty-five years when there was not a sign that it could ever be fulfilled! Imagine continuing to hold on to a promise that contradicted every conceivable human expectation! This was the promise: that Abraham would have a son named Isaac; that from Isaac would come countless descendants; that those descendants would be greatly blessed; that indeed they would become a blessing to the whole world, even including the kings of other nations; that they would possess the Promised Land; and that God would be their God. It is remarkable, on rereading Genesis, to note how many times God repeated this promise in one form or another. It is even more remarkable that Abraham went on believing it, in spite of the fact that he had no children and no possibility of having any.

At length, Abraham, egged on by Sarah, attempted to circumvent God.[2] This is one of the less attractive stories about our ancestral couple. Sarah presented her husband with her nubile slave, Hagar, and Abraham fathered a child by her. God was good to Hagar and her son, Ishmael, giving them a life of their own. In spite of Abraham's insubordinate act, however, God continued to tell Abraham, "My covenant is with your son Isaac" (17:21; see also 21:12), not with Ishmael. In view of the fact that there was no Isaac and no prospect of any Isaac, the whole saga of Abraham up to this point seems downright crazy. How hollow, how false God's promise must have seemed, when Abraham and Sarah were both approaching their hundredth year and Sarah had never once conceived in her whole life! But as St. Paul says, Abraham went on hoping against hope because of the God in whom he believed, the God who calls into existence the things that do not exist (Rom. 4:19-21). Finally, in their extreme old age, Sarah conceived and bore Abraham a son, Isaac — the child of the promise.

---

2. It is crucially important to recognize this failure of faith on Abraham's part. It is a fundamental theological mistake to think of Abraham as one whose heroic faith made God's salvation possible. It was *God* who made the heroic *faith* possible. This is the underlying biblical trajectory that leads to Romans 4 and Paul's climactic definition of God in 4:17.

At last, some measure of peace settles over Abraham's life. The two aged parents watch proudly, we can be sure, as their son grows healthy, happy, and normal. At last it seemed clear that their job was done. A lifetime of obedience had been rewarded; Abraham had remained faithful; at length, God had kept his word.

Then, suddenly, and without any warning, the unthinkable happens. We should understand that it truly is unthinkable, humanly speaking; there has never been another story like this in the whole world. Its uniqueness, in itself, is a cause for wonder. Many times in human history people have had to make terrible sacrifices for some greater cause, but never before or since has a man been asked to kill his own son for no discernible reason whatsoever, except that God wished to test Abraham.

It is extremely difficult for us today to understand this story in the way that it is supposed to function in the book of Genesis. We are so horrified by the thought of a father being commanded to slaughter his own son that we can't think of anything else. For that matter, the ancient writer was horrified, too; we can tell from the way he tells the story. As in all biblical narrative, the telling is spare and economical and remarkably skillful. God says to Abraham, "Take your son, your only son, Isaac, whom you love" (and this language is repeated twice more). It is as if the storyteller were deliberately emphasizing the anguish of the father and the awfulness of the command, but only obliquely, not obviously or with a heavy hand, as a lesser artist would do.

This last climactic story of Abraham is told in the same form as the first:

| | |
|---|---|
| Leave your country, | Take your son, |
| your people, | your only son Isaac, |
| and your father's house | whom you love, |
| and go to the land | and go to one of the mountains |
| that I will show you (12:1) | that I will tell you about (22:2) |

In chapter 12, Abraham is asked to cut himself off from the past; in chapter 22, he is asked to cut himself off from the future.[3]

What sort of God would do such a thing? That is the question we ask. But apparently, according to the story, the answer to the question is that it is the same God that Abraham has known and believed and obeyed from the

---

3. Gerhard von Rad, *Genesis* (Philadelphia: Westminster Press, 1972), p. 239.

beginning. This seems incredible to us, but it is a feature of the story that Abraham seems to believe that God is entirely within his rights to demand this of him.

The most dreadful part of the story, of course, is that Abraham is supposed to do the deed himself. God doesn't ask Abraham to send Isaac out to play in the street so God can come along in a truck and mow him down; that would have been bad enough. What is infinitely worse is that Abraham personally is supposed to slit the boy's throat. The writer does not altogether suppress the human side of this, but the restraint shown in the telling is a clue to us that the meaning of the story lies on the theological plane. Isaac does not function in the story as though he were just a boy; his primary role in the story is as the embodiment of God's promise. This should not lessen the peculiar horror of the situation, however, for the narrator allows us to feel it fully as Abraham makes his three days' journey.

Three days! Conceivably one might carry out an unthinkable order on impulse, in a moment's blind recklessness; but God sends Abraham on a three-day journey to a distant spot so that he will have plenty of time to think about what he has been asked to do. Even Martin Luther quailed at the prospect; he said we could view the journey to Mount Moriah only from a distance, and that he himself could not have been a spectator, let alone a participant or the executioner — in fact, he compares himself and us to the donkeys that were left behind at the foot of the mountain. Again, we emphasize the uniqueness of the story: God asked Abraham to do something that he would never again ask anyone to do. And, be it noted, the hearer of the story is told something that Abraham does not know — namely, that God never had any intention of going through with the killing; he did it to "test" Abraham.

Is this some kind of cruel joke? God already knows everything; why then does he put Abraham to the test? A clue is found in Romans when Paul calls Abraham "the father of us all." The Christian tradition has always known Abraham to be the "father of believers." It is Abraham's faith, the meaning of it, the depth of it, the application of it, and above all the *source* of it that is central to the story of the sacrifice of Isaac.

The depth of Abraham's faith is suggested by the degree of anguish which afflicts him. Typically, the narrator does not describe this directly. Rather, it is implied, hinted at, evoked in the twice-repeated statement that, after the servants were told to stay behind with the donkeys, "the two of them went on together." Some of the greatest imaginations in the world have been applied to the matter of what Abraham and Isaac said to each other as they were "going on together," but once again, the singular artistry of our storyteller defeats all such attempts:

> As the two of them went on together, Isaac spoke up and said to Abraham, "Father?"
> "Yes, my son?" Abraham replied.
> "The fire and the wood are here," Isaac said, "but where is the lamb for the burnt offering?"
> Abraham answered, "God himself will provide the lamb for the burnt offering, my son." And the two of them went on together. (22:7-8)

The reticence and economy with which the journey is described contrasts with the detailed account of the preparation of the sacrifice. The narrative pace slows to an excruciating crawl:

> Abraham built an altar there,
>   and arranged the wood on it;
> He bound his son Isaac,
>   and laid him on the altar,
>     on top of the wood.
> Then he reached out his hand,
>   and took the knife
>     to slay his son. (22:9-10)

And we are to understand, make no mistake, that for Abraham this does not mean the death of his personal hopes only. For Abraham, and therefore for us, the hearers of the story, the end of Isaac means the end of hope for the salvation and blessing of the entire world. It means the end of the purposes of God.

When I went to see my mentor with my fears about nuclear annihilation and the end of civilization, my question was really whether I could go on believing in God in view of what I had seen in my mind's eye when I looked out over the Statue of Liberty. I remember in particular the thought that if there were an all-out nuclear exchange, the survivors would not even be able to find bread or water — let alone wine — to have the Lord's Supper. This seemed to me to be the ultimate in the destruction of a human future.

I'm sure my professor had many things to say that day, but I remember only one. He said, gently, "Fleming, did you think that God had not thought of that?"

I don't know if this works for you. All I can say is that with those simple words my hope in God was restored to me. I realized that, as Paul writes, the God in whom Abraham believed is able to raise the dead and to call into existence the things that do not exist.

Abraham was asked to do something that no one else was ever asked to do, precisely in order to demonstrate to the whole world what hope in God really means. We look upon Abraham's three-day journey with solemn awe. We are amazed by his faith in the God whose promise he had trusted for decades, his obedience to the God with whom he had walked — the God whose gifts and promises are manifestations of pure grace, to be received from his hand in total submission to the One whose will, whether in light or in shadow, is always perfect.

And so, at the very moment that we avert our eyes in unspeakable horror, God acts:

> Abraham put forth his hand, and took the knife, to slay his son. But the angel of the Lord called to him from heaven, and said, "Abraham, Abraham!" And he said [again], "Here I am." He said, "Do not lay your hand on the boy or do anything to him: for now I know that you fear God, seeing you have not withheld your son, your only son, from me."
>
> And Abraham lifted up his eyes and looked, and behold, behind him was a ram, caught in a thicket by his horns; and Abraham went and took the ram, and offered it up as a burnt offering instead of his son. So Abraham called the name of that place "The Lord will provide." (22:10-14)

So Abraham received his son back again from the dead. To "believe in" God, to "fear" God, is to trust him totally and to put oneself in his hands totally, even when the road leads out into God-forsakenness, even when the fulfillment of God's promises seems to have receded into impossibility. Our father Abraham, through his three days' agony, has taught us how to be believers. God knew that Abraham would be faithful; the purpose of the "test" was not for God to gain new knowledge, but for Abraham to bequeath to his posterity a heroic, unparalleled example of steadfast loyalty to God throughout a journey into an apparently hopeless night.

Unparalleled, that is, until the day when God's own Son, his only Son, whom God loved, cried out on the Cross, "My God, my God, why hast thou forsaken me?" For Isaac, there was a substitute — Abraham found a ram in the bush. "God himself will provide the lamb for a burnt offering, my son." But when Jesus was brought to the Cross — the Lamb of God who would bear the sin of the world into fathomless darkness — there was no substitute for him. God did not withhold his Son, his only Son, whom he loved. It is no accident that this story is read during Lent, and also on Good Friday. God the Father and God the Son together, with a single will, offered the perfect sacrifice once for all.[4] What Abraham at the last moment did not have to do, God did.

And what this means for you and for me is that there is nothing so unspeakable that God has not already thought of it, and nothing so evil that God is not victorious over it, however long the journey may be, however indefinitely the fulfillment of the promises may seem to be postponed. What this means is that you and I, as children of Abraham, Isaac, and Jacob, have received our lives from God as pure gift, sustained in his hand, according to his purpose, destined for the completion of his plan, living solely by his grace; and that is the impetus for all resistance — all resistance to the use of nuclear arms and every other form of evil. In the life of faith lived by Christians, we bear witness to the biblical testimony that nothing — nothing at all — can destroy the promised future, because the promised future belongs to our God.

AMEN.

---

4. In the Epistle to the Hebrews, which focuses on the meaning of Christ's sacrifice for sin, the word *ephapax* — "once for all" — is repeated emphatically.

# Does God Need a Name?

*Trinity Sunday 1991*                                                    Exodus 3:1-6

IN THE parish where I first began my ministry, there was a large confirmation class of thirteen-year-olds every year, and we met once a week for seven months.[1] In the beginning of the course, we did a little exercise. Each student was asked to draw a picture of God. As you can imagine, all sorts of things emerged — clouds, suns, circles, triangles, and a preponderance of old men with white beards. When the pictures were finished, we all sat in a circle, and each young person held up his or her picture and explained it.

At this point a clean, empty wastebasket was brought in and set down in the middle of the circle. Each class member, one by one, was asked to tear up his or her picture and drop the pieces into the wastebasket. When they had finished, the Bible was opened, and the Second Commandment was solemnly intoned: "Thou shalt not make for thyself any graven image, or any likeness of anything that is in heaven above, or in the earth beneath, or in the waters under the earth."

Then, as everyone sat around in somewhat abashed silence, a question was asked: "If we can't draw a picture of God, and if we don't know what God looks like, and if God isn't like anything in heaven or earth, then how can we know anything about God at all?" The students were asked to think

---

1. In the eighties, being confirmed in the Episcopal Church was still a status symbol in Rye, New York. Parents gave their children no choice; they had to come to class, just as they had to go to school. The numbers were so large that we split the class into two sections. Those were the days!

about this, and then another passage from the book of Exodus was read. We heard this text read a few minutes ago; it tells the story of the burning bush. We did this exercise every year at Christ Church, and every year the Lord was good enough to give us one or two bright-eyed young people who would catch on. Let me read the crucial parts again. Remember the question: *How do we know anything about God?*

> Moses said to God,
> "If I come to the people of Israel and say to them,
>     'The God of your fathers has sent me to you,' and they ask me,
>     'What is his name?' what shall I say to them?"
> God said to Moses, "I AM WHO I AM. . . . Say this to the
>     people of Israel, I AM has sent me to you."
> God also said to Moses,
> "Say this to the people of Israel, 'The Lord, the God of your fathers,
>     the God of Abraham, the God of Isaac, and the God of Jacob
>     has sent me to you: this is my name for ever.'" (3:13-15)

In the light of the Second Commandment, how do we know anything about God? That was the question. Every year, the story of the burning bush would elicit this answer from one or another boy or girl: "*He tells us! God tells us* who he is!"

It was always a magical moment in the class for those who "got it."[2] The one, holy, catholic and apostolic church rests on this truth: *God has told us who he is.* To use the language of the Book of Common Prayer, he has "made himself known to us . . . in the calling of Israel to be his people, in his Word spoken to the prophets, and above all in the Word made flesh, Jesus his Son." To quote the opening lines of the Epistle to the Hebrews, "In many and various ways God spoke of old to our fathers by the prophets; but in these last days he has spoken to us by a Son, whom he appointed the heir of all things" (Heb. 1:1-2). God *has spoken:* this is the unique feature of the whole Judeo-Christian enterprise.

One of the most important distinctions to be made in the world of religion is the difference between saying "I found God" and "God found me." St. Paul made this distinction when he wrote to the Galatians, "Now that you have come to know God, or rather *to be known by* God . . ." (Gal. 4:9; my italics). Paul is dictating this letter, and he interrupts himself in order to

2. Not everyone gets it. That's the perpetual mystery of faith and the divine election.

make his point; he rephrases his wording, making God the subject rather than the object, so that the Galatians will understand and remember that God is not the object of the human religious journey, but the source and instigator of his own journey toward us. The Bible is sometimes misguidedly described as the record of "man's search for God"; on the contrary, it is the story of God's search for us.

Every year, it is that story that we tell from the lectern and from the pulpit. We hear the story of how God has revealed himself to people who otherwise would never have known who he was or anything about him. For the Christian faith is a *story* more than it is anything else. More than it is doctrine or discipline or worship or philosophy or morality, it is above all a story. It is *a narrative of God,* the *drama of God* and how he came seeking after his disobedient and fallen creatures.

All during this church year, we have been telling the story. The events of the life of Jesus, the Son of God, have passed in chronological order from birth to crucifixion to resurrection from the dead through Ascension and Pentecost. All our church festivals and special days have been centered on this narrative. Only today is different. This is the only day in the church year when we celebrate a doctrine, the doctrine of the Trinity. Many have questioned this. Some have suggested that we should do away with Trinity Sunday. It is not, they say, part of the story.

Well, we can't deny that the doctrine of the Holy Trinity is remarkably unlike the simple story of Jesus in many ways. The quickest way to illustrate this is to ask you to take a look at the back of your Prayer Book, page 864.[3] This is the Athanasian Creed, dating from the fourth century A.D., when the doctrine was being hammered out in its finished form. Let's read just a bit of it (are you ready for this?):

> Whosoever will be saved, before all things it is necessary that he hold the Catholic Faith. . . . And the Catholic Faith is this: That we worship one God in Trinity, and Trinity in Unity, neither confounding the Persons, nor dividing the Substance. For there is one Person of the Father, another of the Son, and another of the Holy Ghost. But the Godhead of the Father, of the Son, and of the Holy Ghost, is all one, the glory equal, the majesty co-eternal. Such as the Father is, such is the Son, and such is the Holy Ghost. The Father uncreate, the Son uncreate, and the Holy Spirit uncreate. The Fa-

---

3. This refers to the Book of Common Prayer of the Episcopal Church.

ther incomprehensible, the Son incomprehensible, and the Holy
Ghost incomprehensible.

It gets worse! Dorothy L. Sayers summed it all up with her wry comment: "The Father incomprehensible, the Son incomprehensible, and the
whole thing incomprehensible."[4]

All kidding aside, though, the Athanasian Creed and the other Trinitarian formulas written out by the Church Fathers, though they sound tor-
tured and preposterous to modern American ears, are some of the most ex-
quisitely wrought intellectual analyses ever produced in the history of the
human race. It's as though God placed before us a gigantic philosophical
puzzle for us to work out, knowing that we would take great delight in doing so. I have heard scientists talk this way about physics and mathematics. I
will never understand physics, but I am prepared to believe what physicists
say, that there is awesome beauty and logic in it. Even though we may not
understand the Athanasian Creed, we can still acknowledge that it is not
only a pre-eminent document in the history of ideas, but also a mental construct of great aesthetic and intellectual beauty.

But is the Trinity just one of many impressive ideas in the history of
ideas? Or is it something more?

Christians believe that the doctrine of the Trinity is, in the final analysis,
the necessary conclusion *from the story*. Had there been no story of Jesus of
Nazareth, there would have been no need to write the Athanasian Creed.
The doctrine of the Trinity was, so to speak, forced upon the church by the
necessity of explaining who Jesus was in relation to God, and how the Holy
Spirit was related to them both. Perhaps the analogy of physics could be used
again: scientific theory does not exist solely for its own sake, but in order to
explain phenomena. Science seeks to understand, to account for the data of
physical existence. Well, the doctrine of the Trinity seeks to explain the data
that we have before us: the church found itself confessing a crucified man as
redeemer of the world, and this confession was, as St. Paul wrote, "an offense
to the Jews and foolishness to the Greeks" (1 Cor. 1:23). It had to be explained. The doctrine of the Trinity emerged from this urgent need to give
an account of the identity of Jesus. In that sense, therefore, the Trinity is not
just an idea in the history of ideas. It has evolved from the self-revelation of
God. It is *given*. As God gave his name to Moses at the burning bush, so he
has given his name to us: Father, Son, and Holy Spirit. We could not have

---

4. Dorothy L. Sayers, *Creed or Chaos?* (New York: Harcourt, Brace, 1949), p. 22.

found this name by ourselves, not even at the end of the longest and most passionate and most single-minded search that religious man is capable of. It had to be revealed. God alone can tell us who he is.

In the Old and New Testaments, God has many names. The Tetragrammaton, YHWH, is an attempt to render the mysterious name God gave Moses — "I AM WHO I AM" — but the ancient Hebrews always considered it too sacred to pronounce. There were other names — Elohim, Adonai, El Shaddai — but the most interesting names of God are not these. The ones that really grab us are the names that connect God with our history, and not incidentally with the history of the Jewish people. You can't get more specific than that.

What is the purpose of a name in the first place? Surely it is to distinguish one person from another in a special way, a uniquely personal way. I remember a classmate from Union Seminary; not long after he graduated, he developed cancer, and he had to go for a long stay at M. D. Anderson, the famous cancer center in Houston. While there, he felt nameless and lost. He felt that he was just a number, just another case to experiment on. He took to wearing his clerical collar around the hospital to try to fight off the feeling of anonymity, to give himself an identity. To become a number, not a name, is to become one of the faceless masses. It is to lose your own personal history.[5]

If God is not given his proper name, he becomes one of a faceless mass of gods, gods with no history. Let me give an example from a recent article by an Episcopal priest in New Jersey, writing in our church's newspaper, *Episcopal Life*. This is an article written to argue that infants should be baptized even if their parents show no inclination to raise them in the church or in the Christian faith. The writer is arguing sincerely out of concern for all humanity, but as I read, you will perhaps notice what has happened to the name and the history of God:

> Among the invisible company [of] sons and daughters known only to God . . . is the African chief on the mountaintop at midnight lifting his naked firstborn in praise and offering to the god of life. Among them is the Iraqi mother turning her child's face to the sun in adoration and joy. Among them also is the Mexican midwife pouring water over the newly delivered child while intoning the an-

5. It is a particularly hideous irony that Jewish prisoners in Auschwitz lost their names and became numbers.

cient prayer to the goddess, "I pray that this celestial water, blue and light blue, may enter into the body and there live. For anew thou art born, purified and cleansed, shaped and engendered by your Mother the Goddess of Water."

Now no one would want to deny that people of all races all around the world experience religious awe and wonder at the birth of a child, and it seems to me that we can certainly affirm — and even insist — that God takes notice of every infant, whether Iraqi or Kurdish or Bangladeshi or Ethiopian.[6] God knows the name of every child, and God in Jesus Christ calls us to have compassion and care for every child. But let us ask ourselves this: What if God did not know the name of every child? Suppose Jesus were here right now, and he called your child Susan when her name was really Emily? Would that make a difference to you? The biblical narratives make a great point of the fact that God knows everybody by his right name, and calls everybody by his right name — Abraham, Moses, Hannah, Samuel, Mary, Martha, Saul. Surely, if God knows our names, we should know his name and call him by his right name.

God's most interesting names in the Bible are the ones that show up where his history intersects with our history. For instance, he is "the God of Abraham, Isaac, and Jacob." That may not sound like a name to you and me, but in the Old Testament — and indeed, in the entire Christian story — it is one of God's most significant names. (We could run it all together to make it a single name: God-of-Abraham-Isaac-and-Jacob.) It distinguishes YHWH from the gods of the mountaintops and the sun and the water, whether blue or light blue. It distinguishes him by his history, his history as it intersects our history, the history of real people in real places — Mesopotamia, Canaan, Judea, New York. And again, it links God with the Jewish people, a particularity which is not found in generic religion.

Another name, or self-identification, of God in the Old Testament, many times repeated, is, "I am the Lord your God, who brought you up out of the land of Egypt with a mighty hand and an outstretched arm" (Deut. 26:8; Jer. 2:6; and scores of other references). The God who has told us who he is is a God who acts, a God who enters the world with power to shape events. He is a God who moves among his people, delivering prisoners, healing the sick, dispensing justice, creating community, overthrowing the proud, raising the dead.

6. These peoples were undergoing extreme hardship at the time of this sermon.

It's very important to get God's name right. Last February there was a much-discussed event at the World Council of Churches Assembly in Canberra, Australia. A young Korean professor, Chung Kyung-Hyung, gave a presentation comparing the world of the Holy Spirit to that of an Asian goddess, Kwan In. An account of this event was published in the magazine called *First Things*. At the end of the article, the author reports that, when he left Canberra, he visited Singapore, where he discovered many signs of Kwan In:

> Kwan In is found on tea mugs, t-shirts, and family altars. People buy joss sticks and burn small sacrifices on street corners or anywhere to earn small favors from her. Pursuing perpetual obeisance to her — and paying "lion dancers" to drive evil spirits out of homes and shops, and burning "hell money" to appease ancestors — [that] is what many [Christian] believers in Singapore and all over Asia have found deliverance from. It is not dissimilar to the deliverance from empty, hopeless secularism that some in the West have experienced. They have forsaken the idols who are but wood, clay, silver, and gold for a living God.[7]

It is important to get God's name right. A few moments ago, we heard of an African chief on a mountaintop lifting his baby in offering to "the god of life." Some say it doesn't matter — it's all the same god in the end. I have heard many African Christians say otherwise. They say that God the Father, Son, and Holy Spirit has been for them the way of freedom and peace. They emphasize the difference between the Father of the Lord Jesus Christ and their tribal deities, who evoked insecurity and fear.

The birth of a child, as we were saying, is indeed an awesome event. The only thing that can beat it is the birth of a grandchild. My husband and I are both amazed at the way we feel about our year-old granddaughter. She seems to us to be the most wonderful creature on earth. When she was baptized, it felt to us like the most important baptism in the world. In whose name was she baptized? We got *her* name right — Alice Dabney, after my mother — but did we get *God's* name right? In what way did it make a difference? Is baptism just something vaguely religious that parents and grandparents like to have done to their children, or is there something real going on?

---

7. Lawrence E. Adams, "The WCC at Canberra: Which Spirit?" *First Things*, June/July 1991.

The faith of the Christian church is that baptism is an act of God — not just any god we choose, but the God who chooses us — the God of Abraham, Isaac, and Jacob, the God and Father of our Lord Jesus Christ. Our granddaughter's baptism brought this home to me in a new way. We would not have wanted her offered to something less than the God who is really God. Anything less than God the Father, Son, and Holy Spirit is worth no more than a piece of paper in the wastebasket. Our God is the God who has told us who he is. Our God is the God who is powerful and able to intervene in our history with his transforming love.

In the book of Daniel, we read the story of Shadrach, Meshach, and Abednego, who refused to bow down and worship King Nebuchadnezzar's god. For this, they were thrown into a burning fiery furnace. In the midst of the fire they sang and praised the God of Abraham, Isaac, and Jacob. When it became apparent that the fire was not going to harm them, the king ordered them released and issued a decree to all the land. On this Trinity Sunday, let his words be our words:

> Blessed be the God of Shadrach, Meshach, and Abednego, who has sent his angel and delivered his servants, who trusted in him, and set at nought the king's command, and yielded up their bodies rather than serve and worship any god except their own God. Blessed be the God of Shadrach, Meshach, and Abednego, for there is no other god who is able to deliver in this way. (Dan. 3:28-29)[8]

AMEN.

---

8. See the sermon "But If Not" for an examination of the problem posed when the servants of God are *not* delivered from the fiery furnace in this life.

# A Way Out of No Way:
## An Easter Sermon

---

*The Day of Resurrection 1999*                                      Exodus 12–14

As a climactic ending to this glorious service on the day of our Lord's resurrection from the dead, we are going to sing the hymn "Come, Ye Faithful, Raise the Strain of Triumphant Gladness!" Let's listen to the words of the first verse; you might want to take your hymnals and follow along:

> Come, ye faithful, raise the strain of triumphant gladness!
> God has brought his Israel into joy from sadness.
> Loosed from Pharaoh's bitter yoke Jacob's sons and daughters,
> Led them with unmoistened foot through the Red Sea waters.[1]

If this was an African-American congregation, I would be able to assume that most of you would understand the connection between Pharaoh and the empty tomb. In largely white congregations, though, there's a lot of mystification about it. During my career as a Bible teacher, I have taken quite a few informal polls, and I've learned that most Episcopalians have only the vaguest idea of the connection between Exodus and Easter. So this is a wonderful day, the best day of all, to enter into the power of our Lord's resurrection through the retelling of the story of the deliverance at the Red Sea.

The Easter story and the Exodus story are about power. Everybody is interested in power. As Henry Kissinger famously said, "Power is the great-

---

1. The words of Hymn 199 were written by John of Damascus in the eighth century. They were translated by John Mason Neale. The tune is by Arthur S. Sullivan (of Gilbert and Sullivan).

est aphrodisiac." Power attracts, power fascinates, power sells, power makes things happen. Powerlessness is very bad for people. The refugees in Kosovo are helpless and powerless, and we feel for them because we have some sense of how awful that is. Many, many times I have heard people say that the worst thing about a bad situation was that they couldn't do anything about it. People whose loved ones are very sick often speak of this feeling. They feel that they can't do anything to help, and they feel impotent. Powerlessness paralyzes people. Many doctors curtail their visits to dying patients because they feel there is nothing they can do.

The story of the Exodus is about the power of God. It is one of the greatest of all the biblical narratives. (I hope you will want to read the whole story in your Bibles when you go home, because there is a lot missing from the portion in your bulletin.) All Bible stories are told with striking economy, with just a few carefully chosen words and details to make the strongest possible impression. Listen to the beginning of the Red Sea story:

> The Lord said to Moses, "Tell the people of Israel to turn back and encamp . . . between Migdol and the sea. . . . For Pharaoh will say of the people of Israel, 'They are entangled in the land; the wilderness has shut them in.'" (14:1-3)

Now the point of this is that the Lord did not bring the Israelites out of Egypt by the normal, direct route. He brought them a roundabout way, which made no tactical sense. "They are entangled in the land; the wilderness has shut them in." We understand from this that the Lord led them to an indefensible position from which there was no way out, no escape, no exit.

The Lord did this deliberately, for a purpose. To Moses he said, "I will harden Pharaoh's heart, and he will pursue them, and I will get glory over Pharaoh and all his host; and the Egyptians shall know that I am the Lord" (14:4). The children of Israel have been led into a cul-de-sac where the Egyptians will come after them from the land, and there is nothing at their backs but the sea.

The story continues:

> When Pharaoh drew near, the people of Israel lifted up their eyes, and behold, the Egyptians were marching after them; and they were in great fear. And the people of Israel cried out to the Lord; and they said to Moses, ". . . What have you done to us, in bringing us out of Egypt? Is not this what we said to you in Egypt, 'Let us alone and let

us serve the Egyptians'? For it would have been better for us to serve
the Egyptians than to die in the wilderness." (14:10-12)

The storyteller has injected a note of rueful humor here. We recognize
typical human nature in the Israelites' lament. Freedom is costly. We think
we want it, but we don't want to pay the price. Whenever there are great
public issues to be resolved, it is easy to get people to sign up for the initial
stages of an effort, but only a few will stay to do the grunt work of the next
stages. Danger sounds glamorous, but after the TV cameras pack up and go
home, not many will want to remain on the barricades. The idea of freedom
is intoxicating, but when real enemies appear, retreat sometimes looks like a
pretty good option. In this case, however, retreat is impossible. "The wilderness has shut them in."

Now listen to Moses. You won't find a moment like this in any of the
Exodus movies. Only in the telling of the story in the midst of the worshiping, believing community do these words come alive:

> Moses said to the people, "Fear not, stand firm, and see the salvation
> of the Lord, which he will work for you today; for the Egyptians
> whom you see today, you shall never see again. The Lord will fight
> for you, and you have only to be still." (14:13-14)

If I stayed in this pulpit all day, I wouldn't be able to tell you how many
times I have drawn upon this verse in my own life. "The Lord will fight for
you; you have only to stand your ground." In times of disappointment, in
times of frustration, in times when I have failed myself, in times when I
could see no way forward, I have called upon this verse. *The Lord will fight
for you, and you have only to be still.*

"Then Moses stretched out his hand over the sea; and the Lord drove
the sea back by a strong east wind all night" (14:21). It has often been noted
that the story is a mixture of the natural and the miraculous. So there was a
strong east wind; what's the big deal about that? The point of the story from
beginning to end, however, is that all the happenings — natural, supernatural, whatever — are the work of God.

There's a song in the animated movie *The Prince of Egypt* that says,
"Miracles can happen if you believe." The Exodus story says something
quite different. The Exodus story says that the miracle will happen whether
you believe or not. "It is fully clear that Israel was not saved because of her
faith. Rather, Israel failed to believe right up until the moment of her deliv-

erance."[2] Moses isn't making this happen, either; Moses is only an instrument. The power is the Lord's. God is doing this, not because Israel has earned it, but because he is a God of deliverance.

It wouldn't do any good for him to be a God of deliverance if he weren't a God of power. There are many theological disputes about this. I'm not going to turn aside this Easter morning to deal with the very serious question about why God so often withholds his power. We spent three hours with that on Good Friday; even so, we barely scratched the surface. Today is the day to glorify the mighty acts of God. Today is the day to say, as the black church does, "The Lord is able." I'll never forget the first time I heard that saying. In 1977 my father was extremely ill in the hospital. I was to be ordained to the priesthood in a few weeks. I was sore afraid that he would not be able to come, that he might not even live. One of his nurses took me out into the hall and said, "The Lord is able." And, yes, my father did get better, and he did come. I know that that nurse would be joyful to hear this story told twenty-two years later on Easter morning.[3]

There is something even better that the African-American church says. I have not entirely tracked it to its original source — it's probably part of the vast rhetorical treasury of the black churches — but Martin Luther King used to say it, and Andrew Young used it as the title of his book about the civil rights movement: "God makes a way out of no way." This is the message of the Exodus.

> The people of Israel went into the midst of the sea on dry ground, the waters being a wall to them on their right hand and on their left. The Egyptians pursued, and went in after them into the midst of the sea, all Pharaoh's horses, his chariots, and his horsemen. And in the morning watch the Lord in the pillar of fire and of cloud looked down upon the host of the Egyptians, and discomfited the host of the Egyptians, clogging their chariot wheels so that they drove heavily; and the Egyptians said, "Let us flee from before Israel; for the Lord fights for them against the Egyptians."
>
> Then the Lord said to Moses, "Stretch out your hand over the sea, that the water may come back upon the Egyptians, upon their chariots, and upon their horsemen." So Moses stretched forth his hand over the sea, and the sea returned to its wonted flow when the morn-

---

2. Brevard Childs, *The Book of Exodus* (Philadelphia: Westminster Press, 1974), p. 239.
3. Even if my father *hadn't* gotten better, faith still says, "The Lord is able."

ing appeared; and the Egyptians fled into it, and the Lord routed the Egyptians in the midst of the sea. . . .

. . . And Israel saw the great work which the Lord did against the Egyptians, and the people feared the Lord; and they believed in the Lord and in his servant Moses. (14:21-31)

Who can make a way out of no way? Only God. The Exodus story is told precisely to demonstrate the power of our God. The American civil rights movement will live forever in the annals of the Christian church because so many of its leaders knew the power of God and depended upon it in their darkest hours. Often we do not actually see the power of God at work. We live in hope of a future we do not yet see except by faith. The Passover and the Exodus, as the church has always understood from earliest New Testament times, were the forerunners of what was to come in full power at the resurrection of Jesus Christ. There is no way out of death. Only God can open that way.

The church is a church of Easter faith. We have seen the evidence of the saving power of the Lord, and we stand upon its promise for a future reign of God. There is more joy here than anyone who does not know God's power can possibly imagine. When the Israelites saw that they had been delivered at the Red Sea, they broke forth into ecstatic praise:

Then Miriam, the prophetess, the sister of Aaron, took a timbrel in her hand; and all the women went out after her with timbrels and dancing. And Miriam sang to them: "Sing to the Lord, for he has triumphed gloriously; the horse and his rider he has thrown into the sea." (15:20-21)

And even skeptical scholars agree — this never fails to give a thrill — that that little fragment of poetry may go all the way back to the event itself.[4]

Singing is empowering. Dancing is empowering. One of the most memorable news stories I ever read in my whole life was a *New York Times* report of a train ride in South Africa right after the collapse of apartheid. On the day of President Mandela's inauguration, a renowned journalist rode from

---

4. "The event itself" — what was it? Was it a humble slog through the low tides of a "sea of reeds"? That is not the point. As in the case of all the biblical narratives, we are meant to give ourselves up to its inner meaning. At the same time, if there is not a core of historical fact at the center of Scripture, the very cross of Christ itself would lose its significance. *God breaks into history* — that is a central affirmation of the Judeo-Christian heritage.

the Soweto ghetto into Pretoria. During the entire three-hour ride, the black passengers celebrated their liberation by singing and dancing in the aisles. It was obvious from the article that the reporter was completely bowled over. He called it a moment of "historic exultation."[5] Who can doubt that their song is joined to the eternal song of Miriam on the celestial shore?

Today, several years later, South Africa, as we know, has a whole new set of problems to deal with. Just so, the Exodus was only the beginning of the Israelites' troubles. We still live in a world of bondage to sin, evil, and death. It has not been easy to write an Easter sermon with one eye on the page and the other on the televised scenes from Kosovo. The ways of Pharaoh still rule this age.

In this world, the last word for you and the last word for me will be death. All the routes of escape have been closed off. In the face of death, ultimate power lies in the hands of Dr. Kevorkian.[6] But listen: there is another, greater Way; there is another, greater Life; there is another, greater Power. St. Paul proclaimed the God "who gives life to the dead and calls into existence the things that do not exist" (Rom. 4:17). This is the God who makes a way out of no way. This is the God whose power raised up Jesus from the tomb as though Death were shredded Kleenex. When all the ways of escape are shut off, when the whole world seems "shut up in the wilderness," when the time comes that you, too, lie helpless before the oncoming night, listen, listen, people of God: "The Lord will fight for you, and you have only to be still."

Listen, listen, people of God — there comes a sound of Miriam's tambourine: "Sing unto the Lord, for he has triumphed gloriously; the horse and his rider he has thrown into the sea."

Listen, listen, O people of God — there comes the strain of a song and the sound of a distant trumpet:

'Tis the spring of souls today; Christ has burst his prison!
From his three days' sleep in death, like the sun has risen!
All the winter of our sins, long and dark, is flying
From his light — to whom we give laud and praise undying.[7]

*Alleluia! The Lord is risen indeed!*

---

5. Francis X. Clines, *The New York Times*, 11 May 1994.

6. "Doctor Death," as he was called, took great pride in traveling all over the country to assist people in committing suicide.

7. This is the second verse of John of Damascus's hymn with which the sermon began.

# A Shield for the Bull-Worshipers

WYCLIFFE COLLEGE, TORONTO

*October 2008*                                             Exodus 32–33:6

WE'VE BEEN in Exodus for a while; many of you will remember the reading for last Sunday, which tells of the golden calf which the people of Israel made in the wilderness while Moses was up on Mount Sinai receiving the Commandments from the Lord. "Up, make us gods!" say the people to Aaron. "As for this Moses, the man who brought us up out of the land of Egypt, we do not know what has become of him." In the fashion of biblical storytelling, the irony in this is only lightly touched upon. We, the hearers, are invited to tease out the paradox: Moses is on the mountaintop in the presence of the God who is really God — the God who revealed himself as I AM WHO I AM — and the people down below are manufacturing gods for themselves.

> And the Lord said to Moses, "Go down; for your people . . . have made for themselves a molten calf, and have worshiped it and sacrificed to it, and said, 'These are your gods, O Israel, who brought you up out of the land of Egypt!'" (32:7-8)

There is a sense in which this is really quite funny. Isaiah sees the joke: "Those who lavish gold from the purse . . . hire a goldsmith, and he makes it into a god; then they fall down and worship! They lift it upon their shoulders, they carry it, they set it in its place, and it stands there; it cannot move from its place. If one cries to it, it does not answer or save him from his trouble" (Isa. 46:6-7). It cannot move from its place! There in two short sen-

[ 83 ]

tences we have the great insight. False gods cannot move from their place. They cannot save in time of trouble.

It almost goes without saying that in America, at least, the great god for quite a while has been The Market. One of my American students in homiletics evoked for us in a sermon the great statue of the bull in Wall Street. Now Wall Street has been shaken, and Bay Street has felt the tremors.[1] I am told that from every pulpit in the States, the refrain has come in one form or another: "Gods of gold cannot save in time of trouble." It may be a decade or more before faith in The Market recovers. In the meantime, some of us, at least, will strip ourselves of our ornaments, like the children of Israel in today's story, and we will reflect upon the ephemeral nature of human institutions.

We read that Moses returned to the top of the mountain and said to the Lord, "Alas, this people have sinned a great sin; they have made for themselves gods of gold" (32:31). We need to reflect upon what a calamity this is for Moses. His history up to the time of the burning bush was checkered, to say the least. (One wag has called him "a stuttering murderer on the run.") But God has forged him into a mighty leader who has faced down the ruler of the Egyptian empire, led the people by their thousands through the Red Sea, and struggled with the burdens of command throughout the wilderness trek. This man has given himself to the service of the Lord with a single-mindedness that stands out even among the many patriarchs and prophets. He has been entirely taken over by his mission; and yet we are given many glimpses of his humanity along the way. Whether Moses is a literary creation or not I will leave others to debate[2] — I say this is a real person whom God took in hand for his incomparable purposes. And by bringing Moses directly into the divine presence — an ineffable favor given to no other — God permits Moses to refract his fierce, dazzling holiness to the people below. Therefore they are without excuse when they turn away to gods of gold.

You have been following your own election here in Canada, so you may not know about all the things that happened in the States since the metaphorical collapse of the Wall Street bull. The rage that rose up against the CEOs of the big corporations caught everyone by surprise and almost scuttled the bailout plan. Even now, every night on the most staid and even-handed cable news channel in the States, the names and faces of these grossly overpaid executives are posted for all to see. These men (and they are

1. This was the time of the Great Recession of 2008. Bay Street in Toronto corresponds to Wall Street in New York City.

2. This is a nod to the context in the University of Toronto.

all men) were pulling in yearly salaries and bonuses in the high mega-millions. Their consumption of houses and lands became legendary. "They sat down to eat and drink and rose up to play" with a vengeance. When almost overnight their glass palaces came crashing down, the ordinary working stiffs of America were ready to stone them, or at the very least to trash their wine cellars. Somehow I don't think the typical Christian congregation in the States has been offering any prayers for the souls of the CEOs, any more than they have been offering prayers for our enemies in Iraq and Afghanistan. "These people have sinned a great sin" — so they deserve whatever happens to them.

But it is at just this point that we learn what the Lord has made of Moses. The man who has been so close to the face of God that his own face reflects the divine glory does something extraordinary. Remember how grievously the people have tested his leadership, and how rebellious, resentful, uncooperative, and ceaselessly complaining they have been. Remember also that he has had precious little help from his second-in-command, his own brother. It's worth recalling Aaron's reaction when Moses first sees the golden calf:

> Aaron said, "Let not the anger of my lord [an obsequious reference to Moses] burn hot; you know the people, that they are set on evil." (32:22)

When in doubt, blame someone else! But Aaron isn't finished getting himself off the hook:

> [The people] said to me, "Make us gods, who shall go before us . . ." And I said to them, "Let any who have gold take it off"; so they gave it to me, and I threw it into the fire, and there came out this calf." (32:23-24)

Don't you love it? Could a five-year-old do any better?

So then, what is this extraordinary thing that Moses does? Listen again to what the Lord tells him:

> The Lord said to Moses, "I have seen this people, and behold, it is a stiff-necked people; now therefore let me alone, that my wrath may burn hot against them and I may consume them; but of you I will make a great nation." (32:9-10)

Over the chastened bodies of the idolatrous Israelites, God declares that Moses will inherit the promise all by himself: "Of you I will make a great nation." Who could resist that? Could I? Could you? Imagine it: all the idolaters, the merchants of greed, and the would-be "masters of the universe" will be passed by, and *you* will inherit their kingdom. I, the true Lord of the universe, have set my favor on *you*.

But maybe you, being Canadians, wouldn't really want that degree of power. No, no, we don't need to be masters of the universe. However, we wouldn't mind getting just a little piece of it. And we surely wouldn't mind if the people who had ruined the covenant through their self-aggrandizement received their just deserts, especially when they have abused precisely the trust that had been invested in them. At the very least, their names should be posted on the Internet, so they could be shamed in front of the whole world.

Here's the extraordinary thing. The morning after the smashing of the golden calf, Moses said to the people,

> "You have sinned a great sin. But now I will go up to the Lord; perhaps I can make atonement for your sin."
> So Moses returned to the Lord and said, "Alas, this people have . . . made for themselves gods of gold. But now, if you will only forgive their sin — but if not, blot me out of the book that you have written." (32:30-32)

Do you see how astonishing this is? This former prince of Egypt, this man who felt entitled to murder a man whom he felt deserved it, this man who was chosen to stand on the mountain before the face of God and bring down the Ten Commandments — this man has become ready to take his place alongside the worst of sinners, even if it means that he will be cast out forever from the blessedness of God's presence.

This partnership that God has created between himself and Moses is a revelation. We saw earlier in Exodus that Moses' face reflected the glory of God. We see it in action, right here, as God responds to Moses:

> "Depart, go up hence, you and the people whom you have brought up out of the land of Egypt, to the land [that] I will give [them]. And I will send an angel before you . . . but I will not go up among you, lest I consume you in the way, for you are a stiff-necked people." (33:1-3)

What is the glory of God? His glory is shown in his mercy. This is the God who protects his own disobedient and ungrateful children by shielding them from his own annihilating holiness. Undeserving as they are, he will nevertheless take them up to the Promised Land — but he will send an angel to go before them, because his own unmediated presence would consume them in the flame of his righteous wrath.

Listen now to some words of another man who, like Moses, was commandeered by God, another man who offered up his own salvation in exchange for that of his unbelieving brothers and sisters.[3] In the fifth chapter of Romans, the apostle Paul wrote a parenthetical comment that is almost always ignored. He wrote, or rather dictated, this parenthesis as a sort of side comment on the main message:

> Rarely will anyone die for a righteous person — though perhaps for
> a good person someone might actually dare to die.

What's the idea here? Paul makes this side comment in order to illustrate from common experience. Not many people will give up their lives for someone else, not even for a very, very good person. Well, maybe — he muses out loud — maybe to save a very, very good and special person, one might be willing to die. That's Paul's parenthesis. Here in the middle of this key passage from Romans, a passage of such radical import that some have called it the heart of the gospel, we find an echo of Moses, who was willing to die not for righteous persons but for the worst of the worst. Here is the whole passage from Romans:

> *For while we were still helpless,* at the right time Christ died *for the
> ungodly.* Indeed, rarely will anyone die for a righteous person —
> though perhaps for a good person someone might actually dare to
> die. But God proves his love for us in that while we still were sinners
> Christ died for us. Much more surely then, now that we have been
> justified by his blood, will we be saved through him from the wrath
> of God. (Rom. 5:6-9; my emphasis)

This is the glory of God. In the next passage from Exodus, God shows his glory to Moses, but he shields Moses from its blinding radiance by hid-

---

3. The reference here is to Romans 9:3, where Paul confesses himself willing to lose his place in the Lord's book if only his fellow Jews will come to Christ.

ing him in the cleft of a rock. When the Israelites started out for the Promised Land, the angel given by God shielded them from God's "consuming fire" (Heb. 12:29). When the fullness of time was come, God sent forth his Son (Gal. 4:4). He sent him in a form that we could see and not be blinded, a form that we could hear and not be deafened, a form that we could receive and not be destroyed. There was to come "a prophet like Moses," but behold, a greater One than Moses is here. He is the One who was shamed in front of the whole world, for us, the ungodly. It is for ourselves, this very night, that the Lord's table of welcome is now spread.

# The Burden of This People

---

*September 1979*                                                    Numbers 11

*This sermon was preached on a Sunday morning when the
new rector (senior pastor) of the parish was to be formally instituted at a service later that day.*

. . . . . . . . . . . . . . . . .

THE LORD of the church arranges things in wonderful ways. Many people
would call it coincidence, but Christians call it Providence when the lessons
appointed for the day turn out to be astonishingly appropriate. The Old Testament lesson in today's lectionary happens to be one that is closely related to
the ministry of the church; in fact, it's among those appointed to be read at or-
dinations. So let's take a few minutes this morning to explore what the Word
of God might be for all of you at this time of celebration in your parish.

The reading is from the book of Numbers. Numbers is about the experiences of the children of Israel as they lived in the wilderness during those
famous forty years. They had been delivered from slavery in Egypt by the
Lord's "mighty hand and outstretched arm." They had been brought across
the Red Sea in safety, and they had danced on the shore to celebrate the victory. As Miriam with her tambourine sang:

"Sing to the Lord, for he has risen up in triumph;
The horse and his rider he has hurled into the sea." (Exod. 15:21)

[ 89 ]

As they came into the arid and barren desert, God supplied them with food and water; they were brought into covenant partnership with him at Sinai; they received blessings and promises of more blessings. Their numbers grew, and the Lord protected them. Yet what did they do? They complained. They complained about everything, but especially about the food. They were sick and tired of manna from heaven; they cried out,

> "O, that we had meat to eat! We remember the fish we used to eat in Egypt for nothing, the cucumbers, the melons, the leeks, the onions, and the garlic! . . . But now . . . there is nothing at all but this manna to look at." (Num. 11:4-6)

In this description of the Israelites in the wilderness, Numbers gives us a detailed picture of human weakness. We see dissatisfaction and greed. We see jealousy and rivalry. We see malicious gossip and back-stairs plots. We see ingratitude, selfishness, and stupidity. In short, we see the kinds of things that go on wherever groups of human beings are gathered together. This is a good time to remember that Israel in the Old Testament is the predecessor of the church in the New Testament and after. So what we really have here in this book of Numbers is a description of the way that the church often behaves. We don't like to think of ourselves that way, but people outside the church don't hesitate to remind us, from time to time, that they get turned off of church at one point or another because they see church people behaving badly. So our text today reminds us of the more unattractive aspects of God's people. The uglier side of ourselves, and of human groups everywhere, is a feature of human life that we would like to ignore but cannot escape from in this life.

Well, as we all know, the leader of the Israelites at the time of the book of Numbers is Moses. He is the one who has been commissioned by God to be the chief of all these thousands. Therefore Moses is the one who has to bear the brunt of all the complaints and all the envy and all the frustration. His own sister and brother — Miriam and Aaron — are jealous of him and accuse him of egotism.[1] Other men in the community plot together to seize power. The people are constantly giving in to superstition and religious quackery, slipping away from the true faith of the one God who brought them out of Egypt. They are never satisfied; they always want more and better.

---

1. "Has the Lord indeed spoken only through Moses? Has he not spoken through us also?" (Num. 12:2).

And so, we are told, "Moses heard the people lamenting, all of them in their families at the openings of their tents" (11:10). You can imagine this scene. It's evening in the Sinai wilderness, the end of another long and exhausting day. Moses has been up since dawn, moving about the camp, attending to everyone's needs, visiting the sick, calling on the shut-ins, meeting with the altar guild, preaching and teaching, examining flocks and herds, checking out buildings and grounds, supervising the Hebrew school, calling in the environmental protection agency about the polluted well, conducting worship, and searching for concealed golden calves. Now it's twilight, and he's on his way home to dinner.

But what does he hear as he passes tent after tent? He hears one gripe after another as whole families join in the complaining, making no attempt to keep their voices down. "How much longer does he expect us to eat this manna?" "Did you see the sloppy way they burned the sacrifices this morning?" "Why don't they play some hymns that we can sing?" "When are we going to get moving to the Promised Land?" "Reuben told me there's going to be a draft-Joshua meeting tomorrow at ten A.M." "My kid didn't get asked to serve at the altar." "He spends too much time on administration and not enough time visiting newcomers." "I liked it better the way it used to be."

And Moses hears it all, and he is bowed down with weariness, sorrow, and discouragement, and he cries out to the Lord, saying these words:

> "Why have you treated your servant so badly? Why have I not found favor in your sight, that you lay the burden of all this people on me? Did I conceive all this people? Did I give birth to them, that you should say to me, 'Carry them in your bosom, as a nurse carries a sucking child,' to the land that you promised on oath to their ancestors? Where am I to get meat to give to all this people? For they come weeping to me and say, 'Give us meat to eat!' I am not able to carry all this people alone, for they are too heavy for me. If this is the way you are going to treat me, put me to death at once — if I have found favor in your sight — and do not let me see my misery." (11:11-15)

In this wonderfully human speech, we learn much about why Moses was such a great and godly leader. *First* of all, he recognized his own inadequacy. We are told in Numbers 12:3 that Moses was the meekest man on the face of the earth. I doubt if any of us think of Moses as being meek, but that's because we aren't accustomed to the biblical concept of meekness, which means humility before God. Moses knew what his limitations and failings were. He had a clear understanding of his total dependence upon God at every moment of his life.

And so the *second* thing we notice about Moses as a spiritual leader is that he goes directly to God in his time of need. He presents his case to God in prayer. He knows where the one and only true source of aid is to be found.

*Third,* Moses understands that he himself is not God. "Did I conceive all this people?" he asks rhetorically, knowing that the answer is, of course, No! Moses knows that only God is great and that it is God alone who can carry out his purposes for his people.

And *fourth,* Moses doesn't attempt to hide anything. He doesn't bury all his anger within himself, where it would fester. Before God he confesses his fear and his weariness. He acknowledges his impatience and disgust with the people's immaturity. He admits that he's sick of the whole business, that he'd really rather be dead than put up with it any longer. He comes before God in true humility, without pretense, not concealing his incapacity.

And God answers Moses, saying:

> "Assemble seventy elders from Israel, men known to you as elders and officers in the community; bring them to me at the tent of the presence. . . . I will come down and speak with you there. I will take back part of that same spirit which has been conferred on you and confer it on them, and they will share with you the burden of taking care for the people; then you will not have to bear it alone. . . ." (11:16-17)

Underlying this whole passage is the great Old Testament truth about the commissioning of persons by the Holy Spirit for God's work. Without God's Spirit, there can be no real *spirit*ual leadership. Whether we know it or not, we have no vocation except insofar as it comes from him. Moses was raised up by God and given power and strength for his task; now God promises to raise up others, to give spiritual commissions to them as well, for the sharing of the work.

> And so Moses came out and told the people what the Lord had said. He assembled seventy men from the elders of the people and stationed them round the tent. Then the Lord descended in the cloud and spoke to him. He took back part of that same spirit which he

had conferred on Moses and conferred it on the seventy elders.
(11:24-25)

Now we've learned something more about the way God intends for his
people to serve him. The leader is not meant to carry the whole burden
alone. Members of the congregation are called to step forward and receive
the Spirit, sharing in the leadership, by submitting to God's guidance. The
Lord does not give power for its own sake; he gives it for the carrying out of
his divine purpose. Most important, though, there is no godly vocation
without the divine gift that makes it possible. We can't attain to it on our
own. Our own talents and skills are not enough. We must wait humbly and
without pretense as the Lord descends in the cloud. It is up to him, not us.
That's what we mean every Sunday, or used to, when we say, "Take not thy
Holy Spirit from us." In saying this, we acknowledge our continual need to
be replenished and renewed for our tasks by his power.

The most interesting part of the story is yet to come. Outside the camp
at the Tent of the Presence, the seventy elders are meeting with God; but
back inside the camp, a completely unexpected thing has happened. God's
Spirit has fallen on two additional men who were not with the seventy elders, and they are prophesying by the power of the Spirit within the camp
while the seventy are still outside. Joshua, Moses' young lieutenant, ran to
Moses and cried, "My Lord Moses, stop them!" Whereupon Moses replied
to Joshua in these wonderful words:

"Are you jealous on my account? I wish that all the Lord's people
were prophets and that the Lord would confer his spirit upon them
all!" (11:29)

In this marvelous response, Moses does several things. He rejects any
suggestion that he should keep all the reins of power in his own hands. He
affirms the Lord's prerogative to pour out his Spirit on whomever he
pleases, not just an elite ordained few. He acknowledges the freedom of
God's Spirit to work in unpredictable ways. And, without realizing it, Moses is looking across the ages into the future, when there will come a time of
the outpouring of the Holy Spirit of God upon all of his people on the day
that we call Pentecost. So rich and so full of meaning is this great saying of
Moses!

It will be clear to all of you by now that there is much in this lesson for
your congregation today. You see the red hangings on the altar and pulpit,

[ 93 ]

red for the Holy Spirit, in anticipation of the commissioning this afternoon of a servant of the Lord. But it is so true, isn't it, that he can't bear the burden of this people by himself! He can't do it without you, and you can't do it without God's continual aid and empowerment. Today I sense that you are all tremendously happy with one another and with God's gifts. Today is a day to rejoice on the shore of the Red Sea with music and dancing: "Sing to the Lord, for he has risen up in triumph!"

But inevitably in the life of every congregation there will come a time when there will be complaining, and division, and tension, and disappointment. Rivalries and jealousies will surface. Try as we will to hide them, our worst qualities will eventually see the light of day. At such times, rectors become weary of their congregations, and congregations murmur against their rectors. And it is at those times that the age-old story comes alive to call us back to the Lord our God. It is at such times that we are summoned to our knees to implore God's mercy in the old words, "Take not thy Holy Spirit from us." Clergy and laity alike, we are needy before God and dependent upon him for our life together.

And so this is a day of re-dedication for all of us, as well as a day of rejoicing. It is a day of commitment — and not just, you understand, to your own congregation, though you love it very much; it is a day of commitment to the Lord of the whole church, the one who alone can give life and health and safety to his people. The greatest thing that you can do for your new rector today is to pledge yourselves together to love and serve the Lord.

Many years after Moses died, when Joshua was an old man, the children of Israel stood together before God in the land that he had given them, and Joshua spoke these words to them:

> "Hold the Lord in awe. . . . Worship him in loyalty and in truth. . . . Choose here and now whom you will worship. . . . As for me and my family, we will worship the Lord." (Josh. 24:14-16)

May it be so for you, and may it be a blessing to your children and your children's children. Praise the Lord!

AMEN.

# To Know the Living God

*September 2000*

*This sermon directly addresses the relationship of the Old Testament to the New. The reader is asked to make a mental adjustment to changed circumstances. The political situation is different today, but the theological message of Deuteronomy is the same, and the issues between Jews and Christians are the same.*

. . . . . . . . . . . . . . . . .

"Keep [these commandments] and do them; for that will be your wisdom and your understanding in the sight of the peoples, who, when they hear all these statutes, will say, 'Surely this great nation is a wise and understanding people.' For what great nation is there that has a god so near to it as the Lord our God is to us, whenever we call upon him? And what great nation is there, that has statutes and ordinances so righteous as all this law which I set before you this day?

(DEUTERONOMY 4:6-8)

HERE IS a political cartoon from the *Palm Beach Post*, reprinted in *The New York Times* last week. It shows a very high mountain, so high that it is partially enveloped in clouds. The summit of the mountain is designated "The Moral High Ground." The Republican presidential candidates are standing up there on the top, peering down through the clouds, where they see a perky, smiling little figure chugging up the slope with some large objects in its arms. "What do we do now, Cheney?" asks George W. "Here comes Joe Lieberman with ten stone tablets!"[1]

As we proceed this morning, I trust you to understand that I am not giving a political endorsement. I'm talking about Lieberman because his selection as the Democratic vice-presidential candidate is a big-time news item and offers an opportunity to address some issues that have been raised in the past two weeks as never before, to my knowledge. Surely the most interesting thing to happen on the American religious scene in some time is the national debate about Senator Lieberman's unabashed faith. One writer even counted up the number of times that Lieberman mentioned God in a speech in a Nashville church (13) and compared that to Abraham Lincoln's great Second Inaugural (14). Every day there have been editorials and op-ed pieces and letters to the editor, arguing about whether or not this is unconstitutional. But the really notable signal was sent by the Jewish Anti-Defamation League when they went after the first Jewish vice-presidential candidate and told him to knock it off. Here was an up-to-the-minute, living illustration of a brand-new book title by a Columbia journalism professor — *Jew vs. Jew*. The reaction of many assimilated Jews to Lieberman's Orthodoxy shows us that the real issues are not so much between Jews and Gentiles, but between secular people and the community of faith. Most of us don't know much about Senator Lieberman yet, but we know that he gives every sign of being a man who knows the living God — and the living God has always made people nervous.[2]

Our texts this morning challenge us to examine Jewish faith and our own faith in a new light. The Old Testament text is from the book of Deuteronomy, that great fifth book of the Torah which Jesus, like all his contemporaries, knew more or less by heart.[3] What's interesting about today's selections is that we read the Deuteronomy text in tandem with some words

1. The cartoonist must have meant to say *two* stone tablets (containing the *Ten* Commandments).

2. As this book goes to press eleven years later, Senator Lieberman's religious devotion has become even more galling to the commentariat (not to mention his political maneuvers, which seriously discombobulated his former Democratic colleagues).

3. And which he quoted to no less a person than Satan when he said, "Man shall not live by bread alone but by every word that proceeds out of the mouth of God" (Deut. 8:3).

of Jesus. We read today's passage from Deuteronomy one way if it is read by itself; if we read it in combination with today's Gospel, however, it takes on a different coloration.

The relationship of the Old Testament to the New is a major issue for both Jews and Christians. From the first century until the present day, there have been disagreements about this. The Episcopal Church has varied in its approach; if you will turn to page 869 of the Prayer Book, you will see what the earliest Anglicans had to say about the matter:

### VII. Of the Old Testament.

The Old Testament is not contrary to the New; for both in the Old Testament and New Testament everlasting life is offered to mankind by Christ. . . . Wherefore they are not to be heard, which feign that the old Fathers did look only for transitory promises. . . . No Christian man whatsoever is free from the obedience of the Commandments which are called Moral [including the Ten Commandments first and foremost].[4]

In practice, however, in recent years, there has been a notable slippage in the knowledge and use of the Old Testament in the Episcopal Church. It is quite noticeable to those of us who travel around the church a lot; the Old Testament is being seriously neglected and in some quarters is actually disparaged. However, there are indications that people are beginning to wake up to the fact that neglecting or disparaging the Old Testament leads not only to ignorance about our own faith but also, subtly or not so subtly, to a form of anti-Semitism. Various signs therefore indicate a resurgence of interest in the Old Testament. The prominent Christian writer Philip Yancey has a popular new book out called *The Bible Jesus Read*. There is now a new Revised Standard Lectionary which is purportedly designed to be more respectful of the Old Testament than the one we have now.[5]

In any case, the combination of Deuteronomy with today's Gospel presents a number of problems and challenges. We find Jesus under attack from the Pharisees, as usual. His disciples have failed to purify themselves

4. The Thirty-Nine Articles of Religion were first adopted in England in 1571. They were established for America, with very minor changes having to do with church polity, in 1801. In recent decades, there has been a wholesale move to discredit the Thirty-Nine Articles, but their importance to the historic Anglican Church is undiminished, and their theological power remains.

5. Ten years later, the revised lectionary has been widely adopted, but I have not noticed any significant increase in Old Testament preaching or emphasis.

by washing before they eat. This is going to take a little extra imagination for you and me to understand, since we know more now than we ever have about the importance of hand-washing for sanitation. In this story about Jesus, however, the issue is not health and hygiene, but moral purification. The "tradition of the elders" required ritual cleansing before a meal. This practice signified respect for God's holiness and righteousness; human beings are constantly in a state of sin and uncleanness, so actions must be taken to make oneself acceptable before God. The Pharisees, please note, were no different from you and me; they sought ways to think well of themselves in comparison to others. We all do this; we all look askance at people who don't behave the way we think they should, and we feel superior to them. "Religion" is based on these distinctions; some people work harder at being religious than others. "Spirituality" seems to be the thing right now; the trouble is that it separates people into more and less spiritual groups, and one can hardly help feeling superior to the other. Self-righteousness is always the greatest danger for religious people, and it particularly afflicted the Pharisees.

Jesus' reply to the Pharisees' accusation about his disciples' not washing goes like this:

> "Hear me, all of you, and understand: there is nothing outside a man which by going into him can defile him; but the things which come out of a man are what defile him." (Mark 7:14-15)

Now it is a very easy matter to slide right over this saying as though it were the most innocuous thing in the world. The Pharisees seem to be saying "You are what you eat," so isn't our Lord just saying "It's the spirit of the thing that counts"? Frankly, I don't think most of us, reading through this passage from Mark, would think Jesus' saying was anything special; I certainly didn't, until I read the commentaries and learned that biblical interpreters all say that it is "radical," "revolutionary," and "shocking."[6]

6. When I read in one commentary that the saying is "revolutionary" (Vincent Taylor), I figured that was just one man's opinion, so I turned to another commentary. There it was again: "revolutionary." I looked at a third. This one said that verse 15 is "one of the most revolutionary statements in the New Testament" (Eduard Reigert in the Proclamation series). Yet another commentator said "very radical" (D. E. Nineham), another "radically new" (Käsemann), and a sixth one (Eduard Schweizer) capped it off with "perhaps the most shocking statement" that Jesus utters in all of Mark's Gospel. By then I was convinced. A more recent commentator, Joel Marcus (a Jewish Christian), is cautious at first but concludes that the statement is "radical" and goes on

But why is it so shocking? Why is it revolutionary?

Because in this saying Jesus sweeps away the distinction between those who are trying to be religious and godly and those who know that they can't manage it. There is no way to overestimate the drastic nature of Jesus' words if we understand them: *There is nothing outside a man which by going into him can defile him; but the things which come out of a man are what defile him.* If you are feeling that you don't get it, don't worry; you are in the same fix as the disciples, who didn't get it, either:

> Jesus said to them, "Then are you also without understanding? Do you not see that whatever goes into a man from outside cannot defile him . . . ? What comes out of a man is what defiles a man. For from within, out of the heart of man, come evil thoughts, fornication, theft, murder, adultery, coveting, wickedness, deceit, licentiousness, envy, slander, pride, foolishness. All these evil things come from within, and they defile a man." (Mark 7:18-23)

Hoo-wee — is that sweet, nice Jesus talking? Sounds as if there's no room here for those who think they can get by with having their hearts in the right place, because the basic problem is that our "hearts" are messed up along with all the rest of us.

To go back to the Articles of Religion (IX and X), all members of the human race suffer, without exception, from an "infection of nature." Our condition is such "that [we] cannot turn and prepare [ourselves] by [our] own natural strength and good works, to faith . . . without the grace of God by Christ [going before] us." The reason that Jesus excused his disciples from the details of the "tradition of the elders" is that strict observance of them would have made it impossible for them to join the Master in his fellowship with contaminated sinners and tax collectors. Keeping fellowship with the contaminated is one of the most characteristic features of Jesus' ministry, and that was what shocked the Pharisees. Jesus seemed to be making a mockery of the sacred laws of religion.[7] That is what was so radical and

---

to speak of Jesus' "apocalyptic vision," observing that "he breaks out of the boundaries imposed by tradition, law, and even logic; the challenge he poses is whether people will continue to take their point of departure from those boundaries, or whether they will learn to see things through his eyes" (*Mark 1–9* [New York: Doubleday, 2000], pp. 454, 461).

7. The "tradition of the elders" was in Jesus' time, and remains, the famous Oral Law, which was later written down as, first, the Mishnah, and second, the Talmud. The "tradition of the elders" was a collection of interpretation and analysis of the Written Law, the Torah (the first five

revolutionary about him. The apostle Paul discovered just how radical it was when he had to fight no less a person than the apostle Peter about this. Peter was sitting at a special kosher table in the Antioch church, and Paul *opposed him to his face* (Gal. 2:11).

So when we read Deuteronomy in conjunction with today's Gospel, we are tempted to cast the Old Testament reading in a bad light. The implication is that there is a sharp contrast: Jesus didn't expect his disciples to keep those bad old Jewish laws. As you can see, this is a very delicate path to tread. There is no denying the fact that there is a radical difference between Christianity and Judaism. It isn't just a matter of accepting Jesus as Messiah; even more, it is this sweeping away of categories of righteousness. Note, however — and this is crucial — that this is not so much what separates Jesus from *Judaism;* it is what separates Jesus from *all* religion, *all* systems of self-improvement and spiritual achievement, including yours and mine. The human heart needs to be changed from the bottom up, but it cannot be changed by our "natural strength and good works." *It can be changed only by the intervening presence of the living God,* and that happens to people who are ritually clean and ritually unclean alike, as God demonstrates his quite shocking indifference to religious propriety.

Now, however, we come back to Senator Lieberman, not as a political candidate but as a faithful reader of the Torah and of Deuteronomy in particular. A friend of mine who is a Jewish Christian and New Testament scholar pointed out to me a long time ago that Deuteronomy is a very special book because of its references to God's intimate relationship to the human heart. Our text today is an example:

> "What great nation is there that has a god so near to it as the Lord our God is to us, whenever we call upon him?" (4:7)

St. Paul, who constantly surprises us with the way that he rebuts the Old Testament by directly quoting from it, calls upon Deuteronomy to make his point about the impotence of righteousness according to religious law. He cites this verse: "The commandment is very near you; *it is in your*

---

books of the Hebrew Bible, or Old Testament). In the time of Jesus, there was controversy about the Oral Law, the "tradition of the elders" — the Pharisees believed it was equal to the Torah, whereas the Sadducees did not. The future was to lie with the Pharisees; the Sadducees later disappeared from history, and in subsequent Judaism, the Talmud did indeed become as important as the Torah, if not more important. See Cecil Roth and Geoffrey Wigoder, editors in chief, *The New Standard Jewish Encyclopedia* (Garden City, N.Y.: Doubleday, 1977).

*mouth and in your heart, so that you can do it*" (Deut. 30:14; Rom. 10:5-13; my emphasis).

So there *is* a difference between Judaism and Christianity, though it is poorly understood in the church. The focus this morning, however, is not on the differences but on something else. The focus is on the living God, who has revealed himself by his Word to Jews and Christians alike. I read a moving description of what happened when Gore announced his selection of Lieberman. Reporters and cameramen were clustered around Lieberman's home, waiting for him to emerge. When he finally came out, in the most unselfconscious way imaginable, he touched the mezuzah on his door and then kissed his fingers. Without doubt, this is what he has been doing every time he comes out of his door for many years. The *New York* magazine reporter (Craig Horowitz), a secular Jew telling the story, didn't see this happen; he heard about it from a rabbi that he had called for a comment. "Did you see? Did you see what he did?" said the elated rabbi. And the secular Jewish reporter (who probably had to ask the rabbi what it all meant) went on to explain that the mezuzah on the door contains the most sacred of prayers, reminding the Jew of the existence, reality, and power of almighty God. And what is that prayer? It is the Shema from the book of Deuteronomy: *Shema Yisroel, Adonai elohenu, Adonai echod:*

"Hear, O Israel: The Lord our God is one Lord;
and you shall love the Lord your God with all your heart,
and with all your soul, and with all your might.
And these words which I command you this day shall be
upon your heart,
and you shall teach them diligently to your children. . . .
And you shall write them on the doorposts of your house and
on your gates." (Deut. 6:4-9)

In his now-celebrated and controversial speech at a Detroit church last Sunday, Senator Lieberman spoke of our "awesome God."[8] This is a word that I do not think would be used by anyone who did not know and love the God of Abraham, Isaac, and Jacob, the God and Father of our Lord Jesus Christ. The New Age gods and spirits of whom we hear so much today are not awesome. They wait to be approached with spiritual techniques; they

---

8. Unfortunately, the word *awesome* has now become so commonplace that it no longer means much of anything.

do not thunder down from Mount Sinai with holy and righteous laws; they do not speak from the whirlwind, as God did to Job; they do not commission prophets to speak to kings, as God did Elijah. The biblical God speaks, and his Word has the power to bring into being that which it describes: "'Let there be light!' and there was light."

How real is God to you? Is he as near to you as your front door? Do you know him as a living reality in your heart? Can you recite his awesome deeds, as every believing Israelite could do? Do you know of his justice and mercy proclaimed in the Psalms? Are you thrilled by the words "Hear, O Israel: The Lord our God, the Lord is one Lord"? There is nothing like the Bible because there is no other god like the God whose Word is alive in it. Let us love the living God; let us praise the living God; let us give glory to the living God. This is what the church is for. Listen to these wonderful words from Deuteronomy:

> "Behold, to the Lord your God belong heaven and the heaven of heavens, the earth with all that is in it; yet the Lord set his heart in love upon your fathers and chose their descendants after them, you above all peoples, as at this day." (10:14)

Think of it: *you* are those chosen descendants of the fathers and mothers. *You* are God's people whom he loves. You have been elected by him to reflect his glory in the world. He lives; he acts; he rules:

> O worship the King, all glorious above!
> O gratefully sing his power and his love. . . .
> His mercies, how tender, how true to the end;
> Our Maker, Defender, Redeemer, and Friend.[9]

---

9. The hymn is by Robert Grant (1779-1838).

# "Whatever Works for You"

## EPISCOPAL HIGH SCHOOL, ALEXANDRIA, VIRGINIA

Deuteronomy 4:5-20

*This was the first in a series of sermons given in 1994 for the Theologian-in-Residence Program endowed by my husband, R. E. Rutledge, Jr.*

. . . . . . . . . . . . . . . . .

IT IS indeed a great joy and privilege tonight to look out at this congregation and see so many old friends, Old Boys and Old Girls, visitors, faculty, and members of the administration. Having said this, however, I must tell you that I will not be speaking to you adults tonight, or tomorrow, or any other time this week. This week is for the *students*. This week is for the boys and girls, soon to be young men and women, of Episcopal High School.

I've given titles to this series of talks. These titles are taken from certain sayings that one hears all the time nowadays. The overall title is "Christian Faith: Who Needs It?" or, alternatively, "Get a Life!" The name of this first talk is "Whatever Works for You," the second is "I Can't Deal with This!" and the third is "Know What I'm Saying?"[1] Many times I have thought to myself that if I had to hear these utterances one more time, I would slip over the edge of tolerance altogether, but on the if-you-can't-beat-'em-join-'em principle, I have decided to make them my very own.

---

1. This is the only one of the three sermons that had an Old Testament text.

You heard two lessons from Holy Scripture tonight, one from the Old Testament and one from the New. They have a common theme: both of them are concerned with what the older generation is going to pass on to the younger. How shall we live? is the question. That is the question that the thinking person has been asking herself since the beginning of civilization. *How shall we live?*

The Hebrew people were profoundly, passionately concerned to address this question and to pass along its wisdom from generation to generation. From the address of Moses to the children of Israel, in the book of Deuteronomy:

"Behold, I have taught you statutes and ordinances, as the Lord my God commanded me. . . . Take heed, and keep your soul diligently, lest you forget the things which your eyes have seen, and lest they depart from your heart all the days of your life; *make them known to your children and your children's children.* . . . [For] the Lord has taken you . . . to be a people of his own possession, as at this day." (4:5-20; my emphasis)

And from the New Testament, the Epistle to the Ephesians:

Grace was given to each of us according to the measure of Christ's gift . . . for building up the body of Christ, until we all attain to the unity of the faith and of the knowledge of the Son of God, *to mature manhood, to the measure of the stature of the fullness of Christ; so that we may no longer be children,* tossed to and fro and carried about with every wind of doctrine. . . . We are *to grow up* in every way into him who is the head, into Christ. . . . (4:7-15; my emphasis)

In both of these passages and in a hundred others, there is a call to maturity, a call to identity, a call to meaning.

It is this call that I am here to represent. Each of you faces a choice. You may make this choice consciously and deliberately, or you can make it by default — that is, by not making it. Most people take the latter route. Most people don't give much thought to what they're doing; they drift into first one thing and then another. The purpose of an education such as you get at EHS is to challenge you not to do that, to teach you to think about the kind of life you want to have, to question the assumptions all around you, to grow up, not into an unexamined life, but an examined one. One of the reasons I'm here this week is to give support to your teachers, who are setting these choices before you and urging you to make them with care, with understanding, with respect for others, and above all with a larger purpose in mind than mergers and acquisitions — of whatever sort.

Now let's get straight to the point. Here we are tonight in this estimable prep school, in this wonderful chapel, where from time to time you are required to come and hear an out-of-town minister say a few inspirational words. You're bound to be asking yourself — at least we hope you are — whether this Christian faith is for you or not. Even if this is the best program of religious education in the American prep-school world, you're still going to find, when you get out of here, that you face intense pressure to allow a serious Christian commitment to slip right through your fingers as you reach for the brass ring. And the insidious thing about this is that you will not even notice that it is happening; the pressure will not even seem to be pressure, but will appear to be a natural movement in the direction that things are already going. Before long, you will have relegated Christian faith to the closet where you keep your stuff. You may have it in the front where you can reach it easily; you may have it in the back with the outworn sweaters. But in either case, Christian faith will have become for you an item in the closet like other items, in the same category as the cross-country skis and the old photo albums — nice to have, fun to bring out from time to time, even life-enhancing on occasion. But still, only one of many adornments in the good American life.

Contrast this with "The Lord your God has taken . . . you to be a people of his own possession, as at this day." Contrast it with "We are to grow up in every way into him who is the head, into Christ." Contrast it with the story you heard this morning if you were in church, about the boy Samuel who was committed to the Lord's service and grew "both in stature and in favor with the Lord and with men" (1 Sam. 2:26). A life of service to God means that religious faith is not one collector's item among many, but a complete way of life, where every aspect of our social, financial, athletic, sexual, domestic, business, and political lives is taken up into the realm of Jesus Christ, who is the fountainhead of all true human growth, all true human maturity. This is what the New Testament means when it calls us "to mature manhood, to the measure of the stature of the fulness of Christ, so that we may no longer be children, . . . [but] are to grow up in every way into him who is the head, into Christ."

Now you may think that I don't have a very good grasp of all this because I am a "churchy" person who hangs around with clergy all the time and am just too spiritual to be true. This is not the case. I spend a good deal of time with secular people. I vividly remember moving to New York from Virginia twenty-five years ago, meeting a famous literary critic who was one of my heroes, and listening to him say with scarcely disguised contempt, "A *Christian!* I don't know *anyone* who is a *Christian.*" Well, this is one of two attitudes that I meet all the time in the secular world, the same two attitudes that you also will meet there, if you haven't already. The first one, the belief of my critic friend, is that a Christian is somewhat lower on the evolutionary scale than the best people. The benighted Christian might actually be a nice person, might even be well-educated, might be cultured and sophisticated in certain respects, but clearly, when it comes to religious faith, the Christian is not as highly developed as the secular person who believes that religion is a sort of self-deception and, as such, is to be barely tolerated. This is one of two ways of saying "Whatever works for you." "I don't need it, dear, and I can't imagine an intelligent person like you falling for it, but if it helps you, that's fine with me."

The other way in which the expression might be used is by the New Age crystals-channeling-and-chanting crowd. When a New Ager says, "Whatever works for you," he is not being deeply patronizing like our secular friend, but is, rather, wholeheartedly enthusiastic about spiritual searches of all sorts and can therefore endorse any and all of them, without distinction.

Both of these positions are inimical to Christian faith, but the second is more so. It is easier to know what one believes when challenged with unbelief than it is to punch one's way through a marshmallow. In either case, however, the young person — or the older person, for that matter — is going to be faced with formidable obstacles if he or she wants to be a Christian. She is going to face a lifetime of being patronized by the sophisticates, on the one hand, and on the other hand, being smothered in sentimental embraces by the indiscriminately religious.

But I am here this week to testify that Christian faith is neither intellectually shallow nor spiritually thin. It is not for people who are looking for an easy way out, nor is it a fashion that one is "into" one month and out of the next. It is neither a hobby nor a collector's item. It is not a spiritual toy, and it is not wishful thinking.

"Who needs it?" Christian faith is not a joy ride. It is not a sugar-coated pill. It is not a tranquilizer. To be sure, it is, as Jesus said, for children in the sense that it requires absolute trust. But it is for grownups in the sense of which we are speaking tonight. Christian believers don't "need" faith in the sense of being more frail than other people and having to lean on it because of our weakness. Christian faith is simple enough to sum up in the words "Jesus loves me, this I know, for the Bible tells me so," but it is at the same time so robust and so intellectually challenging that no one who embraces it will ever be left without rich food for the mind and for the spirit.

Now I want to tell you something quite wonderful. The authors of the book of Deuteronomy (as well as Ephesians) had you in mind when they wrote. They envisioned many days like today, a day far distant in time when an adult would stand before a sea of young faces like Moses standing before the children of Israel, called upon to talk to them about what is really important; about what they need for living; about what they can hold on to in the good times and in the bad times; about what is true, holy, and good; about what you can furnish your mind with so that there will be something strong and nourishing and hopeful in that mind when you have to get out there and cope with everything from failed love affairs to backbiting officemates to corrupt bosses, everything from sexual anarchy to racial prejudice to institutionalized greed to holes in the ozone layer. What furniture are you going to have in your mind and spirit to call upon when you have to deal with the duplicity of a business partner or the unfaithfulness of a spouse or the illness of a beloved family member? What are you going to have in your mind? Astrology? Advertising copy? Beavis and Butthead? Roseanne? *Natural Born Killers? Interview with the Vampire?* (Even Oprah Winfrey walked out on that one.) I am hoping (and I am praying) this week to add my voice to those of others who would commend to you the way of the God of Abraham, Isaac, and Jacob, the God and Father of our Lord Jesus Christ.

Because you see, in the final analysis, Christianity makes a claim that is different. It does not make its appeal on the basis of being religious or spiritual. Christian faith is not worthy of your attention because it is religious or spiritual; it calls you into a lifetime of worship, service, and fellowship *because it is true.* "Whatever works for you" is a barren and empty formulation. I do not proclaim the Christian story to you because it is workable; the faith of the Lord Jesus Christ crucified, risen, and reigning took the Mediterranean world by storm and has never ceased to transform lives, not because it is practical or helpful or useful, but because it is life from the dead.

My husband, Dick Rutledge, devised this theologian-in-residence program for EHS entirely independently of me. I did not even know he was doing it until it was already done. His original idea was that I would be the second or third speaker, not the first. As it has worked out, I am very proud and grateful to be the first, because God has apparently made us a team, after thirty-five years of marriage, in ways that neither one of us could possibly have foreseen twenty or even ten years ago. Dick is a deeply converted man, and he wants to pass his Christian faith on to you. Today on the plane he turned to me and told me what he was hoping to accomplish through this program. He said — these are his exact words — that he hoped you would come to understand that Christian faith is a light for your path, not a program to make you masturbate less. Christian faith is not a device to control your behavior. Proclaiming it is not an offer of "whatever works for you." This is a call to "mature manhood [and womanhood], the measure of the stature of the fullness of Christ."

This very morning at Grace Church in New York where I minister, we had several baptisms because we were celebrating All Saints' Day. One of those being baptized was a man I met in the secular world, a man who has been to the bottom and back. A hard-living journalist most of his life, a serious drinker, married three times, a drug abuser, he nearly died of cancer four years ago. His friends, all of them utterly secular, gave him up for lost in more ways than one. This very morning this man stood forth in the midst of a very large congregation at Grace Church and confessed his faith and received the baptism in the name of the Father, and of the Son, and of the Holy Ghost.

I did not perform the baptism, but I was standing up front where I could see everything. I could look out over the congregation and beyond, and I could imagine the "great cloud of witnesses" and "the angels and archangels and all the company of heaven." There were three little babies baptized, and this one adult. The contrast was amazing. Here were these three untouched infants, to whom God was extending his grace "before they could do anything either good or bad," as St. Paul says in Romans. Their little faces were blank slates on which life had not yet written anything. The grown man, in contrast, had deep lines all over his face — lines made by suffering and, as he would want me to tell you, by sin. Yet here he was, by the grace of God as much a newborn as those three babies. He, with his ravaged face, received the new birth in all its glory equally with the infants in their unmarked state. Then the congregation responded. The moment that I particularly remember is the recitation of the Creed. In full-throated unison, with a vigor that seemed unusual to me even for our enthusiastic Grace Church members, those assembled began to say all together — what?

"Whatever works for you"?

No.

They said, *"I believe in God the Father Almighty, Maker of heaven and earth, and in Jesus Christ, his only Son our Lord."*

May the living God confirm this faith in you, tonight and always.

AMEN.

# Who Redefines God?

TRINITY CHURCH, COLUMBUS, GEORGIA

---

*First Sunday in Lent 2001*                    Deuteronomy 4:39; 26:5-10

BY NOW I expect many of you have seen *Gladiator*. It's a rousing spectacle, guarantees you a terrific night at the movies, and has received many Oscar nominations. On this first Sunday in Lent, however, there is something else about the film that merits our attention.

Those of you who are old enough to remember the Roman sword-and-sandal movies of the fifties — *Ben-Hur, The Last Days of Pompeii, The Robe, Quo Vadis?* and others — will perhaps recall that those older movies had specifically Christian content. Jesus is crucified in *Ben-Hur;* Christians are thrown to the lions in *Pompeii;* people come to faith in Christ in all of them. *Gladiator,* on the other hand, has no references to Christianity whatsoever, even though by the time of the Emperor Marcus Aurelius, the new faith was sweeping the Empire. Marcus Aurelius himself, who is depicted as the moral center of the movie, was indeed a remarkable philosopher-king and admirable in certain ways, but what the moviemakers don't tell us is that he was in fact a brutal and merciless persecutor of Christians who wished to obliterate the movement entirely. Further, and more to the point on this first Sunday of Lent, the Russell Crowe character (Maximus) in *Gladiator* is seen at various crucial moments unwrapping some cherished little figurines of gods, reverencing them and praying to them. These scenes seem to be entirely without irony; we are expected to respect them as history and perhaps even as religion. "Whatever works for you" is the message.

We have entered a new phase in America. The cultural supports for Christian faith that were there when I was an impressionable young person are gone. New trends are at work. You can read about them everywhere. In a recent *New York Times Magazine* article, one of our leading cultural historians writes, "Americans are exploring a new frontier. Though they still believe in God . . . they increasingly decide which God best suits their temperament."[1] And here is *The Wall Street Journal* on the same subject: "Across the country, the faithful are redefining God. Dissatisfied with conventional images of an authoritarian or paternalistic deity, people are embracing quirky, individualistic conceptions of God to suit their own spiritual needs." The *Journal* contacted various figures associated with American religion and asked them, "What is your image of God?" Some of the answers: "God is part of our genes." "[God is] a force field of positive energy." "God is in the buds of the apricot tree." God is definitely a woman, said one. Another said, God is "mysterious, dark, rich and gooey."[2] Sounds like chocolate to me. (I'll take it.)

The first Sunday of Lent may be the best Sunday of the year to address these issues. The meaning of this season is hinted at in the "Faith and Spirit" section of the *Ledger-Enquirer* yesterday, in Allison Kennedy's story about Lenten observance.[3] Pastor Troutman of St. Matthew Lutheran Church is quoted: "In this day and time, the world says, 'Have it your way,' but we say, 'Have it God's way.'" So the question becomes, How do we know what God's way is? The lessons chosen to be read during Lent point the path: We come to know what God's way is by knowing who God is.

The church's tradition from the beginning has been to gather *together* to hear the Scriptures read. God on the golf course, God in the genes, God in the apricot tree — these are not equivalent substitutes for God worshiped in the midst of his people, gathered to hear God speak through his Word. The Old Testament lessons chosen to be read during Lent are bedrock passages because Lent reveals the foundation of Christian faith; the place where we find ourselves at the end of these forty days is the foot of the Cross. Thus it happens that this morning we read one of the mountaintop passages in the Old Testament, often called "the ancient Credo" or "the great Credo," from the book of Deuteronomy.[4] A beloved professor at Virginia Seminary, Murray Newman, for many years required his students to memorize this statement of faith. I had a moving experience last year at

---

1. Alan Wolfe, "The Pursuit of Autonomy," *The New York Times Magazine,* 7 May 2000.
2. "Redefining God," *The Wall Street Journal* (Weekend Journal), 21 April 2001.
3. Allison Kennedy was a member of the congregation.
4. *Credo* means "I believe" in Latin. More generally, a *credo* is a statement of faith.

Trinity Church, New Orleans; I learned that not only had the rector of the parish memorized the passage under Murray Newman, but his assistant, thirty years younger, had done so also. Thus the living faith is passed on from one generation to the next.

The context of this central passage is important. You will see in the passage that the Credo is recited as the people of God bring their offerings to the altar. This is the whole purpose of the offering: that the worshipers should return a portion of God's gifts to the One who gave them. The gifts are not to placate or influence God; they are to acknowledge and thank the Creator and Giver of life. Let's listen again, then, to the Credo — and as we listen, let's remember the questions we've been asking about who God is.

> "A wandering Aramean [that means Jacob, the father of the twelve tribes of Israel] was my father; and he went down into Egypt and so-journed there, few in number; and there he became a nation, great, mighty, and populous. And the Egyptians treated us harshly, and af-flicted us, and laid upon us hard bondage. Then we cried to the Lord the God of our fathers, and the Lord heard our voice, and saw our af-fliction, our toil, and our oppression; and the Lord brought us out of Egypt with a mighty hand and an outstretched arm, with great ter-ror, with signs and wonders; and he brought us into this place and gave us this land, a land flowing with milk and honey. And behold, now I bring the first of the fruit of the ground, which thou, O Lord, hast given me." (Deut. 26:5-10)

You will never find anything like this in the history of religion — in the history of humanity's search for a god. Maximus can set up his little idols from now till kingdom come, and he will never come up with anything like this. Who would have thought it? The answer to the question "Who is God?" is this: God is the One who brought Israel up out of the land of Egypt. This means that God is indissolubly linked to the specific history of a specific peo-ple at a specific time and place, as we have it in the Old Testament. Imagine someone asking you, "Who is God?" The answer is this: "God is the One who brought the Jews up out of the land of Egypt." The fancy academic name for this is "the scandal of particularity," and it's a good name because the particu-larity of the gospel has always been a scandal. In fact, the apostle Paul, when he talks about the Cross of Christ, calls it *skandalon,* which, obviously, is Greek for "scandal." The scandal of the Judeo-Christian tradition is that God is not generic. God is not all-purpose. God is not a religious object. God is not the answer to my needs of the moment. God is not waiting around for me to define him or her. God defines God's self.

Think back to the story of the burning bush (Exodus 3). Moses, stunned to hear the voice of God speaking to him "from the midst of the bush," asks God, What is your name? And God says — you remember? — *I am who I am.* God is who he is in God's self, not who *we* think God is. And then the Lord goes on to tell Moses, "I am the God of your fathers Abraham, Isaac, and Jacob; this is my name forever." Thus the Lord unconditionally binds himself to the children of Abraham, and that means he has bound himself unconditionally not only to the Jews but also to you and me, for as St. Paul says in today's reading from Romans, "There is no distinction between Jew and Gentile; the same Lord is Lord of all and bestows his riches upon all who call upon him" (10:11). The God of Moses, the God of Abraham, Isaac, and Jacob, is not some cruel, harsh "Old Testament God," as some would have you think. This "Old Testament God" is the God and Father of our Lord Jesus Christ.

The God who is really God defines himself. God distinguishes himself from the other gods who are not gods at all. God is independent of our ideas about him; he was who he was before we ever thought of him. But listen to this: God is *independent* of us, but he is not *indifferent* to us. Quite the contrary. Here are some verses from another chapter of Deuteronomy: "Because he [God] loved your fathers [and mothers] and chose their descendants after them, and brought you out of Egypt with his own presence, by his great power . . . know therefore this day, and lay it to your heart, that the Lord is God in heaven above and on the earth beneath; there is no other" (4:37, 39; my emphasis). What does this tell us about God? That God loves us; that God chose us (and that means you and me). That God came down into human history to deliver us from our bondage; and that he did it himself, through his own presence and power. That God is the one and only Lord and that there is no other. "Hear, O Israel: The Lord our God, the Lord is one" (6:4).[5]

We are being told, however, that Americans now want to create God according to our own preferences. The analysts say that Americans do not like being told who God is. Is that true for you? Is it true for your children and grandchildren? I would be very surprised if it was not. We can (and should) delay the impact of cultural forces like television and the Internet when children are very young, but these all-pervasive, ultra-powerful influ-

---

5. The Shema, as this is called, is as central to the Israelite faith as the great Credo.

ences are in the air we breathe. The only antidote for them is another, even more powerful force.

Let us look now at the Gospel reading from Luke, the Temptation of Jesus in the wilderness by Satan, always read on the first Sunday of Lent. In rejecting the devil, our Savior says sharply, "You shall worship the Lord your God, and him only shall you serve." This is a verse from Deuteronomy (6:13). You see, the God of whom Jesus speaks is the God of the Old Testament: *there is no other.* It is by his name and in his power that God the Son renounces Satan and proves himself the stronger. For we are to understand by this story of the Temptation that alone of all human beings ever born, Jesus was able to resist sin and evil on every front. He has entered the battle against Satan on our side and has shown himself to be the conqueror. As Martin Luther writes in his famous hymn, "The Prince of Darkness grim,/ we tremble not for him;/his rage we can endure,/for lo! His doom is sure;/ one little word shall fell him." That "little word" is the word spoken by the Son of God; Matthew gives it to us: "Begone, Satan!" (4:10).

The God who is present in the Word and Sacraments of the church is not at all like the gods that you hear about in the "spirituality" marketplace. The nature of God as love is well-known, but what is not so well-known is that God's love is shown in active intervention: it is shown by "his mighty hand and his outstretched arm," in the often-repeated Old Testament phrase. God is the one who acts. He is a verb more than he is a noun.

Don't get me wrong. It is of course true that, as the Psalms say, "The heavens declare the glory of God." However, that takes us only part of the way. The movement of Lent is to take us all the way. God doesn't just spread out the sky and sit back while we look at it. He doesn't just lean over and fiddle around with things and then go back to his throne room. God has gotten down with us. That is why we must go with him all the way to the Cross. That is the place where Jesus meets Satan for the final and definitive battle. This morning we take our cue from the great Credo: our God is the one who is on the march to overthrow the devil and deliver his children from bondage into freedom. In doing so, he gives us his very self.

I saw in the paper that Hosea Williams died recently. There are wonderful obituaries being written as the heroes of the civil rights movement are being gathered, one by one, to the other side of the River Jordan. The obituaries are full of illustrations of the faith of the black community that God was alive and active in their midst during those days. In 1963, Robert Spike, a white man who was supporting the movement, traveled to Savannah, where Hosea Williams and other young black leaders were leading mass meetings to prepare for dangerous night marches to win the vote. More than five hundred Savannah blacks had already gone to jail. Few white people had ever witnessed anything like those so-called mass meetings, which were not really meetings but occasions for praising God. The preaching was revelatory, and the singing was thunderous. Spike, who knew his Bible, wrote a letter describing the worship: "I had the strongest feeling that I was in Egypt on the night of the Passover. . . ."[6] Thus the old story comes alive again as the power of God makes itself felt, not in airy speculations about the divine but in the midst of the human struggle.

This is the story that is more powerful than any other story. God is not off in the mystical ether; God is in the midst of our very human and very grubby struggles. The reading of the great Credo on the first Sunday of Lent fastens all these particularities into place. Again, St. Paul explains it in the second reading. We do not need to ascend to the heavens or descend into the depths looking for God, he writes (Romans 7–8). Using ideas from Deuteronomy, he continues: "The word is near you, on your lips and in your heart (that is, the word of faith which we preach); because, if you confess with your lips that Jesus is Lord and believe in your heart that God raised him from the dead, you will be saved" (Rom. 10:8-9). Paul is telling us that we do not need to redefine God with some new word, some new story. We have already got the greatest story ever told, the story of the God who is really God and has given us his very self for our salvation.

> "A wandering Aramean was my father; and he went down into Egypt and sojourned there, few in number; and there he became a nation, great, mighty, and populous. And the Egyptians treated us harshly, and afflicted us, and laid upon us hard bondage."

Fellow Episcopalians: when we are gathered together as a worshiping community in our pretty churches, we don't look as if we have any troubles. But each one of us has been or will be in some sort of Egypt. Every human community faces the temptations of the evil one. Each person falls into idolatry of one sort or another. Where is the God who can deliver us? Is it a god that we have projected out of ourselves? But that is not a god at all. The God of the Bible, the God who is the Father of Jesus, comes to us with a power that is not our own:

6. The story is told in Taylor Branch, *Pillar of Fire* (New York: Simon & Schuster, 1998), p. 127.

"Then we cried to the Lord the God of our fathers, and the Lord heard our voice, and saw our affliction, our toil, and our oppression; and the Lord brought us out of Egypt with a mighty hand and an outstretched arm . . . and gave us this land, a land flowing with milk and honey."

God has not yoked himself to us in unconditional love because we are religious, or because we have sought him. He has done it because he is who he is, and because he has sought us. He has yoked himself to us because he is God. He has done it himself, through his own presence and power.

"Know therefore this day, and lay it to your heart, that the Lord is God in heaven above and on the earth beneath; there is no other."

"And behold, now I bring the first of the fruit of the ground, which thou, O Lord, hast given me."

AMEN.

# The Terrors of Grace

*Epiphany 1992*                    Judges 6:21-23; Psalm 111:10

A REMARKABLE short story appeared in *The New Yorker* last year called "The Birds for Christmas." (Not the least remarkable thing about it was that the author is Mark Richard, who is from my very small hometown of Franklin, Virginia.) The story tells of two adolescent boys, both seriously injured, who are in a hospital ward on Christmas Eve. One is white — he is the narrator — and one is black.[1] They have no visitors and no presents. The nurses try to be kind, but they are overworked and preoccupied. The boys, in their boredom and loneliness, swear at the nurses and as a punishment are constantly having their beds rolled out into the hall away from the television. The black boy, whose name is Michael Christian, has one Christmas wish. He knows that Hitchcock's film *The Birds* is going to be on TV that night, and he wants to see it. He says, "I want to see *The Birds*, man. I want to see them birds get all up *in* them people's hair." It is clear, however, that he is not going to get to see it, and a sense of abandonment and hopelessness settles over the scene as the early darkness falls.

But then, suddenly, near midnight, a drunken Santa Claus with a speech defect appears in the ward. He is only a troubled and lonely soul himself, and his Santa suit is askew and none too clean, but he is carrying a

---

1. In 2011, Mark Richard (pronounced "Ri-shard" in the Cajun fashion) published an acclaimed memoir, *House of Prayer No. 2,* in which we learn much more about his frequent sojourns in Crippled Children's Hospital in Richmond, Virginia, and about the development of his Christian faith.

portable television. The night nurse relents and lets him set it up in a place where it will disturb the other patients. The four of them — the night nurse, the boozy Santa, and the two abandoned boys — settle down to watch the movie. A Hitchcock movie would seem to be very unsuitable fare for Christmas Eve, but a serene calm descends upon the little group. Michael Christian's only comment as he watches is "Those birds really messing them people *up*," but it is clear that a small, fleeting moment of grace and mercy has occurred.

The last sentence in Mark Richard's story is taken from the King James Version of the Nativity narrative in the New Testament. When the movie is over and the boys are told to go to sleep, the story ends with the words of the white boy, the narrator:

It was Christmas Eve, and we were sore afraid.

This combination of heavenly grace and earthly fear is one of the most powerful recurrent themes in Scripture, but in our time it has been obscured by current trends toward bland, inoffensive theologies. In the nineteenth century, "the fear of the Lord" was a common phrase among Americans, and it was understood in its biblical sense; today it tends to put people off, so we don't say it. The motif of "the fear of the Lord" appears so many times in the Bible, however, that it requires very fancy footwork to keep out of its way.

The saying that "the fear of the Lord is the beginning of wisdom" appears once in the Psalms (111:10), twice in Proverbs (1:7; 9:10), and once in Job (28:28). Twice in Genesis God is actually called "the Fear of Isaac," as though it was one of God's names (31:42, 53). Sometimes the word *fear* in English means something more like "reverence" or "awe," but very often it means just plain "terror" or "dread." The very worst thing that can happen to God's people is that they should forget the "dread" of the Lord. Jeremiah warns the Israelites, "the fear of me is not in you, says the Lord God of hosts" (Jer. 2:19). What's hard for us to understand today is that when "the fear of the Lord" came upon the people, something beneficial was happening, even though it was terrifying.

This connection between grace and mercy on the one hand, and fear and terror on the other, must be very important, or it would not be repeated so often in the Bible. If I were to read aloud all the verses in the Bible that begin with the words "Fear not," we'd be here an extra half-hour. Frankly, I was amazed when I looked it up; I hadn't realized that the command not to be afraid, in one form or another, ran through the Bible from one end to the other. Perhaps the most familiar example is from the Christmas story:

> And the angel said unto them, "Fear not: for, behold, I bring you good tidings of great joy." (Luke 2:10)

Whenever God shows forth his glory, you're going to find the words "Fear not," or something like them. The glory of the Lord and the fear of the Lord go together. As Annie Dillard has famously written, "Why do we people in churches seem like cheerful, brainless tourists on a package tour of the Absolute? . . . We should all be wearing crash helmets and life preservers."

Today we have two readings about the fear of the Lord, one from the Old Testament and one from the New. The first one is part of the story of Gideon, one of those rousing narratives for which the Hebrew Bible has always been famous. The reading for today tells the beginning of the story; you can read the rest of it in Judges 6–8.

The story begins with the Midianites. Being an Israelite during the invasions of the Midianites must have been a little like being a Kurd in Iraq — constantly in danger of losing everything, always afraid of being uprooted, never secure.[3] We first see Gideon, an untried young man of no distinction from a small Hebrew tribe, threshing wheat in a hidden spot, hoping to hide his meager yield from the Midianites. As he engages in this pedestrian activity, suddenly an angel of the Lord appears to him and says, "The Lord is with you, you mighty man of valor" (Judg. 6:12). I think this is supposed to be funny. Gideon is not in the least a mighty man of valor. He is just a kid, a nonentity. He has the good sense to recognize this himself, for he says to the angel, "My clan is the weakest in Manasseh, and I am the least in my family." But the Lord said to him, "But I will be with you, and you shall smite the Midianites as [if they were] one man" (6:15-16). Notice that, in the Old Testament, "the angel of the Lord" is equivalent to the Lord himself. If the angel is present and speaking, the Lord is present and speaking.

Now Gideon does not quite believe that this is the Lord speaking to him. He asks the angel to wait while he goes inside and prepares an offering

2. Annie Dillard, *Teaching a Stone to Talk* (New York: Harper & Row, Perennial Library paperback version, 1988), p. 40.

3. A few years before, the Kurds had been under murderous attack (Saddam Hussein's Anfal Campaign) and were fleeing by the tens of thousands during the Iran-Iraq war of 1980-1988.

so that the angel can give him a sign that it really is the Lord. This is an exceedingly presumptuous request; we know from other parts of the Scripture that God frequently comes down hard on people who ask for signs. In this case, God demonstrates his freedom, condescending to Gideon's youth and ignorance of his own people's history with God. The angel displays amazing patience: he sits down under a tree and waits for Gideon to go inside and prepare a young goat for cooking, with wheat cakes and broth. This must have taken some time. When Gideon gets back to the tree, the angel is still there; this is meant to amaze us, that the Lord of Hosts would indulge Gideon by sitting around like this. Gideon puts his present of a meal on top of a rock which serves as a table. The angel tells him to pour the broth over the food — to drench it, in other words. Now come the special effects:

> Then the angel of the Lord reached out the tip of the staff that was in his hand, and touched the meat and the unleavened cakes; and there sprang up fire from the rock and consumed the flesh and the unleavened cakes; and the angel of the Lord vanished from his sight. Then Gideon perceived that he was the angel of the Lord; and Gideon said, "Alas, O Lord God! For now I have seen the angel of the Lord face to face." But the Lord said to him, "Peace be to you; do not fear, you shall not die." (6:21-23)

The reaction of Gideon to the presence of God is duplicated over and over in the Old Testament. When God appeared to Isaiah, Isaiah cried,

> "Woe is me! For I am lost; for I am a man of unclean lips, and I dwell in the midst of a people of unclean lips; for my eyes have seen the King, the Lord of hosts!" (6:5)

It's commonplace to hear people declare that "the fear of God" is an Old Testament notion which is out of place in the New. But in our lesson from the Gospel of Luke today, we see how wrong that is. Simon Peter and his fellow fishermen have just spent a very disappointing night out on the Sea of Galilee. Jesus comes along on the shore and, with that air of mysterious authority that characterized him, tells the fishermen to put out into the deep water again, and let down their nets yet once more. Peter is irritated by this. "Lord!" he says. "We've already been out! We caught nothing all night!" Such is the power of Jesus' command, however, that the weary little group of men, no doubt swearing under their breath, haul the heavy nets into the boats again and row out. You know what happens: the catch of fish is so huge that the nets start breaking and the boat begins to take on water.

When the men get back to shore, what happens? Do they whoop it up as if they had just won the lottery? On the contrary. Peter falls on his knees before Jesus standing on the beach and says, "Depart from me, for I am a sinful man, O Lord."

> And Jesus said to Simon, "Do not be afraid; henceforth you will be catching men." And when they had brought their boats to land, they left everything and followed him. (Luke 5:8-11)

Two stories: one about Gideon, one about Peter. God draws near to them both, and both are overcome with terror. At the instant of their fear, however, the word of the Lord comes: Do not be afraid, for I will be with you for the mighty tasks that lie ahead. Luke's story is a parallel to the epiphanies of YHWH in the Old Testament.

What is it about the appearance of God that causes dread? An important German pastor of the nineteenth century, Christoph Blumhardt, wrote:

> There is a question that strikes fear into our hearts, and every honest person will feel it with me. It is this: Will I be able to stand before God? Will I be able to stand before the Saviour? Many people who feel quite reassured because they attend church every Sunday and participate in religious activities . . . would nevertheless be terrified if suddenly they should hear the thunder of the Last Judgment and witness the arrival of our God. They would then come to see their Christian cloak as a filthy garment.[4]

This last sentence is a reference to Isaiah 64:6: "All our righteous deeds are like filthy rags." There's a fundamental sense in which we need to understand that the God who is really God is opposed to us. Over against our littleness is his greatness, over against our impurity is his perfection, over against our sin is his righteousness. This is the reason that God must say to

---

4. This is quoted from *Thy Kingdom Come: A Blumhardt Reader* (Grand Rapids: Wm. B. Eerdmans, 1980), p. 123.

us, "Do not be afraid." If we have never known this, then we must submit to J. B. Phillips, who taught us, "Your God is too small."[5]

The attitudes of God toward us are too much for "unaccommodated man" to bear.[6] The attributes of God toward us are perfect justice and unconditional love — and we cannot tolerate either one. The perfect justice of God would require that each of us be condemned, not only for our own sinfulness, but also for our participation in the human condition in general, as Isaiah recognized when he cried out, "Woe is me! For . . . I dwell in the midst of a people of unclean lips" (Isa. 6:5). Unconditional love terrifies us also. I think of a man I once knew who had a serious car accident which left him helpless for several years. His wife nursed him devotedly and performed all sorts of intimate services for him. When he finally recovered, he left her and married another woman who would not be a constant reminder to him of his weakness and dependency. "Depart from me, for I am a sinful man, O Lord." We don't want to be loved unconditionally; we want to feel that we are *deserving* of love.

Perfect justice and unconditional love are combined in the person of Jesus Christ, who was hastened to his horrific public death by all the best people. The world has never seen his like. In him, God the Father is definitively revealed, in his love and in his justice.

Grace is terrifying. God is opposed to us; he is opposed to our selfishness, greed, idolatry, cruelty, pettiness, pomposity, vanity, and self-deceit. Yet God is for us. He is for us in ways that we can scarcely imagine — indeed, could not imagine if he had not revealed his conquering love in Jesus Christ. It is the love that *not only* opposes all that is harmful in the beloved *but also* has power to make our resistance go up in flames like Gideon's meat and cakes. When God appears, we are filled with fear; but the fear is instantly removed by the enabling word "Fear not." The fear of God is the beginning of wisdom because the awareness of sin comes only to those who are already standing on the firm ground of their salvation. The fear of God is the beginning of wisdom because it cannot come about unless God is present with us and for us.

Like the people Michael Christian was watching in the movie, you and I are indeed "messed up," and our city and our world are "messed up." We are all seriously sick patients in the hospital, swearing at those who would help us, venting our anger on our fellow patients, clutching our privileges to ourselves, increasingly indifferent to the suffering of others, puffed up with

5. J. B. Phillips, *Your God Is Too Small* (1952; reprint, New York: Touchstone, 2004).
6. Shakespeare, *King Lear*, III/4.

an exaggerated idea of our own importance, deficient in giving and — most damaging of all — deficient in receiving love. Yet at any moment, while we are about our mundane daily lives, cleaning our nets, threshing our wheat, doing our income tax, riding the subway, there may suddenly come an irruption of grace — an angel sitting under a tree, a catch of fish, a disheveled Santa Claus, a strain of music, a Valentine, a spurt of energy, unexpected forgiveness, fire leaping from the rock. Count yourself blessed if, when such moments come, you have a sensation of holy dread, a suspicion that what has happened might have come *in spite of* your deserving, an intimation that all good things come not from within ourselves, but as mercy from above.

If your rebelliousness and mine were allowed to play themselves out to the end, we would have our beds rolled out into the dark forever and ever, with no visitors and no presents; but the God who terrifies is also the one who loves us for all eternity. If you come to know the fear of the Lord, count yourself blessed, for the next words that you hear will be

Fear not: for, behold, I bring you good tidings of great joy.

AMEN.

# The God Who Calls,
# the Child Who Responds

*January 1994*                                              1 Samuel 3:10

A LOT of sentimental and fatuous things are written about childhood, especially at Christmas. Those who believe in Jesus as Son of God will understand when we say that, actually, the true meaning of Christmas is more for grown-ups than it is for children.

Having said this, however, we must quickly admit that our childhood experiences mark us indelibly. Biographers nowadays spend a lot more time describing their subjects' childhoods than they used to; we know more now than we ever did about the critical formative role of our early relationships. Wordsworth's saying "The child is father of the man" is more relentlessly true, and far more sobering, than the poet, in pre-Freudian days, consciously knew. "Train up a child in the way he should go," we read in Proverbs, "and when he is old he will not depart from it."

Today we have one of the most famous stories of childhood in the Bible. The narrative of the boy Samuel in the temple of the Lord always had a certain hold on me, but I did not begin to realize until recently that it has a more or less universal appeal for almost all children and plenty of grown-ups. During the past two weeks, I have mentioned to quite a few people that I was preaching on the story of the call of Samuel; I wouldn't be able to count the number of times that I heard the response "Oh, that's one of my favorite stories" or "That's my favorite story." Just a year or two ago, when my sister and I were reminiscing about our early years and the influence of our grandmother and aunt, I was amazed to hear her say that the Samuel story had been the clincher for her. I was awed by this, because the same was true for me, yet she and I had never compared notes on it before.

The beginning of the story, which we did not read aloud this morning, tells of Hannah, Samuel's mother. Hannah was miserable because she had no children; she begged the Lord, and he gave her a son. Hannah dedicated her boy Samuel to the Lord's service from the time of his birth. The story is charmingly told, with details that appeal to children and adults alike. When Samuel is about three, Hannah brings him to the sanctuary at Shiloh where she had prayed to the Lord for a child, and she places him in the care of the old priest, Eli, who had first heard her petition. Thereafter each year she painstakingly makes a little tunic for Samuel to wear, to replace the one he has outgrown from the year before, and she brings it to him at the temple, where she makes her devotions. We are touched by these images of maternal love and filial piety, and we are meant to be, because Hannah and her little boy are the Old Testament prototypes of Mary and her son, Jesus.

The climate in today's church, alas, is such that we would not be surprised to hear that the old priest Eli was a child molester. Such is not the case in the Old Testament narrative, as Eli turns out to be a good surrogate father to Samuel. Do not think the Bible story naïve, however; far from it! The dark part of the story lies with Eli's own sons, who are grown men when we meet them; they are the lurking, sinister counterparts to Samuel's bright, shining young spirit. These two sons were supposed to inherit their father's priestly office, but they were corrupt to the core. We learn that the atmosphere at the Shiloh sanctuary was one of depravity, for the sons of Eli were helping themselves to the collection and sleeping with the women of the altar guild, and all this was going on in the very presence of the Ark of the Covenant. A more appalling atmosphere for a young boy to grow up in could hardly be envisioned. It would not be a great leap of the imagination to picture Samuel caught up in a drugs-and-sex situation of today, and all of it taking place under the auspices of the church. Samuel's self-possession and sense of vocation stand out vividly against this background, like those of today's miraculous young survivors who rise above their surroundings to dazzle us all with their capacity to endure and overcome.

We are led to understand that Eli has been an ineffectual father of his two sons. He has remonstrated with them, but to no avail. It is a picture of a family in which there has been no consistent discipline. Eli has failed with his own sons, but the Lord gives him a second chance. Samuel becomes Eli's true son, and the one to whom the family inheritance passes, with interest. The terrible fate of Eli's sons, and Eli's own sad death, are contrasted with the rising star of Samuel, who has been called forth by God to play a critical role in the history of salvation. It is the story of the call of Samuel that has impressed itself upon so many young minds. To that part of the story we now turn.

Because of the sins of the sons of Eli, the sanctuary at Shiloh has seemingly been deserted by God. "The word of the Lord was rare in those days" (1 Sam. 3:1). The boy Samuel, however, was serving faithfully in the sanctuary under Eli's supervision. It takes a lot of faith and perseverance to continue to serve the Lord day in and day out when he does not give any indication of his presence. A lot of you know that; you have spoken about it from the perspective of your own lives. How hard it must have been for Eli to continue to instill hope in his young protégé when he had so little himself, how difficult to muster the confidence to be a guide to the young boy when his own two sons were violating the Lord's sanctuary on a daily basis. We read that "the sons of Eli were worthless men; they had no regard for the Lord" (2:12). We will learn that to have no regard for the Lord is the foundational offense, the one that defines all other offenses. Eli, however, even in his failure and weakness, continues to live his life in the knowledge of God. This is a guide for us in our own weakness and sin: may we never be so far gone that we have no regard for the Lord.

And so the young boy Samuel grows in the service of Eli. He learns to keep the sanctuary neat and orderly, looking after the rituals, cleaning up after Eli's venal sons, and undoubtedly serving the old man's various personal needs as well. The words that describe Samuel's development will later be used by St. Luke to describe Jesus: "The boy Samuel continued to grow both in stature and in favor with God and man" (2:26). However, the narrator tells us, there is a big blank to be filled in, for "Samuel did not yet know the Lord, and the Word of God had not yet been revealed to him" (3:17). In other words, God was favoring Samuel before Samuel even knew who God was.

The story of the call of Samuel begins with an atmospheric description of the nighttime in the sanctuary at Shiloh. The old priest and the young boy are sleeping in their separate places, apparently some distance apart. It is the dark of night, perhaps toward morning, but "the lamp of God had not yet gone out." On the surface, this refers to an oil lamp on a stand, still fitfully burning; one of Samuel's duties would have been to keep it trimmed and filled each day. Surely, however, we are meant to read this symbolically also, for though it certainly *seemed* that the Lord had abandoned Shiloh, with its corrupt and craven priests, in fact he had not, as we shall see.

Samuel is awakened by a voice calling him. "Samuel! Samuel!" There is nothing so arresting as the sound of one's own name, is there? The child jumps up and, by the light of the flickering lamp, runs to the bedside of Eli. No doubt he had been wakened by Eli's call in the night many times before. His cheerful, ready response warms the heart even across these thousands of years: "Here I am, for you called me." Eli replies, perhaps a bit impatiently, "I didn't call you; go lie down again." So Samuel went back to bed. Again he heard the voice: "'Samuel!' And Samuel arose and went to Eli" (not running this time — like the rest of us, he loses steam). This time Eli responds with an extra touch of gentleness for what he takes to be Samuel's mistake, "I did not call, my son; lie down again." Samuel goes back to his bed, this time, we may imagine, in some bewilderment; but the narrator, in an aside to the reader, has already explained that "Samuel did not yet know the Lord, and the word of the Lord had not yet been revealed to him" (3:4-7).

> And the Lord called Samuel again the third time. And he arose and went to Eli, and said, "Here I am, for you called me." Then Eli perceived that the Lord was calling the boy. Therefore Eli said to Samuel, "Go, lie down; and if he calls you, you shall say, 'Speak, Lord, for thy servant hears.'" So Samuel went and lay down in his place. (3:8-9)

Even over all these centuries, the story still has tremendous resonance, doesn't it? The important thing to understand about it is that it simply does not work, does not operate as a narrative, unless it is understood that it is the Lord speaking, not Samuel's religious imagination. The story demands to be heard in this way. The three-times-repeated call is not there solely for effect; it is there to hammer home the declaration that it is the Lord calling. The theme of the living, vitalizing Word of God is central to the Bible from beginning to end. It is very different from generalized "spiritual" concepts of God. The Bible story refers to the calling of Samuel as a "vision," but there is nothing visionary about it; it is pure audition. It is not a call to be religious; it is a call to speech and action in the world.

> And the Lord came and stood forth, calling as at other times, "Samuel!" And Samuel said, "Speak, for thy servant hears." (3:10)

The Lord "stood forth." The Word of God takes hold of a person. Karl Barth says that Samuel is "commandeered" by the Lord. This is just one of many such stories in the Bible; the Word of God raises up a person and creates the conditions for him to obey.

When this Bible story is told to children, the storyteller usually breaks off at the point where Samuel says, "Speak, for thy servant hears." Maybe that's a good idea — maybe not. Today we're hearing the whole story.

The Lord said to Samuel, "Behold, I am about to do a thing in Israel at which the two ears of everyone that hears it will tingle" (3:11). The message Samuel is to deliver is a message of doom for the house of Eli. No wonder the boy "was afraid to tell the vision to Eli. But Eli called Samuel and said, 'Samuel, my son. . . . What was it that he told you? Do not hide it from me'" (3:15-17). This was Eli's bravest hour, for he must have sensed the boy's fear. So Samuel took courage and told Eli the message: that God had decreed death and condemnation for the house of Eli.

In response to this terrible news, Eli says, "It is the Lord; let him do what seems good to him" (10:18). How are we to interpret this? Is it simply passive resignation? That would not be typical of a biblical character. We know that Eli has been a spectacular failure as a parent, but we have every reason to think that in spite of all, he knows the Lord. He knows the Lord so well that he is able to say, "Let him do what seems good to him." If there is a note of passivity here, there is also an example of faithful trust in the One who, in the end, is in charge of those who have let him down.

"Let God do what seems good to him." Surely this is meant to be a model of faithfulness in spite of everything. To know the Lord, to recognize him when he speaks, and to trust him to do with us and for us that which we cannot do for ourselves — that is true faith, of a sort that even a *good* parent could not outdo. Eli receives a fatal blow not long after, when he hears that the Ark of the Lord has been captured by the Philistines. The death of his sons he could handle, for it was the Lord's judgment on them for their blasphemy, but the loss of the Lord's Ark was too great a sorrow for him to bear, and he dies of a broken neck and a broken heart. But Eli's reward is this: He was the surrogate parent and loving teacher of one of the greatest figures that Israel was ever to know. The child Samuel grew up to be the prophet whose stature was so great that he ranks right behind Moses and Elijah in the history of salvation.

Samuel! Samuel! *God calls people.* He picks them out before they are born, Scripture teaches us, and for reasons known only to himself. Have you ever heard God calling you by your very own name? Well, to tell the truth, neither have I. Never once in my life have I ever heard the Lord speaking to me in the direct way that he spoke to Samuel. And yet I am as sure as I am of anything that God continues to call people. I am certain that, when I was a little girl listening to my grandmother read this story, God spoke to me through it, just as he speaks to you today through this preaching of the Word of God.

We have some letters in our family that my grandmother wrote to my father when he was a young man. Her overriding concern was not whether he was dating the right girl or making top grades or getting a good job. Her great preoccupation was with his knowledge of God. Her greatest fear was that he would have no regard for the Lord. She was by no means a perfect mother; but she gave her son the most important thing of all. When, many years later, that same son was confirmed in the Episcopal Church on the same day as his eleven-year-old daughter (me), her legacy to us was as clear as if we had actually heard the voice of the Lord saying our names.

There is reason to worry about our children and young people today. They do not know the Bible stories. They do not have much opportunity to develop a regard for the Lord. They are bombarded with so many stimuli from every direction; I can see with my own little granddaughter that it is difficult to keep her attention with anything that does not move or talk or pop up or run electronically. But there is one thing in this world that has not changed and that never will change, and that is the power of the combination of unconditional love and the calling of the individual name. Are our children hearing about Samuel and Hannah and Moses and Elijah and our Lord Jesus Christ in that context? Do they know that their very own little personalities are dear to God? Do they know that the Lord speaks to them in the circumstances of their own lives, wherever they are, and that he will guide them every step of the way? How will they know it if their parents and grandparents and godparents and Sunday school teachers do not make it their first priority to teach them? May we each re-dedicate ourselves to do our part with the children that have been given to us so that they will not fail to recognize the voice of the Lord when he calls them by their names.

Our God is a God who calls; our God is a God who establishes by his Word. Not everyone who is here today had a Hannah for a mother; not everyone who is here today had an unconditionally loving father. But God our Father in heaven is the perfect and complete Father and Mother of us all, and he calls each of us by name. He calls you today in the retelling of the story of Samuel, for it is not a human word that the preacher preaches, but the divine Word, which alone has the capacity for making itself present and active in the retelling of the old, old story. The story of Samuel is the story of Israel, and the story of Israel is your story, and mine, and ours — the story of salvation through The Child Who Was to Come, of whom St. Luke says, he "increased in wisdom and in stature, and in favor with God and man."

AMEN.

# Elijah Standing before the Lord

GRACE CHURCH IN NEW YORK

---

*June 1983*                                                    1 Kings 17:17-24

WHAT NAME of a famous person thrills you to the marrow when it is uttered? What person's name calls to mind images of glory, victory, deliverance, an end to oppression, a new and better day?

During the Second World War, that name might have been Winston
Churchill. For centuries of Frenchmen, it was Joan of Arc. In South Africa
today, it is Nelson Mandela. In America, black families display portraits of
Martin Luther King.

What was the name in Jesus' time? What was the Old Testament name
that had the magic? What name more than any other evoked a whole world
of associations having to do with the final triumph of the righteousness of
God, the climax of history, and the destruction of the enemies of Israel?

The name is that of Elijah. To this day, Jews still set out a cup for Elijah
at the Passover Seder; his return would mean that the messianic age of fulfillment had truly arrived. You remember that Elijah had not died in the
usual way; he had been taken up miraculously into heaven by the chariots
and horses of fire. Elijah, in fact, had never done anything in the usual way.
From the beginning of his career, when this strange figure from the desert
suddenly exploded out of nowhere and dared to confront Ahab the king in
his own council chamber, there was an inexplicable aura about him, as
though he had come from another world. And indeed, in a manner of
speaking, he had. Elijah's way of announcing himself was, "As the Lord the
God of Israel lives, before whom I stand . . ." (1 Kings 17:1).

This resonant declaration was peculiarly his own (and that of his disci-

[ 131 ]

ple Elisha), and to this day it carries with it an awesome force. To stand before YHWH — to be present with the thousands and ten thousands of angels attending his throne, to be a servant at his command, to see his holiness and his majesty and to be seen by him in all one's inadequacy and sin and still to be his chosen emissary — to be this kind of a man was all that Elijah cared for. What did King Ahab know of such a God? Ahab and his wife, Jezebel, thought that the God of Israel was a mere god alongside other gods. Under the liberal policies of Ahab and his powerful consort, the great name of YHWH was being cast into the shadows of the lurid flames that sprang up around the sensual rites of the Phoenician and Canaanite deities.

"As YHWH the God of Israel lives, before whom I stand . . . ," declared Elijah to the king. Elijah knew that the idols of Jezebel were impotent and dead. Elijah knew YHWH, the God of Abraham, Isaac, and Jacob, the God who lives: "He who keeps Israel will neither slumber nor sleep" (Ps. 121:4). What was Jezebel's puny god compared to the Lord of hosts?

The only other Old Testament figure who rivals Elijah in stature is, of course, the peerless Moses. Not even Moses, however, casts such a spell as Elijah. Elijah carries around with him an atmosphere of the supernatural. Modern commentators have been bothered by this and have tried to explain it away by referring to Elijah's exploits as legends or fables. The reason this rationalization fails again and again is that the unearthly, numinous aura of Elijah is so clearly derived — according to Scripture — from the nature of YHWH himself, the one and only God, a divinity of ineffable majesty, otherness, and power.

Elijah stood before Ahab, who had done more that was wrong in the sight of God than any other king of Israel, and Elijah said this:

> "As the Lord the God of Israel lives, before whom I stand, there shall
> be neither dew nor rain these years, except by my word." (17:1)

How could Elijah be so reckless? We should not think of him as being a supernaturally powerful man in his own right, so that he had no fear of kings and no hesitance about making preposterous predictions. The apostle James, in the New Testament, wrote that "Elijah was a man just like us." Elijah had not strength of his own, no power of his own, no aura of his own. He was emboldened to stand before the worldly king because he stood before YHWH; compared to the heavenly majesty of the Lord his God, the pomp of Ahab was pretentious and shabby.

Over and over in Christian history, God has raised up men and women to stand before him and serve him. You have known people like this, as I have. They are men and women just like us, yet they are different. They are in no way different in themselves; they are different because of the Lord, the God of Israel, before whom they stand. I can't help thinking of Bishop Festo Kivengere of Uganda and his Archbishop, Janani Luwum, who was murdered by Idi Amin; they were men just like us, with fears, foibles, and frailties just like us, and yet they were able to stand before the fearsome tyrant clothed in the supernatural power of the Holy Spirit. Do you think they stood before the killer in their own human strength? Of course not, as they would be the first to testify. Like Elijah, they bore their witness before the ruler of this world in the name of the Lord, the God of Israel, who lives, and before whom they stood. It is this God who gives power to his servants.

There is something very interesting about people like this. You felt it when Bishop Festo was here with us. We are attracted to such people; they give us hope; they convince us of the reality and power of God. Yet, in some sense, we feel judged by them. It's not that they themselves are judgmental toward us — not at all. Rather, we ourselves are reminded, just by their existence in the world, of the gap between who we are and what we ought to be. Such people reflect the glory of God to us as a prism collects light from the sun. Even a dim reflection of God's holiness puts us in mind of what we lack. Often, this is an irritant, and we want to get away from that person the way Idi Amin wanted to be finished with Archbishop Luwum. In a similar way, Elijah, that incomparable man of God, was not an easy person to be with. We can readily understand why King Ahab didn't want him around, but today's reading tells us how Elijah's presence turned out to be a problem for a God-fearing person as well.

After Elijah told Ahab that God was going to send a killing drought upon the land, Elijah simply disappeared, in that wild, untamed way of his. Ahab had no idea where to find him or when to hope for the word that would send the rain. The word of God had come to Elijah: "Arise, go to Zarephath, which belongs to Sidon, and dwell there. Behold, I have commanded a widow there to feed you" (17:8-9). This cannot have been good news for Elijah. God was sending Elijah to a district where Jezebel had been raised, where the name of YHWH was not honored, where the wicked queen would have spies everywhere. Nevertheless, Elijah went. He had long ago been conscripted. As military men in England used to say, "He knew the service."

The poor widow of Zarephath, when Elijah finds her, is so destitute that she and her son are on the verge of starving to death from the drought.

Yet God has brought Elijah to her hut in order to feed all three of them, and thus it was that the prophet came to live with this humble family. It must have been a dull existence for him, the man of action who challenged a king, called down fire from heaven, confronted political adversaries, and moved with ease in the halls of the mighty. Because he trusted God, however, he stayed there with the woman and her son in obscurity for many months. Eventually, however, something happened which made Elijah's presence a reproach and a horror to the woman of Zarephath, something which robbed her of all serenity and all peace in the presence of the man of God. Her son became desperately sick, and drew near to death. As he lay expiring, the woman bitterly reviled Elijah, saying, "What have you against me, O man of God? You have come to me to bring my sin to remembrance, and to cause the death of my son!" (17:18).[1]

After months of quiet and doing nothing, Elijah and the woman are both suddenly jolted by the tension that inevitably makes itself felt when the reality of the human situation presses in upon us. We are under sentence of death, all of us. Paul, reflecting on Genesis 2–3, writes that "sin came into the world through *one* man [Adam] and death through sin, and so death spread to *all* men because all men sinned" (Rom. 5:12; my emphasis). Death is a malevolent intruder into human life, the cohort of sin. As the apostle Paul says, Sin (understood as a hostile Power) "worked death" in the human race (Rom. 7:13) and infected all human beings. Elijah knows this. Moreover, the death of a young person in Elijah's time was so commonplace that it was hardly worth noting. There was a sense in which death simply had to be accepted.

However, Elijah refuses to accept it. In the terms of the biblical story, what he does next is astonishing. With the same kind of audacity and defiance that he showed two years before in Ahab's council chamber, Elijah snatches up the boy's body and carries it to the upstairs bedroom, where he lays it down on his own bed and then hurls this accusation directly at God: "O Lord my God, have you brought calamity even upon the widow who has taken me in, by slaying her son?" (17:20). We should notice how remarkable this is. Elijah continues to address God as "my God." He speaks to God as though they were on intimate terms. He blames God for what has hap-

---

1. No specific "sin" is mentioned. I am interpreting the woman's lament as if it were a lament for all sin, the power of Sin which deals death to the human race. Paul's teaching leads us to expand the scope of the woman's accusation. The presence of Elijah refracts the inescapability of the nexus of Sin and Death afflicting all human beings.

pened, giving him direct responsibility for "slaying" the boy — not for allowing him to die, mind you, but actually for killing him. We shouldn't let this go by lightly. Serving a powerful God means that there are going to be times when we will accuse God of malice. And that is exactly what Elijah is doing. If we don't recognize that, the force of Elijah's next words will be lost on us.

Continuing to address God as "O Lord my God," maintaining that personal connection that he has claimed all along, Elijah demands that God reverse his own action. "O Lord my God, let this boy's life return to him!" (17:21).

Now for the sake of the meaning of this story, we should take it on its own terms, at face value — that's the way stories work. Here is what we should be asking at this point. Where does Elijah get the idea that he can rage against God and then demand that God roll back his own decision? Where would such an idea come from? Where indeed, in the case of this prophet who stands before the living God? Where but from the living God of Israel himself? That is the thrust of the drama. It is guided by God.

And as the Lord, the God of Israel, lives, Elijah the prophet laid his body over the boy's body three times, and the child's life returned to him.

What we have here in just a few brief sentences is one of the most notable biblical demonstrations of God's ultimate purpose, which is *through judgment to give deliverance, through death to give life.* The boy's death in the presence of God's servant Elijah causes the woman to surmise that the prophet came to her for judgment, and that judgment is the last word spoken by God. We have no idea what the woman's "sins" might have been. That's not important. Sin has us all in its grip. The judgment for sin is death ("the wages of sin is death" — Rom. 6:23), and it seemed to the widow of Zarephath that the prophet of the Lord had visited her with a death sentence.

But Elijah knew something about the Lord before whom he stood. As a prophet chosen and anointed by the Lord, he had a glimpse into God's heart. Therefore he took a step so bold that a person unassisted by revelation could not even imagine such a thing: Elijah demanded that God should behave like God's self — the God who, as Paul puts it, "raises the dead and calls into existence the things that do not exist" (Rom. 4:17). OK, Lord, you've killed this boy — now raise him up!

For this reason, the first thing the widow does after the boy returns to life is not what we'd expect. We'd expect her to rush to her son with ecstatic cries. But that isn't what she does immediately. Her first reaction is an overwhelming response of awe and submission to the presence and power of the living God, and she says: "Now I know that the word of the Lord from your mouth is truth" (17:24).

Now she knows that the purposes of the Lord are for restoration and life, not condemnation and death. Whatever transgressions were gnawing at her soul, they are resolved by what she has seen and acknowledged.

The widow had not come to this state of grace, however, without pain. We cannot deceive ourselves into believing that the presence of God in our lives is always benign. When we are brought to stand before God, we come to feel the laser beam of his holiness, boring through our complacency and exposing our corruption. We don't escape God's judgment; the Bible never promises mere escape. The promise that we may grasp and believe is that God's judgment will for us be life, and not death; mercy, and not condemnation.

A millennium later, Jesus of Nazareth, coming near to the village of Nain, saw a poor widow grieving and mourning for her only son, whose dead body was being carried in a funeral procession. We are not told that this widow had faith, or that she believed in God, or that she was virtuous or charitable or deserving. We are told only that Jesus looked upon her and had compassion on her (Luke 7:13) and that he stepped forward and with a mere word spoke the young man into life.

The presence of Jesus was as disturbing to those who came into contact with him. Even those closest to him felt it; upon seeing one of his Master's deeds, Peter fell on his knees and said, "Depart from me, for I am a sinful man, O Lord" (Luke 5:8). That tells us something about the effect Jesus had on people. Like Elijah, he was not so easy to have around. There was something of another world, another sphere of power that surrounded him, clearly human though he was. No wonder. He brought judgment, not only upon the scribes and Pharisees but upon his own disciples. But when the hour came, he stepped into the place of judgment alone, and took it all upon himself, and then returned with the gift of life eternal.

And what of Elijah? Where do we see him again? You can read about him in the first book of Kings, how he called down fire upon the prophets of Ba'al and the rains came. A thousand years after his translation into heaven in the chariot of fire, Elijah reappeared — twice. All the Gospels in one way or another acknowledge John the Baptist as Elijah *redivivus,* the one who would come to announce the coming of the Messiah. And Elijah himself appeared again. On the Mount of Transfiguration, as Jesus changed in appearance to become a figure of blinding brilliance and divinity, Moses and Elijah came to converse with him. Imagine it! The entire Old Testament summed up — the Law and the Prophets in their two greatest personifications — before the eyes of the awestruck disciples. But Luke tells us that they did not speak of Jesus' glory. They spoke of "his departure, which he was to accomplish at Jerusalem" (Luke 9:31) — his death for sinners.

And then Elijah and Moses, having seen the sight that angels longed to see (1 Pet. 1:12), vanished from sight, so that when Jesus' disciples "lifted up their eyes, they saw no man, save Jesus only" (Matt. 17:8).

# The Little Church in the Wilderness

*July 2003*                                                                                1 Kings 17

*This sermon was preached in a prominent, prosperous church in a university town.*

. . . . . . . . . . . . . . . . .

On the eastern shore of Maryland there is an Episcopal church that has a full service of Morning Prayer each weekday. When I drive down to visit my mother in Virginia, I always stop there. They used to have a decent number of people in attendance, but last week there were only two — two women "of a certain age." It turns out that all the people that used to come regularly had either died or moved away, and they have an interim pastor who does not often attend. Therefore, those two lay women are keeping the doors open and the prayers coming, and this visitor was very grateful. I told them that I was going to put them into my Sunday sermon. In due course you will see what I mean.

This sermon is one of a series, featuring some lesser-known, often neglected biblical characters. My character this morning is like many others in that she is given no name. We know her only as the widow of Zarephath. Now I must tell you that this sermon is something of a Trojan horse. It is indeed about the widow of Zarephath up to a point, but I have smuggled Elijah into the story along with her. It's not possible to talk about the widow without talking about Elijah, and talking about Elijah is a very exciting thing for preachers. For sheer drama, you can't beat Elijah. He delivers more fireworks than all the other prophets put together. Boys today like "action figures" — well, Elijah is one of the greatest action figures of all. One Old Testament scholar calls him the "muscle man" among the prophets of Israel.[1] He challenged the heathen prophets of Ba'al to a duel on Mount Carmel, and when the Lord vindicated him by casting fire on the earth, Elijah, exulting in the sheer power of the Lord, girded up his loins and ran in front of King Ahab's chariot for seventeen miles, all the way from Carmel to Jezreel.

Elijah is big in every way. He thinks big and acts big. He confronts apostate monarchs and hurls threats at heathen prophets. He barges into King Ahab's council chamber uninvited, and the king groans, "Is it you, you troubler of Israel?"[2] to which Elijah replies, "I have not troubled Israel; but you have, . . . because you have forsaken the commandments of the Lord and followed the Ba'als" (1 Kings 18:17-18). The real danger to Elijah, however, is not the king. It is his Lady Macbeth of a wife, Jezebel, the power behind the throne. She has made no bones about her intention to have Elijah killed. Her implacable enmity is a measure of the danger that the prophet posed to her power.

Undoubtedly Elijah had a very large personality which impressed itself upon Israel for all time. Even more than Moses, Elijah remains the figure in Israel's history who carries around with him the atmosphere of the numinous, the preternatural aura of the one who stands before the face of God. Indeed, that is the characteristic way that Elijah introduces himself. Listen:

> Now Elijah the Tishbite, of Tishbe in Gilead, said to Ahab, "As the Lord the God of Israel lives, before whom I stand, there shall be neither dew nor rain these years, except by my word." (17:1)

*As the Lord the God of Israel lives, before whom I stand.* What would Elijah's take-no-prisoners personality have been like if it had been given over to the service of something other than God? He would have been overbearing to an unendurable degree in the service of his own ego. He would have driven all before him. If he had been riding in the Tour de France, he wouldn't have waited for a fallen rider to catch up. If he had been a CEO, there would have been heads rolling all over the place. He would have been insufferably arrogant. He would have been a secretary of war.

---

1. Christopher Seitz (of the University of St. Andrew's, Scotland) wrote this, but I have misplaced the source.

2. In a subsequent meeting, the king says, "Have you found me, O my enemy?"

But Elijah is not in the service of his enormous ego. His ego has been harnessed. He stands before the Lord, the living God of Israel. He bears a divine burden. That's why he's not welcome in Ahab's court. In that respect he is the exact opposite of Billy Graham. I hasten to add that I admire Billy Graham very much in many ways, and I thank the Lord for him, but he himself has admitted that maybe he has been too impressed with himself for getting close to too many presidents. I will never forget the night before the first Gulf War. The Presiding Bishop of the Episcopal Church, a personal friend of the first President Bush, was outside the White House holding a candlelight vigil, and Billy Graham was inside as an invited guest. Which man was most like Elijah that night?

Now for the widow of Zarephath.

Elijah the wielder of power, the fiery antagonist of kings, the flaming scourge of false prophets, the rugged physical presence capable of running at speed for seventeen miles, had to learn humility in the service of the living God. After his first great confrontation with Ahab, we may imagine that Elijah would have been intoxicated with his newly proven capacities. He is able to march in to the king and out again without anyone stopping him! He can tell off the king and get by with it! He is able to start a three-year drought with his mere word! He must be in line to be the next great national power-broker!

On the contrary, Elijah is sent away alone into the wilderness. God comes to him and instructs him to go, anonymous and alone, into a deserted, infertile area where there are no occupants to challenge or dazzle, no Ba'al-worshipers to confront or convert, not even any false prophets to expose and humiliate. He has to sit by a diminishing wadi (watercourse) and be fed by an unattractive and unclean bird. If Elijah was impressed with himself for being able to shut up the heavens with a word, he is not impressed anymore. He in his turn must be brought low. Now he must suffer the effects of the drought like everyone else. This is the Lord's hard way of teaching us our place before him. Beware of the doctor who has never been sick, the prosecutor who has never lost a case, the teacher who always knows the answer, the prophet who is drunk with self-importance. God did not allow Elijah to become intoxicated with his own greatness. After a while — many weeks of enforced solitude, we assume — the brook Cherith dried up, because there was no rain in the land, and Elijah found himself in danger of dying from thirst.

"Then the word of the Lord came to him, 'Arise, go to Zarephath, which belongs to Sidon, and dwell there. Behold, I have commanded a widow there to feed you'" (17:8-9). This is not auspicious. Zarephath is in

Phoenician territory, which is Jezebel's native turf. Moreover, the prospect of being fed by a widow in the midst of a great drought is dismal indeed. Among all the victims of the famine, widows would be among the first to starve. All through the Bible we are made aware of the special vulnerability of widows, who have no one to provide for them or protect them in an intensely male-dominated culture. The plight of a widow with a child to support would be all the more precarious. It is therefore a real test of Elijah's authenticity as a man of God that he should be sent into hostile territory in the midst of a famine with only a widow for support.

About twenty years ago, I happened to pick up a little paperback book called *Elijah the Tishbite*. It's a collection of sermons preached in the nineteenth century by F. W. Krummacher, who, if this volume is anything to judge by, must have been one of the most gifted preachers of all time.[3] He and his great subject are well matched. It is humbling and illuminating to read sermons of this kind. Most preachers today would simply say that Elijah went to Zarephath, saw a woman gathering sticks for fuel, and asked her to give him a drink of water from the town well. But these marvelous old-time preachers see something far more in these narratives. They see the hand of the living God. Krummacher unhesitatingly affirms that the Spirit guided Elijah to this particular woman, and that God told Elijah that since she was the one appointed, God would give her the means to provide for him. Moreover, God has prepared her heart to receive Elijah and minister to him. Listen to Krummacher:

> She seems to know Elijah's name, for how has she addressed [him]? "As the Lord thy God liveth." What an unusual and sweet sound is this in a strange land, in an idolatrous country. Perhaps she is a secret worshiper of the living God — a rose in the midst of thorns — a hidden dove in the cleft of the rock — a *converted* soul, one of the few among the heathen that the word of God has reached. O happy thought, to find a brother or a sister in the land of [Ba'al]![4] And whence does she know that Jehovah [Yahweh] is [Elijah's] God, and that [Elijah] is his servant? Oh, the marvellous disposal of divine Providence![5]

---

3. F. W. Krummacher, *Elijah the Tishbite* (reprint, Grand Rapids: Baker Book House, 1977).

4. Krummacher correctly says *Melech* instead of *Ba'al,* since we are not in Canaan anymore, but for preaching purposes I did not want to confuse hearers with this detail.

5. Krummacher, *Elijah the Tishbite.*

The woman is so moved by the presence of the prophet that she bursts out with her story. She and her son, weakened by years of famine, have reached the last of their meager resources. "As the Lord your God lives, I have nothing baked, only a handful of meal in a jar, and a little oil in a cruse; and now, I am gathering a couple of sticks, that I may go in and prepare it for myself and my son, that we may eat it, and die" (17:12). As Krummacher notes, these pitiful details tug at our hearts even at this remove. Elijah seems strengthened by her sorrowful tale; he discerns through it the plan of God to cause a tiny amount of food to expand beyond human capacity — the power of the same God who many centuries later will feed five thousand people according to the Word of his Son our Lord. And so Elijah, his faith renewed by this unlikely witness, asks the widow to prepare the cakes and serve them, and the meal and the oil did not fail for many months, "according to the word of the Lord which he spoke by Elijah" (17:16).

The towering prophet who comes and goes before angels and kings is now housed in the hovel of a nameless widow, one of the nobodies of the earth. As the world counts success and significance, this household does not even register. Yet Elijah dwells there according to the Lord's will. Listen again to Krummacher:

> Behold, then, this man of God sitting down in her solitary cottage. . . .[6] Well might this poor widow rejoice in the privilege of sitting daily at the feet of this man of God for instruction in divine things! Can we doubt for a moment that the prophet most gladly opened his mouth in divine wisdom, to impart it to the soul of this . . . believing sister? Can we doubt that they prayed together, that they read together out of Moses and the prophets, that they conversed together of the day of Christ, which Abraham saw with gladness? . . . and well might the angels of God have rejoiced, as no doubt they did, over this little church in the wilderness![7]

We have heard the reading of the rest of the story, how the widow's son sickened and "there was no breath left in him" (17:17); how Elijah carried

6. Krummacher continues here: "Indeed our Lord himself thus applies this part of sacred history to the case of the people of Nazareth who refused to receive his ministry: 'I tell you of a truth, many widows were in Israel in the days of Elijah when the heaven was shut up three years and six months; when great famine was throughout all the land, but to none of them was Elijah sent, save unto [Zarephath], a city of Sidon, unto a woman that was a widow'" (Luke 4:25-26).

7. Krummacher, *Elijah the Tishbite*.

the boy up to his own bed and lay down on top of him to impart his own warmth and life; how the prophet cried out to God and demanded that he save the child of the woman whom God had used to save him; how God restored the boy to health; and how the woman praised the God of Elijah, glorifying him for the true Word that he had put into Elijah's mouth.[8]

Now, brothers and sisters, a personal word to you. As I travel from congregation to congregation all over the United States, more and more I sense that a congregation like this one, though you are both prominent and prosperous, is actually a little church in the wilderness. Why do I say that? I say that because more and more it seems to me that the Christian Church in this very religious country of ours is in danger of losing its soul.

Let me explain. At the risk of oversimplifying, I see several groups of churches:

- There are the nondenominational fundamentalist churches, the evangelical churches, the Bible churches, the conservative breakaway denominations, and the larger part of the Southern Baptist Convention. This is the so-called Christian right, identified in the mass media as "evangelicals." They tend to be pro-death penalty, anti-abortion, wary of homosexuality, and fervently patriotic. These congregations tend not to be very interested in social justice because they concentrate on individual conversion. They are extremely generous with their money, however, and they give lavishly not only to overseas missions but also to all kinds of relief agencies.
- There are the old-line Protestants, the mainline churches, often called "liberal" — the Presbyterians, the Episcopalians, the Lutherans, the Methodists, and the United Church of Christ. These are the churches that have been losing members in big numbers. These are the churches that committed themselves to issues of peace and justice in the sixties, seventies, and eighties, but these commitments have waned in many cases because of a lack of theological grounding.
- There are three other bodies that stand apart from these groupings, though to be sure there is some overlap: (1) the traditional African-American churches; (2) the charismatic/Pentecostal churches; and (3) the mighty Roman Catholic Church, which for all of its difficulties has tremendous advantages because of its huge numbers, its global

8. See the sermon "Elijah Standing before the Lord" for a much fuller treatment of the raising of the boy.

reach, and its *magisterium,* which is still able to command attention through the person of the pope.

But there is another category, much smaller and more embattled than any of the others — hence "little churches in the wilderness." Why are the mainline churches having so much trouble? Let's return to Elijah and the way he identifies himself — *As the Lord the God of Israel lives, before whom I stand.* I've been listening to sermons and attending adult education classes all over the mainline churches throughout our country for nine years, ever since I left parish ministry, and very rarely do I hear about a living God. We aren't hearing about the God who actively intervenes for his people through concrete events. We don't hear about "the day of Christ" or "the marvellous disposal of divine Providence." The messages are not about a God who judges and redeems, who causes great movements to come to pass, who puts down the mighty from their seats and exalts the humble and meek. Instead, the messages are about human activity. They are about human potential, human hopes, human wishes, human programs and agendas. Please don't misunderstand me — much of this is important and necessary — but there's a problem here. The problem is that we start thinking that this human activity is what drives the engine of the church. The living God of Elijah does not seem to be in view.

And so we can make a case that the "conservative" churches and the Pentecostal churches are growing because, whatever their failings, there is a sense of a living God. In particular, I think that's been the reason for the strength of the African-American congregations, which have never taken their eyes off the God who "makes a way out of no way."

This particular congregation is positioned to make a great difference. Why? *Because you combine two things* that are not often found together in the mainline congregations today. *First* and most important, you have a tradition of biblical and theological preaching — that is to say, preaching that is grounded in *theos,* the living God, and in the living Word of such a God. And *at the same time* you have a strong tradition of involvement in social justice and a commitment to discerning the action of God in the wider world.

This essentially biblical combination is hard to find in the American churches today. The whole world is looking at American Christianity right now because there is so much talk about God from the administration, but what the world sees is arrogance and swaggering. The world is looking for the compassion and the generosity that President Bush so often mentions, but much of what the world sees is American might without a corresponding commitment to humane values. What American Christianity needs more than anything is congregations that combine an unabashed proclamation of the living God with a witness to God's revolutionary way of sacrifice, service, and selflessness. This congregation, with its traditions, its clergy and lay leaders, may very well find itself called out to stand before kings, so to speak, to tell truth to power not because you are a "peace-and-justice" church or an "inclusive" church or a "Bible-believing" church or whatever may be the code words of the moment, but *because of the Lord, the God of Israel before whom you stand.*

Finally, then, let's look once more at our little church in the wilderness with its three members. One is a celebrity, a world-class prophet, a man with access, yet a man so threatening to the power structure that they seek his life. The others are the widow and her boy. She is a humble, poor, marginalized woman with no standing whatsoever, no worldly resources, no extraordinary gifts — yet her affirmation of the truth of the Word of God spoken through the prophet gives strength to the great man and plays a crucial role in the purpose of God for his Kingdom, so that she is remembered and given honor by Jesus Christ himself and is the subject of sermons to this very day. Doesn't this tell us a good deal about the way the church works? Doesn't this speak volumes about the ways of our God in the world?

We can think of Elijah as representing the public face of the church, the calling of the church to throw down the gauntlet fearlessly before the rulers of this world in the name of the God who calls all human arrangements into question. And we can think of the widow of Zarephath as representing the homely, private, and quotidian face of the church, the ministry that goes on without fanfare — the serving of meals, the reading of the daily office, the visiting of the sick, the balancing of the books, the teaching of the children. There is no one who does not play a part, and the mighty works of God continue apace, and each person may at any time be called out of his or her place to give assistance to God's great enterprise, and the angels rejoice to see the little churches in the wilderness — because *he watching over Israel slumbers not nor sleeps.*[9] Praised be the living God!

AMEN.

---

9. This was the text from Mendelssohn's *Elijah* sung after the sermon.

# The Power That Gives Up Power

1 Kings 19:1-18

*This sermon was originally preached in 2007 at Emmanuel Episcopal Church, Franklin, Virginia. A slightly altered version was preached two months later at Mayfield-Salisbury Church, Edinburgh, Scotland.*

. . . . . . . . . . . . . . . . .

My memories of my hometown have a particular character. When I'm there, I walk through the cemetery almost every day, and it's like a family reunion. I see the headstones of my Sunday school teachers, Mrs. Sue McCann and "Miss Lizzie" Smith. There was no parish house in those days; they taught us while we sat in the pews. I see the stone for Mr. Finley, who was the Sunday school superintendent for decades and greeted every single person in the congregation every single Sunday. And I pay homage to the graves of my grandmother and my aunt, who read the King James Bible to me before I was old enough to understand a word — yet that Word of God was working in me even then. And when I walk down Clay Street, I see the Dutch colonial house opposite the park, and I remember how I was a young guest at a Franklin Book Club meeting in that house when Sally "Shep" Ray gave a heartfelt, unabashed testimony to her Christian faith.

These were not big voices. They were still, small voices. Yet they were voices from God in my life that reverberate in my soul to this day, and I rejoice to remember them.

Today we're going to think about the prophet Elijah. There is more drama in the story of Elijah than that of almost any other biblical character. He was a mighty warrior for the Lord, and we get the impression that he enjoyed it. As we know, every time there's a big hurricane, most people batten down the hatches and leave, but there are always a few who stay because they want to see a hurricane. They want to see something really huge. They want to see *power*. Well, Elijah was like that. He loved it when God fully unleashed his might. He relished the whole idea of calling down fire upon the enemies of God, and he did just that, on Mount Carmel. When Elijah spoke the word, God sent down a thunderbolt and a great storm of rain, and Elijah was exultant. He was a titanic figure, and he had the personality to go with it.

I'm sure many of you have seen the World War II movie *Saving Private Ryan*. One of the minor characters is a rifleman, a sharpshooter. He's a very young enlisted man, almost a boy, really, with an accent straight out of the Appalachian "hills and hollers" where he learned to shoot. He never misses a shot; he picks off Nazis as if he were hunting in his native woods — and while he's aiming his weapon, he's quoting the King James Version of the Bible: "The Lord hath bent his bow, and made it ready. He hath prepared the instruments of death; he ordaineth his arrows against the persecutors" (Ps. 7:12-13).[1] This couldn't have happened — real sharpshooters have scoffed at the scenes — but allowing for dramatic license, there's a similarity to Elijah. After the great contest on Mount Carmel, where the Lord sent down fire and routed the prophets of Ba'al, Elijah pursued the false prophets and killed them all. "Do I not hate them who hate thee, O Lord? . . . I hate them with a perfect hatred" (Ps. 139:21-22).

After the great demonstration on Mount Carmel, the victory over Ba'al, and the massacre of the false prophets, Elijah's adrenaline was pumping. No wonder he ran in front of the king's chariot like a man possessed, all the way to the Valley of Jezreel. Flush with victory, he was ecstatic to think of how the whole nation had now been won for the Lord. Now the wicked queen Jezebel would at last bow down before the one God of Israel. How could God have made his message more plain than he had on the mountain? Surely now the people would return to the One who had redeemed them and forged them into a nation.

---

1. I don't actually remember which Bible verses he quoted in the movie, but this gives the general idea. Later, in the course of the action, he is killed.

But that's not what happened. Here's what happened:

Ahab told Jezebel all that Elijah had done, and how he had slain all
the prophets with the sword. Then Jezebel sent a messenger to Elijah, saying, "So may the gods do to me and more also, if I do not
make your life as the life of one of them by this time tomorrow."
Then he was afraid, and he arose and went for his life . . . into the wilderness, and came and sat down under a broom tree; and he asked
that he might die, saying, "It is enough; now, O Lord, take away my
life; for I am no better than my fathers." (1 Kings 19:1-3)

Among other things, this is sound psychology. Elijah has never been
afraid of the king or the queen before in his entire ministry. He marched
into the king's chambers whenever he had a word from the Lord, to the
point that Ahab groaned, "Is it you, you troubler of Israel?"[2] But now, after the victory over the prophets of Ba'al, Elijah is deflated, demoralized,
and depressed. The mass conversion he was expecting has not occurred.
The king and queen have not been converted, the king's court has not
been converted, and the fickle people have not been converted, either;
they have gone right back to Ba'al worship as if nothing had ever happened. Elijah is experiencing a colossal comedown; his energy and courage have deserted him. You don't want to confront an enraged queen
when you feel like a failure. So Elijah goes off in a fit of gloom, lies down
on the ground, and begs to die, since he hasn't been any more effective
than the prophets before him. Anger causes depression, you know —
maybe Elijah is angry with the Lord because he didn't strike Ahab and
Jezebel dead. After all the fireworks on Carmel, God seems to have fizzled
out. His enemies are as active as ever. Elijah feels there is nothing left for
him to do.

The Lord is gentle with Elijah. Instead of reproaching him, the Lord
sends an angel to feed him, encourage him, and strengthen him. Partly recovered, he pushes on to Mount Horeb, where he takes shelter in a cave. He
doesn't know it yet, but the Lord has brought him on a retreat.

And there he came to a cave, and lodged there; and behold, the
word of the Lord came to him. . . . "What are you doing here, Elijah?" He [Elijah] said . . . "The people of Israel have forsaken thy

2. 1 Kings 18:17.

covenant, thrown down thy altars, and slain thy prophets with the sword; and I, even I only, am left; and they seek my life, to take it away." (19:9-10)

"Only I am left": notice that! How often we feel that way! Nobody is on my side! Nobody understands me! I haven't had any successes! I've knocked myself out for nothing! I've been abandoned! Moreover, Elijah fails to mention the prophets of Ba'al that *he* killed with the sword; he's focused on his own colleagues, whom *Jezebel* killed. He can't see past his own grandiosity. He thinks he's the only worshiper left in Israel. He has ceased to trust God. The Lord's great plan is no longer in his mind.

But again, the Lord is very good to Elijah. He has fed him, strengthened him, and spoken to him. And now God says,

> "Go forth, and stand upon the mount before the Lord." And behold, the Lord passed by, and a great and strong wind rent the mountains, and broke in pieces the rocks before the Lord. (19:11)

This, of course, is Elijah's favorite thing. He's a tornado-chaser; he loves pyrotechnics. When he sees the Lord splitting rocks, it makes him feel better already.

> But the Lord was not in the wind; and after the wind an earthquake, but the Lord was not in the earthquake; and after the earthquake a fire, but the Lord was not in the fire. . . . (19:11-12)

What a disappointment! Where are the special effects?

There is a major lesson here about the nature of God. The Bible teaches this lesson in many places, especially the Psalms. The Lord is the master of creation, but he is not "in" creation. The creation praises God, but it is not itself God; God is not "in" it. The sunset, the mountains, the lakes and rivers, the winds and storms, the mighty ocean and the creatures in it — the Lord God made them all, and they serve him, but they are not God; he is not "in" them.

Where is God, then?

God is in his Word.

The Lord was not in the wind, or the earthquake, or the fire. He came to Elijah another way, in "a still small voice." (In the words of the well-known hymn: "Speak through the earthquake, wind, and fire/O still, small voice of calm."[3])

God does many things to prepare us to hear his Word. Sometimes he gets our attention with big displays, but far more often he wins our hearts and minds with a still, small voice. Sometimes people have "conversion experiences" at big rallies and revivals, but the initial power of such events cannot be sustained without the steady witness of the less flamboyant members of the faithful people of God — the Sunday school teacher, the greeter, the prayer-group leader, the simple, everyday believing Christian. The Holy Spirit blows where it wills.

In the Gospel lesson for today, we read that the people of a Samaritan village refused to receive Jesus. The disciples James and John were seized by vengeful feelings. They said, "Lord, do you want us to bid fire to come down from heaven and consume them?" (Luke 9:54-55). That's just like Elijah, isn't it? Burn up all the enemies! I can't help thinking of Ann Coulter.[4] Shortly after the events of September 11, 2001, she stated that we should bomb the Middle East into smithereens, and then take everybody who was left and convert them to Christianity.

Yes, she really did say that.[5] What's wrong with this picture?

Here's what the Lord said after James and John asked him if they could incinerate his enemies: "Foxes have holes, and birds of the air have nests; but the Son of man has nowhere to lay his head" (Luke 9:58). The Son of God, the incarnate Word, has not come in fire, or thunder, or great demonstrations of power. His power is of another sort. It is the power of the Creator of the world, but it is the power that steps away from power. It is the power that offers up God's self in suffering love: the still, small voice.

What of Elijah, then? He wrapped his face in his mantle, we are told, to hear the Word of the Lord, who gives him his new commission and then says, in effect: "By the way, Elijah, don't be so self-important; you aren't the only faithful servant I have. I have reserved to myself seven thousand people that you didn't even know existed" (1 Kings 19:18). Hearing this, Elijah submits to the voice of God. He has learned humility. Before his career is

---

3. The hymn is "Dear Lord and Father of Mankind" by John Greenleaf Whittier.

4. Ann Coulter is a — what? An ultra-ultra-conservative? A patriot run amok? A verbal terrorist? A flame-thrower? She is a political commentator and "best-selling author." I once heard the ineffable Ms. Coulter define herself on TV as "sort of a mean Christian." Let's hope that's a contradiction in terms.

5. Again, I haven't got the first two-thirds of this quote quite right, but the final third is absolutely right.

ended, he will call down fire from the Lord a time or two more, but essentially he will become a calmer sort of prophet. He will anoint Elisha to be his successor, and he will be a father and mentor to him. He will not be jealous of Elisha, but will rejoice when his disciple receives a double portion of the Holy Spirit. And as his reward, Elijah will be taken up into heaven in the grand manner, by a whirlwind and horses of fire as Elisha watches, overcome with awe, crying, "My father, my father, the chariot of Israel, and the horsemen thereof!" (2 Kings 2:12).[6]

We may learn this lesson from Elijah today. There will be no fireworks this morning, no crashes of sermonic thunder, no oratorical displays. But the Lord is present here. He is present in the preaching of this biblical story because that is what he promised. He is present where two or three are gathered in his name because that is what he promised. He is present in the prayers of his people because that is what he promised. May we, so to speak, wrap our faces like Elijah — wrap our faces in thanksgiving, in adoration, in awe and in humility before the presence of the Lord.

AMEN.

6. The precise meaning of this memorable cry is disputed. Is Elisha likening Elijah himself to a chariot and horsemen, lamenting his departure from Israel, leaving the people without defenses? Or is he simply apostrophizing what he sees? It is striking in any case, and the image has famously lent itself to the great African-American spiritual "Swing Low, Sweet Chariot."

# The Radical Freedom of God

*February 1982*                                                    2 Kings 5:1-15

NAAMAN THE Syrian was a five-star general of the army. He was commander of all the armed forces of the king of Syria. The troops under him had achieved massive victories. We're told that "Naaman was a mighty man of valor." All Damascus stood in awe of him. He could walk right into the king's throne room without an appointment. In fact, Naaman was more powerful than the king, because the king knew very well that the safety of his empire depended on the prowess of Naaman's soldiers. So nothing was too good for Naaman. He had his choice of limousines and secretaries and uniforms with gold braid. There was just one problem. "Naaman was a mighty man of valor — but he was a leper" (2 Kings 5:1).

The CEO of the huge multinational corporation can get the best table at Four Seasons without even calling for a reservation — but his son was hospitalized last year for a suicide attempt. The famous professor is in great demand all over the world for lectures at fees in the five figures — but he's an alcoholic. The celebrated actress can cause every man's head to turn just by walking into the room — but she lives in dread of bright lights and mirrors set at unflattering angles. The beloved pastor brings joy and hope into dozens of lives daily — but his wife despises him. In every life there is a *but*. What is your *but*? What is my *but*? Naaman was a great man with his master and in high favor . . . he was a mighty man of valor, *but he was a leper.*

Back home in Naaman's house, there are trophies of battle. There are cases of medals, closets of uniforms, framed tributes on the walls, art collections brought home as trophies. Naaman has human trophies, too — prisoners of war, refugees, boat people, you might say — the flotsam and jetsam of international conflict. As a matter of fact, Naaman, the general of the Syrian armies, has a slave girl in his household, a prize of war, and she knows his secret: he has leprosy. His leprosy has not yet advanced to the critical state, for if it had, Naaman would not have been able to continue in human society.

Consider Naaman's slave girl. She is a quadruple nobody. She is a *child;* she is a *female;* she is an *Israelite;* she is a *slave.* On the scale of status in Syrian society, Naaman (being free, white, over twenty-one, male, and Syrian) is at the top, and she is so far below the bottom there isn't even a place for her on the chart. She is a nothing.

Now, you understand, there is no cure for Naaman's disease, either literally or figuratively. (As a matter of fact, I read in the *Times* a few days ago that leprosy is on the rise again because it is becoming resistant to the medication we've been using.) Ancient society knew no treatment for the horrifying disease. Even more important, the Bible presents leprosy as a metaphor for guilt, sin, and death. That's why there's a *but* in your life and a *but* in mine. "Naaman was in high favor . . . but he was a leper." No cure, no remedy, no treatment. *Leprosy* is a metaphor for all that is diseased and wrong in human life, for all that is hopeless, for all that is shameful, for all that we seek to keep hidden, even from ourselves, lest the miserable truth be known. The chambers and hallways of Naaman's lavish house in Damascus are expensively furnished and elaborately decorated, but there is a musty, faintly sickening odor drifting through the perfumed corridors.

In this house, this very house where glamour and corruption exist side by side, this house of elegance and of fear, this house of splendor and of death, this very house where there is no cure for what ails the master, a prepubescent female, a foreigner, a slave, a nobody speaks a word of hope from another world. We might imagine her, with her foreign features and strange accent, her poorly fitting clothes and, perhaps, her tear-stained face and red-rimmed eyes — stolen from her parents and native land, brought from Israel to wait on the general's wife. But we are not told these things. What we are told is this:

> She said to her mistress, "Would that my lord were with the prophet who is in Israel! He would cure him of his leprosy." (5:3)

The little slave girl is a voice, the bearer of a strange word, full of promise, from another sphere — and then she disappears, and we do not see her again.

As the Tsarina of all the Russias went to Rasputin, as the Shah of Iran went around the world looking for a cure — looking in vain, in vain! — so the general of the armies of Syria, upon the word of an Israelite slave, drives over to the king's palace, strides past all the guards and the secret service, and tells the king that he has heard that there is a prophet in Israel who can do the undoable.

Now here's a wonderful touch. The king of Syria is told by his general that there is a prophet in Israel who can heal leprosy. We may be sure that the king of Syria wants his general healthy, the way the University of Virginia basketball coach wants Ralph Sampson healthy, because a brilliant general with leprosy is not much use.[1] The king of Syria is ready to go for this cure with every resource at his command, so he does the kind of thing kings always do. He writes a letter to the king of Israel! It never occurs to him to write a letter to the prophet. Kings only write to kings, heads of state want to talk only to other heads of state, CEOs only to other CEOs. If the State Department wants to find out about the human rights situation in Latin America, it asks the generals and the diplomats and the civil servants — it doesn't ask the peasants and the priests (unfortunately). If an American bank wants to present a report on how the bank is doing in South Africa, it asks the bank managers in Johannesburg — it doesn't go looking up Nelson Mandela in jail to ask him.[2] Kings write to kings, not to prophets.

So Naaman sets forth with the king's letter, a hundred thousand dollars, and an entourage of horses and chariots — going to the hospital, so to speak, with bribes for the nurses, presents for the doctors, silk bathrobes, linen sheets, a telex, his personal cook, and a fully equipped bar.

The king of Israel takes a look at all this magnificence. Naaman is an imposing figure even with the beginnings of a dread disease. We may assume that the king of Israel is momentarily flattered that his powerful neighbor has come to call upon him. But not for long. He takes one look at the letter from the king of Syria, which reads as follows:

> "When this letter reaches you, know that I have sent to you Naaman my servant, that you may cure him of his leprosy." (5:6)

Those listening to this story as originally told would have understood that this is a great joke at the expense of the ruling classes. The hearers understood that Naaman was supposed to go to the *prophet*, not the *king*. We are being let in on the joke, but it has very serious theological and political

---

1. Ralph Sampson was the most celebrated college basketball player of his generation, appearing six times in four years on the cover of *Sports Illustrated*.

2. Mandela was not released from prison until 1993.

implications. Imagine the reaction of the king of Israel. His enemy, the king of Syria, is poised on his borders day and night, ready to attack him at any moment with a superior army, and here is his enemy's commander, standing before him with a letter demanding the impossible. The king of Israel looked up from the letter and said,

> "Am I God? To kill and to make alive, that this man sends word to me to cure a man of his leprosy?" (5:7)

With this masterstoke, the biblical narrator sets the real theological question before us. "Am I God, to kill and to make alive?" These are the stakes — not less. Only God has ultimate power over creation. No one can cure leprosy — no general, no king, no potentate. Note the characteristic biblical attitude toward God. There is no hedging against his power, no "what ifs" or "maybes," just the bald presupposition that the God who is really God is able to do anything he wishes — to heal or to destroy.

What, then, will God do? Will he leave the king of Israel to thrash about in his impossible position? Will he remain silent? Will he leave the great Naaman in his deteriorating condition? Will he perhaps strike them both dead, or simply abandon them to their endless, fruitless military misadventures until they kill each other off?

Off in his little house on the edge of town, the prophet Elisha, "the man of God," goes out to buy a newspaper, and he sees the headline — "General Pays Call! King Rends Clothes!" Elisha promptly sent the newsboy to the palace with a message, as follows:

> "Why have you rent your clothes? Let him [Naaman] come now to me, that he may know that there is a prophet in Israel." (5:8)

Now the kings and generals of Syria didn't know a prophet from a sword-swallower, but the kings of Israel did — for better or for worse. After all, Elisha's immediate predecessor was the one and only Elijah, the "troubler of Israel," the whirlwind from the desert who blew in and blew out of the lives of kings and generals as if sent straight from the presence of God. And indeed, that is what the prophets of Israel were — men who stood before God, who heard the deliberations in the heavenly councils, who received messages directly from God to be delivered to his people — from YHWH, the God who can kill and make alive. So when Elisha says, "Let Naaman come to me, that he may know there is a prophet in Israel," he is not saying, "Let Naaman come down here and see what a powerful person I, Elisha, am." He is saying, "Let Naaman come and know the power and the freedom of the God of Israel."

And so Naaman comes, with all his horses, chariots, men, money, uniforms, medals, and all the rest of it. It must have been quite a sight, all that splendor parked in front of Elisha's little house. What must the neighbors have thought? Note that Naaman simply "halts at the door"; he doesn't even dismount from his horse, but waits haughtily for the prophet to come out to him. We can certainly imagine what Naaman was thinking. No doubt he believed the prophet would be very impressed and honored by his visit. Naaman regarded it as Elisha's duty to come out to him, Elisha being his social inferior.

But Elisha does not come out. Elisha doesn't even answer the doorbell. As Jacques Ellul has written, "Elisha remains anonymous and absent, does not even see Naaman, [but] encloses himself in the secret and mystery of the will of God."[3] Instead, Elisha sends his servant to the door with a brief message for the general: "Go and wash in the Jordan seven times, and your flesh shall be restored, and you shall be clean" (5:10).

And Naaman, we are told, "turned and went away in a rage." He said,

> "I thought that he would surely come out to me, and stand, and call
> on the name of the Lord his god, and wave his hand over the place
> and cure the leper. Are not . . . the rivers of Damascus better than all
> the waters of Israel?" (5:11-12)

"Have I come all this way to this hick town to be told such an idiotic thing? If I were going to be healed by anything as mundane as washing in some local wadi, I could at least have stayed at home and done it in the rivers of the great city of Damascus." Naaman had come looking for a top-level consultation with a charismatic healer; he was expecting Sloan-Kettering, Dr. DeBakey, maybe even Oral Roberts. He was counting on a private room, round-the-clock nurses, specialists flown in from all over, the newest experimental drugs sent air express from Brazil and Canada. "Who does the prophet of Israel think he is? *Who does the God of Israel think he is?* I, Naaman, am a great and powerful man; I am supposed to have a great and powerful cure." And so Naaman "turned and went away in a rage" — and

---

3. From Jacques Ellul's *The Politics of God and the Politics of Man,* a splendidly provocative commentary on 2 Kings. (Grand Rapids: Wm. B. Eerdmans, 1972), p. 32.

Elisha, God's man, lets him go. Elisha does not raise a finger to hold him back. Elisha, in fact — like Yahweh, whom he serves — remains invisible, permitting Naaman this liberty to turn away from deliverance. There is no sign from heaven, no thunderbolt, no drop-dead vision, no voice from the sky saying, "Naaman! Go back! This is God speaking!"

Instead, once again, the story turns upon the voice of a nobody. Naaman's servants — not his lieutenants, not his attachés, not his advisors, but his *servants!* — sidle up to him hesitantly. "My Lord!" they say, clearing their throats and shuffling their feet. "Um — that prophet — you know — the prophet of Israel, the guy who just told you to wash. . . . If he had told you to do some great thing, like, say, you know, give him money to build a temple, or go to California to see a psychic, or have a hospital room set up in your house, you would have done it, right? So — um — why not try this little thing he suggested? You can't lose anything just by trying, right?"[4]

Notice the simplicity and the theological inadequacy of this argument. Notice also the tentative and bashful manner in which it is offered; after all, it is not the usual thing for the senior partner to take advice from the man who runs the elevator. We do not expect God to work in this way; Naaman certainly did not. He had thought that Elisha would come out to him and make dramatic gestures and utter eloquent words and treat him in a way that befitted his station in life.

But somehow Naaman is enabled to see some sense in the hesitant speech of his servants. He pulls up his horse and turns back.

> So he went down and dipped himself seven times in the Jordan, according to the word of the man of God; and his flesh was restored like the flesh of a little child, and he was clean. (5:14)

The God who can kill and make alive has given life.

And behold! Naaman the Syrian gets back on his horse and gives the command to his entourage to follow, and he goes all the way back to the house of the prophet who had insulted him by not coming to the door, and this time Naaman gets down off his horse, and this time Elisha comes right out to meet him, and Naaman makes his confession:

> "Now I know that there is no God in all the earth except in Israel." (5:15)

4. This is a paraphrase of 2 Kings 5:13.

Now: think of Naaman for a moment from the standpoint of the Hebrew people, who remembered hearing this story and eventually wrote it down. Naaman was a Syrian — a man of another race, another culture, not one of the chosen people. Naaman was a pagan, an unbeliever, a man who couldn't have cared less for the God of Israel. He was more than that: he was the leader of the forces of Israel's enemies, of the opposing ideology, the hostile nation — he was a Cuban, a Russian, a Libyan.[5] And Naaman was certainly not one of the poor whom God loves, not one of the humble, not one of the lowly. God's "preferential option for the poor" is not at work here.[6] God is, as always, one step ahead of us with his grace. Just as we think we know who it is whom God loves *(us),* he reaches beyond us and brings an outsider like Naaman into his fold.

This is an offense. Lest we should doubt it, the Evangelist Luke tells us that Jesus of Nazareth, when he first appeared in the synagogue in his hometown, said these words:

> There were many people in Israel who had leprosy in the time of Elisha the prophet, but not one of them was cleansed — only Naaman, the Syrian. (Luke 4:27)

And the people who heard Jesus say this were so enraged that they tried to throw him over a cliff — so St. Luke tells us. We do not want to believe that God shows preferential treatment to the foreigners, the pagans, the enemy — let alone an enemy of the ruling class.

How does God show his love to humanity? It would seem that he does it without regard for either rich or poor. Even more drastically, he extends his mercy and works out his plan, more often than not, through the little slave girls and the stammering servants of this world, through the prophets who seek no glory for themselves but remain anonymously in the background.

There is a little slave girl somewhere in your life, bearing a word of hope for your leprosy, for your *but.* Maybe it's your teenage son, come home from a Young Life weekend with a story about how he has met Jesus Christ. Maybe it's the beggar who said "God bless you" yesterday when you gave him a dollar. Maybe it's the preacher whose mannerisms irritate you, or the

---

5. This was the 1980s. Nearly thirty years later, we have different enemies.

6. I'm not calling this watchword of liberation theology into question; there is important truth in it. I am highlighting the freedom that God exercises in his mercy also to the rich, as he chooses.

roommate whose piety drives you up the wall, or the colleague who didn't treat you with the respect you thought you deserved. It may be someone you are very jealous of, or very threatened by, or very scornful of. And the message, when you hear it, will almost invariably offend you by its simplicity, its unexpectedness, its lack of appropriateness as the world understands such things. God shows his love not by overwhelming us with demonstrations of power and majesty, not by clubbing us to our knees, not by staging exhibitions of supernatural strength such as we humans might expect God to do, but rather by coming alongside us with water, and bread, and wine, and the invitation:

> Wash, and be clean;
>   follow me, and be healed;
>     take and eat this, and be fed with the bread from heaven;
>       drink this, and you will never be thirsty again.

# What Job Saw

TRINITY CHURCH, NEW ORLEANS

---

*Second Sunday of Easter 2007*                                    Job 42:1-6

*This sermon should be read as a companion piece to the next sermon, "The God of Hurricanes." "What Job Saw" was preached eighteen months after Hurricane Katrina.*

. . . . . . . . . . . . . . . . .

The biblical text for this sermon is from the book of Job, an unusual and challenging selection for the Easter season. If God wills, something new may come forth from it for us today. I have prayed all last week that the Holy Spirit will be the interpreter, so that the words from the book of Job may become the Word of God this morning for Trinity Church in the beloved, suffering city of New Orleans.

I wonder if we could all take just a moment to see if we can recall an incident when we made a big statement in public about something or other and then found out later that we didn't know what we were talking about. Or maybe we were sounding off about some subject — like the causes of the Civil War, for instance — and then learned that the person across the table from us had written several scholarly books about the Civil War. When something like that happens to us, if we have any sense at all, we feel pretty small and embarrassed.

This morning's text comes at the very end of the book of Job. Job is the man who has lost everything: home, business, family. And now he has got a hideous skin disease. Job's friends come to comfort him, but the more they talk, the more Job resists them and their pious platitudes. Job endures their windy words as long as he can, and then he makes his last-ditch stand. The sum of his passionate outcries is a demand that God respond to him.

Well, God responds to him. God appears out of a whirlwind and addresses Job directly. When this happens, the result is astonishing: Job simply sets aside all his great sufferings and abandons all the many words he has spoken. "I have uttered what I did not understand, things too wonderful for me, which I did not know." After this, Job speaks no more. His mouth is stopped. "I had heard of thee by the hearing of the ear, but now my eye sees thee; therefore I despise myself, and repent in dust and ashes" (Job 42:3, 5-6).

We need to get one problem out of the way to start with. In this translation Job says, "I despise myself." This doesn't go over well in our culture, where we talk incessantly about self-esteem. But many have noted that the Hebrew original really shouldn't be translated that way. Some have suggested "I despise *my words*."[1] My own teacher, who was a noted interpreter of the book of Job, proposed "I melt away."[2] And a respected modern translator puts it this way: "I will be quiet, comforted that I am dust."[3] This makes the point best. What happens to Job is some sort of radical, life-changing humility before God. That's what the book means. God has come to meet Job, and nothing is the same after that.

Job has demanded an answer from God, and God has answered him. God's answer is no answer at all, and yet, much to the mystification of the modern reader, Job seems more than satisfied. His response is so dramatically different from anything that he has been saying before that the careful listener is stunned into silence along with him as he says,

---

1. The Hebrew word meaning "I abhor" has no object, so the object must be inferred. "I abhor *myself*" (KJV) or "I despise *myself*" (RSV and NRSV) are not really the best guesses.

2. There is no consensus on the translation of 42:6. Other suggestions include "I am dissolved," "I am poured out," "I am smitten/struck down," and "I esteem myself dust and ashes" (Marvin H. Pope, *Job,* Anchor Bible series [New York: Doubleday, 1965]). Samuel Terrien, who was my teacher, writes in his commentary that it is not a matter of Job's retracting his words or despising himself. The point is that Job has had "a devastating encounter with . . . the Holy One." (See Terrien's commentary on Job in *The Interpreter's Bible* [New York: Abingdon Press, 1954]). Although *The Interpreter's Bible* fell out of fashion not long after it was published, Terrien's commentary on Job is one of three or four in the twelve volumes widely considered to be first-rate and of lasting value.

3. Stephen Mitchell, *Into the Whirlwind* (New York: Doubleday, 1979). This text was also published with an introduction as *The Book of Job* (San Francisco: North Point Press, 1987).

I have uttered what I did not understand,
. . . things too wonderful for me, which I did not know. . . .
I had heard of you with my ears,
. . . but now my eyes have seen you.
Therefore I will be quiet,
. . . comforted that I am dust.

(RSV and Stephen Mitchell translations)

The season of Lent began on Ash Wednesday, seven weeks ago, with these traditional words: "Dust thou art, and unto dust thou shalt return." Today, on this high holy day of the Easter season, we hear the words "I am comforted that I am dust." The season is bracketed by dust. We human beings begin and end in dust. In the creation story from Genesis we read that the Lord God formed Adam from the dust of the earth. You don't have to reject evolutionary science to understand the symbolic meaning of this. As St. Paul says, the first man, Adam, was "a man of dust" (1 Cor. 15:47). Ashes to ashes. Dust we are, and to dust we return. That is what Paul is saying in his Resurrection chapter in First Corinthians. As creatures of the earth — men and women of mortal flesh — we are subject to Sin and Death. That's why, as Paul writes, "Flesh and blood cannot inherit the kingdom of God" (1 Cor. 15:50). Salvation must come from somewhere else.

At the beginning of this sermon we were remembering times when we made fools of ourselves in front of a group, acting as if we knew something about a subject when the *real* expert was standing right there. What would we do in a situation like that? It would depend on our level of insecurity. We might just shrink back, hoping that no one would notice. We might laugh nervously and try to make a joke of it. We might bluster and say well, actually, we knew the real stuff all along but weren't bothering to say it in this company. Or, if we were really secure in ourselves, we would say something like this: "Look, I'm totally embarrassed. I didn't know what I was talking about, and I retract what I said."

Now multiply that to the *n*th power to understand what has happened to Job. He and his so-called friends ("Job's comforters") have been going on and on for days and days about God and about the meaning of it all, and then suddenly God sends a northeaster ahead of himself to announce his arrival. The friends seem to disappear; we don't know where they went. Only Job is present when God begins to speak. God grants him a personal audience. That's what Job has been demanding all along — that God would hear him, answer him, respond to his cries of distress.

Virtually all interpreters agree that the book of Job gives no answer at all to the problem of suffering. The voice out of the whirlwind passes over it altogether. What God says is, basically, this: "Job, can you create the world that I have created? Look at it! Look at the wonderful things I have made — the snow and the rain, the stars in the firmament, the doors of the sea. Can you make the sun blaze in the heavens or the planets move in their orbits? Can you even imagine, let alone create, all the amazing beasts of the field and the sea? If you can do that, then surely you don't need me; your own flesh and blood can save you!" (40:14).

> Then Job answered the Lord:
> "... I have uttered what I did not understand,
> things too wonderful for me, which I did not know....
> I had heard of thee by the hearing of the ear,
> but now my eye sees thee....
> I am comforted that I am but dust."

All through his long speeches, Job has been struggling against the remoteness of the God who has hidden his face. "This ... eclipse of the divine light is the source of his abysmal despair. And the abyss is bridged the moment [he] is permitted to see ... and this becomes a new foundation."[4]

It's important to notice that although Job says that he has seen God with his eyes, that's a figure of speech. He hasn't "seen" God at all, in the literal sense.[5] When the Bible speaks of people "seeing" God, it means that

---

4. Martin Buber, "A God Who Hides His Face," in *The Dimensions of Job,* ed. N. Glatzer (New York: Schocken Books, 1969), pp. 61-62.

5. In the few references to "seeing God" that we find in the Old Testament, there is always some intermediary manifestation — a sapphire pavement (Exod. 24:10-11), an angel (Gen. 32:30), a "train" of seraphim (Isa. 6:1), a "vision" (Num. 12:8). Not even Moses, to whom God came closer than to anyone else, "saw" God unequivocally, despite the phrase "face to face" (Exod. 33:11), an expression meant to convey the intimate access that God granted to Moses alone among all his servants (Num. 12:8). What he saw was "the *form* of the Lord" (Num. 12:8), or it may have been something like "the *appearance* of the *glory* of the Lord" (Exod. 24:17) — deliberate circumlocutions that manage to convey a sense of the real presence of God while avoiding a suggestion of an *unmediated* presence. When Moses came down from the mountain after talking with God "mouth to mouth" (Num. 12:8), he had to put a veil over his face to protect the people from the blinding glory of the Lord. A fuller account of the impossibility of seeing God directly is given in Exodus 33:20-23: "The Lord said to Moses, . . . 'You cannot see my face; for man shall not see me and live. . . . I will put you in a cleft of the rock, and I will cover you with my hand until I have passed by; then I will take away my hand, and you shall see my back; but my face shall not be seen.'"

their inner understanding has been opened — by God. When John New-ton wrote, in his famous hymn "Amazing Grace," I "was blind, but now I see," he didn't meant that he was literally blind. He meant that the eyes of his understanding had been opened by the Spirit and that he had come to know himself as a sinner redeemed by Jesus Christ. When Job says that he has "seen" God, he means that he has heard and understood God's *voice*. That's really important. We "see" God through his *Word*. And his Word comes to us from the faithful reading and preaching of Scripture. In this liv-ing Word, God makes himself present to us just as surely as he does in the Eucharist.

In the final analysis, the book of Job is asking this great question: Is there a living God beyond what we can imagine? Is there a Being indepen-dent of us, beyond the boundaries of earthly life and earthly struggle? Is there a God who speaks with a voice that is not simply projected out of our human religious consciousness?[6] Is there a God who can deliver us from the dust? Job's great longing is for *revelation*. He craves a God who is really God. He wants to be shown that God has a power that he cannot discern in the world that he knows.[7] That is why he is different from his friends, whose entire message is bound up with their need to believe that there are "expla-nations" for everything.[8]

Now if God had answered Job in the way that we would expect, with soothing explanations and comforting reassurances, then the answer to the question "Is there a God beyond what we can imagine?" would have to be "No." Anyone can imagine a God who does what we expect. The reason that so many people have complained that God's answer to Job is no answer at all is that they want a God who fits their preconceptions. Job, however, is manifestly satisfied. The God who is really God has come to him and has re-vealed himself as the One who was already present, already powerful, al-ready at work before there was anyone to imagine him. God is the author of creation; the creation is not the author of God. This was revealed to Job by the living voice and presence of God's own self. That was enough.

There is a wonderful link between the passage from Job and the Gospel lesson this morning. The disciple Thomas wasn't interested in hearing what the other disciples had to say about the Resurrection. Very much like Job,

---

6. This point is made especially well by Thomas G. Long in "Job: Second Thoughts in the Land of Uz," *Theology Today* 45, no. 1 (April 1988).

7. John Calvin, *Sermons from Job* (Grand Rapids: Baker Book House, 1979), p. 123.

8. And so, at the end of the book God commends Job and rebukes the friends.

he refused to be satisfied until he got a personal response from the Son of God. If he didn't get one, he would not believe. When Jesus therefore came and stood before him, Thomas hushed up in the same way that Job did, and for the same reason: God had revealed himself from a domain beyond the grave that Thomas could not have imagined for himself.[9] The living Son of God had appeared to him personally. Thomas's response is the pinnacle of Christian affirmation, spoken in the highest language of the Bible: *My Lord and my God.*

*I have uttered what I did not understand, things too wonderful for me, which I did not know. . . .* The message of the Resurrection is indeed too wonderful for us. Flesh and blood cannot inherit it. It is grasped only by faith. Through the Word of God the Holy Spirit creates such faith in those who gladly hear the message. It's a strange thing, but throughout the ages Christians have found comfort and hope in the midst of intense suffering simply by contemplating the greatness of God.

Dust to dust, we said earlier. In the context of the agony of New Orleans, it might seem more fitting to speak of beginning in water and returning to water. This, too, is biblical. In the first letter of Peter we read that Christian baptism corresponds to Noah's flood, when Noah and his family were "saved through water" (1 Pet. 3:20-21). God brought them out of the catastrophe into a new life of spaciousness and blessing. Baptism is like this. St. Paul also writes that in baptism [by water] we pass through death into life; we are baptized into Christ's death, so that we may be raised by him into the Resurrection (Rom. 6:3-5). Only God can do such a thing. Only the God who is really God can bring forth new life where there is only death. This is the God proclaimed to us by his Word in our Holy Scriptures.

There is a well-loved hymn that's not in the standard Episcopal hymnal. I suspect it's a bit too "Baptist" for us. But if we listen to these words together, for those who have eyes to see and ears to hear, they will sum up the response of Job:

O Lord my God, when I in awesome wonder
Consider all the works thy hands have made,
I see the stars, I hear the rolling thunder,

9. Notice that in the text, contrary to what the artists of the ages have painted and sculpted, Thomas never touched the Lord's wounds. He didn't have to. The gracious word of Christ was enough.

Thy pow'r throughout the universe displayed;
Then sings my soul, my Savior God, to thee:
How great thou art,
How great thou art![10]

10. The writer Bill McKibben, who is known for his writing about the environment, is a hymn-lover; he directs our attention to "How Great Thou Art" in his marvelous (though admittedly tendentious) little book about God's response to Job, *The Comforting Whirlwind* (Grand Rapids: Wm. B. Eerdmans, 2005).

The origin and history of the hymn is interesting: Carl Gustav Boberg, a Swede, wrote the words ("O Store Gud") in 1885 after seeing a sudden storm arise and subside while walking home from church near his home in Kronebäck. The words were set to a Swedish folk tune. It may have been sung in the Swedish "underground church" during a period when the Baptists were under pressure in Lutheran Sweden.

It was then translated into German by a German Baptist nobleman, Manfred von Glehn, who had heard it in Estonia, where there was a Baptist Swedish-speaking congregation, and it became popular as "Wie gross bist Du." It then traveled to Russia, where it was translated and published in 1912 as "Velikiy Bog" ("Great God") by "the Martin Luther of Russia," a prolific Protestant hymn-writer named Ivan S. Prochanov. It came into English via the Swedish Baptists, the forebears of the Evangelical Covenant Church, now headquartered in North Park, Illinois. The hymn was widely popularized in English by George Beverly Shea during Billy Graham's crusades throughout the world. Today it regularly appears as one of the top two or three favorite hymns in the world. Further interesting details about the competition between numerous English versions are readily available on Wikipedia. The absence of "How Great Thou Art" from the Episcopal hymnal is probably owing to Eric Routley, the eminent English hymnologist (later professor of church music at Westminster Choir College in Princeton), who couldn't stand it and produced a more highbrow version called "O Lord, My God." He re-harmonized the "O Store Gud" tune not long before his death in 1982.

Perhaps the most piquant fact about "How Great Thou Art" is that Elvis Presley's rendition of it repopularized it in Sweden.

# The God of Hurricanes

ST. PAUL'S CHURCH IN NANTUCKET

---

*October 2004*            Psalms 29, 104; Job 38:1–42:6

THE SCRIPTURE readings, the hymns, and the sermon this morning are all chosen to illuminate a particular theme. Here is just a bit of another Psalm that I want to read in the context of Nantucket Island:

> O Lord, how manifold are thy works!
> . . . the earth is full of thy creatures.
>   Yonder is the sea, great and wide. . . .
> There go the ships,
>   and Leviathan which thou didst form to sport in it. (Ps. 104)

The writer Bill McKibben, in his wonderful little book about the book of Job, *The Comforting Whirlwind,* quotes this passage:

> "Leviathan which thou didst form to sport in it" — anyone who has seen a humpback whale breaching understands that phrase, and the world of meaning it conveys. Those who make fun of the "save the whales" crowd make fun of God.[1]

Our first reading was a portion of God's address to Job, from the famous book of Job in the Old Testament. You know how the story goes.

---

1. Bill McKibben, *The Comforting Whirlwind* (Grand Rapids: Wm. B. Eerdmans, 1994), pp. 38-39. "The Comforting Whirlwind" would have been a good alternative title for this sermon.

God and the devil have a wager. The devil bets that if God afflicts his servant Job with all sorts of tragic losses and terrible diseases, Job will curse God. Job's friends come to try to comfort him in his suffering. As long as they keep their mouths shut, they are true comforters, but when they start trying to give theological explanations, they cease to be of any use. Job responds to them with long-winded laments. This goes on for thirty-seven chapters — talk, talk, talk. Then suddenly the Lord God appears to Job in a whirlwind and says, basically, "Where were you, O person of infinite insignificance, when I, the Lord, laid the foundations of the earth?" For some weird reason, this seems to satisfy Job. It wouldn't satisfy you or me, but it seems to satisfy him. He says,

> "Behold, I am of small account; what shall I answer thee?
>  I lay my hand on my mouth. . . .
> I despise myself,
>  and repent in dust and ashes." (Job 40:4; 42:6)

We aren't likely to find that speech in any self-esteem workshops. Yet the writer(s) and editor(s) of this story seem to find it entirely satisfactory. Something about the actual appearance and speech of God to Job has made all the "why" questions irrelevant. The revelation of the overpowering presence and majesty of God lifts Job out of his troubles.

Listen again to some of the rhetorical questions with which the Lord stuns Job from the whirlwind:

> ". . . who shut in the sea with doors . . . ?
> [who] prescribed bounds for it . . .
> and said, "Thus far shall you come, and no farther,
>  and here shall your proud waves be stayed"? . . .
> Can you send forth lightnings . . . ?
> Who . . . can tilt the waterskins of the heavens . . . ?" (38:8-11, 35, 37)

In other words, can you, Job, create a storm? Can you even *manage* a storm? Of course not. So get back in your place.[2]

2. Governor Jeb Bush of Florida grasped the general drift of this theological drama after the assault of Hurricane Charley on his state, though one may legitimately accuse him of oversimplifying it, especially in the immediacy of very real suffering. The governor said, "This is God's way of telling us that he's almighty and we're mortal" (Abby Goodnough, "Florida Digs Out as Mighty Storm Rips Northward," *The New York Times,* 15 August 2004).

When we are in landscapes like Nantucket, we tend to feel that we are somehow closer to God. "God's creation," we call our favorite places — "God's country," "God's acre." Indeed, there are many passages in the Psalms that praise God for his wonderful works shown in the beauty of nature. Look at your own stained glass, with these tranquil scenes of flowers and sky. But this is not the whole story. You don't see any windows of hurricanes or tornadoes in churches, yet just a few moments ago, we read the "Thunderstorm Psalm" (Psalm 29):

> The voice of the Lord is upon the waters;
>   the God of glory thunders. . . .
>   The voice of the Lord breaks the cedars. . . .
>   The voice of the Lord shakes the wilderness. . . .
> The voice of the Lord makes the oaks to whirl,
>   and strips the forests bare;
> and in his temple all cry, "Glory!"
> The Lord sits enthroned over the flood;
>   the Lord sits enthroned as king for ever. (29:3-5, 9-10)

This depicts the people of God not only worshiping God for his power shown in the mighty storm, but even crying out "Glory!" to him in the midst of it.

The biblical testimony about storms raises all sorts of questions. I recently read David McCullough's book *The Johnstown Flood*.[3] In the year 1889, a broken dam in the Pennsylvania hills near Pittsburgh unleashed waters that drowned more than two thousand people and utterly destroyed much of the town. It mesmerized the entire nation to a degree that was almost comparable to 9/11, except of course without television. McCullough reports that "countless sermons on 'The Meaning of the Johnstown Flood' were delivered in every part of the land for many Sundays running. . . . The story of Noah was read from many pulpits."[4] This was a time in America

---

3. Passages from David McCullough, *The Johnstown Flood* (1968; reprint, New York: Touchstone, Simon & Schuster, 1987), pp. 252, 186.

4. Mr. McCullough goes into some detail about the various sermonic angles on the event, and adds that the people of Johnstown were bitterly amused and scornful to think that their misfortune was being interpreted as the wrath of God, because they knew the flood had been caused not by divine Providence but by the heedlessness of some tycoons, including Andrew Carnegie, Andrew Mellon, and Henry Clay Frick, who, in spite of repeated warnings, failed to keep the earthen dam at their elite fishing club above the town in good repair.

when many people had intimate knowledge of the Bible. As the cataracts of water stormed through Johnstown, one group huddled together on the third floor of their house as the Reverend Dr. David Beale read aloud from Psalm 46:

> God is our refuge and strength, a very present help in trouble.
> Therefore will we not fear, though the earth be removed, and though
> the mountains be carried into the midst of the sea; though the waters
> thereof roar and be troubled. . . .[5]

But two passages in particular really captured my attention. McCullough writes that the Reverend T. DeWitt Talmadge, one of the most eminent preachers of the day, took Psalm 93 as his text:

> The floods have lifted up their voice . . .
> the floods lift up their roaring.
>    Mightier than the thunders of many waters,
> mightier than the waves of the sea,
> the Lord on high is mighty!

The Reverend Dr. Talmadge, obviously a man of penetrating theological intelligence, preached that those who want "only the religion of sunshine . . . blue sky and beautiful grass" would discover that nature was merciless. "Let me ask such persons what they make of the floods in Pennsylvania."[6]

Contrary to much popular opinion, the Scripture teaches that God is not "in" nature, is not an extension of nature, is not co-existent with nature. Mountains, rivers, flowers, and sunsets *testify to* God, they *praise* God, they *give glory to* God, but God is not "in" them. God is the *Creator* of them; God is separate from them. The voice of the Lord is not *in* the waters, it is "*upon* the waters." "The Lord sits enthroned *over* the flood."

The second passage that struck me in McCullough's book was this one:

> The flood and the night that had followed, for all their terror and
> destruction and suffering, had had a certain terrible majesty. Many
> people had thought it was Judgment Day . . . that the whole world
> was being destroyed and not just Johnstown. It had . . . come as a de-

5. McCullough, *The Johnstown Flood.*
6. McCullough, *The Johnstown Flood.*

struction from the Almighty. It had been awful, but it had been God-awful.[7]

It is very difficult for us today to think like nineteenth-century American Christians, but I'm trying to suggest that we have something to learn from all this. Today, even knowing what we do about hurricanes, some people simply cannot resist going into harm's way to see the power of nature fully unleashed. Even though they know there will be frightful damage and possibly death, they want to see that power. It is strangely uplifting to catch a glimpse of something that is completely beyond the capacity of human beings to control. The experience offers a fleeting glimpse (emphasis on "fleeting") of a transcendence that we cannot find in a calm sea or a quiet garden. There is a ditty that says we're closer to God's heart in a garden than anywhere else on earth, but in the Bible, it is Satan who seems to specialize in gardens — the Garden of Eden, the Garden of Gethsemane.

In the recent best-seller *Isaac's Storm,* the deadliest hurricane in American history is described. On September 8, 1900, much of Galveston, Texas, was destroyed, and six thousand people drowned. The book creates a remarkable atmosphere of menace and dread as the unforeseen and unnamed storm gathered offshore in the Gulf of Mexico. The descriptions of the implacable forces of wind and water assaulting the city are described with exceptional skill. The passage that remains with me is a description of the ordeal of a man named Samuel Young, who rode out the storm using his bedroom door as a raft. It was an incredibly terrifying experience. For eight hours, in the blackness of the night, he thought he was the only person left alive in Galveston. Yet months later he testified that the sight of the storm in its full power was "the grandest [scene] I ever witnessed."[8]

I would fully expect many of you here to be shocked by much of this. Talking about hurricanes and reading these biblical passages raise many disturbing questions about who lives and who dies, and where God is in the darkness, and whether we can praise God even in the midst of cataclysm. David McCullough continues his story about the Johnstown flood, telling us that the experience of being in the hand of God all night drained away in the morning. When the sun came up and disclosed the devastation, the sight that greeted the survivors was no longer majestically terrifying, but "in

7. McCullough, *The Johnstown Flood.*
8. Erik Larson, *Isaac's Storm* (New York: Vintage, 2000).

the dismal cold was just ugly and sordid and heartbreaking, and already it was beginning to smell. . . ."[9]

The suffering caused by natural disasters raises questions that challenge us at the very heart of our Christian faith, and I am not suggesting that we avoid them. This morning, however, I am trying to focus on just one specific facet of our theological inheritance. If we are truly to understand the miracle of God's mercy and loving-kindness, we need also to know the might, majesty, dominion, and power of God. We can't fully grasp the magnitude of what God has done for us unless we have some sense of the unimaginable power that the Father of our Lord Jesus Christ possesses. This is a very important aspect of the witness of the Old Testament.

Fooling around with nature is analogous to underestimating God. No doubt every Nantucketer has read Nathaniel Philbrick's book *In the Heart of the Sea*. You know that this story of the ship that was attacked by an enraged sperm whale gave Herman Melville the idea for his mighty novel *Moby Dick*. The prize-winning nonfiction book by Philbrick and the masterpiece of imaginative fiction by Melville both have a deep symbolic connection to our theme. Philbrick writes that the deeply religious Nantucket whaling merchants were serenely convinced that they had been called by God "to maintain a peaceful life on land while raising bloody havoc on the sea."[10] When the fire of 1846 destroyed much of this town, the worst damage was done on the waterfront because the sperm whale oil stored there burned beyond the capacity of any human firefighters to extinguish it. It was therefore said, writes Philbrick, that the leviathan had finally achieved his revenge.[11]

For what it's worth, my own study of *Moby Dick* has led me to the conclusion that this heroic novel is Melville's repudiation of the soft and sentimental God that was beginning to predominate in American Christianity in his time and after.[12] If Melville was going to reject God, he was going to reject the towering God of the Bible, not some pale and ineffective substitute who was unable either to judge or to condemn, let alone save. Melville lampoons the "romantic, melancholy" young sailor, apparently common in his day, who signs on for a whaling voyage in order to have some sort of spiritual experience. A sailor of this sort, Melville writes, would rather dream

---

9. McCullough, *The Johnstown Flood*.

10. Nathaniel Philbrick, *In the Heart of the Sea* (New York: Viking Penguin, 2000), p. 9.

11. Philbrick, *In the Heart of the Sea*, p. 222.

12. See especially Ann Douglas's treatment of *Moby Dick* in her now-classic book *The Feminization of American Culture* (New York: Alfred A. Knopf, 1977).

atop the mast than actually see a whale. He writes savagely, "But while this sleep, this dream is on ye, move your foot or hand an inch; slip your hold at all . . . [and] with one half-throttled shriek you drop through that transparent air into the summer sea, no more to rise for ever." And Melville ends with a sardonic thrust at the liberal Protestants of his day: "Heed it well, ye Pantheists!"[13]

It is this dangerous God of storm and wind, waves and water, fire and flood, this God who is infinitely bigger than the sum of all natural phenomena put together, this God who tilts the waterskins of the heavens and speaks to the waves, saying, "Thus far and no further" — it is this God who in Jesus Christ is lying asleep in a boat on the Sea of Galilee. A potentially lethal storm comes up, a storm of the sort that still to this day, I'm told, whips up suddenly on that lake:

> . . . the waves beat into the boat, so that the boat was already filling. But [Jesus] was in the stern, asleep on the cushion; and they woke him and said to him, "Teacher, do you not care if we perish?" And he awoke and rebuked the wind, and said to the sea, "Peace! Be still!" And the wind ceased, and there was a great calm. He said to them, "Why are you afraid? Have you no faith?" And they were filled with awe, and said to one another, "Who then is this, that even wind and sea obey him?" (Mark 4:37-41)

Here's the point. This is what the evangelist Mark wants you to know, here, today, by the power of the living Spirit of God. *"Who then is this, that even wind and sea obey him?"* Jesus of Nazareth is the incarnate Creator. Just as God, in the beginning, said "Let there be light, and there was light," the mere Word of Christ is enough to quiet the storm and bring "a great calm."

Does this action of Jesus mean that we will always be delivered from storms? *No.* Does the knowledge of God as Lord over the hurricane solve the problem of suffering? *No.* Does the glory of the Lord "enthroned upon the flood" deliver us from "the ugly and sordid and heartbreaking realities" of this mortal life? *No.* There are many things in this life that we cannot understand.

But there are some things that we *can* understand. It is good for us to have humility in the world, to know our place, to know that there are powers beyond our control.[14]

---

13. Herman Melville, *Moby Dick,* ch. 35, "The Mast-Head."
14. Nicholas Kristof writes, "A week ago, I took my 12-year-old son out on his third trip

And it is good for us to reflect deeply upon the use that God makes of his power. If you and I had power over hurricanes and earthquakes and tornadoes, what would we do with it? All the evidence suggests that we would unleash it against our perceived enemies. The last thing we would do is give it up and turn ourselves over "to be betrayed into the hands of wicked men." Yet that is what the Son of God did. It is this contrast between the cosmic might of the Creator God and the suffering of the Messiah on the Cross that makes the Christian story unique.

Through these passages today, he speaks to you, the living God of infinite power yet infinite mercy. "The fear of the Lord," says the Scripture, "is the beginning of wisdom." Dear friends, know this: however much the storms of this life may batter you within and without, you may, as the little song says,

"Put your hand in the hand of the man from Galilee."

---

around Mount Hood this summer. The weather was glorious as we started, but by nightfall a cold rain was pounding down on our tarp shelter. The next morning, we found ourselves stumbling through driving snow and wishing we were on a couch watching TV instead. But that's the wonder of the wilderness, an essential part of America's greatness: time in the wild is the best way to temper our arrogance, to remind ourselves that we are temporary intruders upon a larger canvas" (*The New York Times*, 6 September 2006).

# Seeing Sin as God Sees It

I HEARD on the radio this morning that Fred Goldman has made O. J. Simpson an offer.[1] He will withdraw any and all financial claims if O. J. will sign a detailed written confession. He says that the family has never cared about the money; what they want is the confession. I believe him. I think he means it.

In South Africa, the Truth and Reconciliation Commission has been charged with eliciting confessions from all those who seek amnesty from Nelson Mandela's government. No one will receive amnesty unless they are willing to come forward and give an accounting of their crimes. In Guatemala, by way of contrast, the Truth Commission will not hold anyone accountable. They will investigate who died and who disappeared, but not who did it. The perpetrators will never have to admit anything.

*Confession, acknowledgment, apology, remorse, repentance:* these things are powerful. Ash Wednesday is a day set aside in the church year for us to come to terms with ourselves before God. More than any other day, it focuses directly on the theme of self-knowledge. We will shortly read Psalm 51 on our knees. This great Psalm has always been associated with Ash Wednesday. Traditionally it has been attributed to King David at the time of his adultery with Bathsheba. The Bible is full of searingly honest confessions, but nowhere more strikingly than here.

---

1. In case there is anyone who doesn't know, the "trial of the century" involved the famous football star O. J. Simpson, who was tried for (and found innocent of) the murder of his ex-wife and Fred Goldman's son.

The writer Janet Malcolm has written about people who are unable to confess:

> There are a few among us . . . who are blessed or cursed with a strange imperviousness to the unpleasantness of self-knowledge. Their lies to themselves are so convincing that they are never unmasked. These are the people who never feel in the wrong, who are always able to justify their conduct, and who in the end . . . cause their fallible fellow-men to turn away from them.

Malcolm acknowledges that all of us resist self-knowledge. She comments,

> We are all perpetually smoothing and rearranging reality to conform to our wishes; we lie to others and ourselves constantly, unthinkingly. When, occasionally — and not by dint of our own efforts but under the pressure of external events — we are forced to see things as they are, we are like naked people in a storm.[2]

Psalm 51, the Ash Wednesday Psalm, is the acknowledged masterpiece of biblical self-knowledge. "I have been wicked from my birth, a sinner from my mother's womb. . . . I know my transgressions, and my sin is ever before me" (51:5, 3). The Psalmist takes all the responsibility on himself. Never does he say, "I was just doing my job," or "I didn't know," or "I was just following orders." Nowhere does he say, "My mother didn't love me," or "My father didn't understand me," or "The devil made me do it." All these things may be true, but they are not reasons for us to excuse ourselves. All these explanations and excuses dissolve when seen in the white light of the righteousness of God. "You [Lord] are justified when you speak, and upright in your judgment" (51:4). On Ash Wednesday, we come together to acknowledge that God has a case against us, and to throw ourselves on his mercy. We come together to pray Psalm 51, not just as sinful individuals, but as a community of sinners seeking to confess and seek not only amnesty, but restitution.

I believe it was the Duke of Wellington who was supposed to have said, "Never explain; never apologize." That has got to be some of the worst advice ever given. It takes maturity, wisdom, and true manliness to offer a handsome apology. And what's more, people are disarmed by a sincere apology. A woman who had been wronged by her husband said to me, "You

---

2. Janet Malcolm, *In the Freud Archives* (New York: NYRB Classics, 2002), p. 70.

know, I do forgive him. But I wish he would be more sorry. It is so much harder for me because he is not very repentant." A heartfelt confession of guilt and a desire for forgiveness are great things to give another person. The heart-stopping climax of Mozart's great opera *The Marriage of Figaro* comes at the end, when the Count, unmasked, kneels at his wife's feet and sings, *"Contessa, perdono,"* and the Countess sublimely responds, "I do forgive you" *(Più docile īo sono, e dico dī sī).*

There is a strange statement in verse 4 of Psalm 51: "Against you [God] only have I sinned, and done what is evil in your sight." Why does he say that he has sinned only against God? Sin hurts those who are victimized, exploited, used, damaged, scorned, neglected as a result of pride, greed, anger, lust, envy, and self-will. Why does the Psalmist say he has sinned against God only?

The reason for this is of central importance. Sin, at bottom, is not an *ethical* concept at all. It is a *theological* concept. Sin is only understood to be sin when God is understood to be God. The recognition of sin comes as the Psalmist is confronted in prayer with the reality of God, the power of God, and the holiness of God, who has the absolute right to make demands and render judgments. "You are justified when you speak." We need to learn this; we are so accustomed to the kind of reasoning that says, "But I'm not hurting anybody," or "Nobody will know," or "Everybody else is doing it," or "It isn't anybody's business." But in the last analysis, the Bible reveals that every sinful action, every sinful thought, is directed *against God.* Our concept of sin, like our concept of God, is too small until we learn to say with the Psalmist, "Against you [God] only have I sinned, and done what is evil in your sight."

The genius of Psalm 51, and the source of its ageless significance, is this: in its impassioned petitions, the Psalmist demonstrates that *he has learned to see sin as God sees it.*[3] The knowledge of God comes first, before the knowledge of sin. We don't come to God because we fear the consequences of sin. Sermons that whip up a sense of sin in order to introduce the idea of God's mercy are caricatures of the gospel. To know God is to know him as the author of all goodness. When we know this, then it floods in upon us that the goodness of the Lord is the only power than can overcome sin and

3. Kenneth Slack, *New Light on Old Songs* (London: SCM Press, 1975), pp. 110-16. This is a lovely little book. It is gratifying to learn that Slack, an English clergyman known for his broadcasts, derived much encouragement from the writings of the great preacher Alexander McLaren, as have I.

make right what has been wrong. The recognition of sin is the *result,* not the *means,* of coming to know God. On Ash Wednesday, as we look into the depths, not only of our own sin but that of the whole human race, even as we consciously acknowledge the seriousness of our predicament before God, *in that same moment* we recognize God as the one who extends his mercy to us even in the midst of our condition. As Paul wrote, "While we were still sinners, Christ died for us" (Rom. 5:8).

Look at the Psalm again. It begins,

> Have mercy on me, O God, according to your loving-kindness:
>   in your great compassion blot out my offenses.

✳  This is a prayer of a person who knows there is hope, who knows there is mercy, who knows that God is full of compassion. The knowledge of grace has preceded the confession of sin. The person who confesses sin in this free way, holding nothing back, making no excuses, blaming no one but himself, is the person who knows that God is truly able to overcome sin and make a new person out of the sinner. The author of Psalm 51 knows this. He prays,

> Create in me a clean heart, O God, and renew a right spirit within me. (51:10)

So great is his confidence in God that he is able to refer to himself as a "miserable offender" and at the same time say "make me hear of joy and gladness" (51:8). The combination of uttermost penitence and confidence in God's new creation lies at the very heart of the knowledge of who we are before God and what he intends for us.

This is Ash Wednesday. This is the day in the year set apart for the most searching self-inventory before God, the most honest assessment of our sinful nature that we can possibly offer him. Our temptation will be, as always, to try to squirm off the hook in some way. But, you see, all these evasions fall pitifully short of the reality and power and holiness of the living God.

> Against you only have I sinned,
>   and done what is evil in your sight. . . .
> Deliver me from death, O God,
>   and my tongue shall sing of your righteousness. . . . (51:4,14)

In a moment, we are going to read this Psalm together, and then we are going to say the Litany of Penitence. As we reflect on the perfect love of God, we are going to confess lack of love. As we remember how Jesus came to serve us, we are going to confess our failure to serve others. As we acknowledge the faithfulness, the self-giving, the unconditional grace of the Lord, we are going to confess our unfaithfulness, our self-indulgence, our smallness of mind and heart. Our assessment of ourselves and our praise of God will merge in one great corporate act of worship as we "lift up our hearts" to God with the confidence of the Psalmist:

> The sacrifice of God is a troubled spirit;
> A broken and a contrite heart, O God, thou wilt not despise.
>
> (51:17)

Because, you see, God has shown us something. We do not need to surround ourselves with defenses and barricades. We do not need to lie to ourselves and others. We do not need to live out an exhausting, lifelong charade of pretense lest someone discover that we are not what we appear to be. In the Christian community, we can let ourselves be seen as the sinners we really are, because we are not going to be left like naked people in a storm.

There is Another who has taken the sentence upon himself and, in so doing, has nullified it. Jesus, the Son of God, has voluntarily taken our place, naked in the storm. He hung naked on the Cross, bearing in his own body the storm of the wrath of God against sin. Jesus drew into himself the hostility of Satan, and the hatred, envy, wrath, and malice of the entire human race. As St. Paul writes in the Ash Wednesday Epistle, "God made him [Jesus] to be sin who knew no sin, that in him we might become the righteousness of God."

AMEN.

# Whose Righteousness?

## CALVIN COLLEGE, GRAND RAPIDS, MICHIGAN

*January 2005*                                                  Psalm 118; Ezekiel 21

WHENEVER THERE'S a war, the universal human tendency to divide up the world into "we" and "they" becomes even more pronounced than usual. "Our" side is good; "their" side is evil. We measure everything by ourselves, by our own assessment of what is good and right. This has become a hallmark of our present national mood.[1] We are sure that God is on the side of America. After all, we Americans — as the president constantly reminds us — are good people. To use the phrase from Psalm 118, our soldiers on the battlefield dwell "in the tents of the righteous." In his press conference on Wednesday, the president spoke of militant Islamists as "those who have this vision of the world that is the exact opposite of ours."[2] A categorical statement like that, when repeated often enough, creates an atmosphere in which we feel that we are justified in treating our captured prisoners as less than fully human.

When I was asked to choose a text for my sermon on the theme of thanksgiving, I chose Psalm 118. I am now going to embarrass my hosts a little bit, because when I looked at the program for this evening, I noticed to my bemusement that the verses I was going to preach on had been omitted. Do you see those little dots? That's where verses 5 through 7 are supposed to be, but a gremlin has run off with them. Let me read them now:

1. The war in Iraq was dominating the headlines and the national discussion.
2. Transcript, *The New York Times,* 27 January 2005.

[ 180 ]

Out of my distress I called on the Lord;
   the Lord answered me and set me free.
With the Lord on my side I do not fear.
   What can man do to me?
The Lord is on my side to help me;
   I shall look in triumph on those who hate me. . . .

Then we continue with the verses that were read in our service:

All nations surrounded me;
   in the name of the Lord I cut them off! . . .
They surrounded me like bees,
   they blazed like a fire of thorns [wonderfully vivid, isn't it?];
   in the name of the Lord I cut them off!
I was pushed hard, so that I was falling,
   but the Lord helped me.
The Lord is my strength and my song;
   he has become my salvation.
There are glad songs of victory
   in the tents of the righteous. . . . (118:10-13)

Now, on the face of it, this seems straightforward enough. The Psalmist is filled with thanksgiving to God because God is on the side of the righteous man and delivers him from all his enemies. Any faithful Christian anywhere, anytime, can identify with this joyful trust that God is on her side. "The Lord is on my side to help me. . . . This is the gate of the Lord; the righteous shall enter through it" (118:7, 20).

But the word *righteous* in the Scripture is not exactly as it seems. To be sure, the Old Testament, and the Psalms in particular, are full of references to the righteous. We read a verse like this — "The Lord tests the righteous and the wicked, and his soul hates him that loves violence" (Ps. 11:5) — and we think we know what it means. It seems to divide humankind neatly, like Santa Claus, into "naughty and nice." But it is not quite as simple as we think. In Psalm 143, for instance, the Psalmist prays fervently, "Enter not into judgment with thy servant [meaning himself], for before thee no man living is righteous." Think also of the words of Isaiah: "all our righteous deeds are like filthy rags" (Isa. 64:6). And the apostle Paul quotes Psalm 14: "There is no one righteous, no, not one" (Rom. 3:10). Clearly it is not so easy to sort out what is meant by righteous and wicked, good and evil.

And think also of how Psalm 11 says that God hates the one who loves violence. This is confusing. The Old Testament is full of violence committed by those whom God loves. Well, maybe it means not those who *do* violence but those who *love* violence. But any honest observer of the American scene will admit that Americans seem to love violence. I have made a study of what goes on in video games, and it really is almost unbelievable. And what about the movies? When the second *Kill Bill* movie (by Quentin Tarantino) was released, a reporter went to interview the young men standing in line at the box office. One of them said, "I like violence. That's why I wanted to see it. And I don't think that's anything to be ashamed of."[3]

War itself teaches nice American boys — and now, increasingly, nice American girls — to love violence when it is directed against those whom we have identified as our enemies. Many thoughtful writers like Chris Hedges, the war correspondent, and Anthony Swofford, the Marine who wrote the acclaimed book *Jarhead,* have shown us this. So who is it exactly that God hates? And who exactly are the righteous who will enter through the gate of the Lord?

Whenever we speak of war and of making distinctions between the righteous and the wicked, Abraham Lincoln can help us. He saw, as clearly as anyone ever has, the danger in being certain that one is on God's side. During the Civil War he wrote an essay called "Meditation on the Divine Will" containing these words:

> In great contests each party claims to act in accordance with the will
> of God. Both may be, and one must be wrong. God can not be for
> and against the same thing at the same time.[4]

Lincoln struggled with this, knowing that there were deeply religious men on both sides of the conflict. Not everyone is aware that Lincoln was a truly great theological thinker (and clearly Calvinist in his inclinations, by the way). Part of what made Lincoln's thought so profound was that he was able to see several perspectives at once, including the perspective of God — insofar as God has revealed himself in the Bible. He saw that although God does take sides, he does not do it the way we do. And so Lincoln went on to write that since God cannot be on both sides of the Civil War — and here is the real depth of his thought —

---

3. *The New York Times,* 13 October 2003.
4. Abraham Lincoln, "Meditation on the Divine Will," September 1862.

. . . in the present civil war it is quite possible that *God's purpose is something different from the purpose of either party.*[5]

Now the Psalm chosen for this evening's worship is a Psalm of thanksgiving, and in particular it is thanksgiving for God's intervention on the side of the Psalmist against the enemy. The enemy is described as legion — as "all nations." This can be understood in several ways. "Nations" in the Old Testament usually refers to the Gentiles. It refers to everyone except Israel, the elect people. This suggests America today. We have been taught to think of ourselves as the elect, the "indispensable nation." It is therefore an easy step to conclude that God is on our side, even, if need be, against "all nations." But is this really what is meant in the Psalm? Some of you may be reminded of the word spoken by the Lord to Israel through the prophet Amos: "You only have I known of all the families of the earth; therefore I will punish you for all your iniquities" (Amos 3:2). Perhaps the enemy is actually the enemy within one's own society.

In the passage from Ezekiel that was read tonight, we hear another indictment of the chosen people:

The word of the Lord came to me: "Mortal, you dwell in the midst of a rebellious house, who have eyes to see, but see not, who have ears to hear, but hear not; for they are a rebellious house. Therefore, mortal, prepare for yourself an exile's baggage, and go into exile by day in their sight. . . . For I have made you a sign for the house of Israel." (12:1-3, 6)

And a few verses later it gets worse:

". . . Thus says the Lord God concerning the inhabitants of . . . the land of Israel: They shall eat their bread with fearfulness, and drink water in dismay, because their land will be stripped of all it contains, on account of the violence of all those who dwell in it. And the inhabited cities shall be laid waste, and the land shall become a desolation; and you shall know that I am the Lord." (12:19-20)

How remarkable this is. We will know that God is the Lord, not in his blessing but in his judgment. How utterly opposite to the usual rosy picture

5. Lincoln, "Meditation on the Divine Will," emphasis added.

we have of ourselves before God! The picture here is one of *a rebellious house,* an intractable and indeed unredeemable people who have thanklessly appropriated and then perverted the Lord's gifts, who have sunk into appalling idolatry, whose leaders have permitted God's flock to suffer neglect and violence. Moreover, as false prophets have led the people to trust in their own devices, they have thereby drained away their trust in the Lord's promises.

The book of the prophet Ezekiel should be better known among us. It is a difficult book, but it contains many profound passages of Old Testament theology (not to mention passages of great beauty). The prophet continues:

> The word of the Lord came to me: "Mortal, what is this proverb that you have about the land of Israel: 'The days grow long, and every vision comes to nothing'? Tell them, 'Thus says the Lord God: I will put an end to this proverb. . . .' The days are at hand, and the fulfilment of every vision. For there shall be no more any false vision or flattering divination within the house of Israel. But I the Lord will speak the word which I will speak, and it will be performed. . . . In your days, O rebellious house, I will speak the word and perform it, says the Lord God." (12:21-25)

This is the theme of the performative word of God. "I will speak the word and I will perform it, says the Lord." Without this attribute unique to the God of Israel, there would have been no Hebrew prophets. But what is it that the word of the Lord will perform? It will be a prodigious cleansing operation, a wholesale assault on apostasy, a mighty re-orientation of the people's hearts. But it will indeed be wholesale, with no distinctions made. The whole people of God will be judged: "This is what the sovereign Lord says: I will deal with you as you deserve, because you have despised my . . . covenant" (16:59).

There are plenty of places in Ezekiel, as in the Psalms, that seem to speak of a neat division between the righteous and the wicked (chapter 18, for example). That's why all of us who preach and lead God's people need to have a coherent, holistic biblical theology. There are places in Ezekiel where God says "*get yourselves* a new heart and a new spirit" (18:31; my emphasis), and other places where he declares unconditionally, "*I will put* a new spirit within them; *I will remove* their heart of stone and *give them* a heart of flesh" (11:19; my emphasis). Which of these statements should receive priority? Who is the active agent? The overwhelming tendency of the human being is to prefer the first. We are going to do it ourselves. We are going to work out our own salvation. We prefer the satisfaction of deserving God's favor. We want to identify ourselves among the righteous. But here at Calvin College, you have a powerful tradition which celebrates the *prevenient agency* of God — the active agency that "goes before" anything that we can contribute. Ezekiel, who admittedly loves lurid imagery, compares God's people to a newborn abandoned by the roadside, lying in its own mess ("kicking in your own blood" — 16:3-6), utterly helpless and desolate in a condition that we can only call pre-moral, pre-virtuous, pre-righteous. And so the apostle Paul writes, "Before we could do anything either good or bad . . . God's purpose in election" was already at work (Rom. 9:11).

With this background, let's look again at Psalm 118:

> I shall not die, but I shall live,
> and recount the deeds of the Lord.
> The Lord has chastened me sorely,
> but he has not given me over to death.
> Open to me the gates of righteousness,
> that I may enter through them
> and give thanks to the Lord.
> This is the gate of the Lord;
> the righteous shall enter through it.
> I thank thee that thou hast answered me
> and hast become my salvation. (118:17-21)

Do you see how thanksgiving is evoked as we recount the deeds of the Lord? And what is his greatest deed of all? It is making the unrighteous to be righteous. It is taking you and me and, yes, "chastening us sorely," but in doing so he is "opening the gates of righteousness to us so that we may enter through them. I thank thee, Lord, that thou . . . hast become my salvation." The Lord has spoken the word and performed it; "he has reckoned us righteous."

But the tantalizing question still remains: What does it mean to say, as the Psalmist does, that "the Lord is on my side"? I'm sure you know the hymn "Be Still, My Soul." It was written by a woman in German in the early eighteenth century and translated into English by another woman in the nineteenth. It has a lot of wonderful words, as I'm sure you know, but the ones I'm going to quote tonight are from the very first line: "Be still, my soul, the Lord is on thy side."[6]

What does it mean to affirm that the Lord is on your side? Does that mean, as we so often say today, that "the Lord accepts you just as you are"? Well, yes, of course it does mean that. It's clear from the ministry of Jesus that there was nothing whatsoever that could make a person unacceptable to him, no matter what their sin, crime or condition. He had a heart of love equally for every person and, as he said himself, "I did not come to call the righteous, but sinners to repentance" (Luke 5:32). But it is also clear that he did not leave people just as they were. He transformed them. Being reckoned righteous by our Lord does not mean (to continue with lurid imagery) returning like a dog to its own vomit (that's from Proverbs 26:11). Being *reckoned* righteous by Jesus Christ means being assimilated into *his* righteousness.

Think of what Paul says in the great eighth chapter of Romans: "If Christ is in you, although your bodies are dead because of sin, your spirits are alive because of righteousness" (Rom. 8:10). This makes absolutely no sense if we think of righteousness in the usual way — as human righteousness. If we believe that our spirits are alive because we have attained human righteousness, we have abandoned the Christian gospel altogether, and we are thrown back on the "false visions and flattering divinations" against which Ezekiel thunders. There is an awful lot of flattering divination around, isn't there? It's a billion-dollar business; just take a look at the self-help shelf in any bookstore. Even Christian bookstores carry books full of this flattery about how we have the potential within ourselves to be all that we want to be. Let me tell you, when you get to be my age, if you think you've become all you wanted to be, you're a damned fool. May God deliver me from my own righteousness. I don't want *my* righteousness — I want *his* righteousness. And that is exactly what he has promised me. He has promised me himself. I am a *rebellious house* all wrapped up in one person, but through no merit of my own I am being conformed into the likeness of God's own Son. He never stops breathing life into my dry bones.

"I [the Lord] will put a new spirit in [my people]; I will remove from them their heart of stone and give them a heart of flesh. Then they will follow my decrees and be careful to keep my laws" (Ezek. 11:19). The Commandments will cease to be tablets of stone that judge us, and they will be written in our hearts, as Jeremiah prophesied (31:33). My most heartfelt concern for the churches of America is that we would understand better

---

6. "Be Still, My Soul" by Katharina von Schlegel, 1752; translated by Jane Borthwick, 1855.

and proclaim more forcefully that God is on the side of all human beings everywhere. He is on the side of what *he* is doing *in us,* and he is *against* what *we* are continually doing *in ourselves* to spoil his work. And he will win this struggle that goes on within us, because he is God and we aren't, and his word will perform what it requires.

Remember the verse from Ezekiel that we quoted earlier: "I [the Lord] will deal with you as you deserve, because you have despised my . . . covenant." This does not refer to the enemies of Israel. It refers to Israel itself, to the elect people of God. *As we deserve.* If we begin dividing up human beings into the deserving and the undeserving, the righteous and the unrighteous, that means that we have forgotten our own condition before God, and this failure of understanding will show up immediately in our conduct toward others, particularly toward others who are in our power. Tonight, we are all equally powerless before God, yet he loves us all and loves us each, in our singularity and in our solidarity. At his Supper tonight, the distinctions among us are utterly broken down and assimilated into his Body. "Once you were no people but now you are God's people; once you had not received mercy but now you have received mercy" (1 Pet. 2:10). "While we were still helpless, Christ died for the ungodly" (Rom. 5:6).

> Open to me the gates of righteousness,
>     that I may enter through them
>     and give thanks to the Lord. . . .

> This is the Lord's doing;
>     it is marvelous in our eyes.

AMEN.

# Adding Up

*January 1988*                                                           Psalm 130

WE OFTEN hear that "sin" is a truly obsolete topic, along with salvation, justification, redemption, atonement, and so forth. It's curious, therefore, that it keeps popping up, from time to time, in the secular press. For instance, in the *Wall Street Journal* a year or so ago, there was an interview with the world-famous psychiatrist Dr. Karl Menninger, who at ninety-two was more feisty than ever. Dr. Karl stated that neurosis, anxiety, and depression, bad as they are, are not the real problem. Often, he said, they go away in time, like unwanted guests; there are other afflictions, though, that won't get well. Everyday human traits of selfishness, cruelty, hardheadedness — these are the conditions from which people don't recover. Some great impulse toward self-destruction lurks in our hearts, he has written, ever threatening to overwhelm the forces of life and renewal.[1]

In *The New Yorker,* Brendan Gill reviewed a revival of Edward Albee's play *Who's Afraid of Virginia Woolf?* He commented on the play's reception when it first opened years before; its portrait of marriage was so exceedingly unpleasant that many commentators conjectured that it was really about a disastrous homosexual relationship. More than a decade later, Gill notes, this can be seen as a failure of interpretation. I was amazed to read this particular critic's further statement that the subject of the play was not really marriage or sexuality or any other specific pairing off, but rather, that "of which Cardinal Newman was . . . speaking when

---

1. Interview with Dennis Farvey, *Wall Street Journal,* January 1986.

he said of the human race that it was implicated in some vast primordial catastrophe."[2]

In the *National Geographic,* an article about Tahiti describes a seventy-two-year-old Frenchman who has been living as a recluse on the island for twenty-seven years, in search of the ideal of the "noble savage." "My life is poisoned!" laments the hermit. "I've traveled from Paris to Ceylon, but all places are the same. The problem is the pride of man."[3]

These descriptions of the human predicament are classic descriptions of sin. Christians over the centuries have said the same thing by the hundreds and thousands. For example, Dorothy L. Sayers writes, "[Sin is] a deep interior dislocation at the very center of human personality."[4]

All these observations share a sense of universal participation in a common disruption. No one is exempt. As W. H. Auden writes, ". . . even in the germ-cell's primary division/Innocence is lost. . . ."[5] John Calvin calls sin "a contagion that has run riot through every part."[6]

This understanding of sin is almost unknown in the church today. As a Bible teacher, I find that I spend major amounts of time going back over it, again and again and again, in order to try to counteract the false understanding of sin that virtually every one of us began to learn as tiny children. Almost everybody in the church nowadays, Catholic and Protestant alike, grows up believing that "sins" are separate, distinct, identifiable acts of wrongdoing that we can choose to commit or choose not to commit. If we commit one, then we are "bad boys" or "bad girls." If we can convince our parents and our teachers that we have committed only a few of these, then we have attained the precarious status of being "good boys" and "good girls," and we spend the rest of our lives uneasily trying to reassure ourselves and others that we have more credits than debits. This is a very long way from the biblical understanding of sin as a "vast primordial catastrophe" affecting the whole human race.

In our Book of Common Prayer version of the Psalm appointed for today, number 130, the Psalmist cries out to God:

> If you, Lord, were to note what is done amiss, O Lord, who could stand?

---

2. Review entitled "In Vino Veritas," *The New Yorker,* 12 April 1976.

3. "The Society Islands," *National Geographic,* June 1979, p. 863.

4. "Creed or Chaos?" in Dorothy L. Sayers, *The Whimsical Christian* (New York: Macmillan, 1978), p. 45.

5. This quotation is from Auden's *For the Time Being: A Christmas Oratorio.*

6. John Calvin, *The Gospel of John* (Grand Rapids: Wm B. Eerdmans), p. 66.

There are several other English translations of this Hebrew verse. The New Revised Standard Version reads:

If you, O Lord, should mark iniquities, Lord, who could stand?

The New English Bible puts it this way:

If thou, Lord, shouldst keep account of sins, who, O Lord, could hold up his head?

And the New International Version has this:

If you, O Lord, kept a record of sins, O Lord, who could stand?

This is a very sweeping statement indeed. The implication is clear: There is no human being who can come up with enough credits to come into the presence of God as a righteous person. Hamlet says the same thing, in different words, when he instructs Polonius to take care of the visiting Players; Polonius says, in his pompous way,

My Lord, I will use them according to their desert.

And Hamlet retorts,

God's bodkin, man, much better. Use every man after his desert, and who shall 'scape whipping? . . . The less they deserve, the more merit is in your bounty. (Act II, Scene 2)

There used to be a way of teaching all of this from the Book of Common Prayer; in the version that we used until 1976, we said,

. . . we have erred and strayed like lost sheep. We have followed too much the devices and desires of our own hearts. We have offended against thy holy laws. We have left undone those things which we ought to have done, and we have done those things which we ought not to have done, and there is no health in us.

That statement, *there is no health in us,* has been removed from the Prayer Book that we now use. I would not want to go back to the old Prayer

Book for a number of reasons, but the removal of this line has robbed us of a powerful buttress to the biblical concept of sin as a "vast primordial catastrophe." At the same time, the deletion has reduced the honor given to God's mercy, for "the less we deserve, the more merit is in his bounty."

It is very, very difficult to dislodge present-day misconceptions about all this. We are taught from an early age to think in terms of two columns, "naughty" and "nice." If the "nice" column is longer than the "naughty" column, then I can say to myself and others that I am basically a "good person." If one thinks of sin in this way, then naturally a statement like "there is no health in us" becomes unendurable. Any suggestion that the balance is tipped from "nice" to "naughty" would mean that we were in danger of being condemned and rejected.

So it all depends on our understanding of sin. A few months ago, in one of our parish Bible studies, the members of the group were asked to talk about what they thought sin was. One woman said she thought it meant "being bad." I asked her where her idea of being bad came from, and without hesitation she said, "From my parents." Another person spoke up and said that her mother's laws were represented to her as God's laws, and that for a long time she didn't know there might be a difference! In just this way, most of us are mixed up about sin, because consciously or unconsciously we have it confused with trying to measure up to what our parents wanted — and suffering the consequences if we don't.

Two people in the group thought that there was a difference between sin and mere naughtiness. Sin, they thought, was the big stuff: murder, armed robbery, child abuse, arson. Naughtiness was the little stuff — the kinds of things that Episcopalians do. One person said she had trouble thinking of herself as a sinner because she did not think she had ever committed a sin. Before you smile at that, reflect on the fact that there was another phrase in the old Prayer Book that was removed. We used to describe ourselves in the General Confession as "miserable offenders." The liturgical commission thought that was too strong for us merely naughty Episcopalians, so the phrase was dropped.

What was not dropped, however, was the reading of this great Psalm. It is called *De Profundis,* "out of the depths." It begins at rock bottom:

Out of the depths have I called to you, O Lord.

Over the centuries these "depths" have been plumbed by countless sufferers who have cried out to God. This Psalm has been recited by prisoners in solitary confinement, by the incurably ill, by victims of natural disasters, by those condemned to die, and in every other kind of distress and despair. Such use of the Psalm has a long and honored history. However, the "depths" of which the Psalmist is actually speaking here is the depth of the knowledge that he and everyone else is a "miserable offender."

If you, O Lord, kept a record of sins, Lord, who could stand?

Biblical passages like these are the source of the statement "there is no health in us." The idea that we can add up our virtues and balance them over against our faults is decisively repudiated in this verse. Were we to add up all our merits in the sight of the one true God, our response would still be that of the tax collector in Jesus' story: "Lord, have mercy on me, a sinner" (Luke 18:13).

Ever since I was a child, I have been struck by the strangely elevating effect that great plays and films about the human condition have, and I have been perplexed when people would say that they did not want to see anything depressing. It is often said that this is particularly true of Americans. Perhaps there is something analogous here to the message of the Psalm. It seems that there are many who do not want to hear that we are "miserable offenders," and yet those who hear it and believe it find this confession to be the path of life. When we recognize that sin is not breaking our mothers' rules, but estrangement from the God in whom alone there is true redemption, then we are already beginning to move out of the realm of petty record-keeping, of adding up points, onto the world stage where the "vast primordial catastrophe" is met by nothing less than the purpose of an all-powerful Father to redeem his entire creation from its impulse toward self-destruction.

This is the movement of Psalm 130, widely acknowledged to be one of the greatest of all the Psalms. It begins in the depths with unflinching acknowledgment of the wretchedness of all humanity, our total inability to present ourselves righteous before the Lord. Precisely at the point of that confession, the Psalmist is enabled to raise up his eyes in a startling shift of mood:

Out of the depths have I called to you, O Lord. . . .
If you, O Lord, were to note what is done amiss,
   Lord, who could stand?
For there is forgiveness with you;
   therefore you shall be feared. (130:1-4)

If we can only begin to understand what is meant here by the fear of the Lord, we will understand the one thing we really need to know in life and death. The fear of the Lord is the beginning of wisdom, as the Psalms and Proverbs repeatedly say. The fear of the Lord is founded on his absolute goodness. The fear of the Lord arises out of the discovery that he is a God of infinite mercy and compassion. Notice the surprising order of the words: "There is forgiveness with you; *therefore* you shall be feared." The forgiveness of sins does not leave us with a cheerful, domestic idea of God. Rather, it calls forth from us a new respect for the humanly incomprehensible majesty and greatness of the God who can redeem humanity from so grave a predicament.[7] ("The less we deserve, the more merit is in his bounty.") Our understanding of the incomparable glory of God will correspond to our sense of the depths of human pride, disobedience, perversity, and self-will. The fear of God is a very different thing from the fear of our mothers.

We can carry this a bit further. It is drilled into us from childhood that we are to be nice, not naughty — "good girls and boys," not "bad" ones. This leads to our thinking in terms of adding up columns, and the result is that we develop three nasty habits: we attempt to hide our naughty behavior from others and even from ourselves; we seek to assuage our doubts by identifying others as naughtier than we are; and we persuade ourselves that "naughtiness" is not really sin, that it's the little stuff, not in the same class as the big stuff.

It has been the experience of God's people down through the ages that deliverance and new life are to be found in the confession that before God there is something fundamentally, drastically, terribly wrong with all of us — not just the bigots and thugs, not just the pimps and the drug dealers, not just the Nazis and the goons of the gulags, but with us Episcopalians, too, those of us who only do the little stuff. Before God, none of us can hold up our heads. This is not self-abasement leading to paralysis; this is honesty leading to deliverance. Writes Samuel Terrien, "Not the man who is lost, but the man who is about to be saved can understand that he is a sinner."[8]

The Psalm itself is a clear demonstration that the confession of sins before God is an entrance into a larger life. The Psalmist ceases to reflect upon

7. Artur Weiser, *The Psalms: A Commentary* (Philadelphia: Westminster Press, 1962), p. 774.

8. Samuel Terrien, *The Psalms and Their Meaning for Today* (Indianapolis: Bobbs-Merrill, 1952), p. 170.

himself and his own problems, and in beautiful, ecstatic imagery, thinks of himself as a watchman on behalf of *all* the people, straining forward to the approach of the dawn, almost bursting with exalted eagerness to announce to the whole community that

> With the Lord there is mercy;
> with him there is plenteous redemption,
>     and he shall redeem Israel from all his iniquities. (130:7-8)

Many of you who are here today have heard all of this before. I believe that we at Grace Church are very blessed to be in a place where these great and liberating things are taught and preached. Those of you who have been in our Bible studies know that your clergy have found comfort and hope and a deeper knowledge of God in the confession that adding up our merits and demerits will never work, that we come to God trusting that he is "not weighing our merits, but pardoning our offenses," in Thomas Cranmer's unforgettable phrase. In our prayer groups, people are learning to repent of "everyday human traits of selfishness, cruelty, hardheartedness." Each one of us, though, whether we heard it before or not, need to learn it again each day as we come before the Lord in repentance. Only in this way can we be freed from envy, self-righteousness, and indifference to the suffering of others.

There may be some here tonight, however, who have not heard this before, or who have not understood it before. You are spending enormous amounts of psychic energy convincing yourself that you belong on the credit side of the ledger. Your face toward the world is one of smooth, unruffled competence; you exude a certain sense of moral superiority. This Psalm speaks tonight to you, too. Such a way of meeting the world has great cost: either you will find yourself all alone in the depths one day, or you will make other people pay, usually members of your family, who can see only too clearly that you, also, are utterly in need of the mercy of God.

In one of Flannery O'Connor's short stories, an arrogant old man behaves atrociously in front of his young grandson and is caught in the act. The climax of the story comes when he and the boy together encounter the mystery of forgiveness. O'Connor writes,

> Mr. Head [the grandfather] had never known before what mercy felt like, because he had been too good to deserve any, but he knew now. He realized that he was forgiven for sins from the beginning of time

. . . and since God loved in proportion as he forgave, he felt ready at that instant to enter Paradise.[9]

May God grant that not a single one of us today would think himself too good to deserve any mercy, and that not a single one of us would think himself too bad to receive any mercy, and that we all together might go forth in the joyous and liberating knowledge that

With the Lord there is mercy;
with him there is plenteous redemption,
   and he shall redeem Israel from all his iniquities.

AMEN.

9. Flannery O'Connor, "The Artificial Nigger," in *The Complete Stories of Flannery O'Connor* (New York: Noonday Press, 1994).

# Discerning the Mighty Acts of God

## Trinity Church, New Orleans

---

*A sermon for the Trinity Church*　　　Psalm 145:4; Deuteronomy 26:6-11
*Sesquicentennial, 1847-1998*

> *Although the very particular circumstances of this sermon*
> *have been retained — or perhaps because they have been re-*
> *tained — it declares a message for the people of God at any*
> *time and in any place.*

· · · · · · · · · · · · · · · · ·

I WAS privileged to be with your vestry for its overnight retreat, where we
had some significant discussions about the nature of Christian leadership.
Now on this climactic Sunday, I ask you, the congregation of Christ's flock
gathered this morning, to turn with me to the Psalms. The text for this sermon is the verse chosen for your sesquicentennial celebration. This verse is
also the text for the choir anthem written especially by your organist. Here
it is, from Psalm 145:

> One generation shall praise your works to another and shall declare
> your mighty acts.

This is a major theme of many Psalms, not just one isolated verse in
one Psalm. Turn, for instance, in your Prayer Books to Psalm 78, verses 3
to 4:

That which we have heard and known,
and what our forefathers have told us,
   we will not hide from their children.

We will recount to generations to come
the praiseworthy deeds and the power of the Lord,
   and the wonderful works he has done.

And verses 6 to 7:

That the generations to come might know,
and the children yet unborn;
   that they in their turn might tell it to their children;

So that they might put their trust in God,
and not forget the deeds of God,
   but keep his commandments.

Now this is a wonderful thing. Some of you are too young to be parents yet, but God has already planned for your unborn children. Some of you may be anxiously waiting for grandchildren yet unborn. God's care is prepared for them already. The most important thing for these children of the future is not for them to have trust funds, or to be Queen of Carnival, or to have more Beanie Babies than anybody else. The most important thing for these precious children, these generations yet to come, is to *put their trust in God and not forget his wonderful deeds.*

The question now arises, What are the wonderful deeds of God? What are those mighty acts that will inspire future generations at Trinity Church to put their trust in the Lord, as you have done?[1]

If you look further into Psalm 78, you will see that it is a long recitation of the mighty acts of God. It goes on for seven pages. The children of Israel in the Psalmist's time, and in Jesus' time, could say all of this by heart. Turn to Psalm 105 on page 738; here is another Psalm in two parts which recounts the wonderful works of God. Go on to Psalm 106 (page 741), and you will

---

1. In 1961, Langdon Gilkey published an essay ridiculing the whole concept of the "Mighty Acts of God." I am fully aware of his arguments and the influence that his essay has had. From a postmodern perspective, his points seem somewhat dated, but even if that were not so, the foundations of Israel's faith cannot be so lightly dismissed. See, for instance, the sermon "A Way Out of No Way."

see the same pattern. Every child of Israel knew all of this by heart. And what was it that they knew? We can't take the time today to read these long Psalms, but there are many shorter versions of the history of God's mighty acts. Here is the most important one:

> "A wandering Aramean was my father; and he went down into Egypt and sojourned there, few in number; and there he became a nation, great, mighty, and populous. And the Egyptians treated us harshly, and afflicted us, and laid upon us hard bondage. Then we cried to the Lord the God of our fathers, and the Lord heard our voice, and saw our affliction, our toil, and our oppression; and the Lord brought us out of Egypt with a mighty hand and an outstretched arm, with great terror, with signs and wonders; and he brought us into this place and gave us this land, a land flowing with milk and honey. And behold, now I bring the first of the fruit of the ground, which thou, O Lord, hast given me." (Deut. 26:6-10)

Every child of the covenant was brought up knowing this history of the mighty acts of God, and we may be sure that our Lord learned this at his mother's knee. On this Mother's Day, let us pause to honor especially the Mother of our Lord, the archetype of all mothers and fathers who teach their children to recognize the mighty acts of God.

But now we must acknowledge that we, today, children of a somewhat confused American culture, are distanced from these great biblical history lessons. What, exactly, is a mighty act of God? The *discernment* of such acts is a task of the Christian community.

Here is a real-life example. Let us imagine ourselves back in Birmingham, Alabama, in May of 1963. Many of us white folks did not recognize it at the time — our *discernment* was faulty — but one of the great struggles of human history was in progress. All across the South, but especially in Birmingham that month, ordinary black working people were acting out of a courage and resolve that most of us today can scarcely imagine. Police dogs and fire hoses were the least of the dangers; beatings, jail sentences, even death were more tolerable than the ever-present likelihood of being simply ignored and forgotten in the eyes of a nation far more interested in uncovering non-existent communist conspiracies than in the struggles of black people to sit at lunch counters. Remember, this is before the March on Washington: the civil rights movement had not yet entered history. Virtually no white person had ever heard Martin Luther King speak. Most of us

— I include myself as first in that line — most of us white Southerners who lived through that time missed the moment of destiny because *we did not discern* what was happening.

During the struggle in cities across the South, the civil-rights warriors were sustained by the regular mass meetings in the churches — which were really worship services as well as rallies. Only a minuscule number of white people had ever attended such gatherings as these. Many whites, mostly newspaper reporters, were shaken and transformed by the seismic power of the singing and preaching that went on night after night, week after week. One white Northerner wrote back to his colleagues in New York that "I had the strongest feeling that I was in Egypt on the night of the Passover."[2]

Many of the mass meetings were taped, mostly by police departments and FBI looking for communists and insurrectionists. Some of these tapes are in the collection of the Riverside Church in New York. I have not heard them myself, but my closest theological friend has, and he describes one of the meetings at historic Sixteenth Street Baptist this way:

> On the evening in question, [the freedom songs have been sung and the gospel preached] with the contagious emotions found in the midst of struggle. Now it is time to hear from the visitors who have flown in during the afternoon [to add their encouragement]. One of these is a greatly and justly loved figure from the sports world.[3] He begins his speech by remarking, "You people are doing a great thing here in Birmingham." At this, one hears a few feet shuffling back and forth. After three or four sentences he says again, "It is a great thing you people are doing here." Shufflings of the feet, to which is added a few clearings of the throat. Several sentences later, he returns to what is now obviously his theme: ". . . You are doing a great thing here in Birmingham." Now shuffling of the feet and clearing of the throat will no longer suffice. One of the old deacons interrupts the speaker, politely but firmly, by calling out *We are not doing this! God is doing this!*[4]

---

2. Robert Spike, head of the Commission on Religion and Race, National Council of Churches, 1963. Quoted in Taylor Branch, *Pillar of Fire: America in the King Years*, vol. 2: 1963-65 (New York: Simon & Schuster, 1998), p. 127.

3. It was Jackie Robinson.

4. J. Louis Martyn, "From Paul to Flannery O'Connor with the Power of Grace" (emphasis added), *Katallagete* 7, no. 4 (1981).

*God is doing this.* Four months later, it was Sunday morning at the same church. Four young black girls were gathered in the ladies' room in their special white dresses, buzzing with excitement because they were to lead the annual Youth Day exercises. Minutes later, those four children were dead in the rubble of the bomb that exploded at Sixteenth Street Baptist that day. *Where is God now?* was the uppermost question. Dr. King, preaching at the funeral, spoke these words: "History has proven over and over again that unmerited suffering is redemptive. The innocent blood of these little girls may well serve as the redemptive force that will bring new light to this dark city. We must not lose faith in our white brothers [and sisters]. Somehow we must believe that the most misguided among them can learn to respect the dignity and worth of all human personality."[5]

Yesterday at the vestry retreat, the question of *discernment* was raised. How are the leaders of Trinity Church to discern the mighty acts of God? What movement of his Spirit is God calling you to join?[6] It may not be a great and glorious world-historical struggle. It may only be a seemingly small and insignificant skirmish, but nevertheless part of God's great plan. Where, today, is God bringing us "out of Egypt with a mighty hand and an outstretched arm"? What Red Seas are being crossed? How is God leading his people out of bondage into freedom? Where is he leading us "out of error into truth, out of sin into righteousness, out of death into life"?[7] What unmerited suffering can you contribute to God's great purpose for human liberation?

This discernment of God's purpose will be for you, the leaders and people of Trinity Church, to discover together. The visiting preacher cannot do it for you. The visiting preacher has a humbler assignment. What this visiting preacher hopes to do for you in this brief time is to remind you to discern when it is time to shuffle your feet. What this visiting preacher hopes to do is to encourage you to know when it is time to clear your throat. And, if necessary, you might need to holler out *"We're* not doing this! *God* is doing this!" Because as soon as you get the idea that *you* are doing it, you will be back in the house of bondage again — the bondage of spiritual blindness, the bond-

---

5. Quoted in Branch, *Pillar of Fire*, p. 140.

6. Who could have known, when this sermon was preached in 1998, that seven years later Hurricane Katrina would strike the city of New Orleans and the levees would break, leaving 80 percent of the city under water and the population — especially its poorest members — in deepest distress. Trinity Church and the Episcopal Diocese of Louisiana have been front and center in the long and painful recovery. They *discerned* their calling. Indeed, their calling hit them over the head; and they responded with the strength of faith in the God who raises the dead.

7. Eucharistic Prayer B, The Book of Common Prayer, p. 368.

age of moral arrogance, the bondage of self-righteousness that is not able to embrace the brother or sister on the other side of the issue.

At the vestry retreat, we read this biblical passage:

> By grace you have been saved through faith; and this is not your own doing, it is the gift of God — and not because of works, lest any one should boast. (Eph. 2:8-9)

*It is not your doing; it is the gift of God.* What, then, your vestry leaders asked, is the place of human action? If God is doing everything, what is there for us to do? We read on in the passage:

> For we are God's workmanship, created in Christ Jesus for good works, which God prepared beforehand, that we should walk in them. (2:10)

And Ellen Ball, your junior warden, spoke this revelatory word: "It is by God's grace that we do the good works." Yes! *God* is doing it, but human beings are the agents. *We* are not doing this; *God* is doing this. And yet, wonder of wonders, he is doing it *through us, through you* — flawed, yes; sinful, yes; unworthy, yes; but beloved of God and chosen to act for him in the great battle against oppression, sin, and death in which *you* are the Christian soldiers.

So in the final analysis, the mightiest of all God's mighty deeds is this: *By grace you have been saved.* Not "you *might be* saved"; not "you *can be* saved"; most certainly not "you *will be* saved *if* you do enough good works." This gospel has no ifs, no mights, no maybes, no conditions. Just this: *you have been saved.* You have been *saved by grace* — the grace of God through our Lord and Savior Jesus Christ.

Trinity, listen: hear the word of the Lord:

> The Lord heard *your* voice, and saw *your* affliction . . . and the Lord brought *you* out of [your bondage] with a mighty hand and with an outstretched arm.

Praised be his holy Name! Now his arm is stretched out *through you* toward others. Now he is preparing all those good works for you to walk in. Brothers and sisters, this is the freedom train — not just the freedom of those to whom we minister, but your freedom, our freedom. Our God is on the move. You don't want to miss your moment with destiny. The fare has already been paid. The Lord is on a roll. The Kingdom of heaven is at hand.

Just remember, Trinity: *You* are not doing this. *God is doing this.* Tell the children. Tell the children, "so that they might put their trust in God."

Trinity, listen:

From one generation to another, declare the mighty works of the Lord. From one generation to another, praise ye the Lord.

Let all the people say "Amen!" (Ps. 106:48)

# The Man in the Bed

Ecclesiastes; 1 Samuel 16:7

*This sermon was delivered at the conclusion of a conference about the meaning of the crucifixion.*

. . . . . . . . . . . . . . . . . .

It is well known that Americans are optimistic and upbeat. "Positive thinking" is one of our cultural traits.[1] We don't always recognize that people in other parts of the world are not like us. The market for "motivational" and "inspirational" speakers is not as lively in other parts of the world as it is here. The noted public intellectual and New York University professor Tony Judt, when he was in the early stages of ALS (Lou Gehrig's disease), was asked to say something inspirational about his battle with the dread illness. He snapped, "I'm English. We don't do uplifting."[2]

The cultural demand to be constantly uplifted and inspired by positive thoughts works against the heart of the Christian faith. Paul the apostle

---

1. Norman Vincent Peale actually referred to the cross of Christ as "God's plus sign."

2. Quotation from Tony Judt in Barbara Cohen's "Chronicler of the World Now Looks Inward," *The New York Times,* 7 February 2010. (Judt died in August 2010 after dictating a heroic number of analytical essays.) In her recent book, *Bright-Sided: How the Relentless Promotion of Positive Thinking Has Undermined America,* Barbara Ehrenreich makes these points in spades. She is especially exercised about the way that breast cancer patients are made to feel that they can overcome cancer with a "good attitude."

met with problems of this sort. The Christians in the congregation at Corinth were into spiritual uplift in a big way. They thought the crucifixion of Christ was something negative to be set aside. They didn't want to hear about it. Paul nails his colors to the mast in the early part of his letter to them: "I am determined to know nothing among you except Jesus Christ and him crucified" (1 Cor. 2:2). Paul said that sure enough, the Cross was a stumbling block to the Jews and foolishness to the Gentiles, but that for those who believe, the Cross is the power of God and the wisdom of God. Please bear with me today, for I have good news.

On Sunday we reflected on the text "The Lord turned and looked at Peter" (Luke 22:61).[3] We know what the Lord saw when he looked at Peter. He saw a blustering, thoughtless, reckless, overgrown boy, first of all (that's the Peter we all know and love), but more than that he saw a liar and a coward. He saw a man who acted like a stalwart soldier and defender of the faith when he was safe, but who, as soon as he was in danger, became a traitor in order to save his own skin.

What does the Lord see when he looks at us? There's a verse in 1 Samuel that gives us a clue. This is a story about the call of David. "The Lord sees not as man sees; man looks on the outward appearance, but the Lord looks on the heart" (1 Sam. 16:7). Our discussion group was talking yesterday about Rush Week at colleges and universities. What are the fraternity boys and the sorority girls looking for — the outward appearance, or the heart? What are the commercials and print ads pitched to? What are the plastic surgeons making money on? What sells a political figure today: substance or image?

The book of Ecclesiastes is a very important book of the Old Testament. It would be a good thing for our relentlessly optimistic, upbeat American form of Christianity if we all were to read Ecclesiastes once a month. Everybody knows the part about "a time to live and a time to die," but that's the least of the book. The person who wrote it (traditionally Solomon, but we don't really know who he was) was a realist about human life. No pieties for him, no denial, no making nice, no pretense that everything is working out fine. Judy Collins never sang this part of Ecclesiastes:

> This is an evil in all that is done under the sun, that one fate comes to all; also the hearts of men are full of evil, and madness is in their hearts while they live, and after that they go to the dead. (9:3)

---

3. See the sermon "The Lord Looked at Peter" in my book *The Undoing of Death* (Grand Rapids: Wm. B. Eerdmans, 2002).

Qoheleth[4] (that's the name of the writer of Ecclesiastes) is not impressed by riches or social prominence; he has had it all, and he is not satisfied with any of it:

> He who loves money will not be satisfied with money. . . . Here is a man to whom God gives wealth and possessions, so that he lacks nothing of all that he desires, yet God does not give him power to enjoy them. (5:10; 6:2)

Qoheleth would not be at all surprised to see the president of the company laid low by ALS, or depression, or personal tragedy, or failure of any kind. Not even human wisdom works as a bulwark against the whims of a world threatened by meaninglessness:

> One fate comes to all, to the righteous and the wicked. . . . The race is not to the swift, nor the battle to the strong, neither yet bread to the wise, nor yet riches to men of understanding, nor yet favor to men of skill; but time and chance happeneth to them all. (9:2, 11)

This is what Qoheleth sees. What does God see when he looks at us? He sees us running around after success and status and sex and eternal youth, and it is all "striving after wind," in the repeated refrain of Ecclesiastes: "this also is vanity and a striving after wind."

But this is not just a book about old people. Ecclesiastes addresses the young also:

> Rejoice . . . in your youth, and let your heart cheer you in the days of your youth; walk in the ways of your heart and the sight of your eyes. ["I did it my way" *à la* Frank Sinatra!]
>
> But know that for all these things God will bring you into judgment. . . .
>
> Remember also your Creator in the days of your youth, before the evil days come, and the years draw nigh, when you will say, "I have no pleasure in them." (11:9; 12:1)

---

4. Actually, it's not a name. It has traditionally been translated "the preacher," but it means something like "the gatherer," as one who collects wisdom sayings and proverbs. Or, one who gathers the community together.

Even the young, then, though they cannot know it yet, live under this shadow of futility.

Moreover, in the tradition of the Hebrew prophets, Qoheleth goes on to say that heedlessness does not excuse us from participating in a system that elevates the rich and neglects the poor. The judgment of God lies upon such a society:

> In the place of justice, even there was wickedness. . . . Behold, the tears of the oppressed, and they had no one to comfort them! On the side of their oppressors there was power, and there was no one to comfort them. (3:16; 4:1-2)

Do you feel judged by this? So do I. But the worship of the church has made a place for it. When we come into church, we are in company with those who seek to know the truth about human life. Why do big strong men and women get down on their knees and say, "We have followed too much the devices and desires of our own hearts; we have offended against thy holy laws"? Why do we say, "We have left undone those things which we ought to have done, and we have done those things which we ought not to have done"?[5] Why would we say it if it was bad news? Well, it is bad news, of course, but the amazing thing about Christian faith is that the bad news is part of the good news. What did Jesus say? "I did not come to call the righteous, but sinners to repentance."

I wonder if you've had the experience of visiting a socially prominent friend in the hospital. It can be a startling experience. You're used to seeing this person working the crowds, looming over others by force of personality, cutting a figure, working his will. Suddenly there he (or she) is, lying prone on a bed in a hospital gown, pale, hair messed up, arms and throat vulnerably exposed, attached to tubes, perhaps, with a facial expression of discomfort and embarrassment, if not fear. Which is the real person? Is it the senior partner of the law firm, the titan of industry, the *grande dame* of society? Is that the real person? Or is it the frightened, defenseless person in the bed?

No sick person looks vital or vigorous. No dying person looks powerful or commanding. "One fate comes to all," says Qoheleth. We "go to the dead." This is part of what we mean by original sin: something has gone wrong with

---

5. The General Confession in this classic form used to be indelibly inscribed in the memory of every Episcopalian, but unfortunately is not heard much now. It is still to be found in Morning Prayer, Rite One, in the Book of Common Prayer.

the human race, some primordial calamity that disrupted what we were supposed to be. That's the meaning of the story of Adam and Eve. Paul retells that story: *sin worked death* in the human race (Rom. 7:13). We try all our lives to beat back that awful fact, by posing and posturing and throwing our weight around and grabbing after sensation and denying the presence of death, but "one fate comes to all," to the powerful and the weak alike, the rich and the poor alike. "Time and chance happen to us all," and eventually we are all laid low. In the beautiful, poetic, but deeply mournful language of Ecclesiastes:

> ... the keepers of the house tremble, and the strong men are bent, and the grinders cease because they are few, and those that look through the windows are dimmed, and the doors on the street are shut ... and all the daughters of music are brought low ... the grasshopper drags itself along and desire fails; because man goes to his eternal home, and the mourners go about the streets ... the silver cord is snapped, the golden bowl is broken, the pitcher is broken at the fountain, the wheel is broken at the cistern, and the dust returns to the earth as it was, and the spirit returns to God who gave it. Vanity of vanities, says the Preacher; all is vanity. (12:3-7)[6]

Ecclesiastes plays a very important role in Scripture. It asks us to see through the images that we invent for ourselves: images of power and prosperity, youth and beauty, vigor and health, energy and significance. It asks us — indeed, it forces us — to see that we are more like patients in a hospital than masters of the universe. Let's return to the man in the bed. Who is he? Which is the real person? Is it the person who is up and moving, dressed in a power suit, impressing people, totally in command? Or is it the frightened, defenseless person in the bed?

Well, the answer to that, humanly speaking, is of course *both;* but there can be no question as to how God sees us. "Almighty God, unto whom all hearts are open, all desires known, and from whom no secrets are hid"[7] — our Father in heaven sees us in the full dimensions of our weakness and mortality, without pretenses, without defenses; and *he loves us.*

What does God see when he sees the man in the bed, the woman in the ICU? He sees a person that he loves. He sees a person that he loves more

---

6. In order to read a shortened version of the long passage, I have omitted a couple of connecting words.

7. The Collect for Purity, Holy Eucharist I, Book of Common Prayer.

than life, more than glory, more than power, more than riches, more than divinity itself:

> For you know the grace of our Lord Jesus Christ, who though he was rich, yet for your sake he became poor, so that by his poverty you might become rich. (2 Cor. 8:9)

> Christ Jesus was in the form of God, but he did not think equality with God a thing to be grasped, but emptied himself, taking the form of a slave . . . becoming obedient unto death, even to death on a cross. (Phil. 2:6-8)

And why did he do that?

Because he loved you. Because he loved me. He looked at us and he saw our pretensions and our delusions and our false fronts and our sickness unto death, and he loved us. "God shows his love for us in that while we were still sinners, Christ died for us" (Rom. 5:8). What is Jesus doing on that cross? Is it "negative"? Is it frightening? Is it horrifying? Is it ugly? Yes, it is all of those things, but is it not also the greatest story ever told?

We have given our full attention, this week, to "Jesus Christ and him crucified." This has not been easy for everybody, I know. There are those who will flee from this subject, like the Christians in Corinth. St. Paul wrote that "Christ crucified is a stumbling block to Jews and foolishness to Gentiles, but to those who are called, both Jew and Gentile, Christ is the power of God and the wisdom of God" (1 Cor. 1:23-24). This is not "uplift." This is a message from the Most High God (Dan. 3:26; 4:2). I think you are here tonight because you know that this is not "inspirational"; this is not "positive thinking": this is a gospel that addresses us from the heights of heaven into the depths where human motivation and human possibility have exhausted themselves.

Why do we confess our sins whenever we worship? Because it is such a joyful thing not to have to pretend any longer. The Bible teaches us to see ourselves as God sees us. This is the answer to everything: to understand who we are in the sight of God. Without God's mercy, the most that can be said of us is what Qoheleth says:

> It is an unhappy business that God has given to the sons of men to be busy with. I have seen everything that is done under the sun; and behold, all is vanity and a striving after wind. What is crooked cannot be made straight. (Eccles. 1:13-15)

What is crooked cannot be made straight. There is a pall over humanity that was not originally supposed to be there. Even "our *righteous* deeds are like filthy rags," Isaiah writes (64:6; my emphasis). Even the best of our accomplishments are "vanity and a striving after wind." Shelley's famous poem describes the enormous statue of a once-mighty pharaoh, now toppled ignominiously in the desert, where "the lone and level sands stretch far away," mocking our "striving after wind."[8] Even the pharaohs, even the titans of industry, the rock stars and the supermodels, the captains and the kings must all "lie down in darkness" one day.[9] "Lo, all the pomp of yesterday is one with Nineveh and Tyre."[10]

Here is the news from the Cross of Christ. The one and only Master of the universe, the Lord who created the cosmos with his mere word, the almighty and omnipotent Holy One of Israel, the God who parted the Red Sea and caused the walls of Jericho to fall and answered Elijah on Mount Carmel with a bolt of lightning has entered human flesh and laid himself down on our hospital bed. The Son of God has exposed his throat, his arms, his entire body to the scorn and abuse of the multitude. He has taken ultimate shame and weakness upon himself. These are the glad words from the First Epistle of Peter:

> He himself bore our sins in his body on the tree, that we might die to sin and live to righteousness. By his wounds you have been healed. For you were straying like sheep, but now you have returned to the Shepherd and Guardian of your souls. (1 Pet. 2:24-25)

AMEN.

---

8. Percy Bysshe Shelley, "Ozymandias."

9. Taken from the title of William Styron's best novel (in my opinion), *Lie Down in Darkness*.

10. From "Recessional" by Rudyard Kipling. This poem is not as bad as postcolonial opinion would have us think. There is a certain irony in the phrase "lesser breeds without the law." In any case, the refrain pleads, "Judge of the nations, spare us yet."

*In Memoriam*
*Richard A. Norris Jr.*

# Love against the Odds

## REGENT COLLEGE, VANCOUVER: PASTORS' CONFERENCE

---

*May 2009*                    Selections from the Song of Songs

### Prayer of William of St. Thierry

As we approach the epithalamium, the marriage song, the song of the Bridegroom and the Bride, to read and to weigh your work, we call upon you, O Spirit of holiness. We want you to fill us with your love, O Love, so that we may understand love's song — so that we too may be made in some degree participants in the dialogue of the holy Bridegroom and the Bride, and so that what we read about may come to pass within us. For where there is a question of the soul's affections, one does not easily understand what is said unless one is touched by similar feelings. Turn us then to yourself, O holy Spirit, holy Paraclete, holy Comforter; comfort the poverty of our solitude, which seeks no solace apart from you; illumine and enliven the desire of the suppliant, that it may become delight. Come, that we may love in truth, that whatever we think or say may proceed out of the fount of your love. Let the Song of your love be so read by us that it may set fire to love itself within us, and let love itself be for us the interpreter of your Song. *Amen.*[1]

---

1. This prayer, along with the quotation from the Venerable Bede and other references from the early centuries of the church, are taken from Richard A. Norris's magnificent compilation of commentary from the first thousand years in his volume *The Song of Songs,* the first volume in the series called The Church's Bible (Grand Rapids: Wm. B. Eerdmans, 2003). Professor Norris was one of my thesis advisors in 1975, and I am deeply grateful to God that his compendium, with

WHEN I was in theological seminary thirty-five years ago, it was taken for granted by most biblical scholars that the Song of Songs was a collection of erotic wedding poems, without reference to God or the spiritual realm. A collection of erotic poetry. Period. It was decidedly not fashionable to pay any attention to the pre-modern tradition that interpreted the book as an allegory about Christ and his church.

Who would have thought, only three decades ago, that biblical interpretation was about to make an amazing turn! We are rediscovering the fact that during the first thousand years of the life of the Christian church, there were more commentaries written about the Song of Songs than any other book of the Bible except (can you guess?) Genesis and the Psalms. All from the Old Testament! The Venerable Bede, to give just one example, wrote several commentaries on the Song. This extraordinary man of intellect, learning, and piety wrote, "This Song testifies . . . that it intends nothing fleshly or literal when it speaks, but wants to be understood spiritually and typically [typologically] in its entirety." Until quite recently, this view seemed naïve and uninformed to those who were shaped by the historical-critical method.

That was a mistake. For instance, let's look for a moment at what Bede has to say about a verse in chapter 8. In the verse, the bride speaks to the bridegroom as though he were present. She says, "If I met you outside, I would kiss you."

About this, Bede writes, "The Beloved was truly *within* because 'in the beginning was the Word, and the Word was with God and the Word was God' (John 1:1), but in order that he might also be found *outside,* the Word was made flesh and dwelt among us (John 1:14)." So you see, in a one-sentence comment upon one-half of one verse of the Song of Songs, Bede manages to teach us about the Trinity, what it is within itself and what it is in *going out from itself* in the Incarnation of Christ, to live "outside" with us mortal men and women, and to embrace us. Amazing. And that's just one sentence. So we are learning all over again not to scorn the ancient allegorical interpreters, even though we may think we know better.

So, whereas we should acknowledge that the book is indeed a series of erotic wedding poems, we should ask, at the same time, Is that *all* they are? Particularly in view of the long history of interpretation? And, even more important, in view of the place that the Song occupies in the canon of Scrip-

---

translations exemplifying his mastery not only of the ancient languages but also of the English language, should have been ready to hand for my preparation of this sermon on The Song of Songs.

ture? I've come to think that we need to hold both these interpretations in dialogue with one another.

Until I made a point of studying the history of interpretation, I had not realized how frequently we come upon the Song of Songs in the hymns of the church. For example, from our Easter hymns, listen to these words:

Come away to the skies, my beloved, arise. . . .

This joyful Eastertide, away with sin and sorrow,
My love, the Crucified, hath sprung to life this morrow.

And George Herbert, probably the greatest of all Christian poets in the English language, uses the language of the Song of Songs to address Jesus Christ:

Come, my Joy, my Love, my Heart;
Such a Joy, as none can move;
Such a Love, as none can part;
Such a Heart, as joys in love.

So I think that once we've taken delight in these borrowings from the language of the Song in order to express love for the Savior, the Beloved, we won't want to make a strict separation between the carnal meaning and the spiritual meaning. Indeed, as many commentators on the Hebrew text observe, a distinction between secular and sacred is foreign to the Hebrew mind.

A very happy memory of my early ministry seems to me to illustrate the layered meaning of the Song of Songs perfectly. I need to set the stage for you. This was back in the seventies in my first parish position, where for six years I was in charge of ministry to high school students. As I look back on my life, I think of that work as without doubt one of the high points of my thirty-seven years in ordained ministry. At the peak we had about sixty young people, half boys and half girls (really). The amount of *eros* floating around was prodigious. We exploited that shamelessly, using every technique possible to get the boys to come to be with the girls (and vice versa), but we were very strict, too. I learned very early that when we took them for weekend retreats, we had to keep them occupied every waking moment and every supposedly sleeping moment too. We would typically have fifteen adult counselors for the sixty students. None of us got much sleep. You have to be a very young adult to do youth ministry!

Now here's the relevant part. We channeled all that physicality into very well-planned sports, relay races, competitive games, comedy skits — you get the idea. And in particular we channeled their erotic energy into exuberant song, with clapping and stamping and the whole bag of tricks — taking a hint from the Shakers, as it were. We even had steel drums a couple of times. We raised the roof off the chapel. And one of the songs we sang was a direct quote from the Song of Songs. I can still see the faces of those young people as they belted it out:

I am my beloved's and he is mine; his banner over me is love. . . .
He welcomes me to his banqueting table; his banner over me is love.

It really puts a smile on my face to think about that all these years later. The way we sang it, it was a very energetic song with a great beat. Many of the young people probably didn't care that it was from the Song of Songs, but I am sure of this: because they sang it in the context of the communion service, they had at least a clue that the banqueting table was the Lord's Supper, and they certainly had some sense of Jesus as the Beloved, and the wonderful image of "the banner over me" as the love of God was vivid to them as they sang. So I think this little vignette beautifully illustrates how erotic energy can be channeled into passionate love of God, and the Song of Songs surely teaches us something about that.

Focusing now more directly upon the specifically sexual dimensions of the Song, let's hear the voice of the respected Roman Catholic scholar Roland Murphy. This celibate priest had a lot of understanding. He wrote as follows: "The literal sense [of the Song of Songs] seems to be a celebration of the . . . love between a man and woman. . . . Such seems to be the obvious meaning of [the Song], from which we should not depart without a compelling reason. . . . We should not ask, 'How did profane poetry enter the canon?' We should ask, 'What does the Bible tell us about sexual attraction?' A great part of the answer lies in [the Song of Songs]."[2]

In the canon of Holy Scripture of the church, the Song is included among the Wisdom books. That seems a very odd place for it to be unless you consider the role of Hebrew wisdom. Wisdom is derived from Israel's sages. Its purpose was to seek understanding, through reflection, on *the nature of the world of human experience in relation to divine reality.* The folder

---

2. Roland Murphy, "Canticle of Canticles," in *The Jerome Biblical Commentary* (Englewood Cliffs, N.J.: Prentice Hall, 1968).

for this conference features divine Wisdom. Wisdom asks the question, "What does it mean to live wisely before God?"[3]

In Proverbs 9, Wisdom is personified as a noble woman who builds her house of seven pillars and invites her dinner guests to "walk in the way of insight" (v. 6). *Insight* is a word I learned to cherish in the process of seven years of psychoanalysis and training. Seek *insight*, says holy Wisdom. This feminine figure in Proverbs is contrasted with the wanton woman, who ensnares the unwary man with her enticing words: "Stolen water is sweet, and bread eaten in secret is pleasant" (9:17). This is astute psychology. Insight, in this case, requires us to acknowledge the universal lure of the forbidden and the drive for immediate gratification. In fact, one of the highest accolades that can be given today in the supposedly rarefied circles of the cultural elite is that a work of art or literature is *transgressive*. The biblical authors are anything but naïve about such thinking; they lived in the middle of transgression. But the Wisdom tradition of ancient Israel shows how, in the very midst of the highly eroticized religious cults of Canaan, holy wisdom is the only true partner who calls men to life. "Bread eaten in secret is pleasant," says the seductress to the unwise man, and he yields to her:

> But he does not know that the dead are there,
> that her guests are in the depths of Sheol. (9:18)

What, then, is the proper role of *eros* in a life lived before God? The two principal places to look for that in the Bible are Genesis 2 and the Song of Songs. These two portions of Scripture are unique, and they are closely linked. In the creation story in Genesis, we see man and woman (Adam and Eve) delighting in one another physically *without any reference to procreation*. There is no other extended discussion of the male-female partnership in Scripture where this is so except in the Song.[4] Everywhere else it is set explicitly into the context of marriage and family, and Jesus Christ himself gives an unequivocal teaching about that when he says, quoting from the Old Testament,

---

3. From Brevard Childs, *Introduction to the Old Testament as Scripture* (Philadelphia: Fortress Press, 1979), the chapter on The Song of Songs (pp. 571-79).

4. Highly recommended is Karl Barth's wonderful appreciation of The Song of Songs, which appears in several places in the *Church Dogmatics*. I have taken some of these ideas from his discussion, but this little condensation does not even begin to convey the depth and charm of his writing on the subject. See especially vol. III/1.

"From the beginning of creation, 'God made them male and female.' 'For this reason a man shall leave his father and mother and be joined to his wife, and the two shall become one flesh.' So they are no longer two but one flesh." (Mark 10:6-8)

Our Lord is quoting here from the creation story in Genesis 1. It's of great importance that the *imago Dei* (the image of God) is a phrase from that passage:

So God created man in his own image,
in the image of God he created him;
male and female he created them. (RSV)[5]

So God created humankind in his image,
in the image of God he created them;
male and female he created them. (NRSV)

In other words, there is something about the complementarity of male and female that is itself the image of God.[6] The inner life of the Godhead, the blessed Trinity, is imaged among us by when a person *goes out* to the one who is the *other*. And so we find ourselves back with the Venerable Bede once more and his description of the God who goes out from himself toward the other, *outside* — in other words, seeking us *outside* the Godhead.

So we can see that the rapturous love celebrated in the Song of Songs is intended by God for us in the way that the bride and the bridegroom assertively and confidently seek one another, and especially the bride, who is depicted as the equal of the man in every way. Quite apart from any metaphorical resemblance to God and his people, or to Christ and the individual soul, we can see that sexual ecstasy is part of God's plan for man and woman in creation.

But now let's note that word *ecstasy*. Its literal meaning is "to stand outside oneself." Doesn't this once again suggest the *stepping outside of himself* that God accomplished in the Incarnation?[7] There is an analogy here to hu-

---

5. Vernard Eller, in a sophisticated analysis of the way English translations work, has argued (convincingly, in my judgment) that the KJV and RSV versions render the complexity of the Hebrew best. See Vernard Eller, *The Language of Canaan and the Grammar of Feminism* (Grand Rapids: Wm. B. Eerdmans, 1982), pp. 22-32 and *passim*.

6. This interpretation of the *imago Dei* (an interpretation associated with Karl Barth) is persuasive, based as it is on the Genesis text itself and on Jesus' emphatic reference to it in Mark's Gospel.

man love which reaches out beyond itself. It's often been noted that in the Song of Songs, there is much more seeking and longing than there is realization. This is surely true of human life in general. The fulfillment, the consummation — indeed, the transfiguration — of our hopes lies beyond us in the future of God. What we experience in this world is only a hint, a foretaste of what will some day be. The Song of Songs strongly suggests the future restoration of all things by God. The imagery in the poems is that of a restored earth in balance with itself and with its human inhabitants. Ellen Davis, one of the most eloquent modern interpreters of the Song, writes,

> The theological importance of the song is that it represents the reversal of that primordial exile from Eden. . . . The lover's garden is subtly but consistently represented as the garden of delight that Eden was meant to be, the place where life may be lived fully in the presence of God.[8]

So now I address you who are parents of, or counselors to, young people here who need to learn something about how to live such a full life before God. I don't need to tell you that living a godly life is not what our culture is promoting. Unbridled sexual activity is what our culture is promoting. There are a few signs of resistance, however. At Princeton University, there is a group of non-nerdy students who have banded together to support one another in presenting an alternative voice on that high-status campus. They call themselves the Anscombe Society, after the Cambridge Anglo-Catholic Elizabeth Anscombe. One young Princeton woman said that she was deeply offended, as a new student, when she went to a study break in her residential adviser's suite and there on the table "with the soda and the chips was a bowl of flavored condoms." A young man who served as the Anscombe group's spokesman said, "We think the proper human relationship should be one of respect and love, and we think promiscuity and random hook-ups are completely destructive of respect and love. Dignity itself is a moral standard."[9] It takes courage to talk like that at an Ivy League school. But then, the moral life has always required courage.

I am going to speak to you now as an elder, a woman who has been mar-

---

7. This point is emphasized by Ellen Davis in *Proverbs, Ecclesiastes, and the Song of Songs* (Louisville: Westminster John Knox Press, 2000).

8. Davis, *Proverbs, Ecclesiastes, and the Song of Songs*, p. 232.

9. Iver Peterson, "Princeton Students Who Say 'No' and Mean 'Entirely No,'" *The New York Times*, 18 April 2005.

ried to the same man for nearly fifty years. The Song of Songs is about *young* love. I remember that young love very well. The intensity of it does not last — indeed, it cannot. There is a sadness in that, but there is also something fitting in it. As Ellen Davis writes, "The sadness in our world stems from what happened in the Garden of Eden." That is why the note of longing predominates in the Song. It strains forward toward what is not yet, toward that which is not yet consummated. "Love always pushes toward transcendence," Davis comments.[10] ✻

In the meantime, no earthly phenomenon speaks more clearly of the unconditional love of God than a long, faithful marriage. The passion of the early years fades, of course, but it becomes transmuted into a companionship that can be a blessing not only to the couple but also to others. Jane Fonda published her autobiography a couple of years ago. It is full of explicit detail. (One reviewer said that there were a lot of things in it that we never wanted to know about Jane Fonda.) But I heard her on a television talk show, and that was a different story. She spoke about how she had become a Christian through getting to know former U.S. president Jimmy Carter and his wife, Rosalynn. She said she loved being with people who had been married for four and five decades. She spoke how much she wished she had found a lifelong companion.

A lifelong marriage must survive many trials. I don't mean to romanticize it. It's love against the odds. But marriages are sustained in certain ineffable ways. Marriage is sustained, in part, by that happy, binding memory of the "wife [husband] of your youth," as the book of Proverbs says.

> Drink water from your own cistern,
> flowing water from your own well. . . .
> Let [it] be for yourself alone,
> and not for strangers with you.
> Let your fountain be blessed,
> and rejoice in the wife of your youth. . . .
> Let her affection fill you at all times with delight. . . . (5:15-19)

No human relationship is perfect in this life. If what we've said here makes anyone feel uneasy about what is past, let us state without qualification that the grace of God is retroactive.[11] But since God's love *is* perfect and

---

10. Davis, *Proverbs, Ecclesiastes, and the Song of Songs.*

11. The word *retroactive* used to describe the grace of God is taken from an American novel, *Freedomland,* by Richard Price (New York: Broadway Books, 1998), p. 327. Price's most celebrated

*will be* perfected in the saints, we can affirm the message of the Song of Songs: Human love that is *both* passionate *and* faithful is an image of the covenant God has made with us. It is a covenant distinguished above all by its unconditional nature[12] — for better, for worse; for richer, for poorer; in sickness and in health — and then, in the humanly unimaginable word that comes to us from beyond death, God is faithful to us, beyond our deserving, even unto the Resurrection to eternal life, for "my Love, the Crucified, is raised to life this morrow."

He welcomes you to his banqueting table; his banner over you is love.

AMEN.

---

novels — superficially brutal, profane, and violent — are suffused with Christian ideas. The epigraph for *Freedomland* is Psalm 51:17.

12. Some Old Testament scholars have insisted that the Wisdom literature makes no reference to the covenant. I have chosen to go with the larger theological context, as Barth does.

# Last Month of the Year:
## A Christmas Sermon

---

*Christmas Eve 2007*

> Surely for this word [of death] which they speak there is no dawn.
> They will . . . [look] upward [to the stars], and they will look
> [downward] to the earth, but behold, distress and darkness, the
> gloom of anguish; and they will be thrust into thick darkness. But
> there will be no gloom for her that was in anguish. . . . The people
> that walked in darkness have seen a great light: they that dwell in
> the land of the shadow of death, upon them hath the light shined.
>
> Isaiah 8:20-22; 9:1-2

WHEN I was a child at Christmas, I was keenly aware that there was this
thing called "the midnight service." One of my parents would go to it while
the other one stayed at home with me and my sister. It was clearly understood that when we got old enough, we too would be allowed to go to the
midnight service. It was a very big deal. I will never forget the thrill of going
to that service as a young teenager. It began at eleven, so that everyone was
receiving communion at midnight. It was a rite of passage; faith in Santa
Claus was taken up into faith in the Lord Jesus. Those who attended were
all adults and older children, plus a significant number of college students
— many of whom were a bit inebriated, but never mind. There was a glamour and an excitement about it all that remains with me to this day.[1]

---

1. Unfortunately, this thrill has been lost in recent decades. All over America, parents now

I hope you are glad to be here tonight. This service is late enough to qualify as a "midnight service." I hope some of that midnight thrill remains for you. When it is icy and snowing and dark outside, it is all the more wonderful to be together in the church on Christmas Eve.

But for what purpose do we come together? What brings us here? Is it mostly sentiment, nostalgia, and wishful thinking?

Last week in *The New York Times Book Review* section on children's Christmas books, a reviewer had this to say:

> In terms of plain narrative, the Nativity story is hard to beat. It has pretty much everything: a journey, a baby, a mass murderer, music, animals, refugees, the kindness of strangers, and big, big special effects.[2]

This admirable reviewer then goes on to complain about "sappy," sentimental versions of the biblical story, with all the added paraphernalia of baby angels and little drummer boys. She thinks the story from St. Matthew and St. Luke stands best by itself, and surely we must agree. King Herod, the "mass murderer," needs to be in there somewhere too, to remind us of the nature of the world that the Son of God was born into.

There is a great deal to be learned from the words of the genuine Christmas carols. Everybody loves the tunes, but the words can sometimes be genuine revelations. One of my favorite CDs is *Home for Christmas,* a crossover album by the distinguished classical singer Anne Sophie von Otter. Ms. von Otter is Swedish, and her selections are redolent with the atmosphere of a snowbound land where "the great darkness of the Northern winter" reigns for eighteen hours a day.[3]

The highlight on the disk, for me, is "O Holy Night." We think of this number as the soprano showpiece par excellence, but this version is something else again. Ms. von Otter sings it in the original French, and the words are dramatically different from our familiar English ones. Ours begins, "O holy night! The stars are brightly shining;/it is the night of the dear Savior's birth." This puts us in a mellow mood. The original French words, how-

take their children to services at five P.M. — services which tend to be "dumbed down" or chaotic or both — and consequently, attendance at the far more awe-inspiring "midnight" services has shrunk dramatically. The loss of the college-age students at the later service is especially to be deplored.

2. Sarah Ellis, reviewing Frank McCourt's *Angela and the Baby Jesus* in *The New York Times Book Review,* 16 December 2007.

3. The phrase is from Ms. Von Otter's program notes.

ever, are utterly different. Listen to this; it begins this way: "Minuit, Chrétien, c'est l'heure solennelle. . . ." This means "Midnight, Christians, is the solemn hour. . . ."

You'll agree, I think, that this is a startling contrast to the sweet and gentle "O Holy Night." Moreover, the French words when sung sound even more portentous than they do when spoken; the cadence of the four-syllable word "sol-en-nel-le" evokes the tolling of the bell, as if the Day of Judgment were about to strike. Ms. von Otter deliberately darkens her voice and refuses to give us any of the flamboyant high notes that we have learned to expect and wait for.

This Christmas collection overall has the character of darkness. One of the traditional Swedish songs has the recurrent refrain "No daylight is yet to be seen. . . ." Ms. Von Otter sings the American song "Have Yourself a Merry Little Christmas," but she sings it with an ironic twist, especially when she gets to the line "From now on our troubles will be out of sight." You can tell she doesn't believe a word of it. "For this word which they speak there is no dawn." Something more is needed in our world than wishes. The people look upward to the stars for inspiration, the people look downward to Mother Earth for reassurance, but *for this word which they speak there is no dawn.* Something more is needed here than horoscopes and nature rituals.

*The New Yorker* magazine had a startling cover two weeks ago. At first glance I thought it had something to do with the Three Wise Men because there was a midnight sky full of stars, one very big star, and a yellow desert. On second glance I saw that it had nothing to do with the Wise Men at all. It was a picture of a helicopter, dramatically lit from below by a garish yellow light that could be fires, or an explosion. What I thought was a big star was actually the rotor. The picture shows the two gunners and the pilot of the copter looking out grimly from their posts. Inside there is an equally grim-looking passenger. It's Santa Claus. He's in a war zone. He can't use his sleigh. He has to be transported by a helicopter.[4]

This is the world into which our Savior was born. *For this word which they speak there is no dawn.* Something more is needed here than sentiment.

On the radio one time I heard a breathtaking African-American spiritual that I had never heard before. It had a question-and-answer format, or, rather, a call-and-response format:

4. The Iraq war was in its fifth year with no end in sight.

> What month was my Jesus born in?
> Last month of the year.
> What month? January? No . . . February? No . . . March? No . . .
> *Last* month of the year . . .
> Born of the Virgin Mary.

What does this suggest to you? I think it means that the tide of human possibility was running out. Month after month, we thought that we could fix whatever was wrong. New resolutions, new products, new leaders, new technology, new strategies, new medicines, new regimes — surely we can fix it. Month after month the statistics tell the story: better lives for rich Arab sheiks, worse lives for Chinese peasants. Better lives for Scandinavian welfare recipients, worse lives for Congolese children. Better conditions for Baghdad, worse for Kabul and Islamabad. Put your finger in the dike here, and a leak springs over there. *We look to the stars, we look to the earth, but for this word which we speak there is no dawn.* Human potential has been explored to the nth power, and it is a dead end.

> What month was my Jesus born in?
> Last month of the year.
> What month?
> *Last* month of the year . . .
> Born of the Virgin Mary.

What does this suggest? When the tide of human possibility has run out, divine intervention takes its place. On the stroke of midnight, when the executioner is due at the prison door, there is a blaze of light. At the farthest extremity of human hope, the Lord God Almighty slips into the world in disguise. Last month of the year; born of the Virgin Mary. It is no accident that these words appear at this point in the song: the *Virgin* Mary. The singer wants us to know that a miracle has occurred. The early Christians recognized that Isaiah's prophecies meant that something had happened that had its source in another sphere of power. "The people that walked in darkness have seen a great light."[5]

Notice the words of the hymn that we just sang, "In the Bleak Midwinter." Christina Rossetti wrote this; she was a very interesting woman from a

---

5. To prepare for this sermon, I read *The Struggle to Understand Isaiah as Christian Scripture* by Brevard Childs.

fascinating family. She was of Italian parentage but was herself English, a devout Anglo-Catholic Christian. She wrote the words of this hymn in 1872. Listen to the first two verses:

> In the bleak midwinter, frosty wind made moan,
> Earth stood hard as iron, water like a stone. . . .
> [Barren, fruitless, sterile, closed in, shut down, locked. It's midnight.]

> Our God, heaven cannot hold him, nor earth sustain;
> [*The people look to the stars, they look down to the earth, but from these
> sources there is no dawn.*]
> Heaven and earth shall flee away when he comes to reign.
> In the bleak midwinter [last month of the year], a stable
>     place sufficed
> The Lord God Almighty, Jesus Christ.

And so the prophet Isaiah declares, "The people that walked in darkness have seen a great light: they that dwell in the land of the shadow of death, upon them hath the light shined" (9:2).

Is there anything true in all of this? *The Spectator,* an English magazine, recently asked a whole assortment of prominent people whether they believed in the Virgin Birth of Jesus Christ. One of them was a very well-known clergyman in the Church of England. He said categorically that he didn't believe it. He explained that it was "probably legendary." Another English intellectual said contemptuously, "You are going to have a hard time finding any educated person who believes it."

But lying at the heart of the entire Jewish-Christian enterprise are the words at the end of our Scripture lesson from Isaiah: "The zeal of the Lord of hosts will perform this" (9:7). If we do not believe that God does things, performs things, accomplishes things according to his purpose, then the whole story collapses. This is what faith knows: Heaven cannot hold our God, nor earth sustain him. In the last month of the year, "a stable place sufficed [for the birth of] the Lord God Almighty, Jesus Christ." When the very last human hope is gone, *the people that walked in darkness have seen a great light; they that dwell in the land of the shadow of death, upon them hath the light shined.*

Back to the midnight service. Most of us here tonight are far past the age of wishing we could be with the grown-ups. We *are* the grown-ups. We don't necessarily like that. We would rather be back in January, or February, with our futures lying open before us. Frankly, at this point in my life I'd settle for October.

At precisely this point in our lives, whoever we are and wherever we are in our struggles, whatever our disappointments and failures, whatever our anxieties and fears, this Word arrives. In the last month of the year, at the last tick of the clock, at the bottom of the world's midnight, the message comes: Our future is in God through the Lord Jesus Christ, born of the Virgin Mary, "God of God, Light of Light, very God of very God, begotten, not created." These heavens and this earth will flee away, and as the book of Revelation promises, we will receive a new heaven and a new earth. There is no human possibility here. This is the impossibility of God.

> There will be no gloom for her that was in anguish. . . . The people
> that walked in darkness have seen a great light: they that dwell in
> the land of the shadow of death, upon them hath the light shined.
> The zeal of the Lord of hosts will perform this.

AMEN.

# God's Alien Work in the World

Isaiah 28:21; Psalm 88

*Two versions of this sermon were delivered several years apart in very different settings. In a preached sermon, the quotations from Antony Flew and Basil Mitchell would have to be abbreviated. Here, in this written form, I have included almost all of the two parables, since the more of them one hears, the more striking they are.*

. . . . . . . . . . . . . . . . .

IN THE forties and fifties, a group of British philosophers, some of whom were Christians (if you can imagine that) and some not, undertook an extended conversation which produced a publication called *New Essays in Philosophical Theology.* Intellectual fashions being what they are, it is all considered by the academy to be quite passé now, but Christians are constantly in the process of discovering that the old has become new again.

Today's text from the prophet Isaiah comes from a long, challenging section about the mystery of God's ways. One particular verse reads as follows:

The Lord will rise up as on Mount Perazim;
he will be wrathful as in the valley of Gibeon;
to do his deed — strange is his deed!
and to work his work — alien is his work! (Isa. 28:21)

A traditional theological interpretation of this passage speaks of a God whose "proper work" *(opus proprium)* of blessing is often concealed behind his "alien work" *(opus alienum)* of rejecting. Alternatively, we may speak metaphorically of God's two hands: his right hand of creating and redeeming is sometimes hidden in his left hand of judging and destroying.

This brings us back to *New Essays in Philosophical Theology.*[1] The book contains a fascinating exchange between Antony Flew, an atheist, and Basil Mitchell, a Christian. Flew's purpose is to show that all arguments for the existence of a benevolent God break down under close scrutiny. He tells a parable about a Believer who argues for faith in the existence of a gardener who tends his garden lovingly, but has never been seen. The Believer and the Skeptic set all sorts of traps, including an electric fence, but are unable to find any trace of a gardener. The Believer continues to insist that there must be one, even though the garden is full of weeds:

> But there is a gardener, invisible, intangible, insensible to electric shocks, a gardener who has no scent and makes no sound, a gardener who comes secretly to look after the garden which he loves.

At last the Skeptic says in exasperation,

> But what remains of your original assertion? How does what you call an invisible, intangible, eternally elusive gardener differ from an imaginary gardener or even from no gardener at all?

In a well-known formulation, Flew in his role as the Skeptic then asserts:

> A fine brash hypothesis may thus be killed by inches, the death by a thousand qualifications.

He goes on:

> Someone tells us that God loves us as a father loves his children. We are reassured. But then we see a child dying of inoperable cancer of

1. *New Essays in Philosophical Theology,* ed. Antony Flew and Alasdair MacIntyre (New York: Macmillan, American paperback edition, 1964).

the throat. His earthly father is driven frantic in his efforts to help, but his Heavenly Father reveals no obvious signs of concern. Some qualification is made — God's love is "not merely a human love," or "it is an inscrutable love," perhaps. . . . We are reassured again. But then perhaps we ask: What is this assurance of God's (appropriately qualified) love worth? What would have to happen . . . to entitle us to say "God does not love us," or even "God does not exist"?[2]

This parable came up in conversation in a group recently, when this question was posed: Is it true that for the mature Christian believer, nothing can shake his confidence in God's providence — nothing at all? A child is born with a strange disease and receives marvelous healing; God obviously loves the child. The child grows and, as a teenager, makes a profession of faith in Christ; obviously, God loves the child. Then the child develops cancer. Still, the parents insist, God loves the child. The cancer goes into remission, which clearly demonstrates the loving care of God. Prayers of thanksgiving are said, offerings are made, testimonies are given, God's mercy is glorified. Then the cancer returns and kills the child. This time, the parents divide. The father still insists that somehow, somewhere, though there is no evidence at all, the invisible, intangible, inscrutable God still loves the child (and the child's parents). It is different for the mother. She refuses to believe any longer. The affirmation that a loving God benevolently directs the lives of his children, for her, has died the death of a thousand qualifications.

I think we need to take Flew's parable and its challenges very seriously. American Christianity today, especially in evangelical settings, tends to feature personal testimonies about blessings received and victories gained, with the expectation that listeners will be awed into faith in God. But what happens when the blessings dry up and no victories are apparent? Presumably the Christian community continues to affirm its faith. But the Skeptic continues to rear his head, asking insistently, "What would have to occur . . . to constitute for you a disproof of the love of God?"

This is the sort of trap that any Christian gets into when trying to defend God. Those of us who don't care for apologetics — the type of theological approach that tries to give rational, intellectually convincing reasons for belief in Christianity, or the existence of a loving God — believe this is a fruitless endeavor that convinces no one except those who are already look-

2. *New Essays in Philosophical Theology,* pp. 96-99.

[ 227 ]

ing for reasons to believe. In the essay collection, the Skeptic, represented by Antony Flew, is debated by Basil Mitchell, the Believer, who knows better than to be drawn into the apologetic trap set by the parable that Flew tells. Mitchell, a philosopher-theologian from Oxford, responds with a parable of his own, but first with an introduction:

> Flew's [essay] is searching and perceptive, but there is, I think, something odd about his conduct of the theologian's case. The theologian surely would not deny that the fact of pain counts against the assertion that God loves men [*sic*]. This very incompatibility generates the most intractable of theological problems — the problem of evil. So the theologian does recognize the fact of pain as counting against Christian doctrine. But it is true that he will not allow it — or anything — to count decisively against it, for he is committed by his faith to trust in God.

Then Mitchell tells a parable of his own:

> In time of war in an occupied country, a member of the resistance meets one night a stranger who deeply impresses him. They spend that night together in conversation. The Stranger tells the partisan that he himself is on the side of the resistance — indeed, that he is in command of it, and urges the partisan to have faith in him no matter what happens. The partisan is utterly convinced at that meeting of the Stranger's sincerity and constancy and undertakes to trust him.
>
> They never meet in conditions of intimacy again. But sometimes the Stranger is seen helping members of the resistance, and the partisan is grateful and says to his friends, "He is on our side."
>
> Sometimes he is seen in the uniform of the police handing over patriots to the occupying power. On these occasions his friends murmur against him; but the partisan still says, "He is on our side." He still believes that, in spite of appearances, the Stranger did not deceive him. Sometimes he asks the Stranger for help and receives it. He is then thankful. Sometimes he asks and does not receive it. Then he says, "The Stranger knows best. . . ."
>
> The partisan in the parable does not allow anything to count decisively against the proposition, "The Stranger is on our side." This is because he has committed himself to trust the Stranger. But he of course recognizes that the Stranger's ambiguous behavior does count

against what he believes about him. It is precisely this situation which constitutes the trial of his faith.[3]

We are accustomed to thinking of the absence of God in existential terms, a peculiar malady arising in the twentieth century, leaving us abandoned in a fashion akin to that of the bitter, angry minister and his tiny, pitiful congregation in Ingmar Bergman's *Winter Light*. We think of "modern man" as raging against oblivion like a character in Camus or Beckett. We forget that the Bible takes the absence of God with ultimate seriousness; Psalm 88 begins and ends in the utter silence of God, the *deus absconditus*:

> For my soul is full of troubles,
>    and my life draws near to Sheol.
> I am reckoned among those who go down to the Pit;
>    I am a man who has no strength,
>       like one forsaken among the dead. . . . (88:3-4)

> O Lord, why dost thou cast me off?
>    Why dost thou hide thy face from me?
> . . . Thy wrath has swept over me;
>    thy dread assaults destroy me.
> Thou hast caused lover and friend to shun me;
>    my companions are in darkness. (88:14, 16-18)

Whoever put the book of Psalms together saw no need to soften this or give it a happy ending. It is bleak from beginning to end. It begins in the shadow of death and it ends there, in abandonment. Surely a Christian, reading this, will think of the last hours of Christ; but at the same time, this is a Psalm that can be recommended to anyone who doubts the loving care of God and finds no evidence for his presence. As in the case of the partisan in Mitchell's parable, the evidence is overwhelming in the other direction. Yet, like the Psalmist, the partisan hangs on, addressing what must seem like a totally absent God.

How long can the partisan go on like this? "I don't think one can say in advance," Mitchell writes:

---

3. *New Essays in Philosophical Theology*, pp. 96-99.

It will depend on the nature of the impression created by the Stranger in the first place. It will depend, too, on the manner in which he takes the Stranger's behavior . . . it quite obviously won't do for him to say easily, "Oh, when used of the Stranger the phrase 'is on our side' *means* ambiguous behavior of this sort." In that case he would be like the religious man who says blandly of a terrible disaster, "It is God's will." No, he will only be regarded as sane and reasonable in his belief *if he experiences in himself the full force of the conflict.*[4]

In this context, the words of Isaiah are particularly striking:

The Lord will rise up . . .
he will be wrathful . . .
to do his deed — strange is his deed!
and to work his work — alien is his work!

The prophet who wrote that was not speaking in a detached, philosophical way. He knew something in his own person about God's alien work. "He has experienced in himself the full force of the conflict." The wrath of God and the absence of God are familiar to the prophets and Wisdom writers of the Old Testament. In fact, the Old Testament scholar Samuel Terrien argues that the theme of the God who hides himself *(deus absconditus)* binds the Old Testament together.[5] This is an extraordinarily mature theme which takes the human condition and human questioning seriously. We are not asked to gloss over the ambiguities and negation in the life of the world. Our objections and protests are acknowledged, for no one knows the anguish of God's strange work as well as those who have trusted in him. The book of Job is an extended protest against the divine ways. The book of Ecclesiastes is almost entirely written from the perspective of the seeming absence of God. The book of Habakkuk is centered on the question of why God acts as he does and so often withdraws altogether. The paradoxes and challenges of faith are a threat to everything we believe. But the Bible is not written for philosophers to debate in seminar rooms. The Bible addresses itself to those who know the dread of a deathly conflict.

4. *New Essays in Philosophical Theology,* pp. 96-99. I am indebted to Joel Marcus, now professor of New Testament at the Duke Divinity School, for long ago calling my attention to the Flew-Mitchell exchange.

5. Samuel Terrien, *The Elusive Presence* (Eugene, Ore.: Wipf & Stock, 2000).

In those circumstances and under those conditions the Bible introduces the Stranger to us as the One who is indeed on our side. The Bible
does not attempt to defend the proposition. The Scriptures do not give us
any arguments for proof of God's goodness and trustworthiness. The Bible
simply declares him to us, and from time to time his mighty acts of the past
are recalled as the foundation of faith. The prophets testify that even when
God's actions seem most strange and most alien, God is on our side.

And in the fulfillment of time, Jesus Christ, the only begotten Son, came
down into our perilous, death-dealing world and *experienced in himself the
full force of the conflict.* It is because of this that we trust him in spite of what
seems to us much of the time to be his alien work. As the evangelist John proclaims, "No one has ever seen God; the only Son, who is in the bosom of the
Father, he has made him known." In Jesus Christ, God has shown us himself
in his fullness: "The Word became flesh and dwelt among us, full of grace and
truth; we have beheld his glory, glory as of the only Son from the Father . . .
and from his fullness have we all received, grace upon grace" (John 1:15-16, 18).

The writers of Scripture are not philosophers; they are theologians
(*theos:* God; *logos:* word). The theologian does not seek to prove or demonstrate beyond a shadow of a doubt. The theologian works from the perspective of the Word of God and is therefore bound in certain ways to continue
speaking *of* God and *to* God even when there is no evidence, just like the
Psalmist in Psalm 88. Theology, therefore, is a work undertaken in faith —
just as Basil Mitchell says. The theologian recognizes and acknowledges the
fact of pain and understands that it counts against belief in Christian doctrine. But he or she "will not allow [the fact of pain] — or anything [else] —
to count decisively against his belief, for he is committed by his faith to
trust in God."

Twenty-two years ago, George Britt, a pastor in Dallas, lost an eleven-
year-old son to scleroderma. In 2007, another son was murdered. The week
after that son's funeral, Britt found out that he has prostate cancer. He has
concluded that there is no theological explanation sufficient to make him
understand the losses he's experienced. Yet, he says, "I choose to stubbornly
believe that God is good. The book of Psalms is punctuated throughout
with these words: 'The Lord is good,' and there are no qualifiers. . . . I
choose to stubbornly cling to that unqualified goodness — even when
things that happen to me are not good."[6]

That man speaks for many who know God, from Isaiah and Job in the

---

6. DallasNews.com, September 25, quoted in *The Christian Century,* 18 November 2008.

Old Testament to the New Testament apostles Peter and Paul, both of them given up to death in the name of Christ. They never ceased to testify: God is good. They still tell the living story of the Stranger who is on our side. We have met him in the Word, in the Lord's Supper, and in the faith of others, and in those meetings we are "utterly convinced . . . of the Stranger's sincerity and constancy and [we have undertaken] to trust him." May the Lord of life and death strengthen you in that undertaking and give you unshakeable confidence that, even in the midst of his strange and alien work, the purpose that will determine the outcome is inseparable from himself, for his goodness and mercy endure forever.

AMEN.

# God's Right and Left Hands

## GRACE CHURCH IN NEW YORK

*Wednesday night sermon, August 1989*                                    Isaiah 28

THIS IS another sermon in a sequence from Isaiah 28. I admit to being fascinated by this text. All my life I have been gripped by the problem of evil and suffering. These are the kinds of questions that disturb me and many other Christians:

Why does God allow evil?
Why do some people suffer so much, while others seem to glide through life?
Why do so many prayers go unanswered?
If God is in control, why are so many things out of control?

More and more, as I have thought about these questions, I have been drawn to Isaiah 28.

The prophet Isaiah, who was an aristocrat born to privilege, could not have foreseen the kind of life God called him into. Instead of enjoying the comforts and privileges of upper-class life, Isaiah had to spend his entire adulthood preaching to the people about sin and judgment. Of course, that's not *all* that he preached. Please do not think of the Old Testament prophets as harsh and judgmental. There is just as much good news in the Old Testament as in the New Testament, and a lot of it has the additional advantage of being written in poetry. It is no accident that Isaiah is the prophet of the Christmas season — his matchless Messianic prophecies are among the glories of the Christian tradition.

But there can be no denying the fact that Isaiah had a hard message to bring to the people. In a way, his message is no help to us in dealing with the problem of evil, because it is so clear from his preaching that the people of God fully deserved the catastrophe that was to come upon them. They had ceased to trust in the one true God, they had made "a covenant with death" (28:15), and they were "grinding the faces of the poor" (3:15). So the Assyrian invasion, which Isaiah warned against, was a logical consequence of Israel's disloyalty to her God.

But the prophet's words have a wider application. More and more, when I read and hear about awful things happening, I find myself thinking in the terms that Isaiah used. I'm speaking specifically of these verses:

> The Lord will rise up, as he did at Mount Perazim;
> he will rouse himself, as in the valley of Gibeon,
> to do his work, his strange work,
>   and perform his task, his alien task. (28:21)

God's strange work, his alien work — these are terms that have proven to be theologically fruitful. As we've explained before, Martin Luther drew upon this text to develop the idea that God has *proper work (opus proprium)* and *alien work (opus alienum)*. The easiest and most picturesque way of talking about this is in terms of God's right hand and God's left hand. This imagery comes from the Old Testament also; throughout the Hebrew Bible, God's work of deliverance and salvation is referred to as the work of his strong right hand and his outstretched arm. So it makes sense to think of his work of judgment as the work of his strong *left* hand. (I apologize to all the left-handed people present for what must seem to you to be a very unjust metaphor.)

Now it's interesting that God's right and left hands are perceived differently by different groups of people. If there is an airplane crash and some passengers survive while others are killed, the survivors will sometimes say, "God saved me." That's God's right hand at work; we can almost get a sense of it in a literal way, as if God had reached right down into the wreckage and snatched this person out. But what of the person in the next seat who was not saved? His grieving relatives will not see God's right hand at work.

In the book of Exodus, we have the wonderful poem called "The Song of Moses." Moses and the Israelites, having been delivered from Pharaoh's army at the Red Sea, sing a hymn of praise to God:

"Who among the gods is like you, O Lord?
Majestic in holiness, awesome in glory, working wonders —
you stretched out your right hand and the earth swallowed up
    [the Egyptians]." (Exod. 15:11-12)

This is all very well from the standpoint of the Israelites, but we can be sure that the Egyptians did not experience this in the same way. We might say that, to the Egyptians, it is God's *left* hand.

This is a familiar subject for us who are Southerners. For a hundred years or more, Southerners were preoccupied with having lost the Civil War. For white Southerners, their defeat seemed like the work of God's left hand. Black Southerners have seen it very differently; for them, clearly, it was the right hand of deliverance. Then, too, there was an additional complicating factor: generals and soldiers and families and elected officials on both sides, North and South, Blue and Gray, were on their knees throughout the war praying to the same God. So you see the problem.

Studying the Bible and trying to make sense of it in our own lives has been called "thinking God's thoughts after him." The Bible is unique among books because it is written *from God's point of view*. Let's pause over that for a moment, because it is a staggering claim. That claim could not be made if it were not for one conviction: *that God has truly revealed himself in his Word*. If it is true, then the Bible — despite the assertions of a great many textual critics and historians of religion — is written not from the point of view of North or South, Israel or Egypt, Jew or Gentile, but from God's point of view. And God knows what he is doing with his right hand and what he is doing with his left. We don't, but he does. And it is God's right hand that does his proper work, his ultimate work. His left hand is doing his *penultimate* work, his alien work, the work of judgment that will finally be taken up into his saving work, the work of his right hand.

This view, I know, raises many questions. We are not addressing the problem of radical evil tonight.[1] It isn't possible in a short sermon like this to go into all the vexed issues and distressing convolutions. But taking this view has the great virtue of allowing for the perplexity and grief and pain that is suffered on all sides in times of disaster. It is much better than saying either "This was God's will" or "God isn't in control."

---

1. A long chapter on the problem of radical evil, which requires a recovery of the symbol of Satan, is planned for my forthcoming book on the crucifixion. The reader is referred to David Bentley Hart's *The Doors of the Sea* (Grand Rapids: Wm. B. Eerdmans, 2005).

About a decade ago, a great American university had a vacancy in its chapel. Friends of mine who were evangelicals have told me that they sat up all night in a prayer vigil, asking that the Lord send the candidate of his choice. One of them was duly elected, and within a few months he had instituted new policies, such as removing the cross from the chapel for certain services, and omitting the name of Jesus from the prayers on occasion. One of my acquaintances said, in genuine bewilderment, "We prayed all night long, so it must be God's choice; I just don't understand it."

I have spent years of thinking about this, and it seems to me that a way of interpreting it might be as a work of God's left hand. Had he abandoned the Christians who prayed? Had he allowed the Cross to be denigrated? Had he chosen the wrong man? It seems to me that Isaiah's extraordinarily rich, subtle, comprehensive view of history can help here. It is a story told not from the Israelites' point of view or from the invading Assyrians' point of view, but from God's point of view. And God was going to use the Assyrians in his plan whether they knew of it or not. Think of that — what an honor to be used in God's plan without even knowing about it! Maybe that is true of you and me too, and of our enemies at the office and on the playing fields — and even in the churches and chapels.

Every one of you is either going to face these kinds of problems someday, or you are facing them already. You are going to wonder where God is, why he doesn't act, why he seems to do the exact opposite of what you asked, why everything goes wrong. You are going to ask why your most precious dreams burst like bubbles, why your fondest hopes vanished into the air, why your greatest enthusiasms evaporated into bitter disappointments. I do not have an answer for these questions, but I do have a testimony. I believe it is better to be in God's left hand than in the devil's right. I believe it is better to trust the Lord's *alien* work than to give yourself over to the *proper* work of some other lord, some other god. I believe that our greatest sorrow and most excruciating pain are better delivered into the Lord's care than clutched angrily to oneself. He is God. He is righteous, and just, and merciful, and good, and someday we will see that he is. Several decades of wrestling with these questions have deepened my conviction that *both* of the Lord's hands can be trusted. For, as we read in Isaiah 28:29,

All this also comes from the Lord almighty, wonderful in counsel and magnificent in wisdom.

AMEN.

# God's Alien Work in the Church

*November 2003*                                         Isaiah 28:14-22

*This sermon addresses the divisions in the Anglican commu-*
*nion and the American mainline denominations. It was de-*
*livered at Wycliffe College, an Anglican institution in the*
*University of Toronto School of Theology.*

. . . . . . . . . . . . . . . . . .

ON THIS Sunday just past, the last of the Christian year, we focused on Isaiah 10:22 — "Destruction is decreed, overflowing with righteousness." Our
text this weekday, in between the last and the first, continues that theme
from Isaiah, the prophet most associated with Advent and Christmas:

> Therefore hear the word of the Lord, you scoffers, who rule this peo-
> ple in Jerusalem! Because you have said, "We have made a covenant
> with death, and with Sheol we have an agreement; when the over-
> whelming scourge passes through it will not come to us; for we have
> made lies our refuge, and in falsehood we have taken shelter"; there-
> fore thus says the Lord, "Behold, I am laying in Zion for a founda-
> tion a stone, a tested stone, a precious cornerstone, of a sure founda-
> tion: 'He who believes will not be in haste.' And I will make justice
> the line, and righteousness the plummet; and hail will sweep away
> the refuge of lies, and waters will overwhelm the shelter."

[ 237 ]

Then your covenant with death will be annulled, and your agreement with Sheol will not stand; when the overwhelming scourge passes through you will be beaten down by it. As often as it passes through it will take you; for morning by morning it will pass through, by day and by night; and it will be sheer terror to understand the message. . . .

For the Lord will rise up as on Mount Perazim, he will be wroth as in the valley of Gibeon; to do his deed — strange is his deed! and to work his work — alien is his work! Now therefore do not scoff, lest your bonds be made strong; for I have heard a decree of destruction from the Lord God of hosts upon the whole land. (Isa. 28:14-22)

For most of the year the lectionary avoids the note of judgment that runs all through the Old Testament and the New. When you students get out of here, I hope you will remind your congregations that a wrathful Old Testament God has not been replaced by a loving New Testament God. This misapprehension is remarkably widespread. Not only does it lend itself subtly to anti-Semitism; it is also manifestly untrue. This coming Sunday we will hear words of judgment from the mouth of Jesus, as we always do on the first Sunday of Advent. For although the designers of the lectionary deleted wrath and judgment from most the readings for most of the year, Advent has gotten the best of them. We can thank the Middle Ages for this. I commend the medieval carols to you with their unexpurgated references to Satan, hell, wrath, and judgment.

In a time of great unease in the church and in the world, the Word of the Lord according to Isaiah lays down this assurance for us: "Behold, I am laying in Zion for a foundation a stone, a tested stone, a precious cornerstone, of a sure foundation." When the early Christians read this, they were in no doubt about what the Lord God meant by this. The cornerstone, the foundation that was laid, was Jesus Christ. But this great affirmation came with a complicating factor. Both Peter and Paul interpret the cornerstone saying the same way: "Behold, I am laying in Zion a stone that will make men stumble, a rock that will make them fall" (1 Pet. 2:7-8; Rom. 9:33). The coming of Christ divides. It caused a crisis then, and it continues to cause a crisis now. We would rather make "a covenant with death" than "crown him with many crowns."

As a visitor I will tell you that I am troubled. I am troubled (as you are) about the divisions within the church on our continent, and I am worried about the mood in the American body politic. The shouting and name-calling on television, the self-righteous attitudes in the church, the increasing polarization and closing of channels of civilized communication in both church and society — all of this is alarming. It is increasingly obvious that the popular message "God loves everybody" and "Jesus accepts everybody" is simply inadequate to the biblical witness. God *does* love everybody, but that is not the whole story. Jesus did accept everybody — or did he? What about those religious leaders whom he called "whitewashed sepulchers," to whom he said, "Ye serpents, ye generation of vipers, how can ye escape the damnation of hell?" (Matt. 23:33). The biblical message is a great deal more complicated than "Jesus accepts everybody."

> Destruction is decreed, overflowing with righteousness. . . .
>     The Lord will rise up as on Mount Perazim, he will be wroth as in the valley of Gibeon; to do his deed — strange is his deed! and to work his work — alien is his work! Now therefore do not scoff, lest your bonds be made strong; for I have heard a decree of destruction from the Lord God of hosts upon the whole land.

Increased attention has been given lately to the subject of Abraham Lincoln as a theological thinker. It is no exaggeration to say that, although he was not academically trained, he can stand alongside the giants of Christian intellectual and moral history in any language. A book appeared last year which discusses his amazing theological insights. It's called *Lincoln's Greatest Speech: The Second Inaugural,* and it was written by Ronald White, who is the president of the San Francisco Theological Seminary.[1] It has many wonderful things in it, but the most important for my purposes in the present situation is its emphasis on Lincoln's theological struggle to understand what God was doing about slavery and the American Civil War. Much of this thinking is found in his essay "Meditation on the Divine Will," which bears many readings:

> In great contests each party claims to act in accordance with the will of God. Both *may* be, and one *must* be wrong. God can not be *for* and *against* the same thing at the same time. In the present civil war it is quite possible that God's purpose is something different from the purpose of either party — and yet the human instrumentalities, working just as they do, are of the best adaptation to effect His purpose. I am almost ready to say this is probably true — that God wills this contest, and wills that it should not end yet. By his mere quiet

---

1. Since this was written in 2003, White's work on Lincoln's theological depth has become widely accepted as authoritative.

power, on the minds of the now contestants, He could have either *saved* or *destroyed* the Union without a human contest. Yet the contest began. And having begun He could give the final victory to either side any day. Yet the contest proceeds. . . .

Alongside this I want to set another quotation. In 1864, when it was beginning to look as though the North would prevail over the South, a delegation of Kentuckians came to see Lincoln at the White House to ask him why he had changed his mind about slavery. Apparently he satisfied them because they returned home without protest. Soon after he wrote a letter to one of them, a newspaper editor. He said this:

> In telling this tale I attempt no compliment to my own sagacity. I claim not to have controlled events, but confess plainly that events have controlled me. Now, at the end of three years' struggle the nation's condition is not what either party, or any man devised or expected. God alone can claim it. Whither it is tending seems plain. If God now wills the removal of a great wrong, and wills also that we of the North as well as you of the South, shall pay fairly for our complicity in that wrong, impartial history will find therein new cause to attest and revere the justice and goodness of God.

I think you will agree that there have not been any words of that depth from the White House in a long time. The death of Lincoln cost the defeated American South the best friend they could possibly have had. Yet who can doubt that the president, had he known what lay before him, would still have found cause to attest and revere the justice and goodness of God? "Destruction is decreed, overflowing with righteousness."

You will recognize that we are dealing here with the very deepest matters in the Christian faith. Not many will be willing to grapple with these ideas as Lincoln did. Yet there may be some of you here today who will feel called to this task. One who did was Martin Luther. He fastened upon the text from Isaiah that I have read today.

> The Lord will rise up as on Mount Perazim, he will be wroth as in the valley of Gibeon; to do his deed — strange is his deed! and to work his work — alien is his work!

Because of Luther, this passage has been enshrined in the pantheon of significant theological concepts. He gave these concepts Latin names. The alien work of God he called the *opus alienum Dei,* to be contrasted with God's proper work, the *opus proprium Dei.* Sometimes these are referred to as the works of God's left hand and the work of God's right hand. His right hand is often stretched out in the Old Testament for the work of deliverance and salvation. The victories of God on Mount Perazim and in the valley of Gibeon were right-handed works. But now, Isaiah says, the Lord is going to come after Israel with his left hand, in judgment and divine wrath — the *opus alienum,* the alien work, the strange work of God.

This complex of ideas comes from the most radical strain in Christian theology, the mother lode mined by St. Paul in Romans 9–11 when he concluded, "For God has consigned all men to disobedience, that he may have mercy upon all" (11:32). If we could take this text to heart, it would indeed point toward a breakthrough in our common life.

Yesterday I had lunch with a group of clergy and laypeople from a local parish of an evangelical persuasion. For a while the conversation revolved around the state of the church, the marginalization of evangelicals, the blindness of the liberals, and so forth. But then an amazing thing happened. The people from the evangelical parish began to talk about the works of mercy being performed by one of the neighboring "liberal," "revisionist" parishes. By the standard of Matthew 25, they said, the standard of feeding the hungry and visiting the prisoners, the liberal parish was among the "sheep," and their own church was among the "goats."[2] It was one of the most authentically humble confessions I have heard in the church in a long time. Mind you, it did not signal a backing off of commitment to classical Christianity in any way, but the willingness to admit shortcomings and to honor the witness of others was surely a hint of a way forward in the spirit of Christ, who bade us take up the Cross.

One of the crosses that the evangelical community has to bear is the disdain of the other wings of the church. I know something about this. Maybe *disdain* is not the right word. Maybe *dismissal* is more like it. But surely that is part of our vocation. It looks as if God wills this contest to continue. In that respect, his right hand is well hidden in his left. His work feels alien. I do not think any of us know where this will all lead. But God *has laid in Zion a foundation stone, a tested stone, a precious cornerstone* for the most alien work of all was the Cross of Christ, the stumbling stone. The proper work of God — the creation *ex nihilo,* the Second Exodus, and the Resurrection of the dead — did not come about

2. The Parable of the Sheep and Goats in the Last Judgment was another text for the day.

through any means that the religious sensibility of human beings could ever have devised.

> No eye has seen, nor ear heard, nor the heart of man conceived, what God has prepared for those who love him. (1 Cor. 2:9)

Living with the left hand of God calls for a humility beyond what is possible for us without divine revelation. As Paul also wrote to the Corinthians,

> Since, in the wisdom of God, the world did not know God through [worldly] wisdom, it pleased God through the foolishness of what we preach to save those who believe. Jews demand signs and Greeks seek wisdom, but we preach Christ crucified, a stumbling block to Jews and folly to Gentiles, but to those who are called, both Jews and Greeks, Christ the power of God and the wisdom of God. (1 Cor. 2:23-24)

Last week, a woman who has known suffering said to me, "When we cannot see God's hand, we trust his heart." Yes. We know the heart of God because we know Christ crucified, the center of "the foolishness of what we preach, but to those who are called, Christ the power of God and the wisdom of God."

Beloved of God: remember this. You will often feel overwhelmed by God's strange work. You will be buffeted by it, and you will not understand it. It will be for you the left hand of God. But it is better to be struck by the left hand of God than to think that God has no plan. It is better to trust him even in the darkest night than to renounce the Scriptures and conclude that he is impotent. It is better to hurl imprecations at God than it is to trust in "the covenant with death and the agreement with Sheol." We are promised in God's own Word that over and under and through his alien work, his proper work is being perfected.

We do not know how our contests will play out. It is our part to heed the call of God as he gives us light, knowing that though we may be mistaken, God is not mistaken. To follow him in humility, to steel ourselves for the lifelong battle, to serve him in the darkest hours of the night, to trust his right hand when all we can see is his left, "to attest and revere the justice and goodness of God" — this is our high calling. May you always be strengthened and comforted by the knowledge that when *destruction is decreed,* it *overflows with the righteousness of God.*

AMEN.

# Rising Up against the Grave

---

*August 1989*                                                    Isaiah 28:14-22

I DON'T like the way that God runs this world, do you? If I were running it instead of God, there would be no such thing as child abuse. There would be no crack and no homeless people. There would be no mental illness, no alcoholism, no pollution, no racial prejudice, no violence, no war.

Let's see — I could really get into this — if I ran the world, there wouldn't be any heavy metal or self-help books or typographical errors. Everybody would listen to Bach and speak perfect English and raise children with perfect manners and read *War and Peace* from morning to night. I don't need to go on, do I — you are already beginning to get the idea. The most obvious case in point, since I am the editor of the Grace Church bulletin: How come there are so many typographical errors in it? About a year ago, I wrote a fan letter to the editor of a magazine, congratulating him on his proofreaders. About a month after I wrote, the magazine started having all sorts of typos, and it's been that way ever since. So much for the idea of my running the world. Fitz Allison said years ago that typos in the Grace Church bulletin just show that we're human.

Maybe the basic message of the Bible is simply this — Thus says the Lord: I'm God, and you're not. We don't like that, but at least there is a simple clarity about it. *There is a God, and he is not us.* This fundamental declaration divides the God of the Bible sharply from the so-called gods of popular religion, especially the god *within* the creation, the god *within* the self, of which we are hearing so much these days. This distinction is a principal theme of the prophet Isaiah, through whom the Lord declares,

[ 243 ]

✳ "My thoughts are not your thoughts,
  neither are my ways your ways, says the Lord.
As the heavens are higher than the earth,
  so are my ways higher than your ways
  and my thoughts than your thoughts. . . ." (Isa. 55:8-9)

Even the most earnest and most well-intentioned Christians frequently fail to recognize this distinction between God and ourselves. We don't read the Old Testament prophets as often as we should. We have not reflected on the first two commandments as much as we might:

✳ "I am the Lord your God. . . . You shall have no other gods but me."
  "You shall not make for yourself a graven image, or any likeness of anything that is in heaven above or in earth beneath or in the waters under the earth; you shall not bow down to them or serve them, for I the Lord your God am a jealous god." (Exod. 20:1, 4-5)

If we don't do anything else this morning, we will do well if we ponder this one thought: There is one God, and only one. He is known as YHWH, the Lord of Hosts; the Father of Abraham, Isaac, and Jacob; the God and Father of our Lord Jesus Christ. Isaiah calls him "the Holy One of Israel." You can see for yourselves how specific all these titles are. You will never hear any New Age people call God by any of his true names. Why is that? It is because calling God by his true name puts limits on our messing around with the idea of who he is. We do not arrive at the name of God by intuition or imagination or religious consciousness; it is revealed by God himself. The name of God tells us who he is. He names himself: I AM WHO I AM (Exod. 3:14). This means we are not free to imagine him in any way we like. If we are truly to know him, we must stay within the boundaries that he himself has fixed, and this means recognizing that he alone is the Creator, whereas we are mere creatures. We are not creators — or even co-creators, as the current terminology has it; we are distinct from him in that respect above all. God remains separate from what he has made; contrary to popular belief, he has not infused the creation with his divine life. The creation *praises* God, as the Psalms beautifully tell us, and Isaiah — "The mountains and the hills before you shall break forth into singing, and all the trees of the field shall clap their hands" (Isa. 55:10-12) — but God is not *in* the creation. Unlike God, the creation is mortal. God is *involved,* intimately involved, with his creation, but he is not *part of* it. If we can get this right, we will be fortified for the rest of our lives with a true understanding of God that has been the bedrock of the Hebrew traditions from the beginning.

Along with this understanding comes another that is closely related to it. The God who is really God is Lord over his creation and has the right to do anything with it that he wishes. Again, we don't like it, but it does make logical sense. Jeremiah and St. Paul both put it roughly this way: If a potter is making a pot out of clay, he can make it any way he wants. He doesn't have to make a good pot; he can make a bad pot if he wants (Jer. 18:1-6; Rom. 9:19-23). The point that Jeremiah and Paul are both making is that the potter has total right over the clay. Isaiah says the same thing:

> "Woe to him who strives with his Maker, an earthen vessel with the potter! Does the clay say to him who fashions it, 'What are you making?' or 'Your work has no handles'? [I think this is supposed to be funny.] Woe to him who says to a father, 'What are you begetting?' or to a woman, 'With what are you in travail?'" Thus says the Lord, the Holy One of Israel, and his Maker: "Will you question me about my children, or command me concerning the work of my hands? I made the earth, and created man upon it; it was my hands that stretched out the heavens, and I commanded all their host." (Isa. 45:9-12)

But, of course, we *do* say "Your work has no handles." We say to God, "What have you done?" We tell him that we could have done it better. We shake our fists at the heavens and protest against God's ways in the world. Most especially we object when there is serious injustice, random suffering, unpunished villainy. Thank God for the witness of Jeremiah and some of the Psalms; from them we learn that we may indeed lift up our voices to rail against God, to bring our accusations before him. The important thing to remember is that we complain to *him*, not to some other false or imagined god.

I have plenty of complaints against God this week. That's why I began this sermon the way I did; I don't like the way God runs the world. It is true that I have learned the hard way that it's a good thing *I* don't run it — a Christian learns that by taking a hard look at her own sins, failures, and liabilities. Some of you are helping me to do that! Still, the age-old question remains: If God is the kind of god we think he is — merciful, loving, and good — then why is he allowing so many horrors to take place?

Friday's paper contained a description of the death of Yusef Hawkins, the young black man who was killed by the gang of white youths in Bensonhurst. A neighborhood woman, white, named Elizabeth Galarza, who knew how to do cardiopulmonary resuscitation, was on the scene soon after the shooting. This is the way she described it:

> His pulse was still there. He was blinking his eyes. He couldn't talk. The young boy clenched my hand. . . . He was frightened. He had terror in his eyes. He was so young and so frightened. I said, "Come on, baby. You'll be fine. Take small breaths. God is with you."

The youth was, of course, dead on arrival at the hospital — dead because he had gone with three black friends into a white neighborhood to buy a used car.[1]

Was God with him? If God was with him, why did he die? If God is with us, why does he permit such outrages to happen, such vicious, meaningless violence? How can we speak of God at all in such circumstances?

Isaiah, speaking the word of the Lord, said that the people of Israel have made "a covenant with death" (28:15). The white kids certainly made a covenant with death that night as they waited in the street to see what black person might appear. But, as we were saying last week, our whole society has made a covenant with death, because we have allowed this kind of racial animosity to fester among us. Merely to blame Bensonhurst or Howard Beach or rednecks is to "take refuge in a falsehood," as Isaiah says; it is to pretend that "when the overwhelming scourge passes through, it will not come to us" in our more enlightened neighborhoods. The Lord says, "When the overwhelming scourge comes through, you will be beaten down by it."

Isaiah was writing in a time when the nation of Israel was about to be overtaken by disaster because of her sins, particularly her sins of going after false gods in the interests of national security, and consequently of neglecting justice for the poor and the dispossessed. Because of these failures, Isaiah said,

> Your covenant with death will be annulled,
> your agreement with the grave will not stand;
> when the overwhelming scourge passes through,
>     you will be beaten down by it. . . .

1. These details are all taken from a long front-page article by Ralph Blumenthal in *The New York Times*, 25 August 1989.

And it will be sheer terror to understand the message. . . .
For the Lord will rise up as on Mount Perazim,
he will be wroth as in the valley of Gibeon,
to do his deed — strange is his deed!
And to work his work — alien is his work! (Isa. 28:18-21)

Three years ago, I preached on these fascinating words from Isaiah — God's *strange work,* his *alien work.* Now they have come round in the lectionary again, and I am glad to see them. In the three years that have gone by, I have not heard any words from Scripture that more memorably address the dilemma of God's mysterious ways. This was the passage that led Martin Luther to speak of God's *proper work* and his *alien work,* the work of his right hand and of his left.

These terms are still helpful today as we seek to cope with all that surrounds us. We cannot simply say that the hateful murder of innocent people like that in Bensonhurst was God's will, but we cannot say that God somehow let matters get out of control, either — not if we want to be faithful to the God of the Bible. There's another factor in such situations as well: doctrinal theological statements have a hollow sound to them when human beings are suffering. Metaphorical statements are better — God's right hand, his left hand. With his left hand he permits a nation to drift into the catastrophe it chose for itself when it made "a covenant with death." "He rises up as on Mount Perazim" (that was a place where God defeated his enemies — 2 Sam. 5:17-21). He goes into action to do his strange and alien work, the work of judgment, the judgment that the society has chosen to bring upon itself. A society that once imported millions of black people to work as slaves turns its back on those slaves' descendants at its own risk. This is to make "a covenant with death." Here God's left hand is at work. I know this doesn't make complete sense. I am reaching for the biblical metaphors here.

The father of the murder victim spoke out of rage and anguish. "To see my son's life wasted because of some . . . fool with a gun in his hand who saw nothing but a black man is a very, very vile thing to me." And he asked, "Who will pay for this? Who will pay?"[2]

We all know, I think, that in the sense of real reparations, no one will pay. Even if one believes in the death penalty, which many Christians do not, there assuredly won't be any death penalty in this case. Sentences tend

2. Blumenthal, *The New York Times,* 25 August 1989.

to be light in these situations. If anyone pays, it will be our society as a whole, with increased rage and vengefulness and racial hostility. That is what St. Paul meant when he said three times in Romans 1, "God gave them up. . . . God gave them up. . . . God gave them up [meaning the whole people] to a base mind. . . . They were filled with wickedness."

What then? Is there nothing that can be said?

We must approach this whole subject with utmost care. Yusef Hawkins's father said he was sick of hearing people say they were sorry. Unless we ourselves are prepared to feel the full force of the horror of an innocent young person's murder, we had better not say anything at all. We can only speak of God's *right* hand if we are prepared ourselves to submit to whatever his *left* hand may bring us in the way of consequences — not just upon Bensonhurst or Howard Beach or Neshoba County, Mississippi, but upon every person who shares in the lack of national will to bring our society into balance.[3]

This submission to God's judgment is accomplished through repentance. Repentance (*metanoia* in Greek) does not mean saying "I'm sorry," or even *being* sorry. It means something far more radical. It means to turn in the opposite direction. A whole society can repent. Germany has done that.[4] It is surely the part of Christians in America to lead in a movement of national repentance. The issues could hardly be more clear-cut. God does not want this land, which he set as a beacon for the nations of the world, to sink into a pit of racial hatred, crime, violence, drugs, poverty, despair, and armed conflict between the haves and the have-nots. He does not want us to make a covenant with death. If we keep on doing that, we will experience the full force of his left hand, his *alien work*. We will more and more feel that the rising up of God is a rising up in wrath only, to judge and condemn.

But as nations repent, which means that we who are relatively secure make common cause with the most vulnerable members of our society — the ones for whom the Holy One of Israel has a special concern — then we will begin to understand how God's right hand is concealed in his left, how it is that God's judgment is an instrument of his mercy. We may even become agents of God's right hand ourselves. "The Lord will rise up . . . and

3. Howard Beach was another scene of an innocent death in an episode of racial hatred in New York City. Neshoba County was the location of some of the worst racial violence in the civil rights movement.

4. In December 1970, Chancellor Willy Brandt fell to his knees when laying a wreath at the Warsaw Ghetto Memorial, an act that to this day is remembered and evoked as a profoundly significant gesture of acknowledgment, remorse, and responsibility.

then your covenant with death will be annulled. Your agreement with the grave will not stand."

It all depends on how we want to see it. Do we demand to see God rising up in blessing, with instant solutions for all our problems? That is not the way of the God and Father of our Lord Jesus Christ. The Son of God achieved the salvation of the world through suffering and death. He paid — he truly and fully paid — for the death of Yusef Hawkins and every other death. But this payment — this *atonement* — can only be made plain in this world by those who, as St. Paul said, are called to share in the fellowship of Christ's sufferings — on behalf of those who are victims.

A moment ago I said it all depends on how we want to see it. That is not really true, not ultimately. Ultimately it depends, not on us at all, but on the God who is God and not us. His alien work is not the last word. Sooner or later his *proper* work will be revealed behind his *strange* work. Only a "Job's comforter" would say such things to Yusef's grieving father now, but someday it will be revealed that God *was* present with Yusef, perhaps even in the compassionate words of Elizabeth Galarza of Bensonhurst: "You'll be fine, baby; God is with you." Some day the Lord will indeed rise up to annul our covenant with death. He will rise up, and we will see that "death is swallowed up in victory" (1 Cor. 15:54). But for now, we his people have work to do. "Repent, for the kingdom of heaven is at hand" (Matt. 4:17).

AMEN.

# Most Trusted, Most Powerful Name in News

*February 2007*                                                   Isaiah 29:9-20

*This sermon was delivered to a congregation of Methodist clergy.*

. . . . . . . . . . . . . . . . .

Being a news junkie, I flip back and forth among the cable news channels. I've been reflecting on the way that CNN calls itself "the *most trusted* name in news," whereas Fox, not to be outdone, calls itself "the *most powerful* name in news." As best I can figure out, these designations refer to the fact that in a real crisis more people turn to CNN, but week in and week out, Fox News has hands-down more viewers. I think CNN named itself first, and then the Fox people came up with "powerful" as a way of thumbing their nose at "trusted." They would have us know that when it comes to numbers, mighty Bill O'Reilly wipes up the floor with everybody else.

Which is more compelling, power or trustworthiness? Power is a lot — a *whole* lot — more glamorous. When short, homely Henry Kissinger was asked about his ability to get dates with attractive young women, he famously said that power is the greatest aphrodisiac. It's power that attracts us, power that we crave, power that we want to get close to, even if it's only the power of a big fish in a very small local pond. Nobody flocks around trustworthiness. You won't get Angelina Jolie with trustworthiness. No. But think again. Over the long term, who do you want for your doctor?

Your electrician? Your children's baby sitter? Do you want power, or trustworthiness? Or, perhaps, both?

The claim that the Bible makes for itself is that it is *both* powerful *and* trustworthy. I wonder if we've thought about that lately. We live in an age of disdain for such a claim. This scorn is more obvious in New York than it is in the South. The influential journalist Nicholas Kristof scolded his colleagues for this disdain in his column on Sunday in *The New York Times.*[1] Among the cultural elites, as Kristof noted, people who hold to the Bible as *trustworthy* are subject to ridicule. The fashion today is to regard the Bible as a "text," just one among countless others, ripe for deconstruction, neither more nor less trustworthy than any other text. Moving a couple of rungs up the ladder of intellectual chic, the idea that the Word of God is powerful is a truly despised notion. Such a claim smacks of oppression, domination, and "hegemony" — that trendy term in political academia.

But if the Scripture has one controlling presupposition from beginning to end, it is the power of the Word of God. We can't have the Bible without that affirmation. "God *said,* 'Let there be light,' *and there was light.*" A Bible construed without the Word as power is not the Bible at all. Listen to just one among a thousand passages about this:

> The Lord utters his voice before his army. . . . He that executes his word *is powerful.* (Joel 2:11; my emphasis)

He that executes his Word is powerful. He has a host (an army) of angels at his command. The Spirit of God makes the Word live. When the Word of God is *not* understood that way among God's people, when it is suppressed or subverted, a deadly paralysis sets in. Let's hear from the prophet Isaiah about this:

> Stupefy yourselves and be in a stupor, blind yourselves and be blind!
> Be drunk, but not with wine; stagger, but not with strong drink!
> The Lord has poured out upon you a spirit of deep sleep, and has
> closed the eyes of the prophets, and covered the heads of the seers.
> (Isa. 29:9-10)[2]

---

1. "Evangelicals a Liberal Can Love," *The New York Times,* 3 February 2008.

2. The interplay in this passage between "stupefy *yourselves*" and "*The Lord* has poured out . . ." maintains the paradoxical relationship between human responsibility and the action of God. There is rarely a flat-out account of God's action independent of human accountability. One

This is a description of a shortage of the Word of God in the land. Everybody's in a stupor, going in circles, bored to tears. The preaching is so lacking in vitality that the people in the congregations are either text-messaging or asleep. Maybe it's the fault of the seminaries! That's what my husband said to me when I was a student and first started preaching. On the way home in the car, he said, "That seminary is ruining you!"[3] But no, the problem is deeper than that. Isaiah says that the Word of God has been withheld from the educated and the uneducated alike:

> And the vision[4] of all this has become to you like the words of a book that is sealed. When the book is given to one who can read, saying, "Read this," he says, "I cannot, for it is sealed." And when they give the book to one who *cannot* read, saying, "Read this," he says, "I cannot read." (29:11-12; my emphasis)

So, for the educated and the illiterate alike, the Word of the Lord has gone missing. Amos evokes the absence of the Word using different imagery:

> "Behold, the days are coming," says the Lord God, "when I will send a famine on the land; not a famine of bread . . . but of hearing the words of the Lord. They shall wander from sea to sea. . . . They shall run to and fro, to seek the word of the Lord, but they shall not find it." (Amos 8:11-12)

Both prophets speak of the dearth of the Word. The fault is largely in the leadership, but the whole people have gone astray as a result. They are chasing after the living Word of the Lord in nature, in cults, in idolatry, in selfish pleasures, in "grinding the face of the poor" while still persuading themselves that they are true worshipers. Isaiah says this in words that Jesus himself quotes in Matthew 15:7:

---

of the great exceptions is Isaiah 40–55, which fastens into place the theological doctrine of the *prevenient* (going-before), *unconditional* nature of God's action when the human situation is hopeless.

3. That was before Edmund Steimle, professor of homiletics at Union Seminary (NYC), got hold of me.

4. Otto Kaiser in his commentary on Isaiah says that the word *vision* has "the general meaning of *revelation*." See Otto Kaiser, *Isaiah 13–39: A Commentary,* The Old Testament Library (Philadelphia: Westminster Press, 1974), p. 269.

"'This people draws near with their mouth and honors me with their lips, while their hearts are far from me, and their worship of me is according to a commandment of human beings learned by rote.'"

I don't think this is meant as a condemnation of traditional liturgy. The problem is not to be solved by making the prayers extemporaneous or jazzing up the music. Something more fundamental is wrong. The people's hearts are far from God because his Word is sealed. The people *hear* the Word but it does not *penetrate;* it does not change anyone's life; it does not produce fruit; its power *is withheld.* Did you notice that scandalous message? God is in charge of closing the book, and God is in charge of opening it again. God is the one who closes and opens the heart to "hear the vision." Isn't that intolerably capricious? We strenuously object to this. But our objections have already been foreseen. Isaiah says that we have it backwards. We are disrespecting the Author of the Word:

> You turn things upside down![5] Shall the potter be regarded as the clay? Should the thing made say of its maker, "He did not make me"; or shall the thing formed say of him who formed it, "He has no understanding"? (29:16)

I think this is meant to be a little bit funny. Humor disarms, sometimes. We're meant to imagine a little animated pot back-talking to the potter, complaining about the way it's been made. Paul and Jeremiah both use this image of the pot talking back. It's funny, but it's deadly serious too. It all depends on whether there really is a God who shapes all things.

This past summer, after our beloved mother died, my sister and I found a lot of fascinating things in her house. I found a letter written in 1893 by my mother's grandfather, who was brilliant, learned, and what used to be called a "free-thinker."[6] Well, why not? Who would not want to be a free thinker? Who wants to be an imprisoned thinker? Now: I am placing my mother's grandfather side by side in my mind with my father's father, who was a devout Methodist. I found his 1889 hymnal, his name stamped on the

---

5. The exact translation of this is disputed; is it a question or a statement? Anyway, the general idea is clear — the creator-creature relationship has been reversed.

6. His name was Virginius Dabney. His grandson and namesake became a noted newspaper editor and historian.

cover, very worn with use. Two ancestors: the Methodist and the freethinker. I know a great deal more about my great-grandfather the freethinker, because I have typed a hundred pages of his letters. Of my paternal grandfather the Methodist, I know very little; he died in 1918 and left few letters behind, just the hymnal and a stained-glass window in his memory in the Methodist church in my hometown.

I'm going to read two paragraphs from my great-grandfather's 1893 letter. He is writing to his son, my maternal grandfather, who was professor of history at the University of Virginia and a conspicuous unbeliever like his father. Remember that 1893 was the year of the famous controversy in the Presbyterian Church regarding biblical interpretation, with Benjamin Warfield on the conservative side and Charles Briggs on the liberal:

> . . . I do not look upon the acquittal of Briggs as a very momentous event. . . . You must remember that he is acquitted only in New York. In a General Assembly of the Presbyterians embracing delegates from the South & West he would be condemned. When he is tried over again, as I suppose he will be, there will be a chance for a split in the Calvinistic Church — And that will greatly lessen its strength I trust. Like the Republican party the Presbyterian Church has outlived its day of usefulness if such day ever existed. And I suppose we cannot deny that it has struck many a sturdy blow for liberty — But it is time it were gathered to the fathers. . . .

I figure it's a safe bet that a crowd of Methodist ministers would enjoy that! But what a joke the Creator of heaven and earth and Lord of the Church has played on my great-grandfather!

Here's the next paragraph:

> During my idle hours of late I have been reading the Bible systematically. . . . I have been astonished to find it so amazing a jumble. It does not need "modern criticism" to persuade any sane mind that such a mass of confused rubbish could never have . . . issued from the chambers of an omniscient brain. . . .

Now seriously: speaking of the Presbyterians, this has caused me to reflect deeply on the mystery of election. I found this letter and this hymnal at the same time, and I have spent the last few months balancing them against one another and thinking about the questions they raised in my mind. Like many Southern families, we have always been hyper-conscious of family connections. Why is it that my sister and I were both — as far as we can tell — born believers? Why is it that our great-grandfather's "mass of confused rubbish" has been for us both the Word of life from our infancy? Here we have these parallel strands in our immediate ancestry — the faithful Christian and the "free-thinking" scoffer, both of them highly educated. One forebear had ears to hear the Word of God, and the other one did not. How do we account for the appearance of faith in some people and not in others? The book of Isaiah is suffused with that question. Do you know which Old Testament passage is quoted in the New Testament more than any other? It's this one, from the call of Isaiah in chapter 6:

> "Go, and say to this people: 'Hear and hear, but do not understand; see and see, but do not perceive.' Make the heart of this people fat, and their ears heavy, and shut their eyes; lest they see with their eyes, and hear with their ears." (6:10)

The mystery of unbelief! Already in the first years of the Christian community it was puzzling and disturbing. Paul devotes three chapters in Romans to the problem. He concludes, thinking along with Isaiah, that God has his own purposes. There is some reason that unbelief persists in God's world until the Day of the Lord, when all shall be revealed.

Let's read further from Isaiah:

> "[This people's] worship of me is according to a commandment of men learned by rote; *therefore, behold, I will again do marvelous things* with this people, wonderful and marvelous; and the wisdom of their wise men shall perish, and the discernment of their discerning men shall be hid." (29:13-14; my emphasis)

Does this make any sense? Look at that word *therefore.* The people's hearts are far from God, their worship is by rote; *therefore,* the Lord is going to do a marvelous thing. Because faith is dead and the Word brings forth no fruit, *therefore* God is going to open the book again. And when he opens it, the so-called wisdom and learning of the disdainful will vanish, and faith will be called forth from the foolish to whom God has drawn near. That's what God says through his prophet Isaiah. St. Paul says it again in 1 Corinthians:

Has not God made foolish the wisdom of the world? . . . For the foolishness of God is wiser than men. . . . God chose what is foolish in the world to shame the wise. . . . (1:20, 25, 27)[7]

Again, God is the agent. God is the subject of the verbs. "God made, God is, God chose." We're being given a new heart to suspend our objections so that we can just listen to the Word of God speaking. Here's the rest of the passage from Isaiah. Listen for what God is going to do. Remember that the *kerygma* is an announcement — an announcement from the most trusted, most powerful name in news. Listen for the *kerygma*:

"I will again do marvelous things with this people, wonderful and marvelous. . . . In that day the deaf shall hear the words of a book [*the word of God will live and jump off the page!*], and out of their gloom and darkness the eyes of the blind shall see. [*This is not about literal eyesight. Sight in the Scripture is metaphorical; it means understanding, revelation, transformation.*] The meek shall obtain fresh joy in the Lord, and the poor among men shall exult in the Holy One of Israel. [*The great reversal will take place. Those who had no privileges and no prospects will be seized by ecstatic joy.*] For the tyrant[8] shall be no more, and the scoffer shall cease to be; all those alert to do evil shall be cut off — those who cause a person to lose a lawsuit, who set a trap for the arbiter in the gate, and without grounds deny justice to the one in the right." (29:14, 18-21)

Here's news that sounds very up-to-date — news of miscarried lawsuits, bribed judges, corruption in the courts. It's all going to be "cut off." Is this news powerful? Is this news trustworthy? Is this truly a God who is able to keep promises? This passage announces that the right understanding of God's Word means the redemption of society. The Word will leap into the hearts of the deaf and blind. The neglected and downtrodden peoples will greet their deliverance with rejoicing. The scoffer shall cease to be, and the lowly who are waiting for justice will see their enemies "cut off." *The zeal of the Lord of hosts will perform this* (Isa. 9:7; 37:32).

"The scoffer will cease to be." I think of my great-grandfather. Does the

---

7. See also Jeremiah 8:9: "The wise men shall be put to shame, they shall be dismayed and taken; lo, they have rejected the word of the Lord."

8. *Gnaritzim* — Calvin translates this as "violent man."

Scripture mean that he will cease to be scornful, or that he will cease to exist? Will the "cut off" enemies be effectively and permanently *thwarted,* or will they actually be *destroyed?* We do not know. A lot of the language of Scripture about these matters is metaphorical. What we can affirm for sure is that the Word of God is both powerful and trustworthy and that it creates faith where there is no faith, it can grant sight where there is blindness, it can loosen the stubborn heart to praise its Maker.

One final question. Don't we want to be "free-thinkers"? We don't want to be *coerced* into believing, do we? What sort of power does this Word of God have?

"Power largely consists in the ability to make others inhabit *your* story of *their* reality." Speaking for myself, there is nothing in all the world that makes me feel more angry and disempowered than someone else making me inhabit their story of my reality. And there is no more familiar experience in the world, for most of us. Someone wants us to find "closure" before we are ready. Someone wants to tell us we are better off *without* whatever it was we lost. Someone thinks we should be happy in a job that makes us miserable. Someone wants to tell us how to solve an insoluble problem. But the power of God is nothing like that. The power of God moves us into a new place where we can see, perhaps for the first time, what our own true story really is.

There is all the difference in the world between power and coercion, power and force. I don't think we preachers today have enough trust in the power of God to create a *truly* free-thinking person. We've been sold a bill of goods — that if we preach with too much confidence it will be coercive. That's because we're thinking with the thoughts of human beings, not with trust in the promises of God. He is the one who shuts and opens the book. That is not our job. If some of those who listen to our sermons reject the message, that is not our worry — as long as it is truly the *kerygma* that we preach, and not some feeble imitation of it. Rejection is built into the vocation of the preacher. But hear this: The incarnate Word of God is a mighty sword put into your hand. Those who hear it will feel their chains cut off, their prison unlocked, their lungs filled with oxygen:

> With joy you will draw water from the wells of salvation. And you
> will say in that day: "Give thanks to the Lord, call upon his name;

9. I have taken this sentence from Philip Gourevitch, *We Wish to Inform You that Tomorrow We Will Be Killed with Our Families: Stories from Rwanda* (New York: Farrar, Straus & Giroux, 1998), p. 48; italics added. The book was the winner of the National Book Critics Circle Award in 1998.

make known his deeds among the nations. . . . Sing praises to the Lord, for he has done gloriously; let this be known in all the earth. Shout, and sing for joy, O inhabitant of Zion, for great in your midst is the Holy One of Israel." (Isa. 12:3-6)

This, truly, is the most powerful name in news. Let us join then in the hymn written by your own Charles Wesley:

Come, thou incarnate Word,
Gird on thy mighty sword,
Our prayer attend;
Come, and thy people bless,
Come, give thy Word success,
Spirit of holiness,
On us descend!

AMEN.

# The Subject of the Verb

Isaiah 40–55

*This was delivered to a congregation of ordained Presbyterian clergy. It is more a teaching than a sermon, but it has some sermonic qualities.*

. . . . . . . . . . . . . . . . .

ABOUT EIGHT years ago, I was having lunch in New York City with a person well enough known and sufficiently sophisticated to be a bit intimidating. We had recently been introduced and were meeting to discuss some points raised in his latest book. After some discussion of those, he began to ask me some questions about my own work as an ordained minister, and then he cocked his head to one side and said, quite seriously, "Do you believe in God?"

I was not as shocked as you might think. I had been around in the church long enough to know that urbane, progressive members of the clergy believed pretty much anything and everything these days. What saddened me was that my luncheon companion knew this. Indeed, he took it for granted, and seemed to assume that if I did believe in God, I was an exception.

You may think this is extreme. Yet from my perspective it is not. I need to explain that I bring one thing to my task as a preacher that is almost unique. I have probably heard more sermons by more clergy in more churches in more denominations than any other preacher I have ever met. The great majority of the Sundays and holy days of my sixty-five years have been spent not in the pulpit, but in the pew. For instance, last year I preached on fifteen Sundays. The rest of the year I was in a pew somewhere in the United States. I have heard sermons from Maine to Florida, from Boston to Honolulu, from New Orleans to Minneapolis. No exaggeration. Therefore, I speak with a certain amount of authority when I say that there are a lot of clergy out there who give every impression of not believing in God.

By that I don't mean that the word *God* is not mentioned. What I mean is that God plays only a subsidiary or vague role in the messages. (I can say these things to you because I have never heard any of you preach.) Last fall I heard a stewardship sermon with all kinds of inspirational stories about generosity, but not one concrete thing about God. On Christmas Eve I heard a sermon about the faith of Mary and Joseph in which God was merely a bystander. Last summer I heard a sermon about "spirituality" with a lot of references to labyrinths, centering prayer, and techniques of meditation. Last month I heard a sermon about science and faith in which "religion" took the place of God — the preacher's reflections could have been offered in a Buddhist context, or a New Age context, or whatever.

This problem has been on my heart and mind for some years now, but only recently have I been able to give it a shape. I've been puzzling for years to try to figure out what it is that has drawn me all my life to the African-American churches. Is it the music and the enthusiasm? But if so, then why also, sometimes, the occasional conservative-evangelical church? Finally it came to me. The thing about those churches and their preaching — not always, but generally speaking — is that there is a sense of *a living God*. God is the subject of the sentences in the sermons. God is the subject of the verbs. That's what's missing in so much mainline preaching. The subject in so much of our preaching is ourselves — our faith, our "spirituality," our works, our journeys, our responsibilities, our needs, our ministries. The subject isn't God, or at least let's say that God is not the *subject,* but rather the *object* of *our* religious searching. So it is often a tonic to go to a church where the preaching is about God. But then, you see (full disclosure here), I had a Southern Baptist grandmother who talked to me every day about God as a living presence. She died when I was seven — the age at which the Jesuits say their work is done.

Paul the apostle, dictating his fierce message to the Galatians, writes, "Formerly, when you did not know God, you were in bondage to beings that by nature are no gods; but now that you have come to know God, *or rather to be known by God,* how can you turn back again to the weak and beggarly elemental spirits, whose slaves you want to be once more?" (4:8-9). Notice how he quite deliberately changes the sentence so that God is not the object, but the subject. Wouldn't that make a tremendous difference if preachers everywhere did that?

Recently I had an opportunity to meet with about twenty campus chaplains at one of the Ivy League colleges. Among the mainline chaplains there was a single refrain, a single complaint: Most of the students who were interested in Christianity weren't coming to them; they were going to the local nondenominational congregations. The chaplains were accusing these churches of fundamentalism and obscurantism, but I don't think that was the heart of the matter. Later, after talking to some students, my sense was that they were seeking a setting where there is confidence in a living God. Note that I did not say "loving" God. The mainlines are not failing to preach a loving God. The question is not about love. The question is whether God is "living and active" (Heb. 4:12). The issue is whether, as Paul Lehmann used to say, "God is up to something in the world."[1]

The text for this sermon is Isaiah 43:10-11:

> "You are my witnesses," says the Lord, "my servant[s] whom I have chosen, that you may know and believe me and understand that I am He. Before me no god was formed, nor shall there be any after me. I, I am the Lord, and besides me there is no savior."

Actually, it would be more accurate to say that our text tonight is the entire fifteen chapters that make up what we call Deutero-Isaiah, and indeed the whole book of Isaiah. I have long believed that if we preachers spent six months reading Isaiah (particularly chapters 40-55), preaching from Isaiah, teaching from Isaiah, and directing our congregations in small-group work in Isaiah, it would be transforming. I'm quite serious about this. It's all there in those fifteen chapters: creation, fall, judgment, kingdom, redemption, crucifixion, new creation — all of it, the whole story of God.[2]

---

1. The work of the important Presbyterian theologian and ethicist Paul L. Lehmann has been undergoing something of a revival lately under the leadership of Philip Ziegler of the University of Aberdeen and Michelle J. Bartel, whose Ph.D. in theological ethics is from Princeton. They have edited a new collection, *Explorations in Christian Theology and Ethics: Essays in Conversation with Paul L. Lehmann* (Surrey, Eng.: Ashgate Publishing Ltd., 2009).

2. Not mentioned here is the crucial fact that "Second" Isaiah (chs. 40-55) has been identi-

We humans are there too, but not as seekers or questers or co-creators. We are there as *witnesses* and as *servants* — witnesses and servants of the Holy One of Israel. Remember Elijah, who always said, "As the God of Israel lives, before whom I stand. . . ."

Listen to a few verses from Second Isaiah:

> Behold, the Lord God comes with might, and his arm rules for him; behold, his reward is with him, and his recompense before him. He will feed his flock like a shepherd, he will gather the lambs in his arms, he will carry them in his bosom, and gently lead those that are with young. (40:10-11)

> When the poor and needy seek water, and there is none, and their tongue is parched with thirst, I the Lord will answer them, I the God of Israel will not forsake them.
>
> I will open rivers on the bare heights, and fountains in the midst of the valleys; I will make the wilderness a pool of water . . . that men may see and know, may consider and understand together, that the hand of the Lord has done this, the Holy One of Israel has created it. (41:17-18)

These wondrous announcements and promises are indeed among the glories of Scripture, justifiably beloved and cherished. As soon as we read them, however, objections and questions arise. Why do we not see evidence of these things? All over the world, the "poor and needy" live and die miserable lives and wretched deaths, often for lack of clean water, and there is no sign of God. The question at the heart of any discussion of God as living and active remains acute. I recently had a discussion with a professor of religion about this. Identifying himself as theologically "liberal," he said he didn't believe in an intervening God because, as he said, "People get hurt." I am still baffled by this response. Liberal theology, classical theology, evangelical theology — take your choice. People are going to get hurt anyway.

The Hebrew prophets thought about this question long before today's liberal theologians thought about it. Here is what Isaiah says: "Verily thou art a God who hidest thyself, O God of Israel, the Savior" (45:15). God is

---

fied as the mother lode for apocalyptic theology. The concept of the divine intrusion, or invasion, is fundamental to apocalyptic theology.

still active, still living, still in charge, still the subject of the verb: God hides *himself.* God is active even when hidden, even when seemingly absent. "I have tried you in the furnace of affliction" (48:10), says the Lord. Even when the heavens seem shut, the Lord is still the God of Israel, still the Savior. The problem is compounded by the idea of God as the acting subject when we are tried in the furnace of affliction. This has always been a problem, and it points to the necessity of distinguishing between God's intentional will and his permissive will.[3] Knowledge of the living God requires us to wrestle continually with doubt and ambiguity. The Psalms of lament give ample evidence of that. But over and under and beyond it all is the promise of the Holy One of Israel:

> But you, Israel, my servant, Jacob, whom I have chosen. . . . You are my servant, I have chosen you and not cast you off; fear not, for I am with you, be not dismayed, for I am your God; I will strengthen you, I will help you, I will uphold you with my victorious right hand. (Isa. 41:9-10)

But this is only the merest hint of the breadth of the second prophet Isaiah's message. He is living in a civilization that is utterly foreign in every way. He is a member of a humiliated, exiled population, dwarfed by colossal images of imperial might, surrounded by every kind of god and every kind of religious and political excess. He is immersed in a culture where everyone believes the stars and other phenomena have power over their lives. He prophesies in a land of idols, a society that worships forces of nature, graven images, signs, omens, and anything that the empire can turn to its purposes. Here is this lone prophet, a single person calling out from the midst of a lowly, downtrodden population, who has the nerve to call the entire Mesopotamian enterprise into question:

> To whom then will you compare me, that I should be like him? says the Holy One. Lift up your eyes on high and see: who created these [stars and planets]? He who brings out their host by number, calling them all by name; by the greatness of his might, and because he is strong in power, not one is missing.

---

3. Calvin rejects this distinction. I would argue, along with David Bentley Hart, that he was mistaken in this. See Hart, *The Doors of the Sea: Where Was God in the Tsunami?* (Grand Rapids: Wm. B. Eerdmans, 2005).

Have you not known? Have you not heard? The Lord is the ever-lasting God, the Creator of the ends of the earth. (40:25-26, 28)

One of the most striking aspects of Isaiah's prophecy is the mocking of the gods and idols of Babylon. These satirical passages are really funny, and they are meant to be:

The carpenter stretches a line, marks it out with a stylus, fashions it with planes . . . he makes it in human form, with human beauty, to be set up in a shrine. He cuts down a cedar tree . . . part of it he takes and warms himself; he kindles a fire and bakes bread . . . the rest of it he makes into a god, his idol; he bows down to it and worships it; he prays to it and says, "Save me, for you are my god!" (44:13-17)

Over against this target of mockery is the God of Isaiah:

Thus says the Lord . . . : "I am the first and I am the last; besides me there is no god. Who is like me? . . . Who has announced from of old the things to come? Let them tell us what is yet to be. Fear not, nor be afraid; have I not told you from of old and declared it? And you are my witnesses! Is there a God besides me? There is no [other] Rock; I know not any." (44:6-8)

The theme of the *witnesses* is prominent. The witnesses to the idols "neither see nor know" anything that is powerful to save (44:9). Their gods are impotent. But the witnesses to the God of Israel speak the word of a sovereign Lord who is able to shake the foundations of the world:

"For I am the Lord your God, who stirs up the sea so that its waves roar — the Lord of hosts is [my] name. And I have put my words in your mouth, and hid you in the shadow of my hand, stretching out the heavens and laying the foundations of the earth, and saying to Zion, 'You are my people.'" (51:15-16)

This is our faith. God has put his message into the mouths of mere human beings like you and me. He has promised to make himself present in our announcements: "O thou that tellest good tidings to Zion, lift up your voice with strength, lift it up, be not afraid, say unto the cities of Judah, 'Behold your God!'" (40:9).

Not long ago a professor at Howard University gave a speech in which she said that Martin Luther King and the civil rights movement had saved the white church from itself. As a white Episcopalian brought up in segregated Southside Virginia, I think she was exactly right, in a very important way.

Now the American church needs to be saved from itself again. We are in a state of disarray. The mainlines have been sidelined for some years now. Former President Carter pointed out in an op-ed piece before the Iraq war that the leaders of all the mainline denominations had spoken out against a "pre-emptive strike," but no one in Washington paid the slightest attention. The evangelical churches were and are hand-in-glove with the Bush administration for the most part. Large numbers of Catholics ignored the pope's passionate denunciations of this war. African-American Christians largely opposed the war but continue to praise the God who lives. This fragmentation is a perilous state of affairs, it seems to me. I quite seriously propose that a strong dose of Second Isaiah is what we all need. What this "unknown prophet of the exile" sees and proclaims is the most universal vision of God and of human destiny in all of religious history until Paul wrote Romans 11.

> The Lord said to me, "You are my servant, Israel, in whom I will be glorified . . . [but] it is too light a thing that you should be my servant to raise up the tribes of Jacob and to restore the preserved of Israel; I will give you as a light to the nations, that my salvation may reach to the end of the earth." (Isa. 49:3, 6)

In other words, the election of Israel to be God's possession is not for Israel's own sake, but for the sake of the entire human family. Isaiah foresees the approaching deliverance of the entire created order according to the promise and purpose of the God of Israel. This message remains more urgent than ever.

I believe that the American church is suffering acutely from an unwillingness of the mainlines and the Christian right to talk to each other — indeed, in some cases the demonization of one another. If there is one thing we in the mainlines can do to break this impasse, it is a renewal of the knowledge of God and of — dare I say it — the fear of God.

> "I am the Lord, who made all things, who stretched out the heavens alone, who spread out the earth — who was with me? — who frus-

trates the omens of liars, and makes fools of diviners; who turns wise men back, and makes their knowledge foolish; who confirms the word of his servant[s] and performs the counsel of his messengers." (Isa. 44:24-25)

"Do you believe in God?" May the Holy One of Israel, the God of Abraham, Isaac, and Jacob, the God of Elijah and Isaiah, the God and Father of our Lord Jesus Christ confirm his Word in you all. May the God who is the *subject* of the verb act to strengthen you in your several vocations. May he give you such joy in the knowledge of himself that you will let no one despise you. And may the God who lives protect you in every furnace of your affliction until he brings you out into the glorious redemption founded in his promise that cannot fail.

"You are my witnesses," says the Lord. "I am God, and also henceforth I am He. . . . I work and who can hinder it?"

Thus says the Lord, your Redeemer, the Holy One of Israel. . . . "Behold, I am doing a new thing. . . ." (43:12-13, 19)

"For as the rain and the snow come down from heaven, and return not thither but water the earth, making it bring forth and sprout, giving seed to the sower and bread to the eater, so shall my word be that goes forth from my mouth; it shall not return to me empty, but it shall accomplish that which I purpose, and prosper in the thing for which I sent it." (55:10-11)

"The glory of the Lord shall be revealed, and all flesh shall see it together, for the mouth of the Lord has spoken it." (40:5)

AMEN.

# A New Thing

GRACE CHURCH IN NEW YORK

---

IF YOU look at your bulletin, on page 2 in the left-hand column, you will see the calendar of the week. Look at the events for Tuesday. These are the listings: staff meeting, organ recital, social hour, dinner, parish meeting, and "No New Life"!

Now of course what this really means is that the group named "New Life for the Lower East Side" (a wonderful ministry that you might like to hear more about sometime) is not meeting on Tuesday, but what interests me this morning is the way the words look on the page and the thoughts that they suggest. No. New. Life. What does that evoke in your minds?

It is axiomatic in the advertising industry that the quality of newness itself recommends a product. For scores of years, packaging has featured the word "New!" emblazoned across the box, or container, or whatever. Everywhere in the world, new clothes represent excitement, festivity, celebration. Every politician wants to come across as a person with new ideas — everyone running for office wants to offer a New Deal or a New Frontier. A fashion house introduces a New Look; film directors develop a New Wave. It is interesting that, in spite of the contemporary passion for certain aspects of the old, such as retro fashions, Victorian artifacts, oil lamps, classical borrowings in postmodern architecture, and so forth, still we are so thoroughly and ineluctably wedded to our advanced technological society that not even the most ardently nostalgic among us would want anything other than a new camera, a new computer, a new car. Even those of us who are crazy about "ancient music" performed on "authentic instruments" want to have the very latest audio equipment to play it on.

I asked my husband about what the category of the new meant in his business. He said that for him in marketing, "new" had additional implications: It didn't just mean fresh and contemporary; it also implied the vanguard, the frontier of innovation, state of the art, as they say. So "new" doesn't just mean "the latest" or "the most recent." In its most compelling manifestations, it evokes all that we hope for from the future, and especially, in these instances, it conveys a sense of the possibility of unlimited human potential. Even more potent, "new" can suggest "something never seen before."

Some of you were probably fascinated, as I was, by the story in yesterday's *New York Times* of the homeless young people who panhandle by day and live in the Port Authority Bus Terminal by night. The central characters in the article are a group of former crack addicts trying to get hold of a new start in life. One young woman was eager to prove that she had not stolen her little TV set. Offering to show the receipt for it, she said, "We are trying to turn ourselves around." There is something inside all of us, I think, that responds to this. We can understand and even admire the hope, however forlorn, for something better. I was talking with a friend who knows a lot about the tragedy of South Africa. She spoke of the blocked aspirations of the black population and said, "The one thing you must have in order to deal with bad circumstances is the hope that your children will have a better life than you have." When we think about people who must struggle against despair, we can begin to imagine some of the impact the words might convey — No New Life.

The worst thing of all, it seems to me, would be to be in a situation without hope of some kind. This hopelessness can overtake individuals, as in the case of some people with AIDS. It can also attack whole societies, as with the Dalits of India, the refugee camps of Thailand, perhaps the Gaza Strip. It certainly must have assailed the people of Israel in Old Testament times, during the time of the Babylonian Exile in the fourth century B.C. It is hard to convey to an audience today just what that event was like for God's people. They had suffered the loss of home, loss of nation, loss of possessions, loss of the temple, loss of status, roots, traditions, customs, freedoms, identity, sense of belonging. The Babylonians were a great and powerful culture with many great and powerful gods who apparently were able to give mighty victories to their worshipers. Israel, a tiny little nation to begin with, would appear to be almost totally swallowed up by the rich, warmongering Babylonians; and, what was even more significant, Israel's god

Yahweh seemed to have been completely stampeded by Marduk and the other Babylonian gods.

There was, in addition, an even more dreadful factor — a theological one. Here the uniqueness of Israel's faith declares itself. Yahweh, unlike other gods, was a jealous god. He would tolerate no rivals. The Israelites knew that they had brought the catastrophe on themselves, because Yahweh was not capricious; he had sent them into exile as a punishment for their sins of idolatry. They had forsaken him; therefore, it seemed, he had forsaken them. Humanly speaking, there was no hope for Israel as a nation under her God. Humanly speaking, there was no clue that life for the children would be any better. There was no way for an exiled and subjugated people to turn themselves around. The graffiti on the walls of Babylon read, *No New Life.*

In just this situation, the second prophet Isaiah carried out his ministry. His work comes down to us in chapters 40–55 of the book of Isaiah. A very large portion of Isaiah appears in the Old Testament lectionary of the church — more than any other Old Testament book except the book of Psalms; it has always been understood to have profound significance for Christian faith. In a situation of hopelessness, the prophet opens his ministry by addressing the people with these celebrated words of literally unimaginable promise:

> Comfort ye, comfort ye, my people,
>   saith your God.
> Speak ye comfortably to Jerusalem
>   and cry unto her,
> that her warfare is accomplished,
>   that her iniquity is pardoned,
> that she hath received from the Lord's hand
>   double for all her sins. (Isa. 40:1-2, KJV)[1]

When it comes to the frontier of innovation, the vanguard, the state of the art, this prophet whom we call Second Isaiah is in a class by himself. God delivered messages to him that, for sustained sublimity and exaltation of vision, are unparalleled anywhere else. It is this prophet who, in the lesson appointed for today, speaks the Word of God as follows:

---

1. Because these words were set unforgettably to music by Handel in his beloved *Messiah,* the KJV should, in my opinion, be used for the passages from that great work.

"I am the Lord, that is my name;
my glory I give to no other. . . .
Behold . . . new things I now declare;
before they spring forth, I announce them to you." (42:8)

No other part of the Bible puts forward the promise of the new as continually and as rapturously as Second Isaiah does.

This is what the Lord says —
"Forget the former things;
  do not dwell on the past.
See, I am doing a new thing!
  Now it springs up; do you not perceive it?" (43:18-19)

"From this time forth I make you hear new things,
hidden things which you have not known.
They are created now. . . .
  Before today you have never heard of them." (48:6-7)

Notice the most radical announcement here. "Before today you have never heard of" the things that God will do. They are not accessible to human imagination. "They are created now." They are "hidden things which you have not known." This feature of Second Isaiah is what has led interpreters to call this prophet the first apocalyptic theologian — meaning, the first to show in an unmistakable way that God will interrupt the normal progression of things by arriving in — indeed, invading — the midst of human events from a sphere of power capable of calling into existence the things that do not exist (as Paul says in Romans 4:17).

Parts of the book of Second Isaiah are satirical. Yahweh has called the Babylonian gods into his presence, with their worshipers, so that he can be compared to them. They are made of wood and have to be nailed to their platforms so they won't fall over. Yahweh mocks their worshipers unmercifully; over and over, he asks them to do something new, to say something new:

"Present your case," says the Lord. . . .
"Bring in your idols, to tell us
  what is going to happen. . . .
Declare to us the things to come,

tell us what the future holds,
so we may know that you are gods." (41:21-23)

The idols, of course, have nothing to say. Yahweh heaps scorn on them:

You are less than nothing
and your works are utterly worthless!
He who chooses you is detestable! . . .
Those who trust in idols . . .
will be turned back in utter shame. (41:24; 42:17)

Over and over in Isaiah's prophecies, the great division between Yahweh and the idols is described as his ability to call the future into being and their corresponding inability to do so:

This is what the Lord says: "I am the first and I am the last; apart from me there is no god. Who then is like me? . . . Let him declare and lay out before me . . . what is yet to come." (44:6-7)

You and I have idols just as the Babylonians did. New York City is surely a lot like Babylon, with its vast commercial enterprises. We chase after this new thing and that, hoping to find lasting satisfaction, only to discover that something more is continually required in order to feed our appetites for something that will work.

This is what the Lord says. . . .
All who make idols are nothing,
and the things they treasure are worthless.
Ignorant are those . . . who pray to gods that cannot save.
(44:9; 45:20)

"I am God, and there is no other;
I am God, and there is none like me.
I make known the end from the beginning. . . ." (46:9-10)

"From this time forth I make you hear new things." (48:6)

What is the new thing that God is going to do?
Here is a story of two parishioners, just this past week. One was speak-

ing, in the Wednesday women's Bible study, of the recent death of her much-beloved mother. She said that her family had coped fairly well with Christmas; it was New Year's Eve that was the problem. She told how she had been overwhelmed with a longing to hold on to the old year, the year in which her mother had been still alive. Said she, passionately, "I didn't want a New Year that didn't have my mother in it!"

And so the first thing that God must do in order to do a new thing is that he must be able to create something out of nothing: a mother where there is no mother — in short, *the resurrection of the dead.*

Isaiah says,

> The poor and needy search for water,
>    but there is no water;
>       their tongues are parched with thirst.
> But I the Lord will answer them. . . .
> I will make rivers flow on barren heights. . . .
> I will turn the desert into pools of water. (41:17-18)

Water where there was no water! Hope where there was no hope! Life where there was death!

> "I am YHWH, that is my name;
> my glory I give to no other.
> Behold . . . new things I now declare." (42:8-9)

The second parishioner said that when she began to come to Grace Church, she thought she started to hear something new. I asked her to elaborate. She said that she had been taught to add up her faults and sins, balance them against her prayers and good deeds, and present a daily reckoning to the Lord. She thought she was hearing in the preaching at Grace Church that she was free from that, that she didn't have to do it anymore:

> This is what the Lord says. . . .
> "I, I am he who blots out your transgressions for my own sake,
> and remembers your sins no more." (43:25)

> Speak ye comfortably to Jerusalem,
> and cry unto her that her warfare is accomplished,
> that her iniquity is pardoned. (40:2)

For my own sake, says the Lord, not for your sake but for my own sake I will remember your former condition no more. This is the radicality of the gospel in the Old Testament, just as in the New: God's power to call a new creation into being is dependent not upon our merits but upon his own nature, which cannot become inconstant or change.

Words fail me here. I do not know how to convey to you the indescribable wonder of the Word of God written in Second Isaiah. In these ineffable chapters we read of that which is utterly new, unknown to any religion, unimaginable from the human standpoint — creation out of nothing, the rectification of all things, and the total obliteration of evil. God comes to Israel *from the future,* the future where the things that do not exist are called into being (Rom. 4:17). We belong to the future of God, not to the sinful and corrupting past:

"I am the Lord, that is my name. . . .
New things I now declare;
 before they spring forth, I tell you of them."
Sing to the Lord a new song! (42:8-10)

This is what the Lord says. . . .
O Israel, you will not be forgotten by me.
I have swept away your transgressions like a cloud,
 and your sins like mist;
  return to me, for I have redeemed you.
Sing, O heavens, for the Lord has done it! (44:21-23)

But now listen. We have not yet arrived at the deepest place of all in Second Isaiah. We have heard the proclamation of God's new deed; we have been told that it is unimaginable from the human point of view and laughable if attempted by idols. We have heard that Yahweh will bring his people "out of error into truth, out of sin into righteousness, out of death into life."[2] But how is this to be done? Will it be by divine fiat? It certainly sounds that way.

It is no accident that Isaiah 42 is read today. This is the day of the baptism of the Lord. Something is happening today that is so utterly new that the human brain cannot possibly have projected it. God has become man. Yahweh, the Holy One of Israel, the first and the last, who gives his glory to

---

2. From the Book of Common Prayer, Eucharist Rite II, Eucharistic prayer B.

no other, has come down in the person of his Son to be dunked in the muddy waters of the Jordan River for the washing away of sin. What sin? Whose sin? His own sin? Certainly not. Jesus of Nazareth was without sin. Whose sin, then? Listen to these words:

> Surely he has borne our griefs and carried our sorrows. . . .
> All we like sheep have gone astray,
> we have turned every one to his own way,
> and the Lord has laid on him the iniquity of us all. (53:4, 6)

These words, so familiar to us from Handel's *Messiah,* take on an entirely new *(new!)* meaning when heard in their original context. This is Isaiah, chapter 53. At the climax of Second Isaiah's extended, rapturous, ecstatic vision of the paradise that God is going to create, in some of the most exalted language ever produced on paper, suddenly there appears the startlingly, wrenchingly, bafflingly disjunctive picture of what the church has always understood to be the crucified Christ.[3]

The Epiphany season marks the transition from the manger to the Cross. The ultimate glory of God is to be brought about by the ultimate sacrifice. Life is to be wrested from death; sin is to be conquered by the Son of God taking upon himself the sin of the world. This is what the idols cannot do. This is what the various gods of the various religions would never have thought of.

Here is an image. The young woman who lives in the Port Authority Bus Terminal has been a crack addict; she has lied, cheated, and stolen. She has learned to manipulate people. At twenty-six, she has wasted her education and lost several jobs. When she is asleep in her blanket on the floor, there is no way for a passerby to know whether or not she is trying to kick her habit and better herself. Yet, according to the article, she constantly finds that bus passengers put one dollar bill, two dollar bills, even a twenty-dollar bill into her blanket while she is asleep.

Jesus stoops down to us in our miserable condition, bringing the gifts of new life. He does not ask us what we are doing to make ourselves better; he just gives the gift. He does not ask if we are working to turn ourselves around; he does not ask for a receipt; he puts redemption into our blanket. And, having done it, he does not then get on a bus and go to a warmer, more

---

3. Brevard Childs, in *The Struggle to Understand Isaiah as Christian Scripture* (Grand Rapids: Wm. B. Eerdmans, 2004), discusses this at length.

comfortable place; instead, with no place to lay his own head, he gives himself up to suffering and death, paying in his own body the price of sin, idolatry, addiction, greed, pride, and every form of human wickedness. In this sacrifice, toward which the church begins to move in Epiphany, there is a whole new world where everything is changed, where hope appears in the midst of hopelessness, where the promises of God break through to the exiles, where even the smallest acts of human charity signify the coming of the time when water will spring up in all our deserts, the dead will be raised, and all our sins and foolishness will be no more.

AMEN.

# "Spirituality" or Holy Spirit?

FIRST PRESBYTERIAN CHURCH, HENDERSON, NORTH CAROLINA

---

*The Day of Pentecost 2007*                    Isaiah 32:12-20; 44:1-6; Psalm 104

MANY YEARS ago, when our family was going through some bad times, a friend of mine wrote me a long, encouraging letter. It was such an exceptionally good letter that I have kept it all these years. There was only one thing in it that struck a discordant note. She wrote that she knew I would come through the ordeal intact, "because of your spirituality." I think it may have been the first time that the word *spirituality* really came to my attention. I knew there was something wrong with it, but I wasn't sure what.

Today is Pentecost. It's a good day to talk about the difference between "spirituality" and the Holy Spirit of God, the Third Person of the blessed Trinity whose feast day this is.

If you're like me, you find that the Holy Spirit is a much harder reality to grasp than God the Father or God the Son. The Creator we know; Jesus Christ we know. But the Holy Spirit seems more elusive. Jesus himself suggested this when he said to Nicodemus, "The wind blows where it wills, and you hear the sound of it, but you do not know whence it comes or whither it goes; so it is with every one who is born of the Spirit" (John 3:8). It sounds a little spooky. The mainline churches have always been suspicious of the Pentecostal churches, for good reasons in some cases, but we have to admit this: the Pentecostals have us beaten hands down when it comes to understanding the power of the Holy Spirit of God. "Spirituality" doesn't even come close.

Last week I undertook a study of all the Old Testament references to the Holy Spirit. Here's what I found. I found *verbs*. Every time the Spirit of

God is mentioned in the Old Testament, it's connected to all kinds of active, powerful verbs. We read in the books of Judges and Samuel many times that the Spirit of God "came mightily" upon a person. It didn't just *come;* it came *mightily.* Ezekiel says that "the Spirit entered into me and set me upon my feet" (3:24). This Spirit is a mover. When the Spirit shows up, things happen. As you probably know, the word for "spirit" in Hebrew — *ruach* — also means "breath" or "wind." But this isn't just any old breath. This is the power that brought the creation itself into being out of nothing (creation *ex nihilo*). The first mention of the Spirit of God is in the first chapter of Genesis. Here's the familiar translation from the King James Version:

> In the beginning God created the heaven and the earth. And the earth was without form, and void; and darkness was upon the face of the deep. And the Spirit of God moved upon the face of the waters. (1:1-2)

But it can also be translated this way: "a mighty wind from God *swept over* the waters (NRSV alternate). "Swept over" is more forceful than "moved." The Spirit is "mightily" active to create the world "in the beginning." I hope it isn't necessary to say that this is metaphorical truth, not literal truth. The point is this: However the world came into being, God did it.[1] Here's what Isaiah says: "Thus says God, the Lord, who created the heavens and stretched them out, who spread forth the earth and what comes from it, who gives breath to the people upon it and spirit to those who walk in it . . ." (Isa. 42:5).

Psalm 104, the glorious creation Psalm, says this:

> O Lord, how manifold are your works!
>   In wisdom you have made them all;
> the earth is full of your creatures. . . .
>   when you take away their breath, they die
> and return to their dust.
>   When you send forth your Spirit, they are created;
> and you renew the face of the ground. (104:24, 29-30)

---

1. It should always be remembered that the Second Person, or Word, of God is present and powerful at the beginning too, as we read in the Prologue to John's Gospel and the introduction of the Epistle to the Hebrews.

It's right to say that the Spirit of God, the breath or wind of God, is the *energy* of God. This energy, this power, gives life to all things. God is not waiting around for us to develop our spirituality or our "human potential." *God* is the one with the life-giving potency. He is at work "mightily" whether we are ready or not. He is bringing things into being that did not exist before, things that are not dependent on us or created by us. Sometimes the Spirit does things that most of us don't even recognize until they've been accomplished. Think, for instance, of the civil rights movement of forty years ago. Most of us white Southerners — including myself, I am sorry to say — watched the whole thing take place and either ignored it or opposed it. Today, virtually all Christians would agree that it was a great movement of God's Holy Spirit. The black churches knew that all along.[2]

I have been working with the prophet Isaiah for several months. It's an incredibly wonderful book in every way. Isaiah has a great deal to say about the Spirit of God. Listen to this passage from chapter 32 (the prophet is writing in a time of trouble):

> Beat upon your breasts for the [loss of the] pleasant fields, for the [disappearance of the] fruitful vine, for the soil of my people growing up in thorns and briers; yea, for all the joyous houses in the joyful city [have vanished]. For . . . the populous city will be deserted . . . *until the Spirit is poured upon us from on high,* and the wilderness becomes a fruitful field. . . . Then justice will dwell in the wilderness, and righteousness will abide in the fruitful field. And the effect of righteousness will be peace, and the result of righteousness, quietness and trust forever. (32:12-17; my emphasis)

Notice the key verb: the Spirit will be *poured out* from on high. The subject of the verb is God. The passage doesn't say a thing about what human beings are going to do; it says that God is going to pour out his Spirit on his people even though they clearly do not deserve it. The passage speaks of effects and results; these are not the results and effects of human activity, but the blessings of the Spirit. The part about the populous city being deserted might have reminded you of the misfortunes of downtown

---

2. Discerning the Spirit is one of the responsibilities of the Christian community. The apostle John writes, "Beloved, do not believe every spirit, but test the spirits [discern the spirits] to see whether they are of God . . ." (1 John 4:1).

Henderson. Wouldn't it be a good thing to pray that the Lord would pour out his Spirit for a new Henderson built upon the foundation of the old one, but with greatly increased righteousness? Maybe he is raising up servants and leaders right now to do just that, though they may not be aware of it; the book of Isaiah is known for its descriptions of the Persian king, Cyrus, who is acting out the divine purpose even though he does not know God.

The thing to notice in all of Isaiah's passages about the work of the Spirit of God is that *God's power alone* is able to make restoration possible. We human beings cannot do this by ourselves. There is no true justice, righteousness, or peace unless it is given by God. All of us who have safe beds to sleep in should be thanking God every hour of the day. The "quiet resting places" that God promises are not our due; we are not entitled to them; they are his gift, the outpouring of his Spirit. If you and I are resting or shirking or slacking, his Spirit is nevertheless on the move with somebody else somewhere else, for "behold, he that keepeth Israel shall neither slumber nor sleep" (Ps. 121:4). God is always accomplishing his purposes. God is a verb, and the Spirit of God is a verb. The Spirit is not like "spirituality," which, being a noun, just sort of sits there waiting for us to do something with it. God is not waiting. His creative energy is inexhaustible.

Listen to the verbs in the passage from Isaiah 44:

> "Hear this, O Jacob my servant, Israel whom I have *chosen!* Thus says the Lord who *made* you, who *formed* you from the womb and *will help* you: Fear not, O Jacob my servant. . . . For I *will pour* water on the thirsty land, and streams on the dry ground; *I will pour my Spirit* upon your descendants, and my blessing on your offspring. *They shall spring up* like grass amid waters, like willows by flowing streams. . . ." (44:1-4; my emphasis)

All of this activity is the Lord's. He will do these things, and it will be accomplished by the outpouring of the Spirit. And all of it is in the context of some of the most magnificent and most lofty pictures of God that we have in all of Scripture. The promise of the outpouring of the Spirit is set into this context:

> Thus says the Lord, the King of Israel, and his Redeemer, the Lord of hosts: "I am the first and I am the last; besides me there is no god." (44:6)

Isaiah's prophecy[3] is from beginning to end a hymn of praise to the awesome power of God, who by his Spirit brings to light the pretense and impotence of all other so-called gods.

Now, as you know, most of the biblical material about the Holy Spirit is in the *New* Testament, especially the book of Acts, the letters of Paul, and the writings of John. The reason that we've been looking at the *Old* Testament is to show that the Holy Spirit is not something that suddenly appeared at Pentecost. It was there and powerful from the beginning — *"in the beginning."* Why is this important?

When I was here last year, one of your elders asked me a question that interested me. He pointed out that I talked about God a lot, more than I talked about Jesus, and he asked me if this was deliberate on my part. I have been thinking about that ever since. I was thrilled a few weeks ago when I came across just what I was looking for — a passage in something I was reading about John Calvin. (I have the impression that a lot of Presbyterians are embarrassed by Calvin and don't want to claim him. If that's true, it's a big mistake.) It's well-known that Calvin's great theological system characteristically refers to "God." However, and this is the point I want to make, when Calvin speaks of God, he does not typically mean just God the Father, or, if you prefer, God the Creator. He means God in Three Persons.

This is one of the most important things that I can bring you today. Most of the talk about God that floats around in the American atmosphere is vague and shapeless, or, worse, wrapped in the American flag. The word *God* without a context can mean almost anything to anyone. Most often *God* is a projected image of what we want, what we wish for, what we think we need. Christopher Hitchens is right about that God: *that* God is not great.[4] But the God whom Calvin glorified in his superb writings is not projected out of our religious longings. The human imagination is a remarkable thing, but it could not have come up with the idea of One God in Three Persons — let alone the Second Person "crucified under Pontius Pilate." I really would like to hear the enemies of Christianity grapple seriously with that challenge, but they hardly ever do.[5]

---

3. By "Isaiah" I mean the whole book of Isaiah, including "Second" and "Third" Isaiah. Biblical theologians have returned to emphasizing the unity of the book despite its multiple authorship and different settings.

4. Hitchens's book, *God Is Not Great,* was making quite a splash at this time.

5. In order to grapple seriously with it, the atheist challenger would have to spend a lot of time reading Trinitarian doctrine, especially the Church Fathers, and few, if any, would be willing to do that.

Whatever mistakes I make about the Blessed Trinity today, your pastor can straighten out next week on Trinity Sunday. Our church calendar gives us these two Sundays back-to-back so that we can concentrate on this most amazing doctrine. What is the Holy Spirit? The Holy Spirit is the Third Person of the Trinity. The Holy Spirit is the active power of God going out from God's self. Specifically, it's going out from God as the energy created by the dynamic relationship of love between the other two Persons, "proceeding from the Father and the Son," as the Nicene Creed says.[6]

Where is the Holy Spirit at work in the church and world today? Jerry Falwell was certain that the Spirit was galvanizing the anti-abortion movement. Well, maybe.[7] Brother Falwell had his causes — that's for sure. As in the days of the civil rights movement, many Christian people seem to find themselves on opposite sides on the great issues, and the truth emerges later, to the shame of those who took the wrong side. The Civil War is the classic example. I have just come from the cemetery in my hometown of Franklin, Virginia, where a very large stone near my parents' graves commemorates a Confederate officer with the bold inscription "Soldier of the Cross of Christ." On Memorial Day this week, not only American flags but Confederate flags are flying over the graves. That can't be a happy sight for the numerous black people who drive by the cemetery every day on their way to work.

In our own time, the Spirit of God guided the Christians of Poland and Eastern Europe when the Cold War ended, and the largely nonviolent resistance which brought down the apartheid regime in South Africa. In Zimbabwe at this very moment, the Roman Catholic archbishop has defied the disastrous regime of President Mugabe at the risk of his own life, while the Anglican archbishop is in Mugabe's pocket.[8] Whither blows the Spirit?

Just pondering, but today in the pulpits around the land there are sig-

6. The *filioque* ("and the Son") clause is omitted by the Eastern Orthodox Church and has become quite a bone of contention between Eastern and Western churches. The Western argument hinges on the danger of detaching the Third Person from the Son. If the Spirit proceeds only from the Father, then the "scandal of particularity" (the Second Person incarnate and crucified under Pontius Pilate) is lost, with a corresponding lack of emphasis on political ethics, and certainly the history of the Eastern churches would seem to bear this out. I admire the Eastern liturgy and traditions, but there has been no Reformation and no civil rights movement, or anything like them, in the Eastern churches.

7. The Reverend Jerry Falwell had died a few days before this sermon was preached.

8. When this sermon was delivered, the Archbishop of Canterbury was pondering his option of uninviting the Anglican archbishop of Zimbabwe to the Lambeth Conference of Anglican bishops.

nificant challenges occurring. Each of us must discern the signs of the times and make a decision. Not to make a decision is to make one. Whither blows the Spirit of God? What about global warming? A few months ago, the megachurch pastors Rick Warren and Bill Hybels signed a call to action on climate change. The media took note; many observers thought it might be a major turning point in American church life. What about the use of torture? Did you know that the National Association of Evangelicals has unanimously come out against it? This is not just a turning point; this is a seismic shift. Something's going on. If the mainlines can get over their distaste for the evangelicals, we are going to see something happening in American Christianity that we haven't seen for a long time.[9]

Now. Maybe there are a lot of you here who are not up for all this world-historical geopolitical stuff. Maybe you had a hard time just getting out of bed this morning. Maybe your marriage is on the rocks. Maybe someone you love is gravely ill. Maybe you are worried about your future. Maybe you are tired of the role you feel you have to play in order to measure up to somebody else's expectations. Maybe your faith is exhausted. Here's a message for you today.

You are not saved by your spirituality or by your anything else. You have been and you will be saved by God. The Holy Spirit of God is your friend. The Holy Spirit is the love of God reaching out for you when you are too depressed, or too angry, or too tired to reach out. The Holy Spirit is the power of God to set you on your feet when you feel you cannot stand up. Forget your own spirituality. We are talking about *God* today, the force that created the universe yet comes to you personally and intimately with an everlasting and unconditional love whether you believe it or not.

Listen to these words of Paul in Romans 8 (this section of Romans is all about the Holy Spirit):

> We know that the whole creation has been groaning in travail together until now; and not only the creation, but we ourselves, [even though we] have the first fruits of the Spirit, groan inwardly as we wait for . . . the redemption of our bodies. For in this hope we were saved. Now hope that is seen is not hope. For who hopes for what he

9. Four years later, as this book goes to press, it must be admitted that the wind of the Spirit has not been blowing in this direction as dramatically as might be hoped. The split between mainline churches and the Christian Right remains an acute problem. The Epistle to the Ephesians speaks of "grieving the Holy Spirit of God" (4:30) in a similar context.

sees? But if we hope for what we do not see, we wait for it with patience. Likewise the Spirit helps us in our weakness; for we do not know how to pray as we ought, but the Spirit himself intercedes for us with sighs too deep for words . . . because the Spirit intercedes for the saints according to the will of God. (8:22-27)

We do not know how to pray! That's God's verdict on our "spirituality." Even though we look pretty good outwardly, we "groan inwardly," and our prayers are pathetic. But the Holy Spirit prays for us and in us and with us! The energy of the love of the Father and the Son is with you when you pray, even if all you can say is "Help!" Isn't that absolutely wonderful? The Holy Spirit intercedes for us because that is the will of God, to abide with us and in us and to give us strength when we have no strength, faith when we have no faith, hope when we have no hope.

I close with the last words of King David recorded in the second book of Samuel. May these inadequate words from this inadequate messenger be nevertheless for you today the Word of God according to the power of the Spirit.

Now these are the last words of David:
"The Spirit of the Lord speaks by me,
his word is upon my tongue.
The God of Israel has spoken. . . .
he dawns on [us] like the morning light,
like the sun shining forth upon a cloudless morning." (23:1-4)

And all of it is the work of God, Father, Son, and Holy Spirit. May this be his Word for us today.

AMEN.

# A God Not to Believe In

FIFTH AVENUE PRESBYTERIAN CHURCH, NEW YORK CITY

---

*July 2003*                                                     Isaiah 40, 43

SOME OF you may have seen the cover of a recent issue of *New York* magazine featuring "Psychic New York!" Inside there was a full guide to the astrologers, hypnotists, mediums, and tarot card readers of Manhattan. I have subscribed to this magazine for thirty-five years, and I have never yet seen it publish a guide to the Christian churches of New York. Brothers and sisters, we are not in fashion. We live in Babylon-on-the-Hudson.

The prophet that we call Second Isaiah wrote during the period of exile in pagan Babylon (present-day Iraq). "The battering rams of King Nebuchadnezzar" had destroyed the nation of Israel and reduced its deported population to a subject few. The prophet was part of this tiny, squashed company, living in a city dominated by prodigious images of gods and edifices of overpowering mass and scale. The humiliated Israelites were a people of no significance in the presence of the world-dominating presumptions of the Babylonian empire. There was every reason to believe that the God of Israel had lost his might. The covenant appeared to have been abandoned. "Israel's faith was on trial for its life."[1] Imagine now this lone prophet, a member of this discredited minority group. In what has been called the greatest example of *chutzpah* ever, he flings the Word of the God of Israel into the teeth of the Mesopotamian pantheon and all its stargazing mystagogues:

---

1. Quotations from John Bright, *A History of Israel,* 2d ed. (Philadelphia: Westminster Press, 1972), p. 348.

To whom then will you compare me, that I should be like him? says the Holy One [of Israel]. Lift up your eyes on high and see. Who created these [stars and planets]? He who brings out their host by number, calling them all by name; by the greatness of his might, and because he is strong in power, not one is missing.

Have you not known? Have you not heard? The Lord is the everlasting God, the Creator of the ends of the earth. (Isa. 40:25-28)

The mainline churches are going through all sorts of troubles these days. (I'm an Episcopalian who preaches frequently in Presbyterian and Methodist circles — you can't get more mainline than that.) A friend just gave me a Methodist magazine filled with articles about the deep theological split within that denomination. I am sure that many of you saw the story last Tuesday about the Lutheran pastor in Denmark who says he doesn't believe in the God of the Bible. I know quite a few mainline clergy in America who say the same thing, or *think* the same thing, even if they hedge about actually *saying* it — there's an article on yesterday's op-ed page in *The New York Times* accusing the clergy of just that.[2] All of us in the mainlines have been affected by the weakening of traditional faith. I heard an amazing statement the other day. This is a quotation from a professor of religion at one of our Ivy League schools. According to my informant, she told him that she was not an atheist, because, in her words, "You have to take religion very seriously in order to be an atheist." Fifty years of scorn from the intellectual elite has taken its toll. That's why Isaiah has so much to tell us. In an atmosphere of weakened theology, man-made religion, imaginary deities, and imperial cults, the Unknown Prophet of the Exile dares to speak of the God who is really God.

You may have seen the interesting reviews of literary critic James Wood's new novel called *The Book Against God*. Wood grew up in an evangelical family, but, he said in an interview, he tore himself away from a belief in God. However, he has dedicated his book, sincerely and without irony, to his devout Christian parents. He said, "I am grateful to my parents for giving me something to rebel against."[3] That's the idea. I read Mr. Wood's re-

2. This article by a professor of philosophy at Tufts, Daniel C. Dennett, argues that unbelievers of all sorts need to come out of the closet ("The Bright Stuff," *The New York Times,* 12 July 2003). Professor Daniel groups ghosts, elves, and the Easter Bunny together with God among those things that he does not believe in. He proposes that atheists call themselves "brights." Since then, quite a few others have taken up the banner.

3. Dinitia Smith, "Critic at the Mercy of His Own Kind," *The New York Times,* 24 May 2003.

cent article in *The New Yorker* about the King James Version, and it was clear that he had at least some idea of what the Bible is saying about God. It is better to disbelieve in the God who reveals himself in the Bible than it is to make up a God to suit ourselves.[4]

It would hardly be possible to exaggerate the degree of drift away from biblical faith that has taken place in the mainline churches. Your congregation is unusually blessed because you have extensive programs of Scripture study. Really knowing the Bible means that you will have an idea of who the God of Abraham, Isaac, and Jacob is *even if you decide to rebel against him.* The Holy One of Israel is not a therapeutic device, like a spa or a massage or a horoscope. It's vital for the future of the Christian church that we come to grips with the proclamation of God as the powerful deliverer of the poor and the oppressed, rather than a vague, generic deity who sits passively waiting for us to discover him or her at the center of a labyrinth or at the climax of an expensive tour of "spiritual" sites. This is crucial for us to think about in an age when, even within the church itself, the existence and power of the God of the Bible are being called into question. We need to hear the Word of the Lord spoken through Isaiah:

> To whom then will you liken God, or what likeness compare with him? . . . Have you not known? Have you not heard? Has it not been told you from the beginning? Have you not understood from the foundations of the earth? It is he who sits above the circle of the earth . . . who stretches out the heavens like a curtain, and spreads them like a tent to dwell in; who brings princes to naught, and makes the rulers of the earth as nothing. (40:18-23)

> "Before me no god was formed, nor shall there be any after me. I, I am the Lord, and besides me there is no [deliverer] savior." (43:10-11)

The writer (and former Jesuit) Jack Miles deconstructed God a few years ago in his very popular book *God: A Biography.* He argued that Isaiah managed to put together a collection of varying images from different sources to create a mighty *literary* personality that the church now identifies

---

4. In a well-known study, Philip Rieff examined Sigmund Freud's and Carl Jung's idea of God and concluded that perhaps we should "prefer Freud's strong nonexistent God to Jung's weak existent one." See Philip Rieff, *The Triumph of the Therapeutic* (New York: Harper & Row, 1968), p. 91.

as "God." Miles received one of the coveted MacArthur "genius" grants. No one writing from within the church's tradition is ever going to get a MacArthur. In cities like ours, highly educated sophisticates think of themselves as having long since outgrown a need for God. OK, that's the way it is, but let's be sure we redefine the case as we bear our witness. We don't believe in God because we "need" to. That would make our need primary and God secondary. The whole book of Job was written to show that God is *independent of our need.*[5] The prophecy of Isaiah reveals the God who creates, elects, loves, judges, and rescues his people, yes, but not because they "need" him. God does it because it is God's will and nature to do so, and because it shows forth his salvation to the whole world. That is his glory.

> Break forth together into singing, you waste places . . . for the Lord has comforted his people. . . . The Lord has bared his holy arm before the eyes of all the nations; and all the ends of the earth shall see the salvation of our God. (52:9-10)

Once in a while the simple people whom God loves actually break through to make an impression on the sophisticates. I am sure some of you were struck, as I was, by the photograph and story in the *Times* about the "church ladies" of Liberia dancing and praying in the rain. According to the report, these women go out to a field along the main road to Monrovia, and there, every day, rain or shine, they pray and sing to God, asking him to deliver their country from its distress. The headline says, "Liberia's Gentlest Rebels Pray for Peace." The "gentle rebels" part is wonderful. What is the faith of Jesus Christ if not gentle and nonviolent, yet rebellious and revolutionary? But the "pray for peace" part is not quite right. It's too generic. These women are not praying to or for an abstraction like "peace." They are praying to a living, active, *intervening* God to come down and deliver Liberia. In biblical cadences they explained to the reporter what they are doing:

> We are tired.
> We are suffering.
> We are tired of suffering.
> So we come in the sun,
> We come in the rain
> to pray to our God.

5. In his book, Jack Miles misses this point altogether.

*Their leader chants:*
   Liberian mothers thank you, Jehovah God.
*The women respond:*
   Thank you, Jehovah God, thank you.
*The leader calls:*
   Thank you, God, for intervention.
*The women call back:*
   Thank you, Jehovah God, thank you.

Now the reporter who wrote this article tells us that these women are regarded by some as slightly crazed. They are "Liberia's peaceniks, a radical — some would say delusional — breed." Nevertheless, somehow the reporter manages to convey admiration for them. Their prayers are specific and practical, just as biblical prayers should be. "Tell our international brothers [and sisters] to come quickly and stop the killing," said one woman. "Even if right now, as I am speaking, if they could hear us, and come right now, right now, we would be so happy. . . . We want the oppression of women to stop in our country. . . . What is going on now, this raping, this abduction of our children, these are the reasons we are on the streets."

Will the Holy One of Isaiah come down to deliver Liberia? Will he hear the prayers of these mothers? Will he comfort his people? Will all the earth see the salvation of our God? We saw it in South Africa with the end of apartheid; we saw God in action there; we saw God do a mighty work; we saw his deliverance and his salvation; and the people of South Africa rejoiced in it. Will we see it in Liberia? Listen, listen to what those Liberian women, the prayer warriors in the rain have to say. One of them said, "We know God will not come down. *But he will pass through people to help us.*"[6]

The secretary-general of the United Nations, Kofi Annan, meets with President Bush tomorrow.[7] If he succeeds in his mission to convince the Western community to help Liberia, will that be God's doing? Or will it be Kofi Annan's doing, or President Bush's, or Condi Rice's?[8] If such a thing by the grace of God comes to pass, it is a thing certain that the praying

6. Somini Sengupta, "Liberia's Gentlest Rebels Pray for Peace," *The New York Times,* 1 July 2003; emphasis added.

7. By 2004, with the assistance of the UN, the situation in Liberia had improved somewhat, and the problem of sexual abuse and violence was addressed. Since most African countries live with the threat of instability much of the time, however, improvement is incremental, and there remains much to be done.

8. Condoleezza Rice, Secretary of State under George W. Bush.

women of Monrovia will *thank* America, will *thank* the UN, will *thank* the peacekeepers — but they will *praise and glorify* God. They are not primitive and stupid. They do not expect God to come down in a literal sense. But *God passes through people* to bring forth justice and righteousness in the earth.

> Thus says the Lord, your Redeemer, the Holy One of Israel: "For your sake I will send to Babylon and break down all the bars, and the shouting of the Chaldeans will be turned to lamentations. I am the Lord, your Holy One, the Creator of Israel, your King." Thus says the Lord, who makes a way in the sea, a path in the mighty waters. (Isa. 43:14-16)

Chaldeans and Babylonians lived in what is today called Iraq, but that is incidental; the point is that when God intervenes, it means judgment on someone. It might mean judgment on America too. Abraham Lincoln wrestled with that in his Second Inaugural Address. You know that Lincoln was a very great Presbyterian theologian.[9] All during the Civil War, he struggled and agonized, trying to make sense of so much suffering. The address is much too complex and subtle to examine here, but — here's the point — Lincoln was convinced that the war was a judgment of God upon both South *and North* for the sin of slavery, and that it was better to believe this and to know that there was a transcendent purpose behind all the suffering than it was to retreat into bitter recrimination, reprisal, and revenge.

The God of Abraham Lincoln is the God of the Bible, huge, vast, cosmic in dimensions, yet calling forth "malice toward none and charity for all," requiring care for "the widow and orphan," commissioning us "to do all which may achieve and cherish a just and a lasting peace, among ourselves, and with all nations."[10]

Here is a challenge for you as a notable congregation, making a powerful witness when many other churches are in decline. God has placed you in a strategic position for his Kingdom in your splendid building on one of the most famous streets in the world. But like all congregations in all parts of the world, large and small, the danger always lurks: Will you become proud

9. It is often pointed out that Lincoln never joined a church. That does not change the fact that he was a great theologian and that he derived some of his understanding of God and the Bible from listening to sermons in the Presbyterian Church.

10. Quoting from the Second Inaugural Address. See Ronald White's excellent theological study of this address, *Lincoln's Greatest Speech* (New York: Simon & Schuster, 2002).

and self-satisfied? Will you forget the women praying in the rain? I have visited churches all over this country, and many times I have seen powerful
congregations totter in a matter of months from loss of leadership. As you
know, you cannot count on charismatic leadership alone to guide you indefinitely.[11] In the last analysis, it is the *congregation* that must grow in awareness of its greatness, not its greatness as the world measures such things, not
its greatness in buildings and endowments and programs, but its greatness
in the sight of God. Because when churches become powerful, it is not their
own doing; it is God's doing.

This is a crucial time in American history. Many say that we have become an imperial power, with all the arrogance and heedlessness that goes
with hegemony. The more powerful and dominant we become, the more
God is invoked at every hand. But Isaiah reminds us:

> All the nations are as nothing before [God], they are accounted by
> him as less than nothing and emptiness. . . . Scarcely are they planted,
> scarcely sown, scarcely has their stem taken root in the earth, when
> he blows upon them, and they wither, and the tempest carries them
> off like stubble. (43:17, 23-24)

America had, I believe, a divine founding. Call it American
exceptionalism if you like. But that makes America all the more vulnerable
to God's judgment if we become accustomed to glamorizing war, excusing
lies, and parading our might and dominance. Who is going to be the
counter-voice? Who is going to remind the powerful and the great that God
loves the poor and the small? Who will defend the homeless people and the
veterans languishing in hospitals and the prisoners at Guantánamo?[12] Who
is going to be the unpopular voice that says God loves justice for all people
everywhere, not just America's allies of the moment? Who is going to protest that God requires mercy? Who if not the church?

In an atmosphere of weakened theology, imaginary deities, imperial cults,
and man-made religion, hear the Word of God to us who are here today:

> "You are my witnesses," says the Lord, "my servant[s] whom I have
> chosen, so that you may know and believe me and understand that I

---

11. Ironically, it was not long after this that Fifth Avenue Presbyterian lost its charismatic
pastor. The congregation experienced serious difficulties, but endured.

12. The photographs from Abu Ghraib did not become public until 2004.

am He. Before me no god was formed, nor shall there be any after me.
I, I am the Lord, and besides me there is no savior." (Isa. 43:10-11)

Facilities and numbers and dollars are beside the point. *The Lord, he is
God.* I believe you have some sense of that. I rejoice to have some small part
in the great enterprise of your Christian discernment, not falling in line
with what the culture tells you, but identifying what God is doing in the
world and running with joy to meet him there. There is no mission so great
as this, no security equal to this, no ideology that can touch this.

"I am the Lord, your Holy One, the Creator of Israel, your King. . . .
I am about to do a new thing; now it springs forth, do you not perceive it?" (Isa. 43:15, 19)

# On the Palms of God's Hands

*May 2008*                                                            Isaiah 49

*This sermon was preached for Christ Church-Trinity Lu-
theran, a small conjoined congregation in western Massachusetts. It is relatively healthy, but most churches in New England are struggling with declining membership, as noted in
the sermon.*

. . . . . . . . . . . . . . . . .

PRINTED BIBLICAL readings, like the one you received this morning, are
used by many churches, but they have disadvantages. Today, for example, it
would be much better if you could have an actual Bible with you, because
some things are missing from the printed excerpt. It ends with these words
from Isaiah 49:

Can a woman forget her nursing child,
or show no compassion for the child of her womb?
Even these may forget,
yet I will not forget you.
See, I have inscribed you on the palms of my hands;
your walls are continually before me.

The next sentence isn't on your page:

Your builders outdo your destroyers,
and those who laid you waste go away from you. (49:15-17, NRSV)

That verse is really important, and we'll be incorporating it into the sermon this morning.

Another thing that the printed excerpt doesn't give you is the context. It begins with a rapturously joyful passage, so it's hard for us to realize that the setting in life is one of deprivation and despair. The proximate verses speak of waste and desolate places, a devastated land, bereavement and barrenness, a city of old people and no children, like a dwindling congregation where there are no baptisms taking place. That last part is the most important. Israel is in exile, in Babylon. The Lord's household appears to be barren. There isn't any next generation coming along. Back in Judea, the temple has been destroyed, and the people have been completely demoralized. The words of Isaiah are spoken into that situation.

In the book of what's sometimes called Second Isaiah (beginning with chapter 40), the people's suffering and despair are addressed in many ways. The passages alternate among different voices. Sometimes the people speak; sometimes the prophet speaks; sometimes God speaks directly. Here in today's selection, the people speak in just one verse:

But Zion said, "The Lord has forsaken me, my Lord has
forgotten me." (49:14)

The people are personified as one entity, *Zion,* which has the same meaning as Jerusalem, Israel, Judah — just different names for the same thing. *Zion* means "the people of God." So it is the people of God who say, "The Lord has forsaken me." It's easy to overlook that one verse in your printed text because most of the selection is a rapturous vision of the promised future. I'd like to read you something from a commentary on Second Isaiah: "It is hard to grasp that anyone could walk the hard, dark road that was Deutero-Isaiah's lot and sing with joy as he does."[1] When we read the glorious promises that make this book famous, we must always remember that they come out of a context of apparent hopelessness. A lot of articles have been written recently about the rapidly diminishing congregations of Christians in the Middle East. What must it be like for them? This congre-

---

1. James D. Smart, *History and Theology in Second Isaiah* (Philadelphia: Westminster Press, 1965), p. 215.

gation in Sheffield is healthy, praise the Lord, but all around us in New England, and in the Great Plains, and other places, churches are dying; congregations are just melting away.

Worse still is the moral condition of the church. I have here a clipping from the front page of *The New York Times* a few days ago. It's a story about violence directed against churchgoers in Zimbabwe. The church in Zimbabwe is politically divided because the president of the country, Robert Mugabe, has turned his back on his formerly progressive policies and has focused instead on power for himself. The Anglican bishop, Nolbert Kunonga, is one of Mr. Mugabe's best buddies, with a two-million-dollar farm and seven-bedroom house to show for it. Bishop Kunonga has been removed from his post by the Archbishop of Canterbury, but he is still there in Harare and still in Mugabe's pocket.

The great hope in Zimbabwe was the Roman Catholic archbishop, Pius Ncube, whose opposition to Mugabe at the risk of his own life was extraordinarily inspiring, along the lines of Desmond Tutu. It was, that is, until the government recently got hold of some photos of Bishop Ncube in a compromising position with a married woman. (We can all be thankful that it wasn't a child! But even so, his future as the leader of the church's opposition came to an abrupt halt.)

So what are we to think of this church that God has attached himself to? What does the world think of us? We are quite sheltered, here in the Berkshires, from the stress and strain of what's going on in the national Episcopal Church these days. The Lutherans are relatively quiet at the moment, but no denomination is going to rest easy in these times. The pain and anger, hurt and misunderstanding, self-righteousness and vindictiveness, and general bad behavior that is going on among people that I know and love around the country is just indescribable, and it's taking a tremendous toll. We can therefore find some common thread in the lament of the demoralized Hebrews in their exile: "The Lord has forsaken me, my Lord has forgotten me."

It helps to remember that the ancient Hebrew mind did not make the distinction between the individual and the group that the American mind typically makes. In the world of the Bible, an individual without a community would be a person inconceivably deprived, hardly a person at all. When the biblical writers say "Israel" or "Zion" or "Joseph," they mean the community; yet — get this — they say "he" or "she" instead of "we," to show that the individual has not become absorbed into an undifferentiated blob of faceless humanity. Here in our text, Zion laments, "The Lord has forsaken *me, my* Lord has forgotten *me.*" So it works at both levels, *both* the individual *and* the communal, but never the individual *without* the communal.

To this lament of Zion about being forsaken and forgotten, the Lord speaks directly to his people (through his prophet) in words of astonishing intimacy:

Can a woman forget her nursing child,
or show no compassion for the child of her womb?
Even these may forget, yet I will not forget you.

This is remarkable. Usually God speaks to Israel as a father or a husband. In this exceptional case, God chooses to compare his love for his people in the strongest possible image: that of the mother who bears her child for nine months within her body and nurses the infant with her own milk. As one of the old theologians writes, "What amazing affection does a mother feel toward her offspring, which she . . . watches over with tender care, so that she passes sleepless nights, wears herself out by continual anxiety and forgets herself!"[2] This is the image that God uses to convey his love. And even if a mother forgets her child, says the Lord, I will not forget. Even though there are, as we know, some mothers in this world who are so crazed or depraved that they abandon their own children, the Lord promises never to forsake or forget his people, whom he loves and cares for as a father and a mother.

And so these promises of God are not made to individuals existing in isolation from other individuals. They are made to a community of individuals who have become organically connected to one another like a family, with God as their common father and mother.

We have all heard of groups that function like families. Cancer support groups, company employees, teams of rescue workers, groups of hikers or bikers or bridge players or any number of other groups sometimes say about themselves, "We are family." (I think even Barney the dinosaur said that.) But the family of God is not like these other human groups. In God's family, we don't choose our brothers and sisters according to mutual interests or activities. In the church, our brothers and sisters are chosen for us, given to us. I suppose the biologists would tell us that we are a family

2. John Calvin, *Commentary on the Prophet Isaiah,* Calvin's Commentaries, vol. 8, 2nd vol. (Grand Rapids: Baker Book House, 1984), pp. 30-31.

because we have common ancestors back in prehistoric ages, but that's not the same kind of family as the one that has a living Father who loves all his children as much as a mother and a father combined, only much more so because this Father is not only able to *make* divine promises but also *to cause them to come true.* Like a human parent, he has the love and the will to do good things for his children, but he has something inconceivably greater: he has the power to do those good things. The church, unlike human institutions, has a divine origin, a divine mission, and a divine destiny. The promises of God to the church are not contingent upon the church being a model of virtue. The promises made to the church are based in the faithfulness of God.

The church is always addressed as the whole church. The wheat and the chaff are growing together. It is impossible to separate them in this life, and God does not separate them. The church will always have sin and sinners in her midst until the great day of our Lord's coming. But listen again to this verse that's not on your printed sheet:

Your builders will outdo your destroyers.

The church is full of those who would destroy it with sin and selfishness. And we shouldn't make the mistake of thinking that only applies to *other* people. Every one of us has at one time or another offended a brother or sister, or failed to welcome a visitor, or neglected to offer comfort, or overlooked a wrong. Even a congregation as healthy as this one has its faults, its strains and tensions. But *your builders will outdo your destroyers.* There are severe divisions and problems in the American churches, but the builders will outdo the destroyers. The church around the world suffers greatly, but its builders will outdo its destroyers.

How do we know that? How can we be sure of it? There is only one way, the way of faith. But this is not generalized faith with a vague object. This is faith in the promise of the living God of Israel, the God who created heaven and earth with a purpose, who, "when we had fallen into sin and become subject to evil and death," sent his only Son to offer himself as a living sacrifice and put the entire creation on a new foundation. Isaiah saw the purpose of God by revelation and faith. God's promise comes from the grave of human hopes.

"It is hard to grasp that anyone could walk the hard, dark road that was Deutero-Isaiah's lot and sing with joy as he does." That is the wonder of this biblical book. In chapters 40–55 of the book of Isaiah, we have reached the summit of the Old Testament. We know this unknown prophet of the Exile only as Second Isaiah, but no one else among the prophets has such a universal vision of redemption and new creation. But we should never forget that the vision was held in tandem with suffering and death. Only God can conquer the sorrows and evils of this world, let alone do this with such poor builders as we are.

Yet he wants us as builders! In spite of our obvious weaknesses, he intends to use *you* as builders. The merger of the two congregations here is surely a sign of *building,* for this Lutheran congregation was hanging by a thread for several years. The merger is not a finished product, of course; it's not completed; there will be challenges, there will be disappointments, there will be losses. But listen to this word from the Lord:

> . . . I will not forget you.
> See, I have inscribed you on the palms of my hands;
> your walls are continually before me.
> Your builders outdo your destroyers. . . .

"I have inscribed you on the palms of my hands." What an extraordinary thing the Lord says here! Why on the palms? Because of all places on the body, the palms are always visible to their owner, and they are always working. We hear the refrain all the time in the Old Testament: the Lord has done something "with his mighty hand." Does this mean that God has hands? Of course not, but he uses images and figures of speech that we can understand. God never forgets us because his palms are always before him, always seen by him, never forgotten by him. Even if a mother forgets her child, I will not forget you, says the Lord. But not only does he not forget us, he is working on our behalf with his mighty hand, making use of us as his builders. Most of us can't build the way that the carpenters, electricians, and masons among us can build, but each of us is able to make a contribution to the upbuilding of this congregation because that is God's purpose. The walls of the church are ever before him, as though the Great Architect had the plans engraved on his palms. The builders will outdo the destroyers. (And don't forget, paraphrasing Woody Allen, that eighty percent of building the church is just showing up.)

The sociologists and the statisticians and the futurists are predicting the death of the church. The church in New England is in exile in the very land of its birth. Yet into this decline, this estrangement, this bereavement, the One who has demonstrated his power to raise the dead and pour out his

Spirit upon the church even in the wilderness speaks to you and to me this very day as if for the first time:

> . . . I will not forget you [says the Lord].
> See, I have inscribed you on the palms of my hands;
> your walls are continually before me.
> Your builders outdo your destroyers.

AMEN.

# The Father Who Does Not Devour

---

*October 1994*                                                                    Isaiah 53:3-6

MOZART'S OPERA *Idomeneo* has a plot taken from the period of the Trojan war. The story tells of Idomeneo, king of Crete. When his life is threatened by a storm at sea, he makes a vow to the god Neptune to sacrifice the first person he meets. As he is washed up safely on shore, the person who first appears turns out to be his own son.

In the Metropolitan Opera production, the entire stage is dominated by a colossal head of Neptune. He has eels and other sea creatures for hair, huge black holes for eyes, and an enormous, cavernous, devouring mouth. We get the message: Neptune's wrathful power constantly looms over the land and people of Crete. The libretto speaks of the "inexorable god" who "does not cease to threaten," "fierce Neptune" in whose presence no one can be at peace for long. The chorus of Cretans laments, "Have mercy! Pitiless fate thrusts us into the arms of dreadful death. . . . What is our sin, that heaven rages?" The High Priest appears and addresses Idomeneo, demanding that he keep his vow to kill his son in order to turn away the rage of the god: "Who is the victim, and where is he? Render to Neptune that which is his."[1]

Variations of this story about human failure and a vengeful God who has to be appeased run through the entire history of myth and world religion. The basic motif is familiar to us from a hundred sources. Something is terribly wrong in human life: storms devastate, plague spreads, violence destroys. The god is angry and demands to be placated. Ordinary sacri-

---

1. *Idomeneo* translation by Lionel Salter from the Italian by Giambattista Varesco.

fices will not avail; only the life of a human being will avert the wrath of the deity.

Now, we should bear in mind that people who went to the opera in Mozart's time did not believe this sort of thing any more than you or I do. The story of Idomeneo was part of the heritage from classical antiquity, not a literal description of the way that gods need to be bought off. We are moved by the drama, not because we believe in Neptune, but because of the beauty of the music and the universal themes of war and peace, vengeance and mercy, retribution and self-sacrifice. In other respects the presuppositions of the story leave us untouched. We do not believe in angry gods who demand human sacrifice.

Or do we? Perhaps the ancients were not so naïve as we might suppose. After all, we still speak of Oedipus and Electra complexes when we want to talk about the most basic, most formative influences in the development of human character, the relationship with the parents or parent figures. Every parish priest will tell you that there are countless numbers of big, strong, grown men who have achieved great things in the world and yet remain terrorized in their inner selves by the fear of a condemning father or punitive mother. The giants and ogres and wicked witches of the fairy tales still have universal power because they are really projections of the fearful aspect of our parents. I once asked a powerful, self-confident man to tell me the most frightening moment in his life. I expected him to tell me something from the Vietnam War. Without hesitation, he said, "When I was a little boy, my father ordered me to jump into a pond where he knew there were snakes." The devouring mouth of Neptune is still with us. In the movie *The Great Santini,* there is a scene of sheer terror. The young boy through whose eyes the story is told dares to try to compete with his Marine Corps father on a basketball court. The father, taking the ball and repeatedly bouncing it off the boy's forehead, verbally berates, ridicules, and humiliates him. To me, that episode was more violent and horrifying than a hundred scenes of gore and mayhem. Fear of condemnation by a wrathful father (or mother) is one of the most fundamental of human emotions, and it drives us all of our lives, whether we know it or not.

So it seems that we do believe in angry gods who demand human sacrifice, after all. The Christian story throughout the ages has often been cast in terms of an enormous, devouring maw that threatens to consume and destroy everybody within reach. Even people who know virtually nothing about the Bible will speak of "the Old Testament God" of wrath and judgment. As they speak of this supposed God, they will make it clear that they do not believe in him. Yet very often their actions belie their words, for they demonstrate in their behavior and attitudes the same problem that the rest of us have — namely, the fear of not measuring up, the struggle to believe that one is good enough to pass muster before some dreadful Judge with a cavernous mouth. Ten thousand times ten thousand wise words have been written about this; one quotation will suffice as an example, from Joseph Conrad's famous character Marlow in *Lord Jim:* "Nobody, nobody is good enough."

The Christian church knows what to do about this fear. We put it into our confession of sin. Something is, indeed, terribly wrong with human life. That's why we say in the General Confession, "We have left undone those things that we ought to have done, and we have done those things that we ought not to have done." (Like a great many Episcopalians over sixty, I for one still add, mentally, those omitted words "and there is no health in us.") We have reason to think that there is a huge God ready to devour us all. If we are terrified of our fathers and mothers, it is because somewhere down deep, most likely below the surface of conscious awareness, we are afraid that we have done something irretrievably bad. We have good reason to think that there is going to be a human sacrifice required, and that it is going to be us.

Recently, as Billy Graham's Parkinson's disease has grown worse, there have been a number of articles about his son Franklin. When Franklin Graham was a young man, he was a hell-raiser, a rebel. He smoked, drank, collected guns, rode a motorcycle, and was not at all a model son. One day (he can date it to July 22, 1974), his life changed. His father took him out to lunch in Lausanne, Switzerland, where they both were staying. I think every one of us can envision such an occasion. We can readily imagine the fear of being eaten for lunch by an enraged parent. I am sorry to say that my own children have sometimes experienced me this way. As Franklin Graham tells the story, Billy Graham told him that day at lunch in Switzerland that he sensed his son was going through some sort of spiritual struggle, that he should know his parents were praying for him, and that he would always be welcome in their home, no matter what.

Two weeks later, Franklin Graham underwent a conversion experience, getting down on his knees and receiving the forgiveness of sins from the Lord Jesus Christ.

Amazing grace! The fearsome ogre turned out to be the loving father of the prodigal son. Mercy evoked repentance, not the other way around. The unconditional love of the father won the battle for the son's heart and mind. The gift of the father's understanding was the occasion for a new creation. When the son knew he was safe from the devouring mouth, he was able to receive forgiveness and a transformed life.[2] The space of grace that had been opened for him enabled him to understand for the first time that the words of the prophet Isaiah were about the Lord Jesus:

> Upon him was the chastisement that made us whole, and with his stripes we are healed. All we like sheep have gone astray; we have turned every one to his own way; and the Lord has laid on him the iniquity of us all. (53:5-6)

We are not going to be eaten for lunch. Instead, in a reversal that has no parallel in the history of religion, the incarnate Lord gives his own body and blood to be heavenly food *for us.* As Christ said of himself, "The Son of Man also came not to be served but to serve, and to give his life as a ransom for many" (Mark 10:45).

The Christian story is not about "the Old Testament God." There is no Old Testament God different from the New Testament God. The Old Testament God is the God of the prophet Isaiah and the Father of our Lord Jesus Christ: "Hear, O Israel: the Lord our God, the Lord is one" (Deut. 6:4). He is the God to whom Jesus prayed in the garden, "Abba, Father." He is the God who says through his Old Testament prophet, "Upon him was the chastisement that made us whole, and with his stripes we are healed" (Isa. 53:6b).

With all due respect to the religions of the world, there is no other story like the Christian story. The god who thunders, the god who persecutes and condemns, the god who wreaks vengeance — yes, we know this god from the caricatures. We know this god from the old paintings. We know this god from hearing continual references to "the Old Testament God." But this is not who God is. "The Old Testament God" is the one who has come down from his throne on high into the world of sinful human flesh and of his own free will and decision *has come under his own judgment* in order to deliver us from everlasting condemnation and bring us into eternal life. He has not *required* human sacrifice; he has himself *become* the human sacrifice. He has not turned *us* over and forsaken *us;* he was *himself* turned over and forsaken. This is what the Old Testament prophet Isaiah says:

---

2. In the years since this sermon was preached, Franklin Graham has said things — about Islam, for instance — that many people have found offensive. That does not change the power of the father-son story.

Surely he has borne our griefs and carried our sorrows; yet we esteemed him stricken, smitten by God, and afflicted. But he was wounded for our transgressions, he was bruised for our iniquities; upon him was the chastisement that made us whole, and with his stripes we are healed. (53:4-5)

We are not going to be eaten for lunch. Instead, in a reversal that has no parallel in the history of religion, the incarnate Lord gives his own body and blood to be heavenly food *for us.* "The Son of Man also came not to be served but to serve, and to give his life as a ransom for many." Our heavenly Father has not ordered us into the water with the snakes. He has gone into the water with the snakes himself.

# O Beulah Land!

*Second Sunday after the Epiphany 2007*     Isaiah 62:1-5; Job 2:13; 40:15

ALMOST FORTY years ago, I used to go regularly to a dry cleaner in our New York suburb where an elderly woman from somewhere down South occasionally worked. One day I asked her what her name was. She cast her eyes down and said, "Beulah." I started to say "What a wonderful name," but she spoke first, saying in a low voice as if she were ashamed, "It's a country name." She did not know what it meant, and at that time I was not confident enough in my knowledge of the Old Testament to tell her. I have thought of her a hundred times, wishing that I could see her again and tell her that her name is glorious.

The main character in Nathaniel Hawthorne's novel *The House of Seven Gables* is named Hepzibah Pyncheon. Those were the days when everyone knew the Bible through and through and named their children from it. Anyone walking through a nineteenth-century cemetery will see "Obadiahs" and "Calebs" and "Tabithas" by the score. These Americans read only one Bible, the King James Version; and their version of Isaiah 62 said this:

> Thou shalt no more be termed Forsaken; neither shall thy land any more be termed Desolate: but thou shalt be called Hephzibah, and thy land Beulah: for the Lord delighteth in thee, and thy land shall be married. (62:4)

---

The sermon title echoes the title the first of five serial novels by noted writer Mary Lee Settle. She knew the Bible well.

It's really important to understand the context of these words. They were written by a prophet of Israel whose people were utterly downcast and despairing. The Israelites had been conquered, humiliated, and carried off captive by the Babylonians. They were hauled away to mighty Mesopotamia (modern-day Iraq), where the colossal Babylonian gods looked scornfully down on them as if to say, "Where is your God now?" That was a very difficult question to answer. The Hebrew captives asked it themselves, repeatedly. "How long, O Lord, will you remain silent?" We hear this despairing lament over and over in the later parts of the Old Testament. It is a question that every person in this place of worship today has asked, or will someday ask. Where is God? Why doesn't he do something?

When God finally did do something, moving the heart of the Persian king to let them go home, it seemed as though their prayers had been answered and the Lord's name vindicated. But what a devastating homecoming it was! The people lament:

Thy holy cities have become a wilderness, Zion has become a wilderness, Jerusalem a desolation. Our holy and beautiful [temple], where our fathers praised thee, has been burned by fire, and all our pleasant places have become ruins.[1] Wilt thou restrain thyself at these things, O Lord? Wilt thou keep silent, and afflict us sorely? (Isa. 64:10-12)

A commentator puts it this way:

The country is inhabited. People live in the ruins of Jerusalem. Farmers and vine growers carry on their work. . . . But it is a broken and oppressed community, burdened with rapacious rulers from beyond its borders and even more by its own consciousness of God's hand resting heavily upon it in judgment. As time passed, the latter deepened into a despairing sense of Godforsakenness. . . .[2]

So, if we can put ourselves into the place of those who heard Isaiah's prophecy, if we can imagine ourselves as those who have been lamenting for a long time that God is unresponsive, that we cannot reach him, that he

1. At the time of this sermon, paramount in my thoughts was New Orleans, a city that had given me more joy than any other American city. For those who made their homes in the drowned parts of town, all the pleasant places had become ruins.

2. James D. Smart, *History and Theology in Second Isaiah* (Philadelphia: Westminster Press, 1965), p. 264.

does not show his face, that he is silent, then the words of the prophet are electrifying:

For Zion's sake I will not keep silent . . . (62:1)

This announcement is meant to strike our ears as though someone had sounded a bugle in the church. For your sake, for our sake — that's what Zion means — for the sake of the people of God, the prophet raises his voice in a clarion call. I will not keep silent! God has given me something to say!

Nothing in the Bible makes any religious sense unless we are people of faith who believe that God's own self speaks to us in this living Word. Well, maybe there's one exception, and that's the mournful book of Ecclesiastes. Ecclesiastes makes plenty of sense if there's no word from God. It's a very important book, Ecclesiastes. One of the most beautifully written portions of the Bible, it lays it all out before us, a world where one meaningless event follows another, where all is vanity and "striving after wind, and there is nothing new under the sun" (2:11). We are supposed to set Ecclesiastes alongside the writings of the prophets. Isaiah is the one who brings the astounding announcement:

"Behold [says the Lord], I am doing a new thing." (43:19)

"For Zion's sake I will not keep silent." That is the rallying cry of Christians over the centuries who have not kept the gospel to themselves. The good news is proclaimed: the Lord has turned to his people. "No more will you be called Forsaken [*Azubah*], and your land shall no more be termed Desolate [*Shemamah*]; but you shall be called My Delight Is in Her [*Hephzibah*], and your land [shall be called] Married [*Beulah*]; for the Lord delights in you, and your land shall be married" (62:4).

It might have been a bit difficult to explain to Beulah in the dry cleaners' what her name was supposed to mean. She looked to me as if she'd seen a world of trouble, and maybe a bad marriage had been part of that. It takes a bit of effort for any one of us today to understand why the name *Beulah* is wonderful. We need to know less about *man* (in both senses of that word) and more about *God* and his covenant with Israel. We need to know that God betrothed himself to his people in the wilderness, promising to be faithful to them and bless them forever. We need to recall the way that the children of Israel turned their backs on the covenant the way a husband walks out on a wife, or vice versa. We need to know about the prophet Hosea, who has his own book in the Old Testament. Hosea was told by God to go and redeem the woman whom he had married, a harlot who had abandoned him. *Redeem* — that's a word with a world of meaning. To redeem something means to buy it back at a price. Hosea did that. Following the command of God, Hosea followed his wife into the sinkhole where she had gone and paid the price to her pimp.

Why did Hosea do that?

It was an image of God. The Holy One of Israel, as Isaiah calls him, would not give up on his people. His heart yearned after them. He would not let them go. God would pay the price for them. Then he would marry them and be their God forever. Listen to Isaiah again, speaking to God's people:

> For as a young man marries a young woman, so shall your builder marry you, and as the bridegroom rejoices over the bride, so shall your God rejoice over you. (62:5)

The image of marriage is one that God has chosen for himself and his people. All through the prophetic literature of the Old Testament, we hear the imagery of God as the husband of his people. This takes a wondrous new form in the New Testament, where the church is called the Bride of Christ, and our Lord calls himself the Bridegroom. In the midst of irrevocable dissolution, in a situation of God-forsakenness, in the miasma of depression and despair, at the extremity of loneliness and hopelessness, the word comes: I love you. I am coming to you. I am going to restore everything that you have lost.

But now, wait a minute. How does this announcement change anything? The world still looks a whole lot more like the world of Ecclesiastes than it does like the promised Kingdom of God. The oppressed are not free, the poor are not rich, and the dead are not raised.

I have been working for a year on a chapter about evil and suffering. In a sense I have been working on it all my life. If there is one thing that can be said for certain, it is this: No one understands the mystery of evil and suffering. Moreover, no one can explain why God — if there is a God — allows the things he allows. No one can explain why God seems to be silent when we most need to hear from him. In fact, the best stance to take in the time of extreme suffering is "rage against explanation." I didn't make up that phrase; it comes from a book by a Christian theologian who wrote a book about the mystery of suffering and the apparent silence of God.[3] In such sit-

---

3. David Bentley Hart, *The Doors of the Sea: Where Was God in the Tsunami?* (Grand Rapids: Wm. B. Eerdmans, 2005).

uations, "rage against explanation" is the right posture to take, and people who offer explanations to sufferers would be more helpful if they, like God, would remain silent. We read in the book of Job that after calamity came to Job, his friends came to comfort him:

> And they sat with him on the ground seven days and seven nights, and no one spoke a word to him, for they saw that his suffering was very great. (2:13)

This has come down in the Jewish tradition as "Sitting Shiva" — "sitting seven." The *silence* of Job's friends was helpful to him; the trouble began when they started to *talk* and find explanations. Job's rage against explanation is, in a perverse way, a sort of model.

And what finally comforted Job?

The voice of God. But God does not say anything we would have wanted to have him say. He says nothing at all about Job's suffering. He says, basically, "Job, behold the hippopotamus [KJV: "Behold now Behemoth"[4]]. Can you make anything like that?" (40:15). And Job says, "I won't say another word, because I have met God."

God is God. He is not us. As Isaiah says, his thoughts are not our thoughts, and his ways are not our ways. But once you have grasped even a tiny bit of the greatness and majesty and otherness of God, then the news from God is all the more staggering and awesome:

> As the bridegroom rejoices over the bride, so shall your God rejoice over you.

These are intimately personal terms. Like a young man passionately in love, God loves us and rejoices in us. The prophetic books abound in this personal imagery: God is the father of the fatherless (Hos. 3:14, KJV); he calls Israel his "darling child" (Jer. 31:20); he has written us "on the palms of his hands" (Isa. 49:16); he lifts up his children and carries them like a mother (Isa. 63:9). And our Old Testament ends with the promise that the coming God will turn the hearts of the children to the parents and the hearts of the parents to the children (Mal. 4:6). O Beulah land!

---

4. In spite of humorous attempts to render this ("Look at the hippopotamus!"), the word *behold* simply must be retained. In both Hebrew and English, the word *behold* has a revelatory quality. It is a word of awe, having nothing to do with human seeing.

In the final analysis, in this world there is nothing to sustain any of this except faith and hope. The prophet Elisha brought the son of the Shunammite woman back to life from the dead (2 Kings 4:8-37). There do not seem to be any Elishas among us today. There is no human explanation for these matters.

But the story does not end here.

The story comes to its appointed consummation with a Redemption greater by far, a price paid that is infinitely higher than that paid for Hosea's wife. This time it is not one wife who is bought back, but the whole world. "The Son of Man came not to be served but to serve, and to give his life as a ransom for many" (Mark 10:45). "God gave his only-begotten Son" (John 3:28). "I am the Resurrection and the life, saith the Lord; he who believes in me, though he were dead, yet shall he live . . . and I will raise him up at the last day" (John 11:25-26).

And so this is the message to those here today who have even the smallest seed of faith in the Son of God:

As the Lord spoke through his prophet Isaiah, pledging gifts of eternal love to his people, so he speaks and acts still, through those who draw near to him. Your smallest action might be life itself for someone. I read an article the other day about a prominent man in desperate financial trouble. All his friends had abandoned him. He had not heard from a single one. His words were poignant: "If only there had been even one call," he said, "just one message at midnight, wishing me the best. I would have been so happy."[5]

You, too, can be the messenger at midnight. That is the way God works. The silence of God is broken by God's speech. It is not the human speech of Job's friends, who tried to give Job comfort where there was no comfort, and explanations where there were no explanations. The speech of God is not the language of explanation. It is the language of promise — promise that God will give a family to the desolate, joy to the despairing, and a new creation bursting with the wonders of his love:

5. This man was Alberto Vilar, who to this day remains the third-largest donor in Metropolitan Opera history. He gave twelve million and pledged many millions more, which he was then unable to pay. His fall was complete. He was convicted of securities fraud and sentenced to nine years in prison. His name was removed from the Grand Tier of the opera house. While awaiting trial, he found some solace at St. Thomas, Fifth Avenue. (See James B. Stewart, "The Opera Lover," *The New Yorker*, 13-20 February 2006.) There is no doubt about Vilar's culpability, but he is in some ways a sympathetic crook, because he truly adored the arts and was so clearly addicted to philanthropy. One ex-friend said that asking Vilar for money for the arts was like offering an active alcoholic a drink.

For Zion's sake I will not keep silent . . .

No more will you be called Forsaken [*Azubah*], and your land shall no more be termed Desolate [*Shemamah*]; but you shall be called My Delight Is in Her [*Hephzibah*], and your land Married [*Beulah*]; for the Lord delights in you, and your land shall be married.

For . . . as the bridegroom rejoices over the bride, so shall your God rejoice over you.

AMEN.

# God's Justice Is a Verb

ST. PAUL'S CHURCH, RICHMOND, VIRGINIA

---

*2009*                                                              Jeremiah 9:23-24

FIFTY YEARS ago, being a political junkie then as now, I used to sit up in the balcony of the Legislature over here at the Capitol watching the Byrd machine at work, and listening to all the speeches against miscegenation and amalgamation; and believe it, there was no person at that time and in that place who could possibly have foreseen a day when the state of Virginia would help to elect a president who was the son of a white mother and a black African father. John Hope Franklin, the great African-American historian who died this week, said that the election of Barack Obama was the closest thing to a peaceful revolution this country had ever seen.[1]

On the night when Dr. Franklin was awarded the Presidential Medal of Freedom, he was honored at a celebratory dinner at the elite Cosmos Club, where he had been the first black person to become a member. After dinner, a white woman approached him. She thought he was the coat-check man. As Franklin later reflected, she was unable to see a black man in any role other than that of a person whose purpose in life was to serve her. If that is true for a man like Professor Franklin, how much more true is it for a black person in a more humble station in life. More about that shortly.

During the civil rights movement, the marchers and protesters and re-

---

1. The fact that Obama, as this goes to press, has disappointed many of his supporters cannot take away from the historic nature of his campaign and election.

[ 311 ]

sisters, almost all of them brought up in the black church, were sustained all the way through by the Word of the Lord. For instance, this passage from Jeremiah:

> Thus says the Lord: "Let not the wise man glory in his wisdom, neither let the mighty man glory in his might, let not the rich man glory in his riches: But let those who glory, glory in this, that they understand and know me, that I am the Lord who exercises lovingkindness, judgment, and righteousness in the earth: for in these things I delight, says the Lord." (9:23-24)

"I am the Lord who exercises lovingkindness, judgment, and righteousness in the earth." In most popular American religion, all the emphasis is on the lovingkindness. We habitually speak of God as a loving, embracing, forgiving, "inclusive" God. But without judgment and righteousness, nothing else can flourish. The distinguished New Testament scholar Reginald Fuller, who was here at St. Paul's Church in his latter years, said something important and perhaps surprising. He explained that forgiveness is too weak a word for what God does.[2]

Support for that view comes from an unlikely source: the famous atheist, writer, and provocateur Christopher Hitchens. Hitchens has said, with his typical disdain for Christianity, that forgiveness is immoral. Well, oddly enough, he has a point there. The New Testament does not avoid the concept of vengeance. St. Paul counseled his congregations to repay no one evil for evil, and never to avenge themselves, but this is not freestanding advice! It is grounded on God's affirmation: "'Vengeance is mine, I will repay, says the Lord'" (Rom. 12:17-21). True forgiveness is possible only because the Christian knows that God is just, and that his Kingdom is a Kingdom of justice, and that his Kingdom will come.

Now there's a basic verbal fact underlying all of this. This sounds academic and professorial, but if you remember it, it will unlock all kinds of doors. In Hebrew and Greek, *justice* and *righteousness* are the same word. Two words in English, but one word in the biblical languages. So, in both the Old Testament and the New, *justice* and *righteousness* mean exactly the same thing.

Even more important, though, is the way the biblical word works. The

---

2. Reginald Fuller, *Interpreting the Miracles* (London: SCM Press, 1963), p. 51. I also heard Dr. Fuller say this in person, more than once.

justice of God sounds like a noun, but it acts like a verb.[3] The righteousness of God is a *verb.* What does a verb do? It works. It does something. It's not static: it doesn't just sit there like a concept asking to be understood. It's not passive: it doesn't wait for you or me to get into the right frame of mind. The righteousness of God, the justice of God is out there ahead of us because *God* is out there ahead of us. Great social movements for freedom, for equality, for justice originate not in humanity, but in God. Human participants climb on board a train that's already moving. Gandhi knew that. Martin Luther King knew that. Lech Walesa knew that. Their peaceful revolutions were not their work, but God's.

The *righteousness* and *justice* (same thing) of God can't be separated from the *be-ing* of God. God *is* (that's the verb *to be,* the strongest of all verbs) the righteous Judge of all the earth. Much as we don't like the idea of judgment, there isn't any biblical ethics without it. Everything is weighed before the *judgment* of the God, who *is righteous.* In our text, we see this. Notice how the "lovingkindness" of God is linked to his judgment:

> "I am the Lord who exercises lovingkindness, judgment, and righteousness in the earth: for in these things I delight, says the Lord."

Notice that God *exercises* lovingkindness, judgment, righteousness. They are more verbs than they are nouns. God is *doing* them, making them happen.

The great theologian Karl Barth often included newspaper reporters in his prayers. The best newspapers, the best columnists, the best journalists are God's allies in God's exercising of "judgment and righteousness in the earth." They are a voice for those who have no voice. They see the people no one else sees. I always think of the late, great Mary McGrory of the *Washington Post.*[4] When she accepted the Fourth Estate Award from the National Press Club, she proudly said this:

> "No great men call me. You know who calls me? Losers. I am their mark. If you want to abolish land mines, if you want to reform cam-

---

3. The Greek word *dikaiosune* (righteousness) is used as a verb by St. Paul. The traditional translation is "justify," but a better one is "rectify," meaning "to make right what is wrong."

4. She wrote for the *Washington Star* for decades before it closed, and then she went over to the *Post.*

paign spending, if you want to save children from abuse, or stupid laws, or thick-headed judges, you have my phone number."[5]

Mary McGrory: there was a true fighter for God's justice and God's righteousness.

Justice is about truth. Wherever the truth prevails over lies, there is the presence of the One who said, "I AM the Truth" (John 14:6). Here's a story about justice and truth from the *Norfolk Virginian-Pilot*. It's about an African-American man from Suffolk.

As we listen to this story, let's notice some things. First of all, this story is about injustice and lies. Notice that there is nothing that any human being can do to undo the injustice and the lies. Nothing can give back the lost years. Nothing can restore the strength of youth or the presence of one long dead. There is *nothing* in the human sphere that can make those things right. So this is not meant to be an inspirational, feel-good story. There's judgment in this story. We don't like the biblical language of judgment, but there's plenty of it here. Without a good judge and hard-working *pro bono* lawyers, this story would not be what it is. This is a story about how *partial* justice, *partial* righteousness, plus a strong dose of courage and faith, can open a window in this sinful world to the Kingdom of God that will someday come.

The black man's name was Julius Earl Ruffin. In 1982, when he was a young man working in maintenance at the Eastern Virginia Medical School, he was accused of a brutal rape of a white woman. In spite of the weakness of the evidence, he was convicted by an all-white jury largely on the basis of the woman's doggedly insistent visual identification of him as her assailant. He was sentenced to five life sentences at the Virginia State Penitentiary — terrible years during which he wept and prayed during many long nights when he was often the victim of prison violence. His sister never stopped visiting him in spite of humiliating searches by the prison guards.[6] His mother never lost faith in his innocence, but she died in 1994, the twelfth year of his captivity.

Twenty-one years after Earl Ruffin entered the prison, in early 2003 — you can guess it, can't you? — the new technology was brought to bear. His DNA did not match. The DNA of another incarcerated man did. Through

---

5. Obituary for Mary McGrory, *The New York Times,* 23 April 2004.

6. His son was eight years old when his father was sentenced, and he never forgot the trauma of the prison visits.

science, God did something that was unimaginable when Earl Ruffin was first convicted.

But that's just the beginning. The white rape victim, whose name was Ann Meng, did an extraordinarily courageous thing. She wrote him a letter expressing her profound remorse for misidentifying him. She went to meet with him in 2004, after he was released, before the state government hearing designed to discuss reparations for him, and she sat next to him at the hearing. She testified before the panel, and this is what she said:

> I feel a personal responsibility for Mr. Ruffin's incarceration. However, our system of criminal justice also must bear some responsibility. There was no one on [that white] jury who saw themselves, or their son, or their brother, when they looked at Mr. Ruffin.[7]

What was Earl Ruffin's response to this? You know that forgiveness and redemption are major themes in the African-American church, but this would seem to be beyond human forgiveness. This would seem like a good example of Christopher Hitchens's idea that the injustice done to Earl Ruffin was so great and so irreparable that forgiveness would be immoral. Easy talk about forgiveness is out of place in such cases. Forgiveness is a mysterious gift. Forgiveness is very costly, and no one can force it on anyone else. There are evils which cannot be redressed by any means that this world has to offer. Forgiveness is truly possible *only* in the confidence that there is a righteous Judge and a coming Kingdom in which all wrongs will be made right.

Forgiveness there was. Earl Ruffin accepted the apology. How was that possible? At the hearing, *he began by thanking God.* The struggle for justice arises out of the nature of God. We should not romanticize the black church or any other church, but in that black church tradition there is a deep repository of faith in the God who makes a way out of no way, who creates hope out of no hope.

God's way of doing justice in this deeply disordered world is always imperfect, because he does it through deeply flawed people. Many people in this story acted wrongly, and the system acted wrongly. But in the actions of otherwise imperfect people we see God at work through his human instruments. Ann Meng did a morally heroic thing. State Senator Ben Lambert

7. Tim McGlone, "State Urged to Pay for 21 Lost Years," *Norfolk Virginian-Pilot,* 4 February 2004.

sponsored a bill to pay reparations to Earl Ruffin. Governor Mark Warren gave him an Absolute Pardon. Nothing could restore the lost years. Nothing could bring back the departed mother who kept faith with her son. But how unspeakable it would be if no one had done *anything*. The bill for reparations to Earl Ruffin was passed by the state legislature on April 15, 2004. I found the bill on the Internet, and it makes compelling reading. Thanks be to God for the lawyers and the legislators who put it together.[8]

Righteousness belongs to God. We have no righteousness of our own. Rather, the human being is taken up into the righteousness of God and established in it.[9] The righteousness of God is already present and active. It does not wait for the final day. It is powerful now. Grasped by faith, it becomes a present reality. There is not one person in this space today who cannot be an instrument of the justice of God. Nobody can do everything, but everybody can do something. Who in Richmond is voiceless? Who is invisible? Who is suffering from neglect, from discrimination, from the legacy of slavery that lingers in spite of the election of a black president? The righteousness of God — the justice of God — is there ahead of us, awaiting our witness.

> [For] thus says the Lord, "Let not the wise man glory in his wisdom, neither let the mighty man glory in his might, let not the rich man glory in his riches: But let those who glory, glory in this, that they understand and know me, that I am the Lord who exercises lovingkindness, judgment, and righteousness in the earth: for in these things I delight, says the Lord."

AMEN.

---

8. See http://leg1.state.va.us/cgi-bin/legp504.exe?041+ful+CHAP0880.

9. Otto Schrenk, *dikaiosune,* in *Theological Dictionary of the New Testament,* vol. 2 (Grand Rapids: Wm. B. Eerdmans, 1964), p. 203. St. Paul gleaned this great insight from the Old Testament.

# The Lord of the Dance

*May 2005*      Jeremiah 31:10-14; Psalm 30:11-12; Lamentations 5:15-16

*This sermon was first written and preached in Canada for
graduate students of homiletics and clergy engaged in continuing education. Shortly after, it was adapted for an American audience with a similar constituency.*

....................

IN NEW YORK CITY there is a prominent Episcopal parish called the Church of
the Heavenly Rest. This name has always evoked a certain amount of gentle
ridicule, and I certainly don't know of any other churches that have chosen the
name. It is popularly known as the Church of the Celestial Snooze.

The phrase "heavenly rest" derives from the fourth chapter of the Epistle
to the Hebrews. "There remains a sabbath rest for the people of God; for whoever enters God's rest also ceases from his labors as God did from his" (Heb.
4:9-10).[1] What does it mean to enter God's rest? Emily Dickinson wickedly
mocked the idea in one of her incomparable letters: "It will take so many *beds!*"
She was not at all attracted to the idea of having "Sunday — all the time." A lot

---

1. The passage continues with a word that all preachers should take to heart: "Let us therefore
strive to enter that rest, that no one fall by the same sort of disobedience. For the word of God is living and active, sharper than any two-edged sword, piercing to the division of soul and spirit, of joints
and marrow, and discerning the thoughts and intentions of the heart. And before him no creature is
hidden, but all are open and laid bare to the eyes of him with whom we have to do" (vv. 11-13).

of people would agree with her. The idea of a literal rest of everlasting duration has been off-putting. Two millennia of speculation about this have not cleared up the problem. The notion of heaven as a place where everyone lounges about in the clouds, plunking idly on harps, has persisted throughout the years as a standard setting for cartoons in *The New Yorker* magazine.

Over the centuries, many images of heaven have competed within the Christian tradition. The pictures of paradise that appear in the great hymns of the church are mostly taken from the liturgy of the celestial city in the book of Revelation. The redeemed people of God are pictured worshiping God with thunderous acclamations of ecstatic praise: "Holy, holy, holy, all the saints adore thee, casting down their golden crowns around the glassy sea." An alternative view appeared during the Protestant ascendancy of the seventeenth and eighteenth centuries. The industrious Puritans and their heirs could not bear to think of heaven without work. They emphasized growth, learning, service, and even progress in heaven.[2] From the nineteenth century up to our own time, the emphasis has been on reunion with loved ones. In passing I can't resist quoting Karl Barth, who was asked, "Dr. Barth, will we meet our loved ones in heaven?" He replied, "Not only our *loved* ones!"

But to return to the idea of "rest" in heaven, the matter really does call for some interpretation. The Hebrews text suggests that the Sabbath rest, or "heavenly" rest, derives from the seventh day of creation, when God rested from his labors. This is a poetic description, not to be taken literally — but at the very least, the promise of rest does not support the idea of continuing to work toward an incomplete project, does it? Quite the opposite, in fact, since the work of creation was finished. But then what sort of rest does it mean? If we are not to think of God literally lying down and taking a snooze, what *are* we to think?

Some of you may know the traditional English carol "Tomorrow Shall Be My Dancing Day." The words are medieval, so they have to be read with pronunciations that sound odd to us today. It goes like this:

Tomorrow shall be my dancing day;
I would my true love did so chance

2. The great nineteenth-century preacher Charles Spurgeon was among those who believed in continual progress and improvement in heaven. Writing after World War I (*And the Life Everlasting*), John Baillie saw that this was anthropocentric and culture-defined. Still, he agreed that paradise involved motion, activity, and energy. It was development *within* fruition, however, not *toward* fruition. See Colleen McDannell and Bernhard Lang, *Heaven: A History* (New Haven: Yale University Press, 1988), pp. 276-306.

To see the legend of my play,
To call my true love to my dance.
*Chorus:*
Sing, oh! my love, oh! my love, my love;
This have I done for my true love.

Then was I born of a virgin pure,
Of her I took fleshly sub-*stance* [rhymes with "dance"];
Thus was I knit to man's na-*ture* [rhymes with "pure"]
To call my true love to my dance.

In the original version, which is never sung on the commercial disks, the carol goes on for eleven verses, telling the whole story of Christ's life imagined as a dance. I wish we had leisure to go through all the words, because some of them are remarkably subtle and theologically suggestive.[3]

The Cross itself is depicted as essential to the dance:

Then on the Cross hangèd I was,
Where a spear my heart did glance,
There issued forth both water and blood
To call my true love to my dance.

The carol continues with the descent into hell, no less (imagine singing that at Christmas! those medieval Christians were a lot more tough-minded than we are), then with the Resurrection, and then finally with the Ascension:

Then up to heaven I did ascend,
Where now I dwell in sure sub-*stance*
On the right hand of God, that man
May come unto the general dance.

The modern song "Lord of the Dance" is based on some of these same ideas, but it is by no means as rich in biblical and theological imagery. All those references to the "substance" of Christ suggest a familiarity with the teaching of the Church Fathers that would baffle most Christians today.

---

3. One of the original verses of this carol is unacceptable today because of the prejudicial use, typical of the Middle Ages, of the term "the Jews" to identify the enemies of Christ. We have since learned how crucial it is to identify *ourselves,* not "the Jews," as his enemies.

In any case, my listening to this carol started a process of thought about our promised eternal life in God. Why might it be compared to dancing?

My *principal* text for today, as it happens, is not Hebrews 4 after all. It is Jeremiah 31:10-14 (my emphasis):

> Hear the word of the Lord, O nations. . . .
> For the Lord has ransomed Jacob,
> *and has redeemed him from hands too strong for him.*
> They shall come and sing aloud on the height of Zion,
> and they shall be radiant over the goodness of the Lord . . .
> and they shall languish no more.
> *Then shall the maidens rejoice in the dance,*
> and the young men and the old shall be merry.
> I will turn their mourning into joy. . . .

Let's focus on the two most powerful ideas in the passage. The first is that *the Lord has redeemed us from hands too strong for us.* The second is that this redemption will be joyful beyond measure, and the concrete sign of this radiance in the goodness of the Lord will be *rejoicing in the dance.* We also find this theme in Psalm 30:11-12:

> Thou hast turned for me my mourning into dancing;
>    thou hast loosed my sackcloth
> and girded me with gladness,
>    that my soul may praise thee and not be silent.
> O Lord my God, I will give thanks to thee for ever.

References to the motif of the dance are not particularly frequent in Scripture, but the mentions are significant because they are part of a united picture of the joy that is to be in heaven, along with other motifs such as singing, feasting, and other forms of merrymaking. Over the centuries in Christian art, dance has appeared numerous times in pictures of paradise.

Now we should ask, what sort of dance is it? Let's say first what it is not. It is not like the club dancing of today, where each dancer is only minimally connected to others, where each individual is essentially "doing his own thing," "expressing herself." Nor is it ballroom dancing, with everyone paired off. Nor is it performance dance, with a few doing the dancing and everybody else watching. No, the heavenly dance is more like a folk dance where everyone participates. An exquisite fresco by the Renaissance painter Fra Angelico depicts saints and angels hand in hand in a round dance.[4] The circle dance suggests many things: equality, inclusion, fellowship, harmony, security. Many years ago I went to a little Greek restaurant where they had bouzouki music, and everybody there got up out of their seats and did that wonderful "Zorba the Greek" dance where everybody puts their hands on the shoulders of the two people next to them. It was an ecstatic experience that I have never forgotten, sheer abandon — "On with the dance! let joy be unconfined."

Now, dancing is not exactly *resting,* is it? But it is not *working,* either. What comes to mind? If the heavenly rest is like the rest of God on the seventh day after he finished the work of creation, the thing that comes to mind is *enjoyment.* God saw, and it was good. Our calling in this world and in the world to come is "to glorify God and *enjoy* him forever."[5] The round dance symbolizes not only the joy in God's glory that we will share but a *mutual* joy, uninterrupted human fellowship in his presence. Everything that is gracious and happy and exuberant in this present life is only a minuscule hint of what God has in store for us in heaven.

There's a line from the U2 song "Vertigo" — "They know that they can't dance." Whoever "they" is, the meaning seems pretty obvious: not being able to dance is not a good thing.[6] Not to be asked to dance, not to be able to dance, not to be included in the dance — that is misery. Even worse than not being *able* to dance, however, would be a stubborn *refusal* to join the dance. We need only to think of the elder brother of the prodigal son: "Now [the] elder son was in the field; and as he came and drew near to the house, he heard music and dancing. . . . But he was angry, and he refused to go in" (Luke 15:25, 28).

Maybe some of you will remember the power of the last cantos of Dante's *Paradiso* (Paradise). They convey the most astonishing sense of movement and energy. As the various saints appear in the concentric circles

---

4. Matisse's famous painting of a circle dance hangs in a place of honor in the Museum of Modern Art.

5. Augustine said that in heaven "we shall have eternal leisure to see that he is God" (*City of God* 22:30). When he imagines someone asking, "What will I do? There will be no work for our limbs. . . ." Augustine answers, "Is this no activity: to stand, to see, to love, to praise God?"

6. Back in my New York City ministry, I was meeting with a man who seemed to be very angry. He didn't seem to have anything to be especially angry about, and he was not able to identify anything in particular. I went regularly to a psychoanalyst for help with problems like this, so I asked him why he thought this man had so much anger. He said, "Because he can't dance like Fred Astaire." This was a figure of speech, obviously, but it is striking how *dancing* stands for all that is joyous, excellent, admirable, and sublimely free.

of the redeemed, they are continually turning, wheeling, circling. This motion radiates from God's inexhaustible source of energy and ecstasy, and it is continually directed outward toward others, as God himself is. In Canto X, we meet the Circle of Twelve Lights. These are the glorified bodies of great teachers and wise men of the church — Solomon, Thomas Aquinas, the Venerable Bede, and nine others. The infused love and energy of the blessed Trinity keeps them in motion, alight with the flames of the Spirit. Indeed, in a striking passage in *Mere Christianity,* C. S. Lewis writes of the Trinity itself in these terms: "God is not a static thing [or] person, but a dynamic, pulsating activity, a life, almost a kind of drama. Almost, if you will not think me irreverent, a kind of dance."[7] Since the promise of the Resurrection is the eternal life of God, and the very inmost nature of God is relational activity, it is not wrong to think of heaven in terms of motion, movement, dance, if you will — entirely moved, as Dante wrote, by the power of Love emanating from the heart of the Trinity.

Now we're going to make a huge downward turn. This turn is analogous to that which was made by the Second Person of the Blessed Trinity as he stooped down from heaven and took upon himself the form of a slave in corrupt human flesh. He entered the realm of the Powers of Sin and Death. Sin has sometimes been described as the perversion of the good. I never particularly understood that, nor was I ever attracted to it as a definition until a few days ago, when I read a news story.

The news story tells how the American Civil Liberties Union has obtained some previously classified documents as part of a lawsuit intended to determine the extent of abuse and torture in Iraq and at Guantánamo. We were not meant to see these documents. They show that some U.S. marines in Iraq were convicted in military courts of committing a variety of abuses of captured Iraqis. This happened in April 2004 in Baghdad. One method of abuse involved suspending a prisoner by the wrists over an electrified drum. He would attempt to keep himself pulled up so as to avoid the shocks, but inevitably he could not continue to do so, and as his feet hit the drum, he would receive repeated shocks. This was called "making him dance." Two Defense Department officials had objected to the treatment. They were threatened by interrogators and told to keep quiet.[8]

7. C. S. Lewis, *Mere Christianity* (San Francisco: HarperSanFrancisco, 2001), p. 136.

8. Neil A. Lewis, *The New York Times,* 15 December 2004; see also Kate Zernike, "Newly Released Reports," 6 January 2005.

This sermon originally contained these words: "America is going through a convulsion, I believe, but no one is listening and no one is noticing. Only a very few courageous journalists are

We read in Genesis 6 that the Lord, looking down from heaven, "saw that the wickedness of man was great in the earth, and that every imagination of the thoughts of his heart was only evil continually" (v. 5). In the book of Lamentations, we read,

> The joy of our hearts has ceased;
> our dancing has been turned to mourning.
> The crown has fallen from our head;
> woe to us, for we have sinned! (5:15-16)

There is not going to be any heavenly rest or heavenly dancing without an intervention from God. The human heart is too far gone in callousness, in indifference, in apathy. Canadians cannot think themselves superior to Americans. No one can exempt himself or herself from the general indictment. "'My people are skilled in doing evil [says the Lord], but how to do good they know not.' . . . The heart is deceitful above all things, and desperately corrupt, who can understand it?" (Jer. 4:22; 17:9).

That's from Jeremiah. Let us return to our text (my emphasis):

> For the Lord has ransomed Jacob,
> *and has redeemed him from hands too strong for him.*
> They shall come and sing aloud on the height of Zion,
> and they shall be radiant over the goodness of the Lord . . .
> and they shall languish no more.
> *Then shall the maidens rejoice in the dance. . . .*

There is a unified message here from the Old and New Testaments alike. There can be no rejoicing in the dance unless the Lord redeems us *from hands too strong for us.* That old Adam has us in a stranglehold. We cannot defeat him.

Yet in the midst of this sickness unto death the announcement comes: Jesus Christ is Lord. He has bound the strong man. He has done this for us in order that we should be remade according to his image and likeness. The life of the Resurrection is made incarnate even now in the life of the church. We are free now from the fears that bind us. The voice of the church is

---

pushing this, and the churches are almost entirely silent. I don't know what is wrong with us." At the time of publication of this book of sermons, torture and abuse by the United States remains one of the great unaddressed subjects in the nation's pulpits.

needed in our world, not just for the soothing of souls in conventional American congregations, but also on behalf of those around the world who suffer from the indifference of Christians. It is believed by many observers of the Rwandan genocide that if the churches in Rwanda had stood fast against the rising tide of hate, the massacre of 800,000 could not have happened. Similarly, in America, if the churches nurture a protest against secretive American policies, they can be changed.

✳ Rabbi Arthur Hertzberg has said that the sign of true religion is the defense of the defenseless.[9] As soon as a combatant becomes a prisoner, he is defenseless. A sign of the Resurrection is mercy for prisoners. A sign of the Resurrection is concern for those who are not like us. A sign of the Resurrection, dare I say it, is love even for the enemy — for we ourselves, left to ourselves, would be the enemies of God.

Someone in Christ right now is taking up the banner on behalf of those who suffer from the neglect of the developed world, for the Lord will not leave himself without witnesses. Someone, somewhere, is taking up the cause of civilians who are caught in the cross fires of our wars, and people who are being held without charges in our prisons, and children who are either traumatized or starving or both. Someone in the name and in the power of Christ is taking up the cause of those who are in need of encouragement, or assistance, or a voice raised on their behalf. You are those voices. The life of the Resurrection constrains us. This is the work of God in us, and the work of God cannot be stopped. Let us pray that we will be among those who participate, and not among those who stand aside while God's procession passes.

May it be so.

By the grace of God may it be so.

For the Lord has . . . redeemed us from hands too strong for us.
We shall come and sing aloud on the height of Zion,
and we shall be radiant over the goodness of the Lord. . . .
Then shall we rejoice in the dance. . . .

AMEN.

---

9. From a conversation with Arthur Hertzberg in the mid-nineties.

# Jeremiah and the Human Dilemma

Jeremiah 15:15-16; 17:5-10; 31:27-31

*This sermon was preached at a conference of clergy and lay leaders in 2009.*

.................

THE PROPHET Jeremiah, who lived in the sixth century B.C., is tremendously interesting to modern people. For many centuries, Isaiah was the most beloved Hebrew prophet, and he is still read in the church far more than any other. In modern times, however, Jeremiah has become a favorite. The reason is that Jeremiah shows us his heart. He has left numerous descriptions of his state of mind in his own words. We know more about Jeremiah from the inside out than any other Old Testament figure.[1] That's what interests us in our day. We are more attracted to human psychology than we are to divine revelation.

But this would have dismayed Jeremiah. He would never have wanted to be remembered for himself. Like all the other Hebrew prophets, he was a God-intoxicated person. He lamented and complained mightily, but there

---

1. I am aware of current developments in Jeremiah studies which devalue the autobiographical aspects of the prophet's legacy. See, for instance, Walter Brueggemann's *Commentary on Jeremiah: Exile and Homecoming* (Grand Rapids: Wm. B. Eerdmans, 1998), pp. 11-12 and *passim*. For many Bible readers, however, the intimate glimpse into the depths of the struggle to be faithful in this passage and others like it in Jeremiah will always be a comfort and an inspiration.

was no doubt of his overriding devotion to God and to the mission that God had given him. Here is just one example of his personal struggle, in his own words. Note how his moods change almost from line to line, as he passes from indignation to submission to lament:

> O Lord . . . remember me and visit me,
> and take vengeance for me on my persecutors. . . .
> For thy sake I bear reproach.
> Thy words . . . became to me a joy
> and the delight of my heart;
> for I am called by thy name,
> O Lord, God of hosts.
> I did not sit in the company of merrymakers,
> nor did I rejoice;
> I sat alone, because thy hand was upon me. . . .
> Why is my pain unceasing,
> my wound incurable, refusing to be healed? (Jer. 15:15-18)

This sort of thing comes up time after time in the very long book of Jeremiah. We can't help feeling for him. His life was largely a misery to him. He struggled for years to call the people of Israel to repentance, knowing all along that it was a fruitless cause. He lived through the Babylonian invasion and the fall of Jerusalem, which for him would have been like our 9/11, though on a much larger scale, because it meant the downfall of a whole nation and people.[2] Through it all, he kept heroically to his calling.

The book of Jeremiah is very difficult to teach. I have taught almost every book of the Bible, and this is the only one that I felt I had to break up into various pieces according to themes, rather than taking it verse by verse. It just doesn't seem to have any logical progression from one chapter to the next. We think it was put together from various portions of the prophet's teaching over a period of decades, without much coherence. However, more and more in recent years I have come to believe that the shape of the book as we have it is part of the Holy Spirit's intention. For example:

> Thus says the Lord: "Cursed is the man who trusts in man and makes flesh his arm, whose heart turns away from the Lord. He is like a

---

2. Rembrandt's painting of Jeremiah lamenting as Jerusalem is pillaged and burned gives the idea.

shrub in the desert, and shall not see any good come. He shall dwell in the parched places of the wilderness, in an uninhabited salt land.

"Blessed is the man [person] . . . whose trust is the Lord. He is like a tree planted by water, that sends out its roots by the stream, and does not fear when heat comes, for its leaves remain green, and is not anxious in the year of drought, for it does not cease to bear fruit."

The heart is deceitful above all things, and desperately corrupt; who can understand it? "I the Lord search the mind and try the heart, to give to every man according to his ways, according to the fruit of his doings." (17:5-10)

The first two parts seem logically connected. The person who trusts in human potential instead of God's life-giving power is like a scrubby plant that can never thrive because it's in the desert. (This is not like the beautiful Sonoran desert that blooms — the barren Judean wilderness is meant.) This is contrasted with the lovely image of the person who trusts in the Lord. Such a person is like a tree planted by an unfailing source of life-giving water.

But then Jeremiah suddenly says, "The heart is deceitful above all things, and desperately corrupt; who can understand it?" This sweeping, all-inclusive statement doesn't seem to have any connection to the image of the thriving green tree by the stream. Moreover, he then goes on to transmit the Lord's warning: "I the Lord search the mind and try the heart, to give to every man according to his ways, according to the fruit of his doings." That makes me feel very uneasy. If the human heart is corrupt and deceitful beyond all things, and if God is going to assess everyone according to his or her doings, then what confidence can we have? The same indictment of the human heart appears in various other places in the Bible:

The Lord saw that the wickedness of man was great in the earth, and that every imagination of the thoughts of his heart was only evil continually. (Gen. 6:5)

The hearts of men are full of evil, and madness is in their hearts while they live, and after that they go to the dead. (Eccles. 9:3)

God looks down from heaven upon the children of men to see if there are any that are wise, any that seek after God. They have all fallen away; they are all alike depraved; there is none that does good, no, not one. (Ps. 53:2-3)

According to the Scripture, there is a vast disruption in the creation that has affected every human being ever born. The apostle Paul picks up this theme in Romans, citing Psalm 53: "There is no one righteous, no, not one" (3:10). This is a central teaching in biblical faith. We surround ourselves with all sorts of defenses against these bleak truths, but in our essential selves, we are dislocated; we are estranged; we are essentially alone; we "go to the dead."

During Oscar week, the whole country goes completely crazy. There were something like 60 million hits on the Oscar Web site this year. I read an article about the millions if not billions spent on dermabrasion, Botox, teeth whitening, and tattoo removal. And that's for twenty- and thirty-year-olds! It's truly pitiable. What of shaven-headed Britney Spears, the formerly virgin idol of my granddaughter and her friends? "Where have all the flowers gone?" Poor Anna Nicole Smith: she had a bodyguard, she had a personal nurse, she had a supposedly devoted gentleman friend; but she perished all alone in a hotel room. "In the midst of life we are in death," says the Prayer Book. What about the astronaut Lisa Nowak? And Governor Eliot Spitzer? And the golden idol, Tiger Woods?[3] "Madness is in the human heart . . . who can understand it?"

But, we protest, *we* are not crazy or obsessed or out of control; *we* are upstanding members of our decent and orderly communities. Here is the challenge for us as Christians: No matter how upright our lives may appear to be, we share in the human condition. The prophets and apostles summon us to an understanding of this reality, so well described in the famous words of John Donne: "No man is an island, entire of itself. . . . Therefore do not ask for whom the bell tolls; it tolls for thee."

We are all involved willy-nilly in a worldwide web of human folly and misery, no matter how much we may think we have nothing to do with the corruption of the larger powers. A few days ago on NPR there were a number of interviews with people who had been fired from their jobs. As I listened, I began to have the overwhelming impression that almost all of us would do almost anything to keep from being fired from our jobs, especially if we had no other immediate prospects. This fear keeps us from speaking out, taking a stand, disturbing the peace. Maybe our company is involved in dishonest practices; maybe a fellow employee is being mistreated; maybe it's necessary to fool around with the figures just a little; maybe a little bribe isn't so bad. Take this all the way up the ladder, and we arrive at Halliburton

3. All three were disgraced to one degree or another by sexual scandals.

and other contractors in Iraq, where hundreds of millions have simply disappeared — and Blackwater, where civilians are wantonly killed and the corporation simply closes ranks, clams up, and protects its own.[4] It has been noted a thousand times: Most of the evil in the world takes place because good people do not speak up.

Above all things, I seek to share an abiding love for the greatness of the Bible. It is titanic; its words are filled with power and majesty; yet it tells the truth about the smallest incidents and most insignificant people. Every person in it is recognizable in one way or another. We see ourselves, yet without pretensions. The Bible's depiction of the human condition is ruthless and relentless. It is a long saga of idolatry, apostasy, chicanery, cowardice, incest, rape, violence, deceit, betrayal, murder, and the well-deserved judgment of God. It omits nothing.

And yet . . . and yet.

Since, unfortunately, we don't have time to look at the intricacies of the entire book of Jeremiah, or even of one whole chapter, we're going to leap over thirteen chapters and read one of the most important passages in all of Scripture. Let us hold in our minds the picture of the human heart, "deceitful above all things, and desperately corrupt." We are skipping over whole chapters describing the determination of the people to pursue their course of self-destruction. Remember the words "I the Lord search the mind and try the heart" — so reminiscent of our Collect addressed to the God "to whom all hearts are open, all desires known, and from whom no secrets are hid." Recall also the concluding words of our reading: God searches our hearts "to give to every person according to his ways, according to the fruit of his doings." Do you — do I — think we can stand up to that? I know I can't. We are up against a stone wall here. The human heart is desperately corrupt and beyond self-help. The history of biblical Israel proves it. The tabloids prove it. The nightly news proves it.

Jeremiah, chapter 31: the whole chapter is incredibly beautiful; how good it would be to read the whole thing! We will begin, however, with verse 27:

> "Behold [says the Lord], it shall come to pass that as I have watched over [Israel] to pluck up and break down, to overthrow, destroy, and bring evil, so I will [in that day] watch over them to build and to plant, says the Lord. . . .

4. These are well-known phenomena from the period of the war in Iraq.

"Behold, the days are coming, says the Lord, when I will make a new covenant with the house of Israel . . . not like the covenant which I made with their fathers when I took them by the hand to bring them out of the land of Egypt, my covenant which they broke. . . . But this is the covenant which I will make with the house of Israel after those days, says the Lord: I will put my law within them, and I will write it upon their hearts; and I will be their God, and they shall be my people. . . ." (31:27-31)

Jeremiah 31:31 — the New Covenant passage. Here is the plan and purpose of God to overcome the resistance of the human heart. Here is the great action that the Lord is preparing to redeem his creation from its bondage to sin. Here is the renewal of the world and the salvation of the human race, the healing of the human heart and the re-ordering of all human relationships. For you will recall the words of the Lord Jesus, how he said, "This cup is the new covenant in my blood. Do this, as often as you drink it, in remembrance of me" (1 Cor. 11:25).

This is the best possible illustration of the necessity of the Old Testament. The New Testament (the New Covenant) simply does not work without the Old Testament. The Old Testament is the operating system of the New. The words of Jeremiah from the sixth century come true in the words and actions of our Lord Jesus Christ in the new century of the new era. God's covenant is written on the human heart. How Jeremiah must have rejoiced in heaven to know this!

In the Cross of Christ, in his life poured out for the making of the New Covenant, in his death on our behalf and in our place, a transaction of unimaginable grace and mercy has taken place. Our condition was hopeless, but now it is taken up into Christ's divine life. Everything is changed for us. There is a new promise written in the blood of Christ. In his saving recapitulation of the human story, we see the future of God's redeemed creation.

And so the next time we are tempted to go along with whatever the corrupt world is doing, we can say to ourselves, "I am a creature of the New Covenant. God has written his commandments in my heart. I am not the same person that I was. I have been planted by the stream of living water, and if there is a drought, I will still be fed by the unconquerable purpose of God." Every Christian who lives by this promise is a sign planted by God in this world that groans for its redemption.

"Blessed is the man [woman] . . . whose trust is the Lord. He [she] is like a tree planted by water, that sends out its roots by the stream, and does not fear when heat comes, for its leaves remain green, and is not anxious in the year of drought, for it does not cease to bear fruit."

AMEN.

# Beyond Hope

*Lent 2009*

The word of the Lord came to Jeremiah a second time, while he was still shut up in the court of the guard: "Thus says the Lord who made the earth, the Lord who formed it to establish it — the Lord is his name: Call to me and I will answer you, and will tell you great and hidden things which you have not known."

(JEREMIAH 33:1-3)

Abraham . . . is the father of us all . . . in the presence of the God in whom he believed, who gives life to the dead and calls into existence the things that do not exist. In hope he believed against hope, that he should become the father of many nations: as he had been told, "So shall your descendants be."

(ROMANS 4:16-18)

Let's think for a moment about hope and hopelessness. "Where there's life, there's hope," the saying goes; yet even life itself can seem hopeless. We've all heard about the suicides of people who have suffered catastrophic financial losses during these last few months.[1] The suicide rate in the U.S. Army has been escalating for some time. Even very young people can experience

---

1. The Great Recession of 2008 was in full force.

hopelessness; we have all known of teenagers who have committed suicide, often because they have been rejected by a girlfriend or boyfriend. The famous lines from Dante's epic poem, "Abandon hope, all ye who enter here," appear over the entrance to hell. Life without hope is truly unthinkable. When a dream expires, when the life savings are gone forever, when there is no further treatment for an illness, the words strike like the blows of an axe: "It's unrecoverable"; "It's incurable"; "It's hopeless." Such words seize the heart in a grip of ice.

In the crucial fourth chapter of the letter to the Romans, the apostle Paul retells the story of Abraham and Sarah, whose situation was definitely hopeless from any human point of view. God had promised Abraham that he would have an heir, and that through this heir, Abraham's descendants would be a blessing to the entire human race. Yet decades have passed, and nothing has happened. Abraham is a hundred years old, and his aged wife, Sarah, has never been able to bear a child in her entire life. There is no heir. It's a hopeless situation. Yet in this chapter, Romans 4, Paul writes that "Abraham believed in hope against hope."[2] People still use that phrase today — "hoping against hope."

It's customary to say that Abraham's *faith* was what kept him going, but actually, that isn't quite right. We often say that people are saved by faith, or saved by prayer, but faith and prayer are not anchored in anything without the power of the God who gives them. So it's not Abraham's *faith* that counts, but Abraham's *God. Our* God: the God of Abraham, Isaac, and Jacob, the God and Father of our Lord Jesus Christ. Paul identifies God this way:

> . . . the God in whom [Abraham] believed, who gives life to the dead
> and calls into existence the things that do not exist. . . .
> In hope [Abraham] believed against hope. (Rom. 4:17-18)

This is one of the greatest texts in all of the Bible, yet many do not know it. Let's hold it in our minds as we think about the nature of God in hopeless situations. Abraham's God, our God, is the one "who gives life to the dead and calls into existence the things that do not exist." This is not the

---

2. Actually, the Greek is probably best translated "In hope he believed against hope" (RSV). The KJV has "against hope [he] believed in hope," which does not convey the sense properly. The NRSV renders it "Hoping against hope." A literal translation would be "beyond hope" *(par elpida),* which is our theme.

language we use about God as a general rule. We speak of God as loving, forgiving, embracing, inclusive, and so forth, but that doesn't convey the unique generative power of a God who can call things into existence when they do not even exist.

My sister was with our beloved mother when she took her last breath in this life. She said to me later, "There is all the difference in the world between a breath and no breath." Yes. When there is suddenly no breath, you become aware that *there is no life there anymore.* You can say "No!" and "Don't leave me!" and "Come back!" all you want, but it's hopeless. There is nothing anyone can do. Life has simply vanished beyond recall.

Into this void the apostle speaks of hope against human hope, hope in "the God who raises the dead and calls into being the things that have no being."[3]

The prophet Jeremiah speaks of God in a similar way. Jeremiah lived a life that was hopeless by any human standard. Jeremiah's entire existence was given over to his vocation of warning the people of Judah to repent of their ways and return to God before it was too late, but — and this is the terrible part — he knew they wouldn't do it. He knew that his prophecies wouldn't be taken to heart. He knew that the Babylonians were going to come and sweep everything away. He knew it was hopeless. His life was a misery. One of the greatest Old Testament interpreters writes,

> These men [the Hebrew prophets] placed themselves first and foremost under the judgment.... They became poor, lonely, indeed ridiculed, spat upon and beaten; and in [their suffering] they did not proudly preserve their souls in philosophical immovability [like Socrates, for example]. No, they participated in the suffering and let it flood over them. Step by step they descended into the night of God-forsakenness and walked the road on which Jesus Christ . . . descended into the lowest depths of darkness. . . .[4]

And yet Jeremiah had a hope that was beyond hope. Listen to what God said to him:

> The word of the Lord came to Jeremiah . . . while he was still shut up in the court of the guard: "Thus says the Lord who made the earth,

---

3. This is a variant translation.

4. Gerhard von Rad, *God at Work in Israel,* trans. John H. Marks (Nashville: Abingdon Press, 1980), p. 170.

the Lord who formed it to establish it — the Lord is his name: Call
to me and I will answer you, and will tell you great and hidden things
which you have not known." (Jer. 33:1-3)

Jeremiah was shut up in the court of the guard. This was one of many
times that he suffered abuse and imprisonment. The cataclysm is coming;
Jerusalem will fall; the temple will be destroyed and the people taken off to
live as exiles in a godless land. Yet the Creator of the universe speaks to Jeremiah, the Lord who formed and established the earth, the God to whom
mighty Babylon is but a drop in the bucket (Isa. 40:14). The faith of Jeremiah, like the faith of Abraham, was not worked up out of human religious
consciousness. Faith is called into being by the Word of the Lord. The
noted preacher Will Willimon says rightly that everything depends on
these words: "Thus says the Lord."[5] And God said to Jeremiah: "Call to me
and I will answer you, and will tell you great and hidden things which your
human imagination cannot produce."

The key that unlocks the hope beyond hope is the knowledge of God.
No matter what the various "spiritual" experts tell us in all of their various
talk shows, best sellers, and expensive retreats, God is not a product of the
human religious search. God is the One who was already there before we
started searching for him. He was there before human imagination existed — the One who is, and who was, and who is to come (Rev. 1:8). God
is the One who will reveal great and hidden things *which we have not
known,* things that we cannot devise or create. That is the door of the divine hope.

As we grasp this hope which is beyond hope, we learn to loosen our grip
on our own hopes. Our idea of what to hope for is limited by our human
horizons. We think we know what we want, what is best, what will make us
happy, what we need. Most theologically dangerous of all, we think we
know *what God owes us.* All of that has to go. We need a larger sense of the
God who reveals great and hidden things that we do not know! Our God is
so small! Have you ever noticed the sameness of a lot of prayer today?
"Lord, give us safe travel!" — I hear that a lot. But what if there is a wreck?
Early in my ministry, an elderly woman who admired me extravagantly
(that was her first mistake) was on her way to visit relatives, and she asked

---

5. To be absolutely accurate, Willimon says that everything depends on the words "And God
said . . ." (He's quoting Genesis 1; I'm quoting Jeremiah.) See *Conversations with Barth on
Preaching* (Nashville: Abingdon Press, 2006), p. 12 and *passim.*

me to pray for her safe travel. On the way she had a bad accident and was seriously injured. I went to visit her, and she refused to see me. She would never speak to me again. Literally.

When we pray, we need a larger view of the God whose thoughts, as the prophet Isaiah said, are not our thoughts, whose ways are not our ways (55:8). At the end of our services, Episcopalians sometimes hear the verse from Ephesians: "Glory to God, whose power working in us can do *infinitely more than we can ask or imagine*" (3:20; my emphasis). That's the idea.

As the Day of Resurrection approaches, we need to think about these things. I visit a lot of different parishes in different denominations. On a recent Sunday, I worshiped in an Episcopal church. In the bulletin there was an announcement of an adult class about the Christian and Jewish festivals of the season, and this is what it said: "Passover and Easter celebrate spring and hope."

What's wrong with this picture? Well, for one thing, Passover and Easter in the Southern hemisphere take place not in the spring, but in the autumn. Most of the biblical imagery of Resurrection is about harvest, not spring.[6] But the more serious error in the bulletin announcement is the idea that Easter is a celebration of a generic hope detached from the knowledge of God. Springtime is indeed glorious — the merry month of May and all that — but it's not a surprise. We expect it. We know that it's going to come. The God of Abraham, the God and Father of Jesus Christ, is doing great and hidden things beyond what we know, beyond what we expect, beyond what we can imagine. Passover celebrates the mighty acts of a God who takes hold of a band of wretched slaves and makes them a proud, free people. Easter is the feast of the God who gives life to the dead.

Faith in God is not faith which gives up when God seems to be silent. That would be mere human faith, grounded in human hopes and expectations — expectations that God will answer our prayers in exactly the way we want. Last week, a woman told me a story of going to pray with a member of her church who was facing very serious surgery. She held the woman's hand,

---

6. One of our greatest Easter hymns, by the fine poet Christopher Wordsworth (nephew of William), is entirely built around the imagery of harvest:

Christ is risen, Christ the firstfruits of the holy harvest field,
Which will all its full abundance at his second coming yield;
Then the golden ears of harvest will their heads before him wave,
Ripened by his glorious sunshine from the furrows of the grave.

Christopher Wordsworth (1807-1885), Hymn 191

and they prayed together. After the prayer, the woman who was to have the operation thought for a while and then said, "You know, I don't know how this is going to come out. But now I know that *either way,* I'm going to be all right." Those women knew the Lord. They were holding on to the hope that is beyond hope.

On the final day of Resurrection, the Lord will gather in the harvest of all those who have hoped in him. But *not only* those who have hoped in him at the level of an Abraham. Do you know someone who feels hopeless? Are you wondering about someone who has no faith? Is there someone dead whose presence you desperately miss? The God who is powerful to call into existence the things that do not exist is also powerful to create hope where there is no hope, faith where there is no faith, and life where there is no breath. The hope that is beyond hope is the hope that refuses to let go even when the cold clasp of death seems to be the last word, for this is the eternal God who raises the dead. "The Lord is his name."

AMEN.

# The Evolutionary Ladder

Ezekiel 1:28; 2:1-7; 3:1-3, 10-11; 36:14-36

*In the case of this sermon, the context is important. It was preached to a congregation of aspiring young people in New York City — actors, artists, students, writers, musicians — working in various jobs to support themselves while pursuing their calling. There were also young bankers, lawyers, teachers, and so forth. They came expecting a substantial sermon every Wednesday evening.*

. . . . . . . . . . . . . . . . .

I SOMETIMES ask a wise psychotherapist of my acquaintance for suggestions. She is Jewish, but she respects the Christian gospel and wants to see it well presented. Let me give you an example of her advice. A few weeks ago I had to preach a funeral sermon to a congregation that was about 90 percent Jewish. I asked the therapist how she thought I should go about it. She said I should remember that secular people, whether Jewish or not, although they may be interested in religion in a general way as one subject among many, believe that they are a little higher up on the evolutionary ladder than religious people. They (and I suspect she included herself, though she would never have said so) believe that they have outgrown any need for religious belief.

That really got me to thinking. I turned to Freud's *Future of an Illusion*, which I always go to at such times because it gives the evolutionary argu-

[ 338 ]

ment against religious faith as well as it has ever been given. It shakes my faith every time, and as a result I understand better the resistance to the gospel that one finds among the intellectual elite, especially here in New York City. As a result of two things, the psychoanalyst's comment and my reading of Freud, I realize now as never before that the polite silence of many of my secular friends when I say something about God is actually a mask (a courteous mask, but a mask nevertheless) for their feelings of superiority. They're actually thinking, "She seems like an intelligent person, but she seems to believe this Christian stuff." Bill Buckley observed that if one mentioned God more than once at a New York City dinner party, one would never be invited back.

When the Lord commissioned the prophet Ezekiel, he warned him ahead of time that his message would meet with scorn and contempt. The Lord strengthened Ezekiel with these words:

> "Mortal, be not afraid of [those who reject your message], nor be afraid of their words, even if briers and thorns are with you and you sit upon scorpions; be not afraid of their words, nor be dismayed at their looks. . . . Mortal, you shall speak my words to them, whether they hear or refuse to hear; for they are a rebellious house." (2:6-7)[1]

In a strange way, I find these words very comforting as I go about my work of bearing witness to Jesus Christ. That is your work too, by the way, as Christian people. It is not for clergy only, for as Karl Barth has written, "The ministry of witness is the primary determination of Christian existence."

For all of us who recognize this situation as we go face to face with the sophisticates of New York City, the book of the prophet Ezekiel has a message. If you can show me anything else in world literature like the book of Ezekiel, I would like to see it.

> God said to me, "Mortal, stand upon your feet, and I will speak with you. . . . Mortal, I send you to . . . a nation of rebels, who have rebelled against me; they and their fathers have transgressed against me to this very day. The people also are impudent and stubborn: I

1. *Mortal* was traditionally translated "son of man," but after the time of Ezekiel the title became Messianic and was applied to Jesus to mean that he was the heavenly figure foreseen in Daniel 7. In Ezekiel, "son of man" simply means "human being."

send you to them; and you shall say to them, 'Thus says the Lord God.' And whether they hear or refuse to hear (for they are a rebellious house) they will know that there has been a prophet among them." (2:1-5)

What's important here? What's the first principle, so to speak? Is it the rebelliousness of the Israelites? Is it their tendency to reject their prophets? No, the first and foundational fact here is the Word of God. The entire Bible is founded upon these words: "Thus says the Lord God."

We don't have to believe this, of course. Most of the people you know in New York City take pride in not believing it. It is a fact that from the beginning, people have refused to hear. But here's the challenge for us: we want to be sure that they are refusing to hear the real thing and not a pale imitation of it. The real thing is God saying to Ezekiel, "Mortal, stand up on your feet. I'm speaking to you." Without this, the Bible is a religious text among other religious texts. It's always surprising to me that so many readers of the Bible don't recognize that the whole thing is built upon the words that appear in the third verse of the first chapter of Genesis: "And God said, 'Let there be light,' *and there was* light." The Word of God is *performative* — that is to say, it is actively at work making itself happen. The great theologian Karl Barth, who produced many massive volumes of *Church Dogmatics,* based his entire enterprise on this foundation. The first two enormous volumes are called *The Doctrine of the Word of God.* Only then did Barth produce two more enormous volumes called *The Doctrine of God.* The meaning of this is that we wouldn't have a clue about the God who is really God if God hadn't spoken to us first. *God spoke first.* Every one of those three words is vital — "*God* spoke first," "God *spoke* first," "God spoke *first.*" Here's what that means:

1. It is *God* who speaks and not a deity projected out of human religious consciousness.
2. God *speaks.* God is not a deity who shows up in visions. There is no vision in the Bible without audition.
3. God speaks to the human being *first, before* the human being can say anything or prepare herself in any way.

And so God said to Ezekiel, "Mortal, stand upon your feet, and I will speak with you." The tone is peremptory, isn't it? Well, God can talk any way he chooses. We might prefer for him to be a bit less bossy, but God doesn't act according to our preferences. He acts according to who he is in himself. Who is he in himself according to this passage? We've already seen that the first disclosure is that he *speaks*. He communicates, not in riddles or conundrums, but in plain words meant to be understood by his creatures.

The second disclosure is that God is a *sending* God. "Mortal, I send you to . . . a nation of rebels, who have rebelled against me." This is the classic prophetic commission. God doesn't speak directly to his calf-worshiping people from Mount Sinai; he sends Moses as his messenger. God doesn't speak directly to the heedless apostates from his throne room; he sends Isaiah. God doesn't thunder down against the idle rich from his place above the firmament; he sends Amos. We could go on and on like this. If we don't recognize that the God of the Bible calls and sends human beings — "mortals" — to deliver his messages, then we aren't reading the Bible rightly. Again, we don't have to *believe* that God does this — we have to keep saying that — but the Bible demands to be read that way, "whether we hear or refuse to hear." In other words, the Bible wants to be read like a story. If you are engrossed in a whopping good story, you aren't stopping to ask every minute, "Is this true?" or "Did this really happen?" or "Do I believe this?" You are swept along in the direction that the storyteller carries you.

For this reason, Bible-reading should begin very early in life, and classic children's literature should be read along with it. If you're reading a classic fairy tale to a child, you don't stop every few paragraphs to say, "Now this didn't really happen" or "We don't really believe this, do we?" Stories have a power of their own, and the Bible, which is essentially one prodigious story ("the greatest ever told"), has a power uniquely its own.

Therefore, when we read that the Lord spoke to the prophet Ezekiel during the mournful time when the people were in exile in pagan Babylon without hope, without resources, without options except to turn to the Babylonian gods, we suspend disbelief until we have absorbed what God says through his messenger:

> And [the Lord] said to [Ezekiel], "Mortal, eat what is offered to you; eat this scroll, and go, speak to the house of Israel." So I opened my mouth, and he gave me the scroll to eat. . . . I ate it; and it was in my mouth as sweet as honey. And he said to me, "Son of man, go, get you to the house of Israel, and speak with my words to them. . . ."
> Moreover he said to me, "Son of man, all my words that I shall speak to you receive in your heart, and hear with your ears. And go,

get you to the exiles, to your people, and say to them, 'Thus says the Lord God'; whether they hear or refuse to hear." (3:1-4, 10-11)

Did he really eat a scroll? How could anybody eat a whole scroll? He would choke! See what I mean? We can't read this "literally." We read it with our imaginations working. We understand that Ezekiel is absorbing the fierce words of God and is amazed to find them sweet. So it is that we who read the book of Ezekiel with faith will "receive in our heart and hear with our ears." The order of these two phrases is suggestive. Why doesn't he say them in the usual sequence — "hear with your ears" first and *then,* as a consequence, "receive in your heart"? Doesn't this suggest that the reception comes before the hearing — that is to say, faith before understanding? Indeed, that's a famous theological formulation: *Credo ut intelligam:* I believe in order that I may understand.[2]

Many of you talk to us, your clergy, about your struggles to defend your faith in the midst of this very secular city. You know how tempting it is to capitulate to the indifference and, sometimes, the disdain of your co-workers and secular friends. You come here not once but twice a week, or more, to hear again the Word of the Lord and to be strengthened by it. The prophet Ezekiel, read with faith and hope, is a great comfort. Ezekiel, like Isaiah, "saw the Lord" (Isa. 6:1); yet he did not really see him, but saw something "as it were," in what is perhaps the most thrilling vision of God in the Bible (Ezek. 1:4-28). He takes twenty-four verses to describe what he saw. Read it when you go home! At the end of this astonishing, unforgettable vision, we read this:

Such was the appearance of the likeness of the glory of the Lord.

Do you sense the way in which Ezekiel distances himself from the actual sight of God? He doesn't see God. No one can see God. He sees the "glory" of God. No, he doesn't exactly see that, either. He sees "the *appearance* of the *likeness* of the glory." So he stands three times removed from actually seeing God. All those wheels and eyes and strange living creatures that he sees give only an impression. We can't build a knowledge of God on that. What then can we build on? Ezekiel tells us:

2. Typically in formulating theological statements, we have to balance one with another: *Fides ex auditu* — Faith comes from what is heard. This does not contradict *credo ut intelligam,* but balances it. "What is heard" is the gospel itself, and it comes with power to create faith where there was no faith.

And when I saw [the appearance of the likeness of the glory of God],
I fell upon my face,[3] and I heard the voice of one speaking. (1:28)

Tonight, you hear the voice of One speaking. "Whether you hear or refuse to hear," this is the Word of God. We said earlier that we need to read
the Bible imaginatively, and this is profoundly true — up to a point. The
point where imagination fails is in the revelation of God's self. Only God
can communicate himself. We cannot imagine him. He has come forth
from his place to tell us who he is. This is the claim that lies behind, before,
above, and beneath everything in the Scriptures. This is the foundation of
biblical faith, and the power behind all Christian witness. And those here
tonight who receive this Word in faith will hear with your ears and believe
with your heart these promises to the exiles that God made through his
prophet Ezekiel:

> ". . . I will not let you hear any more the reproach of the nations, and
> you shall no longer bear the disgrace of the peoples and no longer
> cause your nation to stumble, says the Lord God. . . .
>
> "For I will take you from the nations, and gather you from all the
> countries, and bring you into your own land. I will sprinkle clean
> water upon you, and you shall be clean from all your uncleannesses,
> and from all your idols I will cleanse you. A new heart I will give you,
> and a new spirit I will put within you; and I will take out of your
> flesh the heart of stone and give you a heart of flesh. And I will put
> my spirit within you, and cause you to walk in my statutes and be
> careful to observe my ordinances. . . . And you shall be my people,
> and I will be your God." (36:15, 24-28)

In these words, your eyes have seen the glory of the coming of the Lord.
His glory is cosmic, encompassing all nations and all peoples, and yet at the
same time it is intimate and personal, like a favorite teacher walking among
his students and imparting all that he knows to them. God's presence stuns
and frightens, so that reassurance is necessary, but at the same time God embraces his people with an everlasting love that is capable of reconstituting
them as they are supposed to be. That is the promise. It is not a human
promise, which may or may not be kept. Human promises are so often

---

3. The sermon "The Terrors of Grace" takes up the theme of holy fear such as we see here in
Ezekiel.

made out of wishes; we wish something would happen, so we promise it. Then we can't keep the promise, or something changes, or we don't love the person anymore that we made the promise to. The divine promise is not like that. The divine promise is faithful in and of itself because God is faithful; and what's more, God is powerful and able to make his promises come to pass, even his promise to make all things new:

> "Thus says the Lord God: On the day that I cleanse you from all your iniquities, I will cause the cities to be inhabited, and the waste places shall be rebuilt. . . . Then the nations that are left round about you shall know that I, the Lord, have rebuilt the ruined places, and replanted that which was desolate; *I, the Lord, have spoken, and I will do it.*" (36:33-36; my emphasis)

AMEN.

# Nothing More True

*March 2008*                                        Ezekiel 37; John 11

As a guest preacher, I don't have any way of knowing you, or what brought you here today, or what is in your hearts this morning. What I do know of you, and what you know of me, is reflected in the two majestic Scripture lessons that we have just heard. This is what we know about each other: we're all going to die.

The poet Philip Larkin writes these lines:

Unresting death, a whole day nearer now,
Making all thought impossible but how
And where and when I shall myself die.
Arid interrogation: yet the dread
Of dying, and being dead,
Flashes afresh to hold and horrify.
. . . Not to be here,
Not to be anywhere,
And soon; nothing more terrible, nothing more true.

And so, as the funeral service tells us, "In the midst of life we are in death." The season of Lent is a time to reflect on this, beginning with the ashes of Ash Wednesday.

Listen to these additional lines from the same poem. The fear of death, Larkin writes,

... is a special way of being afraid
No trick dispels. Religion used to try,
That vast, moth-eaten musical brocade
Created to pretend we never die. . . .[1]

Is this worship today in this cathedral a "vast, moth-eaten musical brocade," and are we here to pretend? Let's hold that question in our minds for a few minutes as we look at our two readings.

It is rather unexpected to find two of the greatest of all Resurrection texts here in the middle of Lent. The Old Testament book of the prophet Ezekiel has some of the most glorious, most extravagant passages in all of Scripture, and at the same time a good many of the most perplexing and provoking. The famous vision of the dry bones, however, presents no such complications. Let's pay attention to the context first. The first part of the prophet's book is an extended indictment of God's people and their leaders. Without going into lurid detail (and some of Ezekiel is indeed lurid), the people whom God has chosen and nurtured and loved and protected have given themselves up wholesale to idolatry and apostasy. The verdict of the Lord is, "You want idolatry, you will get idolatry — raised to the nth power." The people are dragged off as captives to an unthinkable place: mighty Babylon, dominated by colossal statues of brutal and capricious gods. It's a city at the furthest possible remove from the worship of the one true God.

In this lamentable situation the prophet Ezekiel speaks to the exiles. But it's not really Ezekiel speaking. The undergirding foundation of all the prophetic books is *the speaking of God*. The entire Scripture rests upon this one presupposition: *The Lord said . . .* And so the Lord said to Ezekiel:

> "These bones are the whole house of Israel. Behold, they say, 'Our bones are dried up, and *our hope is lost; we are clean cut off.*' Therefore prophesy, and say to them, Thus says the Lord God to these bones: Behold, I will cause breath to enter you, and you shall live. And you shall know that I am the Lord, when I open your graves, and raise you from your graves, O my people. And I will put my Spirit within you, and you shall live, and . . . *you shall know that I, the Lord,* have spoken, and I have done it, says the Lord." (37:11-14; my emphasis)

---

1. From "Aubade," in *Philip Larkin: Collected Poems* (New York: Farrar, Straus & Giroux, 2004).

Let us take away just one thing from this amazing text. The Israelites have done less than nothing to restore God's faith in them. He does not raise them from the dust because they have repented. He raises them from the dust because he is their God. This is the theme of Ezekiel. "When I raise you from your graves, O my people, you shall know that I am the Lord." The promise is unconditional. God's action in reconstituting the people Israel is not a reward due them. It proceeds from his nature as the one who raises the dead.

It would be a very good thing if Jews and Christians could spend more time reading this passage about the dry bones together. In its context in the Hebrew Scriptures, it is a promise to the Hebrew people. Christians hearing it with a Jewish sensibility can perhaps think of it in the context of the Holocaust: *our bones are dried up; our hope is lost; we are clean cut off.* The passage is not about the resurrection of individual souls; it is about the remaking of God's people Israel, the restoration of their identity, the reinstatement of their hope. Christians read it differently: we think of it in a more universal way, having to do with Jews and Gentiles alike. The interpretation of the passage at any time by any particular group gives it specific shades of meaning. We've learned something about the spirituals that came out of the slave communities in the South. They weren't just songs of individual longing. When they sang "de footbone connected wid de anklebone," they were thinking of themselves as a community in exile, a people enslaved, an oppressed race to whom the promise comes. "Dem bones, dem bones, dem dry bones, We gonna walk again wid-a dry bones . . . *now hear de Word of de Lord.*"[2]

I wish that we could linger with Ezekiel this morning. But we must hasten on to the New Testament lesson, the equally towering story of the raising of Lazarus.

Lazarus and Martha and Mary of Bethany were like Jesus' family. We have the impression that his visits to them in their home were the only times of peace in his entire adult life. It is therefore very strange that when the sisters send him a message that Lazarus is seriously ill, he postpones going to them. The Evangelist implies that Jesus does this for two specific reasons: to show his glory, and because he loves the family.[3] We could have a

---

2. See www.Negrospirituals.com for the full text of this song. See also the marvelous "'Zekeil saw de wheel, way up in de middle of de air," based on Ezekiel 1.

3. John links verses 5 and 6: "Now Jesus loved Martha and her sister and Lazarus. So [*hos oun*] when he heard that he was ill, he stayed two days longer in the place where he was."

whole sermon on God's timing. He delays precisely in order to show his love. What he plans to do for Lazarus is infinitely greater than what Mary and Martha had prayed for. Two days later he says to his disciples, "Lazarus is dead, and for your sake I am glad that I was not there, so that you may believe" (John 11:14-15). Here the Lord restates his purpose. The raising of Lazarus is to be a sign, the last and greatest of all his signs, the one that will most definitively reveal him as the Son of God, the sign that will set in motion the plots that lead to his death.

When Martha, the active, assertive sister, heard that Jesus was coming, she ran out to meet him and reproached him: "Lord, if you had been here, my brother would not have died." But then she hints that she trusts in him: "Even now I know that whatever you ask from God, God will give you." And Jesus says to her, "Your brother will rise again" (John 11:21-23).

It's important to get the inflection right in the next verse. Martha says to Jesus, "I *know* that he will rise again in the resurrection at the *last day*" (11:24). She's rebuking him; she thinks he's not taking her seriously. Most pious Jews of Jesus' time believed that there would be a general resurrection on the Day of Judgment.[4] Martha is saying, in effect, "I know Lazarus will rise at the *last day*, but that's no use to us *now!*" And the Lord says:

> "*I am* the Resurrection and the Life; he who believes in me, though
> he were dead, yet shall he live, and whoever lives and believes in me
> shall never die." (11:25-26; my emphasis)

In these two majestic verses, Christ tells Martha three things. He declares that he himself *is* Resurrection and Life, already, now, in the present, and death can have no dominion over him. He pronounces that even in the midst of death, he is able to give life. And he promises that he freely gives this life to anyone who trusts in him.

Are we here today to pretend that "this vast, moth-eaten brocade" is true because we want it to be true? I ask myself that question every day in the face of "unresting death."

Here is the story of someone who knew that he was to die.

Helmuth James von Moltke is not as well known as Dietrich Bonhoeffer, but he should be. He was a young German aristocrat, a member

---

4. The belief that there would be a general resurrection was very late, appearing in the period between the Testaments. It appears scarcely at all in the canonical Old Testament. In the time of Christ, the Sadducees continued to reject the concept (Matt. 22:23).

of the ancient Prussian nobility, tall, strikingly handsome, a brilliant law-yer.[5] Unlike most people, very early in the 1930s he saw that the rise of Nazi power would be a catastrophe. He was appalled by the Nazi-controlled Olympic Games and horrified by the enthusiasm of the general population. He worked tirelessly during those years to save the lives of prisoners of war held by the Germans and to help Jews get out of Europe. He became the leader of a resistance group who met at his country estate, Kreisau (the group became known as "the Kreisauers").[6] Moltke was a deeply committed Christian who read the Bible regularly and devotion-ally and loved to sing hymns. He believed that the German churches could be mobilized against the Nazis and was in contact with church lead-ers throughout Europe. George Kennan, the celebrated American diplo-mat, wrote that Moltke, "one of the few genuine Protestant-Christian martyrs of our time," was "the greatest person, morally, and the largest and most enlightened . . . that I met on either side of the battle lines in World War II."[7]

Moltke considered himself a "very average" person. Using biblical lan-guage, he called himself "a humble earthen vessel." Kennan described him as "lonely" and "struggling." He did not make a big decision to be a moral hero. He made small decisions and took limited actions, day after day, for more than ten years. He traveled, meeting people and talking to them, try-ing to get them to understand. At any time, he wrote, one word from his wife, Freya, would have called a halt to his activities. But she was as much a resister as he; she saw him through to the end. Moltke's letters to his wife were published in English in 1990 in a volume called *Letters to Freya*.[8] On

5. Helmuth James von Moltke inherited the title of Count. His father was the great-nephew of Bismarck's legendary field marshal, "the Great Moltke." His illustrious name pro-tected Helmuth for a time, but in the end it only exacerbated the Nazis' determination to exe-cute him as a traitor. Himmler would eventually refer to his class as "blue-blooded swine." See the introduction to *Letters to Freya,* trans. and ed. Beata Ruhm von Oppen (New York: Knopf, 1990), p. 21.

6. The complex, detailed, harrowing, morally uplifting history of the Kreisauer group (many of whom lost their lives) and of Moltke's leadership are only hinted at here. His principal project was to rally the humane institutions of Germany, including the Roman Catholic and Protestant churches, to reconstitute Germany after the defeat which he knew would come. Unlike Bonhoeffer, he did not participate in the plots to kill Hitler (though several "Kreisauers" did); his astute political sense told him that a military coup d'état, even if successful, would lead to dire un-intended consequences.

7. George F. Kennan, *Memoirs, 1925-1950* (Boston and Toronto: Little, Brown & Co., 1967).

8. Freya von Moltke, who disdained the title of Countess, died in 2010 at the age of ninety-

the morning he was sentenced to death by the Nazis, Moltke wrote his farewell letter to Freya and his two little boys. Here is a very small part of that letter:

> Your husband stands before [the judge] not as . . . a big landowner, not as a Prussian, not as a German . . . but as a Christian and nothing else. . . . For what a mighty task your husband was chosen; all the trouble the Lord took with him, the infinite detours . . . all suddenly find their explanation in one hour. . . . Everything which was hidden acquires its meaning in retrospect. . . . The refusal to put out [Nazi] flags or to belong to the Party . . . it has all at last become comprehensible in a single hour. For this one hour the Lord took all that trouble. And now, my love, I come to you. . . . And we were allowed finally to symbolize this fact by our shared Holy Communion, which will have been my last. . . . The task for which God made me is done. . . . There is a hymn which says, "For he to die is ready/Who, living, clings to Thee."[9]

This husband, this wife, were not pretending. In the midst of life, they were in death; in the midst of death, they were in life. Death had no dominion over them.

Adolf Hitler tried to cut off the hope of the Jews and nearly succeeded. But the God of Israel is the One who reconstitutes a slain community. All the powers, religious and secular, joined together to crucify Jesus of Nazareth. But the God and Father of the Incarnate Word is the one who raises the dead. There is One who is *more true* than death.

*And the Lord said:*
"I am the Resurrection and the Life; he who believes in me, though he die, yet shall he live, and whoever lives and believes in me shall never die. Do you believe this?"

Here is the reason for the sermon, and the worship, and the communion today — that you who are in this congregation will hear the question

---

eight. She won much recognition in her own right for her courage and her lifelong commitment to humane, democratic principles. She later helped to form the Kreisau Foundation for European Understanding.

9. This letter is a hundred times more extraordinary than this tiny excerpt can suggest. I have made some very slight alterations in the word order.

addressed to you by the living Jesus Christ in the power of the same Spirit that breathed upon the dry bones:

"Do you believe this?"

May the Spirit move our hearts today to join Martha in her confession:

"Yes, Lord; I believe that you are the Christ, the Son of God, the one who comes into the world" (11:27).

AMEN.

# Patriotism and Prophets

GRACE CHURCH IN NEW YORK

---

*July 1991*                    Ezekiel 2:3-7; Amos 3:2, 7:14; Zephaniah 3:8-20

THIS IS the weekend of our most important national holiday. It's a good habit always to reread the Declaration of Independence every Fourth of July. This incomparable document is without question one of the greatest ever produced in the history of the human race. When this period of contempt for Western culture that we are enduring right now is past, the Declaration will still stand, unparalleled, the noblest of all recorded affirmations of human rights and freedoms, the beacon and proving ground for the aspirations of all human beings everywhere — *all* races, *all* cultures, *all* creeds, and *all* faiths. It is not for nothing that people from all over the planet make pilgrimages to Monticello.[1] The Founders could not have known fully what they were doing for the world, but the work of the Signers of the Declaration and the Framers of the Constitution has endured as the foundation of a society that continues, against all fashionable left-wing predictions and expectations, to represent hope for all the nations of the earth. Anyone who doubts this need only read the daily accounts of the desire of peoples all over the world to emigrate to America, at whatever cost, through whatever danger, despite whatever hardship. Anyone who doubts it need look no further than the recent recapitulations of the life and work of Thurgood Marshall, about whom one civil rights veteran testified this week: "We didn't know about the Constitution. He [Marshall] brought us the Constitution . . . like Moses brought his people the Ten Commandments."

---

1. This is even more true today than it was in 1991.

[ 352 ]

All these things and more need to be said at the outset so that no one will be in any doubt about this preacher's love for America. I continue to believe that God ordained a special providential role for this country. If that is "exceptionalism," so be it.

American patriots, however, often seem to be suffering from insecurity more than they should. No matter how carefully one professes one's loyalty to the U.S.A. prior to offering a few doubts and misgivings, backs stiffen and arms cross as though preparing to resist the most abominable desecrations. During the war in the Persian Gulf, I had an opportunity to speak to an old friend who is senior pastor of a church near one of our most important army bases. With considerable trepidation and after much prayerful soul-searching, he had decided to preach a sermon encouraging his parishioners to keep patriotism in perspective. He told me that, as soon as the congregation that day began to suspect what he was up to, faces hardened, arms crossed, and expressions froze in a way that he had never before seen from the pulpit. He said that he felt real hatred, for the first time in his ministry. Weeks and months later, he was still dealing with the backlash.

I asked him to send me a copy of the sermon. Knowing that this man is one of the most mild-mannered, reasonable people you could imagine, I wanted to see what he had said that was so infuriating. When I read the sermon, I couldn't believe it. It was the opposite of a fire-breathing rant. It was extremely thoughtful, careful, and modest in its presentation. Those who objected to it must have been beyond the range of hearing.

> And [the Lord God] said to me, "Mortal, I send you to the people of Israel . . . and you shall say to them, 'Thus says the Lord God.' And whether they hear or refuse to hear (for they are a rebellious house), they will know that there has been a prophet among them. And you, son of man, be not afraid of them, nor be afraid of their words, nor be dismayed at their looks, for they are a rebellious house." (Ezek. 2:3-7)

The Hebrew prophets were a unique breed, and we are not going to see any more of them in this life. God spoke through them directly in a way that he has not spoken through anyone else since the apostolic age, for the Hebrew prophets were authorized to speak, not only in God's name but in his very words, in the first person. People exercising prophetic ministry today don't do that. Ours is a derivative authority, based on the original voices of the Old Testament prophets and the New Testament apostles. Nevertheless, prophetic ministry in our own day is very real. One thinks immediately of Martin Luther King Jr., for instance. Equally striking is the fact that many ordinary Christians have been called on occasion to prophetic roles, even though they may not have considered themselves prophets in the least. I can easily imagine my friend the preacher protesting like the prophet Amos, "But Lord! I am no prophet or even a prophet's son! I'm just a pastor!" But, Amos goes on, "the Lord took me, and the Lord said to me, 'Go, prophesy to my people Israel'" (7:14).

There is a great deal of self-righteous talk in the church nowadays about prophetic ministry. I used to do this myself when I was younger and less experienced. Many clergy and lay leaders will appropriate the title "prophet" for themselves when they have something to say that they know will offend. You get the feeling that they are proud of themselves for this. The trouble with this is that it does not fit what we know of the Old Testament prophets. They did not leap up and volunteer for the post of prophet; they were hauled into it, kicking and screaming. Even Isaiah, who is famous for having said "Here I am; send me," had to have his tongue burned first. Jeremiah protested vehemently against his vocation all his life. Amos we just heard about, and Hosea's prophetic ministry was a misery to him. The Hebrew prophets were dragooned, so to speak; they were overpowered by God's purposes, against their natural inclinations. For this reason, it seems to me, a reluctant and measured sermon by a hesitant but principled pastor has a better chance of being genuinely prophetic than the gleeful, microphone-grabbing sound bites of our self-styled contemporary "prophets."

Now the Word of God, we need to remember, does not issue forth in a vacuum. It intersects with our world, with human history. Karl Barth is supposed to have said that preaching is done with the Bible in one hand and the newspaper in the other.[2] All the Hebrew prophets were called to do their work in the context of specific events and particular public figures. Elijah and Elisha repeatedly confronted kings; when the Presiding Bishop of the Episcopal Church lets the President know that he doesn't agree with his decision to go to war, he is in the great prophetic tradition. Whether we agree or disagree with his particular point of view, there certainly can be no doubt that a bishop has a right to challenge a political leader on a matter of Christian conscience. Isaiah and Jeremiah and Daniel and the others did it all the time. When the lectionary readings for a given Sunday bring the

---

2. No one has been able to track down this often-quoted dictum, but it sounds like Barth, who often prayed for journalists.

prophet Ezekiel together with an American national holiday, it would seem to be the right time to examine our American consciences in light of the powerful tradition of the prophets of Israel.

Our text from Ezekiel this morning puts the most important fact right up front. God sent the prophets to Israel because they were his most favored nation. He didn't send them to Egypt or Persia or Iraq or other villainous heathen nations; he sent them to his own special, chosen people. Being the most favored nation was no Fourth of July picnic. I seem to hear the voice of Tevye *(Fiddler on the Roof)* in my ear, saying "Lord! Once in a while couldn't you choose somebody else?" Great privilege means great responsibility.

God instructs Amos to say this to Israel:

> You alone have I known of all the families of the earth; therefore I will punish you for all your iniquities. (3:2)

Sounds as if it's a privilege to be chastised, doesn't it? And indeed, that's exactly what the Word of God to Amos means. So if it is true that America has any sort of special status among the nations of the earth — and I believe the evidence of this continues to be undeniable — then the testimony of the Hebrew prophets is that special status means special accountability.

There is something terribly wrong in the United States these days, and you don't have to be a Hebrew prophet to see it and be horrified. All over this city and all around the country, the news is about poverty, crime, homelessness, drug abuse, family violence, gunfights, and inadequate health care. I don't need to spell it out; each of us knows what is going on. What Christian congregations do not necessarily know these days, however, is the biblical evidence about God's judgment upon his own people for allowing a great gap to develop between rich and poor. We don't know our Bibles very well, even in our churches; many Christians are not aware that the prophets repeatedly denounced the most favored nation for spending money and energies in foreign wars while neglecting problems of poverty and injustice back home. These themes were very familiar in the sixties; many Christians seem to have the idea that they were made up by wild-eyed hippies and bleeding-heart liberals. Now it sometimes seems as though the churches have turned their backs on the prophetic motifs of peace, justice, and a more equitable distribution of wealth, as though orthodox, evangelical Christianity needed to be purged of such suspiciously left-wing notions.

But this is not true. I know it's not true when I see a pretty young woman, obviously mentally ill, sitting on the steps of the Met Life building in dirty clothes, with tears running down her face as pedestrians hurry past with eyes averted. I know it's not true when I see a man begging for money and using for bait a small child with a hunted expression. I know it's not true when I see a young couple asleep under filthy blankets in the middle of a very hot day on the porch of St. George's Church.[3] When I see these sights, and when you see these sights, we know in our heart of hearts that these lost creatures are God's most special concern, and that he addresses us not only as individuals, *but also* as a nation — a nation that, Garry Wills writes in his most recent book, is still a powerfully Christian nation in some respects.

When I first came to Grace Church almost exactly ten years ago, the conscience of this congregation was stirring. I remember joining with a sizeable group of parishioners for the massive anti-nuclear-arms march. I remember our chapter of Evangelicals for Social Action. I remember our AIDS ministry. I remember when the Grace Opportunity Project began to burgeon into the fine program it is today. I remember our close affiliation with Habitat for Humanity. And I remember how, back in 1982, a group of passionately concerned young (and not-so-young) activists (yes, activists — right here at Grace Church!) began setting things in motion for a shelter for homeless men.

Not all of these ministries have continued to be vital at Grace Church. To tell the truth, there have been times when I have been so discouraged by the seeming lack of progress with regard to the homeless situation that I have been tempted to say, "What's the use?" It is at such times that I am reminded of the men in our shelter. Many would scoff at our shelter; it accommodates only six guests. It is rather luxurious for a shelter; many would say that we are spoiling the men and making them dependent. Maybe we are. And yet over the years I have come to believe more and more that our shelter is a gift to us from God to keep us from being isolated from the plight of his beloved poor. It has been a blessing for us that we have been able to keep it open with volunteers 365 days a year for several years, and there has been at least one significant success story that we know of. What would future generations think of us as a Christian congregation if all we had to show for ourselves during our period of stewardship was an improved physical plant? Thank God, we will not have to enter the twenty-

3. These sights largely disappeared from the streets of New York City in the boom years of the nineties. That doesn't mean the misery wasn't there; it was just hidden.

first century with the reproach hanging over us that we did absolutely nothing for our fellow creatures during a time of national disgrace.

Did that phrase — "national disgrace" — jar you? This is supposed to be a time of American pride and self-esteem, not disgrace. But it was at precisely such times that many of the Hebrew prophets were sent to address Israel, "whether they hear or refuse to hear, for they are a rebellious house." It was in times of national *prosperity* that the warnings of God about economic and social injustice were most pointed.

The prophets must have been at times a group of exceedingly discouraged men and women. They often did not live to see their prophecies come true. They were despised and vilified by patriots. They were ostracized and ridiculed. They were thought of as a danger to national life. The last and greatest of them, John the Baptist, was thrown in a dungeon and beheaded by the government. As for the Messiah of Israel, he was put to death on a charge of sedition, for being a danger to the Roman Empire. This is the history, this is the tradition, in which you and I as Christians stand.

But as the Epistle to the Hebrews puts it, God has spoken to us "in many and various ways by the prophets; [and] in these last days he has spoken to us by a Son" (1:1-2). He has spoken to us of our permanent citizenship in another city, another country. He has told us of our calling to be builders of a society that has its foundations not in the past, but in the future. He has told us of his Kingdom; what's vastly more, he has come in person to begin to establish that Kingdom through the faithful deeds, the prayers and faith, the witness and proclamation of his people.

Each of us knows the thrill of seeing the Star-Spangled Banner unfurled. It takes considerably more imagination to see the Kingdom of God made incarnate in a simple act of resistance to the idolatry of power, money, status, and self-righteousness. "For not with swords' loud clashing, nor roll of stirring drums, but deeds of love and mercy, the heavenly kingdom comes."[4] It is profoundly true that, as Christians, we always see our citizenship in this world in the light of the world which is to come, but this does not mean abdication of our worldly responsibilities. It is remarkable how the prophetic proclamation of the future Day of the Lord always maintains that striking connection between the purposes of God and the lowly ones of the earth. This Fourth of July weekend, you and I, gathered here today as

---

4. These words are from the hymn "Lead On, O King Eternal" by Ernest W. Shurtleff. He wrote it in 1888 for the commencement ceremony at Andover Theological Seminary when his class graduated.

a small remnant of our total, but nevertheless representative of the whole people of God, may play our part by quietly but firmly resolving to put our prayers and faith and deeds not on the altar of our country, not even so great a country as the United States of America, but on the altar of the God whose Day we await. The prophet Zephaniah calls us to our eternal citizenship in the city of God:

> "Therefore wait for me," says the Lord,
>     "for the day when I arise as a witness.
> For my decision is to gather nations,
>     to assemble kingdoms. . . .
> Yea, at that time I will change the speech of the peoples
>     to a pure speech,
>         that all of them may call on the name of the Lord
>         and serve him with one accord. . . .
> On that day you shall not be put to shame
>     because of the deeds by which you have rebelled against me;
> for then I will remove from your midst
>     your proudly exultant ones,
> and you shall no longer be haughty
>     in my holy mountain.
> For I will leave in the midst of you
>     a people humble and lowly. . . .
> And I will save the lame
>     and gather the outcast,
>         and I will change their shame into praise
>             and renown in all the earth . . .
>         at the time when I gather you together.
> Yea, I will make you renowned and praised
>     among all the peoples of the earth,
>         when I restore your fortunes
>         before your eyes," says the Lord. (Zeph. 3:8-9, 11-12, 19-20)

AMEN.

# But If Not

BACCALAUREATE SERMON FOR GORDON COLLEGE,
HAMILTON, MASSACHUSETTS

*May 1988*                                                    Daniel 1–3

SHADRACH, MESHACH, and Abednego! They don't tell 'em like that anymore. Even from a purely literary point of view, it is everywhere acknowledged that the stories of the Old Testament — of which our text is a pre-
mier example — are incomparable masterpieces of narrative art. If we judge
the story of the three young men in the fiery furnace for its political and
theological impact as well as its artistry, then, like so many of the other great
biblical stories, it must be counted in a class by itself.

To begin, then. Shadrach, Meshach, and Abednego, along with their
even more prepossessing companion, Daniel, were young graduates like the
men and women gathered before us today. They had been sent to the best
college in Babylon for several years, and they had been educated for success.
They had been groomed to step into fast-track jobs that would lead to high
posts in Mesopotamia, Inc.

Shadrach, Meshach, and Abednego were actually their Babylonian
names. Their real names were Hananiah, Mish'a-el, and Azariah, for they
were Hebrews. They had been brought all the way to Babylon as captives
from their homeland in order to be indoctrinated into the glamorous, advanced, powerful culture of the Babylonian Empire, compared to which Judah must have seemed like the sticks. They had been chosen for this special

---

As indicated, this sermon was delivered at Gordon College, an evangelical liberal arts college.

education precisely because they were bright, alert, and full of promise. It must have been a program similar to that of the Soviets bringing youths from Afghanistan to Moscow.[1]

I don't know much about what it would be like to be an Afghan youth in the Soviet Union. I really cannot say that I know much about what it was like to be a young Hebrew in Babylon. But I do know something of what it is like to be a young Christian in America, because I am a minister in a parish full of young evangelicals in the midst of New York City, and I suspect that maintaining a Christian identity in the midst of a largely pagan society is very likely the most difficult challenge that you will face in the years ahead.

The young Hebrew men who were brought to the king's court in Babylon were assigned to the chief eunuch, who was ordered to spare no expense in converting these fresh, bright kids from the boondocks into aggressive Babylonian go-getters. We might think of a football coach who has been given all kinds of money under the table in order to recruit the best high-school players with parties, cars, women, dope, and celebrities.

But Daniel, Hananiah, Mish'a-el, and Azariah resisted. They refused to smoke the dope, drink the booze, or bed the women. King Nebuchadnezzar, clearly fascinated by these clean-living young Hebrews, sent down some caviar and champagne on a silver platter, but they rejected that too — which was about the same as having the President of the United States call up to congratulate you on winning the Olympic medal and your refusing to take the call. Apparently, though, the king never found out about their renunciation of the royal favor, because the chief steward protected them. He passed them carrot sticks and fruit juice when no one was looking, and they were healthier and smarter and quicker than any of the other young men in the Babylonian court, and they got promoted rapidly. That's what happens in chapter 1.

Now, I was going to skip over chapter 2, but after the events of the past two weeks here in the U.S.A., I can't resist taking a quick peek. Nebuchadnezzar, ruler of the Babylonian Empire, has a bad dream. You know about this dream — it's the one about the statue of a man who has a head of gold and a chest of silver and legs of iron and — yes — feet of clay. Nebuchadnezzar didn't like this dream at all. He suspected it might have something to do with world events, as indeed it did. So he called in the very best that Mes-

---

1. This is the sad prequel to the war in Afghanistan that the United States is waging in 2011 as this book goes to press.

opotamia had to offer in the way of Chaldean wise men, enchanters, magicians, sorcerers, and — you guessed it — *astrologers.*[2]

And, of course, the astrologers don't know anything about the dream and can't tell anything about the dream. So Daniel offers himself as interpreter, and he is brought in to the king, and Daniel speaks to the king these memorable words:

> "No wise men, enchanters, magicians, or astrologers can show to the king the mystery which the king has asked, but there is a God in heaven who reveals mysteries, and he makes known to King Nebuchadnezzar what will be in the latter days." (2:27-28)

So Daniel tells the dream and interprets it; we won't go into that now, except to say that it's not as bad as the king had feared, and he rewards Daniel accordingly. Daniel doesn't forget his three friends; he brings them up with him, into the realms of the power brokers and the deal makers and the inside traders. And there we find them at the beginning of chapter 3.

It's been said of a number of the fallen television evangelists that they just couldn't handle the temptations of power and money. No doubt you and I think that we could handle them just fine. But many good men and women have fallen prey to it. Sometimes it seems that we should be asking whether the whole Christian community in America hasn't fallen prey to it — the gospel of prosperity, the gospel of success, the gospel of happiness in this world, the gospel of answered prayer, the gospel of Mesopotamia first. Sometimes I wonder if American culture might not be even more seductive than King Nebuchadnezzar's realm. After all, it was clear to the young Hebrews that Babylon really was pagan. YHWH of Israel, called the Most High God in the book of Daniel, was not worshiped in Babylon; his name was not known. In our country today, however, there is still a perceptible overlay of religion. Sometimes it's hard to find the boundary between the authentic worship of the God who is really God and something else that masquerades under that same name.

When King Nebuchadnezzar erected an image of gold on the plain of Dura, in the province of Babylon, however, there could have been no doubt in the minds of Shadrach, Meshach, and Abednego about whether it was really the Most High God wrapped in a Babylonian flag. It wasn't. It was an

---

2. First Lady Nancy Reagan had been consulting astrological charts to help her husband make important decisions.

*idol,* pure and simple. Even so, there was a fairly potent threat attached to it. If they didn't bow down to it and worship it, they were going to be thrown into a fiery furnace on the instant. No three-month probationary period, no house arrest in the pleasant vicinity of the Hanging Gardens, no temporary ban, no early retirement with opportunities to go on the lecture circuit and write a book. Nothing of the kind — instead a hasty, painful, and unpleasant execution, generally thought of as the most effective deterrent to undesirable behavior.

So what supernatural power gripped those young men? We're not told in any detail; we are told only that they were "servants of the Most High God." How did they find the courage to do what they did? How could three young men who had risen together through the ranks through sheer fiber and grit suddenly find the fortitude to renounce everything they had won and even life itself? They had everything to live for — Babylon was their oyster, so to speak. What was their secret?

Let's imagine the scene for a moment as the narrator gives it to us.

Old Testament *poetry* depends largely upon repetition for its effects, but no other *prose* account relies as exclusively upon repetition as does this story. To our modern ears, it sounds almost comical. Why are we told *three times* about "the satraps, the prefects, the governors, the counselors, the treasurers, the justices, the magistrates, and all the officials of the provinces" (3:2, 3, 27)? It may simply be a stylistic device, but it impresses upon the hearers (and of course these biblical stories originated as oral recitations) the breadth and depth of the power arrayed against Shadrach, Meshach, and Abednego. The technique of rhythmic repetition greatly increases the sense of their isolation and uniqueness among these hundreds of supposedly consequential people who are only too ready to bow down to whatever idol offers them personal or ideological advantage.

And why are we told no fewer than *four times* about all those "horns, pipes, lyres, trigons, harps, bagpipes, and every kind of music" (3:5, 7, 10)? Is it just for fun, to increase our admiration for the facility of the storyteller? Your guess is as good as mine, but I think it creates a kind of hypnotic, numbing, almost totalitarian effect. Music can be used that way to elicit a mindless response from a large crowd. The most extreme example of this would be the giant rallies in Nazi Germany. Closer to home would be certain rock concerts. Some would even say — forgive me for this — that the simple, repetitive chants sung over and over at some types of Christian worship services produce the same sort of groupthink and loss of discernment. In any case, it is clear that every device available to "the rulers of this age" (to use St. Paul's language in 1 Corinthians 2:6-8) has been brought to bear against our three young men.

Now it's time to direct our attention to an often overlooked but most crucial part of the story. Listen carefully to the singular statement of Shadrach, Meshach, and Abednego as they confront the king.

The king says:

> "Is it true, O Shadrach, Meshach, and Abednego, that you do not worship the golden image which I have set up? Now, when you hear the sound of the horn, pipe, [trumpet, trombone, saxophone, tuba, snare drum, kettle drum, electric guitar, and electronic synthesizer], if you are ready to fall down and worship the image which I have made, well and good; but if you do not, you shall immediately be cast into a burning fiery furnace; *and who is the god that will deliver you out of my hands?"*

And Shadrach, Meshach, and Abednego answer the king:

> "O Nebuchadnezzar, we have no need to answer you in this matter. If it be so, our God whom we serve *is able* to deliver us out of the burning fiery furnace, and he will deliver us out of your hand, O King. *But if not,* be it known to you, O King, that we will not serve your gods or worship the golden image which you have set up." (3:13-18; my emphasis)

This truly is one of the more extraordinary utterances in the Bible. "Our God *is able* to deliver us and our God will deliver us; but *even if he does not* deliver us, we will not bow down to any other god." This is a statement of ultimate trust in God *for his own sake,* a statement so radical as to make other statements about God look conditional, self-serving, and half-baked in comparison. This is not the familiar evangelistic technique of winning souls by recounting one tale after another of prayer requests answered. If everybody who went on the 700 Club talked like Shadrach, Meshach, and Abednego, contributions would dry up overnight. When you think about it, their statement is almost too unconditional to be borne. God is God, whether he chooses to intervene on the human stage in a particular way or not. His majesty, his righteousness, his worthiness to be worshiped does not depend on any given set of conditions that human beings might devise. The three young men believed that it was infinitely better to die praising the living God than it was to compromise his honor by acting as though he were no better than Nebuchadnezzar's image — a god bound to and limited by the needs and demands of his followers, a god who would be at the beck and call of those who claimed to worship him.

> "O Nebuchadnezzar . . . our God whom we serve *is able* to deliver us out of the burning fiery furnace, and he will deliver us out of your hand, O King. *But if not,* be it known to you, O King, that we will not serve your gods or worship the golden image which you have set up."

Well, you know the rest of the story. Nebuchadnezzar's storm troopers stoked up the furnace and forthwith threw the three young men into it, bound hand and foot. The flames of the furnace were so hot that they jumped out of the oven door and burned up the executioners. Nebuchadnezzar, sitting nearby in order to watch the grisly scene, jumped up in astonishment:

> "I see four men, loose, walking in the midst of the fire, and they are not hurt; and the appearance of the fourth is like a son of the gods."
> (3:25)

Shadrach, Meshach, and Abednego stepped out of the furnace with not a hair on their heads or a thread of their garments so much as singed. And all of the satraps, governors, magistrates, and so forth saw it happen, and saw the power of the God of the three young men.

And Nebuchadnezzar the king said,

> "Blessed be the God of Shadrach, Meshach, and Abednego, who has sent his angel [that would be the fourth man] and has delivered his servants, who trusted in him and who set at nought the king's command and yielded up their bodies rather than serve and worship any god rather than their own god."

And Nebuchadnezzar made a decree that no one was to speak anything against the God of Shadrach, Meshach, and Abednego, for *"there is no other God who is able to deliver in this way"* (3:28-29; my emphasis).

What we need now to remember about this magnificent story is that it was part of a literature written for the encouragement of the faithful who were undergoing fierce persecution. Throughout the centuries, this story has found its home in communities of believers who were probably *not* going to be delivered in this world. The book of Daniel is part of the literature of martyrdom. If we remember this, we can understand with new clarity how the center of this story is this ringing declaration:

> "Our God whom we serve is able to deliver us . . . out of your hand,
> O King; but [even] if not, let it be known to you that we will not . . .
> worship the golden image which you have set up."

God is supremely able, and worthy of worship for his own sake. Deliverance in this world is a sign of his greatness and "his mercy toward them that fear him," but it is not an end in itself. In those little words, *But if not,* a whole history of pain, suffering, ambiguity, and seemingly unanswered prayer is summed up. In those little words, *Even if not,* the determination of the Christian community to hold fast to the name of the Lord in spite of everything finds its noblest expression.

To the class of 1988:

You are going to go out from here into Babylon. In a sense, you have been in Babylon all along, because the Christian community cannot really isolate itself in the midst of the larger society; we must work out our relationship to the world around us.

Now, in American society today, no one is going to do anything so crass as to set an idol before you and say "Worship this!" (Well, I take that back — maybe the advertising agencies will.) But for the most part, the idols are going to be masquerading as good things in life which are compatible with Christian faith; you can have God, and you can have all these other things too. You can pursue whatever style of life is most pleasing and enjoyable, as long as you practice personal piety. The young people in our New York parish talk about this dilemma all the time, but you can be sure it is not peculiar to New York.

In chapter 4 of Daniel, we find Nebuchadnezzar in a humbled condition, seeking counsel from his young Hebrew aide. What Daniel advises the pagan king is simply this: "Practice righteousness, and show mercy to the oppressed" (4:27). Here is the link between the worship of the one true God and the way of life that God requires. This linkage of worship and ethics pervades the Bible from end to end. In a society riddled with greed and self-centeredness, the surest path is not mere religiosity, but a holy life, and active compassion toward those who are disenfranchised and dispossessed

— those groups for whom the story of the deliverance of Shadrach, Meshach, and Abednego has always had a special meaning. In Babylon, the great temptation is always to follow these on the way up, those who are surrounded by the trappings of worldly success, especially if there is a veneer of religion to go along with it; but the biblical story proclaims to us a God who, in St. Paul's words, "has chosen what is weak in the world to shame the strong, has chosen what is foolish in the world to shame the wise. . . . The rulers of this age . . . are doomed to pass away" (1 Cor. 1:27; 2:6). —

I address you tonight as young American Christians, or as young Christians from other countries who have received a good dose of American Christianity while you have been here. As you go out from Gordon College, you go out into a world which, by and large, feels deeply ambivalent about America. On the one hand, our country still represents for many the greatest hope of the free world, a trust we have received from the God of our fathers. But on the other hand, we are regarded with deep suspicion, and, often, with outright hostility, because of the arrogant self-righteousness of our foreign policy in so many parts of the globe, a policy that seems to many to be lacking in basic American decency and forthrightness.[3] We must acknowledge also that there are many in our society who find themselves on the outside looking in; for them, the American dream exists only as a flickering image on a TV screen. One cringes to think what the prophet Amos would say were he to walk the streets of any of our cities today; never has the gap between rich and poor been so glaringly apparent, never has it been so easy to "pass by on the other side." Our entire middle-class culture is in danger of losing its soul. American values are being shaped to an unprecedented degree by inane movies pitched to the lowest common adolescent denominator, by music videos, by soap operas, and it is all happening almost imperceptibly, so that Christians are able to discern the difference between what is Christian and what is merely cultural only by exercising perpetual vigilance.

But that is precisely what your education at Gordon College has been for: not to equip you for a job and for worldly success, but to train your mind for discernment, for vigilance, and, it may be, for resistance to "the rulers of this age."

Will the members of the graduating class of 1988 please stand:

I don't suppose that any of you are going to be asked to jump into a fi-

---

3. And this was only 1988. After the American invasion of Iraq in 2003, the situation described here became exponentially worse.

ery furnace, although you never know. Here are some of the things I am *sure* you are going to be faced with:

- You are going to be tempted to believe that the end justifies the means in a hundred areas, ranging from your personal relationships to your political commitments.
- You are going to be tempted to forgo the disciplines of reading and thinking for the easy passivity of being a couch potato in front of the tube.
- You are going to be tempted to take the line of least resistance in raising your own children.
- You are going to be tempted to retreat to a purely individualistic view of Christian faith that concentrates exclusively on the state of the self without any reference to the needs of society as a whole, and particularly the oppressed within that society.
- You are going to be tempted to think of your own, very probably homogeneous Christian community as representative of the whole church.
- You are going to be tempted every day to think of prayer as a means of getting things to work out, of worship as a technique for manipulating God, of being a Christian as a path to the good life.

In these ways and in countless others, you will meet turnings in the road every day, turnings which, if taken, will lead you farther and farther away from the living God, deeper and deeper into the worship of the gods of the image-makers. As you come to these turnings in the way, perhaps you will think from time to time of Shadrach, Meshach, and Abednego, and how they said, "Our God is able to deliver us . . . but if not, be it known to you, O King, that we will not serve the image which you have set up."

For you see, ultimately the story of the three young men in the fiery furnace, for all its thrilling qualities, is a story not of glory, but of the Cross. The story of Shadrach, Meshach, and Abednego has maintained its power over the centuries as a story cherished by those who would walk into the flames and would not come out again on this side — martyrs, slaves, prisoners, those who bore their witness in the midst of the world that hates God.

I myself will confess to you that I do not find this so easy to listen to, let alone live by. I like the pleasures of this world as much as the next person, and more than some. But this story, which I have loved since I was a little girl, goes out ahead of me, claiming me by its power. It goes out tonight ahead of you, calling you to march under the banner of the Most High God. For the story gains its significance in each new generation of Christians as we recognize that the worship of the living God may not bring us prosperity, may not bring us success, may not bring us advancement in this world, but that he alone is worthy of worship for his own sake, he alone keeps his promises in the way that is best for us, he alone can and will vindicate the cause of his people.

And for those who believe this, no road is too long, no fire too hot, no night too dark, no sacrifice too great, for truly, as King Nebuchadnezzar was forced to admit,

"There is no other God who is able to deliver in this way."

May the Lord God of Hosts defend you for all your days and fill your hearts with the peace that passes human understanding. In the name of the Father, and the Son, and of the Holy Spirit.

AMEN.

# The Apocalyptic Man

MARYHOUSE: THE CATHOLIC WORKER, NEW YORK CITY

---

*September 1980*                                                    Daniel 5

*The Catholic Worker movement is celebrated for its radical
stance toward politics — hence the tenor of this sermon,
which was intended to honor and encourage the workers.*

. . . . . . . . . . . . . . . . .

About halfway through the Old Testament, it becomes possible for discerning readers to see that a brilliant new thread has made its appearance in
the fabric, and that, furthermore, it runs here and there throughout the
subsequent portions of the Hebrew Scriptures until ultimately it becomes
at least the warp, if not also the woof, of the entire New Testament tapestry.
How remarkable, therefore, that many devout Bible-readers have never
seen it. I certainly never saw it until I was trained to look for it. Like everybody else in the modern, post-Enlightenment age, I was conditioned not to
see it. The closest I ever got to it was laughing at cartoons of little bearded
men carrying signs that said "Get Ready for the End of the World." I was
told quite early in my life that modern educated Christians do not believe
in the End of the World.

And so, like most mainstream twentieth-century church members, I
read the Bible for many years without ever realizing that there was this
apocalyptic thread running through it. Of course, one of the problems was
that I had been taught to equate apocalyptic thinking with various quaint

notions about Armageddon, the Rapture, pre- and post-millenarianism, and so forth. Only those on the margins believed such things. (We should have taken a hint from that, since the Bible is through and through concerned with the marginalized.)

There has been an explosion in biblical studies in the twentieth century, however. It has been re-learned in our time what Paul the apostle knew from the beginning, and the prophet we call Second Isaiah before him. Apocalyptic theology has to do with God, with history, with ethics, with living, with suffering, with dying, with war and peace, and above all with the human future. We discover this by divine revelation, and that is what the word *apocalypsis* means in Greek — revelation, unveiling, or disclosure. More than that, it means invasion from a sphere other than this one. The *apocalypse* of God comes to us with life-transforming force. The apocalyptic unveiling of which we read in the Scripture requires — no, it *creates* — a radical alteration in our perception of the world and of our lives.

In recent times we have seen a marked acceleration of interest in the apocalyptic dimension of the Judeo-Christian tradition. This isn't a mere cyclical fluctuation in public taste. The re-discovery of apocalyptic in our time is related to the post-Constantinian condition of the church, the memory of the Holocaust, the decline of the West, and the global threat of environmental or nuclear disaster. It is in this world threatened with annihilation of various sorts that the recovery of apocalyptic is taking place. It's taking place for reasons intimately connected to the circumstances of our lives, just as the appearance of the apocalyptic thread in Scripture was related to the conditions of those times and those places.

The apocalyptic thread of which I am speaking began to work its way to the very center of the pattern of biblical thought at just about the time when the period of our Old Testament was coming to an end — namely, about 160 years before the birth of Christ. The world of that time was like our own in certain interesting respects. The conquests of Alexander the Great had paved the way for the spread of Greek culture throughout the entire Mediterranean; Alexander had dreamed of the *oikoumene* — one world — and after his death, the process he began did indeed continue to bring diverse populations into one common culture, a kind of synthesis of the Greek and the Oriental that we call Hellenistic civilization. Just as today we travel the world around and see people wearing jeans, listening to rock music, and drinking Coca-Cola, so in the Hellenistic period we could have seen Greek statues in Egypt, Greek clothing in Syria, and Greek theaters in

Persia. Above all we would have heard the Greek language spoken everywhere, as English is today.

Because Hellenism served as the first world culture, so to speak, races and people were brought out of parochialism onto a vast international stage. Sophisticated Greek manners and learning became available to people from various ethnic backgrounds, particularly those of the upper class. Many embraced Hellenistic culture with complete enthusiasm, seeing in it a means of advancement, of broadening horizons, of increasing knowledge, of exchanging a dull provincial life for an urbane, fashionable one — like coming to New York from the various provinces of the Deep South or the Great Plains.

Now picture, if you will, the position of the Jews in such a world. The chief characteristic of the chosen people of God has always been their "holiness," their "set-apart-ness," their distinctiveness. In a world of cultural synthesis, what would they do? For a while, after Alexander, pious Jews were allowed to live as they pleased, and many of them became thoroughly Hellenized, particularly the aristocratic class, since their intellectual and commercial interests coincided with so much of Hellenism, and no conflict was seen between faith and culture. The similarity to today's American church is obvious; one may attend worship services in prosperous suburbs for years on end and never perceive any tension whatever between the values espoused by the community as a whole and those being held up by the congregations. It has become "the absorbed church."[1]

Then as now, however, there were groups and sects who refused to go along with this kind of cultural assimilation. In the time of which we are speaking, a small group, remembering Elijah and the other great figures of the past who had warned Israel of cross-cultural apostasy, began to form a kind of resistance movement. These were the Hasidim, the "Faithful Ones," the "Pious Ones."[2]

The Hasidic movement was obscure at first; but then something happened which changed everything. Antiochus Epiphanes, an exceptionally vicious tyrant by any standard, came to power, and suddenly the easygoing atmosphere of Hellenistic religious toleration disappeared, a casualty of Antiochus's megalomania. Suppression of the worshipers of Yahweh was

1. This phrase is borrowed from an article by Charles Kinzie in *Sojourners,* July 1978. Thirty-something years later, the situation differs in detail (we are much more multicultural now), but not in urgency, as American Christians continue to struggle with the temptations of assimilation.

2. This is not the same Hasidic movement that we know today, which arose much later. There is the same commitment to separation, however.

part of his strategy to extend and consolidate Hellenistic culture. He issued an edict to the effect that everyone in the kingdom should have one religion, with himself as a member of the pantheon.

This is the point at which the Hasidim emerge into the full light of historical attention. They would not submit to Antiochus's edict. Therefore, the king proceeded to more cruel measures, and the most ferocious persecution of the Jews to ever take place up to that time was launched. Anyone who was found observing the Sabbath, circumcising a child, or eating kosher food was liable to be burned alive. It was a capital offense just to own a copy of the Torah. Many terrible things happened: Jerusalem was pillaged and the temple treasures were carried off; thousands were massacred; circumcised children were slaughtered and hung around their mothers' necks. Worst of all, in the eyes of the believing Jews, the king built an altar to the pagan god over the sacred altar of YHWH in the Jerusalem Temple (this is the "abomination of desolation" referred to in Daniel 11:31 and Mark 13:14). Under the fearsome threats of Antiochus's persecution, every Jew in the area of Jerusalem had to decide whether to deny his heritage and be Hellenized, or be killed.

Think of it: how easy it would have been to compromise! What difference did it make what one ate? Was it really necessary to say the Sabbath prayers publicly? Couldn't one give lip service to Antiochus and still remain faithful to Yahweh in one's heart? Many Jews compromised in this way, were Hellenized, and escaped. Many others, like the Hasidim, stood firm; it is a matter of historical record that many Jews were martyred for their faith under Antiochus Epiphanes, during the period of the famous Maccabean revolt.

It is during this period of unprecedented horror for God's people that the thread of apocalyptic which had been running through the tradition all along suddenly appeared in full-blown color. Most of the apocalyptic literature of the period never made it into the Old Testament, but the great masterpiece of the genre did.[3] In 164 B.C., when the pressure on the Jews to go Hellenistic or die was at its most intense, an unknown Hasidic author, working with traditional materials but in the grip of some transcendent, visionary power, produced for the encouragement of his people the document known to subsequent generations as the book of Daniel.

And so we read that King Belshazzar of Babylon held a feast for a thou-

---

3. This was surpassed later only by the "Synoptic apocalypse" of the Gospels and the book of Revelation.

sand of the nobles of his realm. From the description in the fifth chapter of Daniel, it sounds like an affair that the *Penthouse* paparazzi would have liked to cover; apparently the only women present were the king's concubines and a number of call girls. We're told that there was a lot of liquor flowing, and all in all, it sounds pretty much like a good old-fashioned orgy.

After Belshazzar has been drinking for a while, he reaches out for a grand climactic gesture, a display that will really raise his celebration to the next level. He orders the gold and silver vessels from the temple in Jerusalem to be brought in.

This would be like using the communion chalices of the church for beer mugs at a fraternity initiation, only this is a whole lot worse because this is a king doing it. Most important, though, the original readers of the book of Daniel would not fail to catch the allusion to Antiochus Epiphanes. Just as King Belshazzar of Babylon is described as profaning the sacred vessels of the temple, even so Antiochus had desecrated the altar and treasures of the house of God. The author of the story sets up a parallel which his Hasidic audience would recognize immediately. The God of the Jews, Belshazzar clearly believes, is impotent, and Antiochus thought so too. Who could expect the king to believe in a God who apparently was unable to protect either the honor of his people or his own honor? Why not make a public display of the powerlessness of such a God? Why not humiliate him and his people by putting his consecrated vessels to sacrilegious use? And so Belshazzar the King summoned his servants to pour wine into the cups, and the nobles began quaffing Babylonian vintages from the vessels of the Holy One of Israel.

Immediately, the Scripture tells us, the king saw "the handwriting on the wall." A disembodied hand — or rather, a hand that is attached to and set in motion by a Power invisible to Belshazzar — appears and writes mysterious words on Belshazzar's palace wall; and the king, drunk as he is, begins to tremble. Such is the artistry of the story that we are not yet told what the writing is; instead, we hear the king hollering for the cryptographers, for the CIA and the FBI, for the consultants and the pundits and the psychics. But nobody can tell him anything about the handwriting. The king becomes panicky, and the whole company is in confusion. At this dramatic moment the one person who has access to the king without invitation comes sweeping into the hall, having heard the uproar — namely, the queen mother.

"O King, live forever! Do not let your thoughts alarm you or your color change. There is in your kingdom a man in whom is the spirit of the holy gods. . . . Let Daniel be called, and he will show the interpretation." (5:10-12)

"There is a man!" What sort of man was this Daniel? The queen mother remembered him from the days of her husband, Nebuchadnezzar. There is a man! A man who would not eat Nebuchadnezzar's non-kosher food; a man whose friends would not bow down to Nebuchadnezzar's god; a man who stood before Nebuchadnezzar and said:

> "No wise men . . . or astrologers can show to the king the mystery which the king has asked, but there is a God in heaven who reveals mysteries, and he has made known . . . what will be in the latter days." (2:27-28)

There is a man! A man who, because he would not compromise in the lesser things, could be trusted with the greater; a man who would continue to pray to Yahweh in public, though all the officials of Persia were watching in order to trap him; there is a man![4]

Daniel is brought before Belshazzar. It has been many years since Nebuchadnezzar's time, many years since Daniel has had anything meaningful or rewarding to do, many years since he has received the praise of men. "Look, uh, Daniel," says the king, "if you can read that handwriting on the wall, I'll give you a Mercedes with a chauffeur and set you up in the corner office right down the hall from me."

Then Daniel utters one of the great speeches of the Bible:

> "[O King], let your gifts be for yourself, and your rewards for another; nevertheless I will read the writing. . . . You have lifted up yourself against the Lord of heaven, and the vessels of his house have been brought in before you, and you . . . have drunk wine from them, and you have praised the gods of silver and gold . . . which do not see or hear or know, but the God in whose hand is your breath, and whose are all your ways, you have not honored. From his presence the hand was sent. . . ." (5:17, 23-24)

And this is what it wrote:

---

4. Reading this sermon thirty-something years later, I feel sure that I must have borrowed the repetition of "There is a man" from the repertoire of some hallowed preacher of days gone by. Unfortunately, I do not remember who it was or where I found the venerable sermon.

*Mene* [Numbered]
*Tekel* [Weighed]
*Parsin* [Divided]

And Daniel interpreted:

"God has numbered the days of your kingdom and brought it to an
end. You have been weighed in the balances and found wanting.
Your kingdom is divided and given to the Medes and Persians."
(5:26-28)

And that very night Belshazzar the Chaldean was slain, and Darius the
Mede received the kingdom.[5]

Let's pause a moment to let this sink in. Can you imagine the effect of
this story when it was first told in the days of the persecution of Antiochus
Epiphanes? Despite all the appearances to the contrary, the God of Israel is
the God of all the nations of the globe. God's power cannot be thwarted, no
matter how much the mighty of the earth may swagger and boast and lift
themselves up against the Lord of Heaven. "We are in the presence of the
ultimate judgment on history."[6] YHWH, he is God! The future belongs to
him. The empires of this world belong to him:

"The Most High rules the kingdom of men, and gives it to whom he
will, and sets over it the lowliest of men." (4:17; 5:21)

"The lowliest of men . . ." Ah, there is the critical point. Remember
those marginalized people? The lowly, humble servant of God is more than
all the kings and generals and presidents and dictators of the world. No fol-
lower of the living God of Israel would fail to understand; Antiochus, with
all his worldly power and pomp, was doomed. What really mattered, what
really lasted, was the faithfulness of God's people even unto death.

In a very real sense, Daniel represents all the people of God, to whom
God has revealed his mysteries, to whom God has made known what will be
in the latter days. You understand that it was no easier to resist cultural
pressures in those days than it is in our own time. After all, what was a single
Jew, or a handful of Jews, in the vast sweep of empire? Was it so terrible to

5. One of the most spectacular biblical paintings in the world is Rembrandt's *Belshazzar's
Feast* in the National Gallery in London. No reproduction can capture the eerie light of the hand
writing on the wall or the terror it evokes in Belshazzar.
6. Norman Porteous, *Daniel* (Philadelphia: Westminster Press, 1965), p. 83.

skip a couple of Sabbath services? Couldn't a person simply go private with his faith and wait until the danger was past? For countless Christians in our own time as in Antiochus's time, the book of Daniel has been a towering bulwark for faith under extreme pressure. Its readers have trusted the message and known what the end would be. God would vindicate the loyalty of his servants, though all the fury of a Nero or a Hitler or an Idi Amin or a military-industrial complex be unleashed against them.

The genius and the significance of apocalyptic do not really lie in its depictions of the End of the World. The unique importance of the apocalyptic mentality, which eventually comes to pervade the entire New Testament, is this: it enables believers to see two levels of reality at one and the same time — to see, as it were, both what is going on and what is *really* going on.[7] Did Belshazzar and Nebuchadnezzar really have control over Daniel? Did Antiochus really determine the destiny of the people of God? Does the fate of the poor really rest with the federal bureaucracy? Does the future of the world really depend upon the President of the United States and the leaders in the Kremlin? Or is it all part of "the form of this world" which, as St. Paul tells us, "is passing away" (1 Cor. 7:31)? Apocalyptic thinking tells us that the most High God rules over the kingdom of men and gives it to whom he wills, and sets over it the lowliest of human beings, men and women alike. It is in the witness, the faithfulness, the testimony of the lowliest of his servants that the Lord works. That is what is real; that is what is lasting.

Can we believe this? Can we believe in a God who vindicates his servants when all appearances are to the contrary? In the aftermath of Election Day 1980, the only handwriting on the wall visible to the unaided eye appears to be directed against liberal Democrats. Belshazzar has not been slain; his kingdom has not been toppled. Tyranny and oppression reign across the world as before. But I said "unaided eye." That is precisely the point. Apocalyptic vision is unveiled vision. God has ripped apart the curtain and permitted us to see "what must take place" (Rev. 1:1). "Behold, I have told you all things beforehand" (Mark 13:23).

God has not revealed these things, however, for us to enjoy passively, as though they were motion pictures. The apocalyptic writings are "a call for the endurance of the saints" who obey God's commandment and remain faithful to Jesus (Rev. 14:12). The difference between knowing what is happening and knowing what is *really* happening — that is, knowing that the

---

7. I have proposed that this be called *apocalyptic transvision.*

Most High God rules over the kingdom of men — can be costly and dangerous, and very often it feels as though it is being undertaken in the dark. The day after the takeover of the military junta in Bolivia in July, *The New York Times* reported that twelve Roman Catholic priests who had been active on behalf of the poor had disappeared. Where are they now?

Knowing the Most High God is to see things that cannot be seen by the unaided eye. The things of God can be seen only by faith, faith in the God who revealed to Daniel that "his dominion is an everlasting dominion, and his kingdom one that will never be destroyed" (7:14). In this world, the Christian community lives and acts in the dark, defended by a power that to "the rulers of this age" (1 Cor. 2:8) is invisible and nonexistent. For those whose eyes have been opened, it is God's invading grace that enables us to see in the dark, to become children of light (Eph. 5:8), to do battle with "this present evil age" (Gal. 1:3), to "take no part in the unfruitful works of darkness, but instead expose them" (Eph. 5:11). You here at the Catholic Worker have known these things for a long time, and here on the margins you have ministered to "the lowliest of men and women." Wherever this takes place, the Most High God is present in power. It was this apocalyptic literature that made way for the time when Daniel's vision would come true, and the disciples of Jesus of Nazareth with opened eyes would read the book of Daniel and know of a truth whose coming it revealed:

> "I saw in the night visions,
> and behold, with the clouds of heaven
> there came one like a Son of Man,
> and he came to the Ancient of Days
> and was presented before him.
> And to him was given dominion
> and glory and kingdom,
> that all peoples, nations, and languages
> should serve him;
> his dominion is an everlasting dominion,
> which shall not pass away,
> and his kingdom one that shall not be destroyed." (7:13-14)

May we bear our witness to the Son of Man in such a way that it will be said of us all, "There was a man! There was a woman!"

AMEN.

# Prophet of Amazing Grace

*June 1978*                                             Hosea 3:1–6:6

Children often go through periods of disliking the names they were given. Most parents these days try to avoid saddling their children with embarrassing names, so that you don't run into too many children named Hezekiah or Petunia. In earlier times, though, great men did not have such sensitivities about their children's social life. Names had a larger significance. Names could have political, social, or historical meaning. One of the signers of the Declaration of Independence from South Carolina, Henry Middleton, named his daughter Septima Sexta, Latin for "Seventy-Six."

In the eighth century B.C., the great Hebrew prophet Hosea had three children, and their names were chosen for them by the command of the God of Israel. The first, a son, was named Jezreel; that was the name of a valley where a massacre had taken place, so it was a warning that God was about to send destruction on the people. The second child, a daughter, was named Lo-ruhamah, which meant "Not-pitied" or "Not-loved." The third child, another boy, was called Lo-ammi, meaning "Not-my-people." These children with their strange, frightening names were meant to be walking, living testimonies to Hosea's neighbors that Israel's God was very angry. Every time the children's mother took them to the market and people heard her saying, "Not-loved, put those dates back in the bin!" it was supposed to remind them that God had turned against them, against the nation of Israel, and that whereas once they were the chosen people of Yahweh, now they were not his people any longer, not loved and not pitied by him anymore.

Why was God angry with his chosen people, so that the prophet (God's mouthpiece) felt he was called to give such forbidding names to his children? In order to find out, we turn to the book of the prophet Hosea, from the Old Testament, where we hear one of the most memorable stories in the prophetic literature of the Bible.

God is angry, says Hosea, because his people have been disobedient and disloyal; they have gone after other gods. The Hebrew people were living alongside the Canaanites, who had a vibrant, erotic nature religion that was very easy to assimilate. The Canaanite deities, called Ba'alim, were being worshiped in conjunction with the one and only YHWH as though there were no conflict between them. The Hebrew people knew so little about their God that they got him all mixed up with a whole host of other gods who supposedly were able to provide them with personal blessings, security, status, money, prosperity in business, and an exciting sex life. Very much like ourselves today, the Hebrew people saw no harm in partaking of the religious smorgasbord that they saw all around them, and they lost all sense of the unique majesty, holiness, and purity of YHWH, the "jealous" God of their forefathers, who forbade his children to have other gods beside himself. The Hebrew people no longer knew their God, so they no longer saw any difference between Yahweh and the Ba'alim, and could not believe that the difference would matter, even if there were any. Being religious was the main thing; the nature of God was a secondary issue, being a matter on which there could be a variety of opinions.

Hosea knew better because, like all the great Hebrew prophets, he had been commandeered by the direct intervention of the living God of Israel, who had a message to be delivered. With passionate indignation and withering sarcasm, Hosea described the Israelite worship of Ba'al:

> They ask advice from a block of wood, and take their orders from a fetish. . . . What sort of god is this bull? It is no god; a craftsman made it!
>
> . . . You have forsaken your God, you have loved an idol. . . .
>
> For their evil deeds, says the Lord, I will drive them from my house, I will love them no more. (4:12; 8:6; 9:1,15)

Hosea's children, with their foreboding names, signified the judgment of God on his faithless people. Hosea could see the approaching clouds of doom coming from the direction of Assyria, the menacing foreign power. He knew that God was preparing to punish the Israelite nation for forsaking true worship. He tried to warn the people, using his children's names as well as his own prophetic voice, but it was too late: the worship of Ba'al was too appealing; the urge to make deals with foreign states was too powerful; the general air of religious amalgamation was too heady. They would not listen; perhaps they could not. Hosea laments:

> Their misdeeds have barred their way back to their God: a wanton spirit is in them, and they care nothing for the Lord. . . . They go with sacrifices of sheep and cattle to seek the Lord, but they do not find him. He has withdrawn himself from them, for they have been unfaithful to him. (5:4, 6)

The sins of Israel in Hosea's time were essentially two, and in both cases we can see a similarity to Christianity in America today. First, Israel saw nothing wrong in supplementing the religion of YHWH with other religious ideas from the surrounding culture. Just as we mix in a little astrology, a little science fiction, a little transcendental meditation, and a little patriotic fervor with our Christianity, the Hebrews thought a little Ba'al worship, a little temple prostitution, and a nature festival now and then could only enhance the worship of Israel's God. But Israel's God holds otherwise. Through Hosea he declares:

> Israel has run wild: the wind shall sweep them away. . . . They will find their sacrifices a delusion. . . . They have broken my covenant, they have played me false. (4:19)

The second sin of Israel was that she put her trust as a nation in foreign alliances and treaties, in military strategy, and in political solutions, instead of calling upon God. Therefore this is what the Lord says through Hosea:

> They made kings, but not by my will: They set up officers, but without knowledge of me. . . . There is nothing but talk, imposing of oaths and making of treaties, all to no purpose. . . . Because you have trusted in your chariots, in the number of your warriors, the tumult of war shall arise against your people . . . the king of Israel shall be swept away. (8:4; 10:4, 13-15)

So today, America, a nation that prints "In God We Trust" on its coins, is a nation that has become arms manufacturer to the world and does not seem to be able to stop the escalating billions of dollars for weaponry.

Israel sows the wind and reaps the whirlwind. . . . Israel is swallowed up, lost among the nations, a worthless nothing. (8:7-8)

In both of these ways — in worshiping false gods and in abandoning God's will for the nation he brought into being — Israel shows that she has lost her most priceless possession: her knowledge of God. This is the theme of Hosea's book. Israel is faithless because she no longer knows the Lord:

> Hear the word of the Lord, O Israel, for the Lord has a charge to bring against the people of the land: There is no good faith or mutual trust, no knowledge of God in the land . . . my people are ruined for lack of knowledge . . . a people without understanding comes to grief. . . . I long to deliver them, but they tell lies about me. . . . I desire steadfast love, not sacrifice: not burnt-offerings but the knowledge of God. (4:1, 6, 14; 7:13; 6:6)

Knowledge, in the Hebrew language and tradition, is not at all the same thing as mere information. You could know things *about* God and still not know *him*. This is what had happened in Israel. The people had *information* about God but did not *know* him. Knowledge, in the Hebrew Bible, has a far more personal, more involving connotation than "knowledge" as we use the term. We are able to learn a great deal about the gods of the Ancient Near East by studying the myths of the region, but that wouldn't mean knowledge of the gods in the biblical sense. Knowing God meant being in a close, intimate relationship with him, a relationship of deep commitment and intense personal awareness, a bond, a covenant, a connection of the heart, mind, and will that is like a . . . well, that is like nothing else in human experience so much as it is like a marriage. The relationship of God to Israel is like a marriage, said Hosea, and he was the first ever to say so. He was the first of a long line of biblical writers to describe Israel as the marriage partner of YHWH and, correspondingly in the New Testament, the church as the bride of Christ. Israel was sworn to fidelity to YHWH, her spouse, and he had bound himself to cherish her and be her Lord forever.

But God's "wife," Israel, was unfaithful and went after other gods. Hosea says she played the harlot and committed adultery, breaking the sacred bond between herself and her covenant Lord:

> "She decked herself with earrings and necklaces; she ran after her lovers and forgot me: this is the very word of the Lord." (2:13)

Now, Hosea preaches, Israel thinks she can come back to God with religious ceremonies and insincere words of flattery borrowed from her other alliances, but she cannot:

> For I desire steadfast love and not sacrifices to the Ba'alim. She ran after her lovers and forgot me. I will show her up for the lewd things she is, and no lover will want to steal her from me. (6:6; 2:13, 10)

Here is the truly fascinating part of the story. Hosea himself had a wife, the mother of those three children that we were talking about. Her name was Gomer. Hosea loved her and was a good and faithful husband to her. Gomer, however, was not faithful to him. She became involved with other men. Her adultery was so flagrant that finally Hosea sent her away; that was the law of Israel in those days concerning an adulterous wife. In his unhappiness, Hosea meditated on what it was like to be betrayed by the one you love, and he began to enter into God's own pain and suffering, his sorrow and indignation at the infidelity of the bride he cherished in the wilderness:

> I came to Israel like grapes in the wilderness . . . but they resorted to Ba'al. . . . For their evil deeds I will drive them from my house, I will love them no more. (9:10, 15)

All the bitterness of unrequited love, all the anguish of betrayal, and all the righteous wrath that God felt toward his faithless wife Israel, Hosea shared. He understood from his own experience how God could threaten:

> "I will make her as bare as the wilderness, parched as the desert; and I will leave her to die of thirst." (2:3)

But one day there came a command from God to Hosea:

> "Go again, and love a woman loved by another man, an adulteress, and love her as I, the Lord, love the Israelites, although they resort to other gods and love the raisin-cakes offered to idols." (3:1)

And so — picture this! — the spurned and humiliated husband, the one who was sinned against, the one who was betrayed, goes from his own decent, quiet home into the indecent, brawling marketplace to seek his wife, who has by now sunk into the depths. When at last he finds her, she has become the property of another man, perhaps a pimp, and Hosea "redeems" her — he buys her back and brings her home and re-instates her as his wife. And we should note that this domestic drama was played out in full view of the community, for prophets of Israel were highly public figures. The message was there for all who had eyes to see: God's love is invincible and unconquerable; God's faithfulness to Israel is stronger than her unfaithfulness to him; God's grace will seek after and redeem the beloved. The Hound of Heaven will track down the one who flees from him; the Good Shepherd will not rest until he has found the lost sheep; the God of Israel will save his people when they cannot save themselves. Hosea is the first prophet of the unconditional love of God. When Israel is unable to turn back to her Lord, her Lord goes to her:

> "Now listen: I will woo her, I will go with her into the wilderness and comfort her . . . and there she will answer as in her youth . . . on that day she will call me 'my husband' . . . and I will wipe from her lips the very names of the Ba'alim; never again shall their names be heard. This is the very word of the Lord." (2:14-17)

No biblical writer has spoken more eloquently, with more feeling, of the tender love of Yahweh for his people than Hosea. He is famous for it. He is truly a prophet of God's amazing grace. But note this: the reason that Hosea's depiction of God's grace is so amazing is that it is set in direct connection with God's judgment, so that *both* the judgment *and* the love are seen to be part of God's redemption. Israel suffers from her adultery: she is taken into exile by the Assyrians. But the experience is redemptive: God cleanses Israel in the wilderness, as in the old days, and once more Israel comes to the knowledge and love of God. God's wrath and God's mercy go hand in hand to restore the fallen sinner.

Seven hundred years later, there was a group of religious leaders called Pharisees whose learning and rectitude were so manifest that they thought that they were somehow exempt from the wrath of God. They went to church every Sunday, and they were very good at identifying other people as sinners. Since they had spent their lives in religious studies, they could talk about God all day; they were confident that they "knew" God quite well. It was the wrong kind of knowledge, however, because they failed to recognize the presence of God when he stood right in front of them. They were shocked and angered when they saw God's love at work redeeming notorious sinners. "Look at that," they said. "That man who acts as if he's the Messiah is sitting at the table with the worst people in town."

And Jesus of Nazareth, looking steadily at these highly religious men, said:

> "Go and learn what this means [in the book of the prophet Hosea]:
> 'I require mercy, and not sacrifice.' I did not come to invite virtuous
> people, but sinners." (Matt. 9:13)

# What Is the Source?

GRACE CHURCH IN NEW YORK

---

*September 1983*                                   AMOS 5:21-24; 8:11-12

IN LAST week's *New Yorker* magazine, there is an arresting article in "The Talk of the Town." It is about two "Marches on Washington" — the great and famous one in 1963 and the anniversary one this year. Here are the opening sentences in the article:

> What are the sources of fundamental change in our society? From what spring will justice roll down like water? That mighty stream of righteousness — how do we find it?[1]

The *New Yorker* article does not mention the prophet Amos, but that is who the writer is quoting. Amos was a prophet in Israel in the eighth century B.C., which means that he appeared on the world scene much earlier than Socrates or Buddha or Confucius.[2] Like those other figures, he is sometimes described by historians as a "religious genius." No title could have displeased Amos more; he knew that he was neither a genius nor "religious" but that he

---

1. Bill McKibben wrote this in "The Talk of the Town," *The New Yorker,* 12 September 1983. McKibben has since become world-famous for his many writings about ecological/environmental issues, but he has retained his interest in the Bible. As noted earlier, his book about Job, *The Comforting Whirlwind,* is idiosyncratic but well worth reading and pondering.

2. The utter originality and specificity of the eighth-century Hebrew prophets confute all claims that there was a worldwide, culturally universal time of religious genius, as Karen Armstrong, among others, proposes. Amos and his contemporaries cannot be conflated into a generalized religious scheme.

had been seized in the middle of his business day, so to speak — commandeered by God right out of the sheep-breeding trade and into the dangerous occupation of being a prophet. A prophet was a spokesman from God, a person bearing a commission from the Lord, a man with a message.

Amos's message was not a pleasant one. Through his servant Amos, Yahweh was declaring himself to be sickened by the worship that was being offered to him by the people of Israel. Yahweh was nauseated, according to the graphic biblical imagery, by his people's hymns and prayers and offerings — for three principal reasons:

> *First,* although the court of Israel was supposed to be the place where the poor man could be confident of having his rights defended and his cause upheld, the judicial process had been corrupted to the point that only the powerful and well-to-do could be certain of receiving justice.
>
> *Second,* Israel's affluent upper classes lived in luxurious disregard of the deprivations of their fellow citizens. They celebrated their own prosperity in isolation from the hardships endured by those who were on the lower levels of society.
>
> *Third* and worst of all, Israel's religion had become one of self-love. The interests of the privileged classes became identified with the blessings of Yahweh, and the prosperity and prestige of the nation were unhesitatingly equated with the will of God, so that worship of Yahweh was really no more than worship of what the economic and political rulers of the nation wanted for themselves.[3]

If this sounds familiar, it is intended to. In all three areas — (1) the failure of the courts to give even-handed judgments, (2) an increasing gap between rich and poor, and (3) the identification of the nation's success and prosperity with the purpose of God — the nation of Israel in Amos's day was very much like America in our day. It is in this context that God speaks his famous words through his prophet:

"I hate, I despise your feasts,
    and I take no delight in your solemn assemblies. . . .
Take away from me the noise of your songs;

---

3. The three points are taken from James L. Mays's commentary on Amos (Philadelphia: Westminster Press, 1969), pp. 11-12.

to the melody of your harps I will not listen.
But let justice roll down like waters,
    and righteousness like an ever-flowing stream." (5:21-24)

Amos's message from God to the people of Israel was that their worship was a sham because it came from hearts that were idolatrous, self-satisfied, complacent, and hardened against the sufferings of the poor. This same message was rephrased eight hundred years later in the New Testament, when James wrote, "Be ye doers of the word and not hearers only" (1:22), and "faith apart from works is dead" (2:26).

The *New Yorker* writer is aware of this biblical material, and he sees Martin Luther King Jr. as a sort of latter-day "religious genius" ("saint" and "giant" are the terms used in the article) who was able to tap the deep sources of justice and righteousness and get that mighty stream flowing. The "Talk of the Town" article is unutterably sad because it evokes the overwhelming sense of loss experienced by those on the twentieth-anniversary march:

The men and women who spoke in Washington last month are courageous and hard-working and better by far than most of us. But their voices seemed to blend together. They are not saints and they are not giants . . . only the greatest leaders allow history to leap ahead with bounding strides. When a tape of King delivering his "Dream" speech was played to close last month's march, the people gathered by the reflecting pool could hardly bear even to look at each other, they felt so lost.[4]

I would like to suggest that this analysis sounds somewhat like a modern, "existential" version of the fate that Amos says is going to befall the people of Israel. The prophet warns the nation that God is going to judge it harshly for its neglect of God's righteous will; he piles up images of wreckage and ruin, but the most devastating judgment of all will not be the destruction of the economy or the ravages of military invasion, though they are also predicted, but the withdrawal of the life-giving Word of God:

"Behold, the days are coming," says the Lord God,
    "when I will send a famine on the land;
not a famine of bread, nor a thirst for water,

---

4. McKibben, "The Talk of the Town."

but of hearing the words of the Lord.
They shall wander from sea to sea,
   and from north to east;
they shall run to and fro, to seek the word of the Lord,
   but they shall not find it." (8:11-12)

The Word of Yahweh — that is what has the power to create and to destroy, to preserve and to cut short, to save and to judge. To lose one's job and one's house and one's family and even one's nation is terrible, says the prophet, but the most fearful loss of all is the loss of the life-giving Word of God, whose mere absence (let alone antagonism) creates the most death-dealing void that humanity can ever experience.

Now, of course, the *New Yorker* writer doesn't put it this way. He writes not of the absence of the Word of God, as Amos did; he writes of the loss of the voice of Martin Luther King. Still, there is a certain connection here. If you read the *New Yorker* article from the standpoint of biblical faith, you can see how it was that this man, Dr. King, was a man seized and overpowered by his vocation from God. It was his vocation to proclaim deliverance to the captives, so that he became one who in our time declared the Word of God to a population enslaved: not only black people enslaved by white people, but also — and Dr. King was explicit about this — white people enslaved by racial hatreds. From a biblical point of view, it is impossible to hear his refrain — "I have a dream today!" — and not be profoundly aware that Martin Luther King was gripped not by a mere human dream, but by the reality and power of the coming Kingdom of the sovereign Lord God. When such a preacher speaks, even "the rulers of this age," as St. Paul called them (1 Cor. 2:8), must shut their mouths and give heed, as all the world did on that world-historical day in front of the Lincoln Memorial.

The *New Yorker* article talks about Dr. King as though he were a saint. In the crucially important New Testament sense, it is profoundly true that Christians are all saints. But in the usual sense of the word, Dr. King was no more a saint than you or I. His greatness lies not in some imagined saintliness, but in his embodiment of the power of God that puts down the mighty from their seats and exalts the humble and meek. When his voice was stilled, many people — though they could not identify it as such — felt as though it were a loss of the voice of God, a far worse loss than that of material fortune.

Perhaps some of you may be shocked by the suggestion that a human being like Martin Luther King could actually speak the word of God, and it is true that John the Baptist was the last of the actual prophets. But this is the way God has chosen to work, through human voices, or else we preachers could not stand in our pulpits. Amos spoke of the experience of being overmastered by the Word of God when he said,

"The Lord roars from Zion,
    and utters his voice from Jerusalem. . . ." (1:2)

"The lion has roared;
    who will not fear?
The Lord God has spoken;
    who can but prophesy?" (3:8)

As St. Paul wrote hundreds of years later, "Necessity is laid upon me; woe is me if I do not preach the gospel!" (1 Cor. 9:16). And Jeremiah said, speaking of the Word of God, "There is in my heart as it were a burning fire shut up in my bones, and I am weary with holding it in, and I cannot" (Jer. 20:9).

The Word of God as it came to Amos revealed that God loves the poor, the weak, the oppressed, and those who have no one to plead their cause. Through Amos, God disclosed his righteous anger at the privileged classes:

Because you trample upon the poor
    and take from him exactions of wheat,
You have built houses of hewn stone,
    but you shall not dwell in them;
You have planted pleasant vineyards,
    but you shall not drink their wine.
For I know how many are your transgressions,
    and how great are your sins —
You who afflict the righteous, who take a bribe,
    and turn aside the needy in the gate. (5:11-13)

Sometimes Amos sounds so contemporary, you'd think he had been looking at the ads in *Vanity Fair:*

Woe to those who lie upon beds of ivory,
    and stretch themselves on their couches . . .
who drink wine in bowls,
    and anoint themselves with the finest oils. . . . (6:4, 6)

The fate of these affluent ones will be dreadful indeed:

> "On the day that I punish Israel . . .
> I will smite the winter house and the summer house. . . ." (3:14-15)

Many of you are probably too young to remember how widely Amos was quoted during the late sixties. "The prophet of social justice," we called him. When I was a half-baked, late-coming crusader for civil rights in those days, I knew certain parts of Amos by heart. The book of Amos was a Bible within the Bible for my friends and me. We loved to go to church meetings and quote self-righteously, "I hate, I despise your feast days. . . ." Ask any clergy who were around during the sixties. They'll tell you what a hot ticket Amos was in the seminaries back then. Certain parts of Amos, that is. When I was re-reading *the whole book* of Amos prior to writing this sermon, I was forcibly struck by a theme that I had completely missed in those earlier days, a theme that matches social justice verse for verse in significance for the prophet Amos.

This overlooked theme is nothing less than the "might, majesty, power, dominion, and glory" of the Lord God of hosts. For instance:

> "Prepare to meet your God, O Israel!"
> For lo, he who forms the mountains, and creates the wind,
>    and declares to man what is his thought;
> who makes the morning darkness,
>    and treads on the heights of the earth —
> YHWH, the God of hosts, is his name! (4:12-13)

And here is another verse, often read for the evening office:

> He who made the Pleiades and Orion,
>    and turns deep darkness into the morning,
>    and darkens the day into night,
> who calls for the waters of the sea,
>    and pours them out upon the surface of the earth,
> YHWH is his name! (5:8)

Can you share with me, then, my astonishment as I pondered these passages, as I realized that Amos has a *double* theme — social justice *and* the power of God — and then suddenly and providentially I flipped through *The New Yorker* and saw these words:

> What are the sources of fundamental change in our society? From what spring will justice roll down like water? That mighty stream of righteousness — how do we find it?

These questions spring from a mind and a heart agonizing about the apparent inability of the human race to make lasting changes without unique charismatic leaders — who themselves are flawed, vulnerable, doomed to pass on and to leave their followers bereft. Yet the entire trajectory of the *biblical* story is that the charismatic leaders are not simply comets blazing and dying, but servants of *God's* mighty purpose for justice and reconciliation. Therefore, their example, their leadership, their movements belong to God and cannot be defeated even when the leaders raised up by God are assassinated, or executed, or martyred, as they have been more often than not — just look at the roll call of the heroes of faith in Hebrews.

"From what spring will justice roll down like water? That mighty stream of righteousness — how do we find it?" The Holy Spirit that animated Amos and the other prophets tells us. The wellspring is God. It is from him that we yearn for the mighty stream of righteousness in the first place, from him that we receive inspiration for joining his cause, and from him that we find the strength to continue. YHWH, the God of hosts, is his name! *God* is the spring of justice. *God* is the ever-rolling stream of righteousness. *God* is the mighty source. The Word of God — *that* is the power behind "fundamental change in our society."

Great voices like that of Amos, and great preachers and leaders like Martin Luther King, come along only rarely; but the Word of God is never still. God is on the move. He cannot and will not tolerate injustice. He is the source of righteousness. He is the source of love for the poor and the forgotten. There are hundreds of ways, large and small, for us to align ourselves with God's great movement. The former senior warden of this parish, Whitney North Seymour, fought hard, all of his professional life, to establish the Legal Aid Society and set it on a firm foundation, seeking justice for all Americans. On October 3, this congregation will open its shelter for six homeless men of New York City.[5] The members of our chapter of Evangeli-

---

5. The shelter at Grace Church came about as a result of the forceful leadership of a few laypeople. It was in operation for about eight years, overseen by one of the clergy. It had beds for

cals for Social Action tell me that they have had a "phenomenal" response to their program for feeding the hungry. These are just a few of the ways that God has used us in this parish for his mighty purpose of declaring deliverance to the captives and good news to the poor.

Deliverance to the captives, good news to the poor. The *New Yorker* writer says that this will require nothing less than a transformation "among us in the majority, that we should sacrifice some portion of our standard of living." And he says sadly, "Such transformations may no longer be possible."[6]

Jesus of Nazareth said to his disciples, "With men, it is impossible, but not with God; all things are possible with God" (Mark 10:27). The source of transformation is God. The fountainhead of the mighty stream of righteousness is the Lord of hosts. The power behind social action for justice, whether it be small, unpretentious acts or huge international movements, is the God who lives.

And now hear this: the wellspring of all love for the poor is God's love *for us all;* for ultimately, as Flannery O'Connor once wrote, we are *all* "the poor." We can carry that even farther. We are all "the *undeserving* poor." This is the gospel; this is the good news. Not one of us deserved the love that has been shown to us in the sacrifice of the Son of God; not one of us has any riches to offer the Lord of all the universe; not one of us could by any stretch of the imagination be called a saint except through the mercy of Jesus Christ — and yet we too are called by that same Lord to praise him and glorify him and give thanks to him with angels and archangels and all the company of heaven, the saints and martyrs of all ages, most certainly including Martin Luther King, who is purged of his sins even as you and I are being purged of ours. For even the book of Amos, most doom-laden of all the prophets, ends — incredibly! — with a promise of restoration and blessing for sinful, disobedient Israel — totally undeserved, totally unmerited, totally unearned.

---

six men, who were brought each night from a central New York City reception center. It was staffed by volunteers from the congregation and their friends. It was open 365 nights a year, and in that respect was a standout among church shelters in the city. Many of the men were with us for a number of months. Most were suffering from mental instability of one sort or another, but the stability of the shelter made a difference for some of them, at least. In one case, the Grace Church shelter made all the difference in the life of a disabled man, who became a member of the church along with his young son. When the father died as a result of his chronic illness, the son — a young teenager — was taken under the wing of a young couple, members of the parish, who shepherded him through his graduation from Fordham University.

6. McKibben, "The Talk of the Town."

Having heard this news, having known this love, having received this Word, is there any one of us who cannot now go forth from this place strengthened for the service of the one true God who is the powerful source of all charity, all mercy, and all reconciliation? May it be so.

AMEN.

# Blessed Are the Poor

*September 1995*                    Amos 5:11-15; 8:4-8; 22:24

> *More than any other sermon in this volume, this one addresses a particular congregation at a particular time. It is very personal in some ways. After reflection, I have resisted the temptation to disguise this feature of the sermon. I retain it as an illustration of the way that a specific congregation wrestled with, and took seriously, the need to express its evangelical faith by heeding the prophetic message.*

..................

IT IS now exactly two decades since the beginning of what has generally been called the renewal at Grace Church. In 1975, I have been told many times, the choir almost outnumbered the congregation. Since that time, this parish, which in the nineteenth century was the most socially prominent in Manhattan, has regained much of its eminence, though in a vastly transformed style from the era of Edith Wharton. It is hard to believe, today, that the shift from rented pews and morning coats took place so recently. I never cease to marvel at the recollection of the late Whitney North Seymour, Esq., one of New York City's most prominent citizens, who was senior warden here for upwards of twenty years, and the largeness of soul he exhibited in benevolently welcoming a host of new young people in jeans to the venerable pews of Grace Church in the late seventies and early eighties.[1]

What caused Grace Church's explosive growth? Very simply put, it was the telling of the Bible story. It was the preaching and teaching, in passionately accessible terms, of the gospel of the unconditional grace of God in Jesus Christ, in the context of a welcoming community and an atmosphere of fearless intellectual inquiry. This congregation was one that studied the Bible together, prayed together, and shared the most basic aspects of its life together. When I came here in 1981, it seemed to me that I had found something akin to New Testament Christianity, with all the freshness and excitement that implies.

As most of you know, I am winding up fourteen years in this parish. It is not possible to come to such a place in one's pilgrimage without giving thought to what one might say in the way of valedictory. I have four more Sunday sermons to preach at Grace Church, and I want to give you my very best. This challenge has been in my heart and mind for several months now. I pray that the Lord whose Word we proclaim from this pulpit will be my guide.

You know, one does not preach the same way in every parish or at every season. The preacher tries to discern what the particular congregation might need at the particular time. Most of my preaching, both here and away from Grace Church in past years, has tended to be on the bedrock. I think of the bedrock as the verse from Romans that former assistant Paul Zahl, now Dean of the Birmingham (Alabama) Cathedral, loved so much: "There is therefore now no condemnation for those who are in Christ Jesus" (8:1).[2] I think of the verse, also from Romans, that Joel Marcus, now Associate Professor of New Testament in Glasgow, so frequently called upon: "God has consigned all men to disobedience in order that he may have mercy upon all" (11:32).[3] I think of St. Paul's two references, yet again from Romans, to *the justification of the ungodly,* identified by the great evangelical New Testament scholar F. F. Bruce as the heart of the gospel — words which have been my own personal comfort through self-doubts and failures of every kind for many a year and through many a trial. I always

1. Whitney North Seymour was one of the most honored lawyers in New York City history, but was extraordinarily free of self-importance. More of him later in the sermon.

2. Paul F. M. Zahl earned a Ph.D. in Tübingen from Jürgen Moltmann, was Dean of Trinity School for Ministry, and later retired as rector of All Saints, Chevy Chase.

3. Joel Marcus later became Professor of New Testament at Duke Divinity School and is the acclaimed author of the two-volume Anchor Bible commentary on Mark.

thought I would preach on those texts as my final sermons, and in a very important sense, I will.

In another sense, though, I will be ranging afield somewhat. In the four sermons remaining to me, I will be preaching *as though to a theologically mature congregation.* I don't know if I am right in doing that or not. Very few of you who are here today were here twenty years ago, and not all of our members are engaged in intensive Bible study and theological work. Thanks be to God, many of you are brand-new to our midst. Still, it is the case that after a while a community takes on a certain coloration, a certain emphasis, so that even newcomers will be aware that this congregation has been somewhere and is going somewhere. I have seen some things happen during my fourteen years here, barely perceptible at the time, but becoming visible now, which seem to me to be fruits of the Spirit.

Theological maturity, however, is not necessarily the same thing as other kinds of maturity. If I pay us the compliment of preaching as to a theologically grown-up parish, I do not mean to suggest that we are necessarily mature in every respect. There are other areas where we could use some improvement. When I say *theologically mature,* I mean just this: formed by the Bible, proudly Trinitarian, grounded in justification by grace through faith, dedicated to the person of Jesus Christ, convinced of his incarnation as Son of God, recognizing his death on the Cross as redemption from sin for the whole world, boldly convinced of the truth of the Resurrection, and committed to a worldwide mission of witness in Christ's name. One of the blessings about being at Grace Church is that we do not have to re-establish and re-argue these foundations over and over; they have become part of our common life. I don't mean that every individual at Grace Church understands these articles of faith identically or relies upon them equally, but I do believe that our community taken as a whole has been shaped by them in an unmistakable way. This will be my assumption in these four final sermons.

All over the United States today, Episcopalians and all the other denominations that use the common lectionary are reading the same lessons from the Bible. In thousands of churches, from coast to coast, in cities and towns, in great landmark buildings like this one and little frame structures, in old-line suburban WASP churches and inner-city ethnic churches, a passage from the prophet Amos is being read this morning. Many sermons across the land this morning will be based on the living Word of God through his prophet Amos, the sheepherder from Tekoa who was sent by the Lord to the cities of the northern part of Israel to declare that God had seen the conditions there and would not tolerate them any longer.

According to Amos, what did God see? This is what he saw: he saw the misery of the poor and the luxury of the rich. He saw a population of haves and a population of have-nots. God saw the suburbs of Samaria with their swimming pools and their wine-tasting parties, and he saw the homeless people in the streets and the children afraid to go to school because of the guns and the drugs, and he said:

> "I will smite the winter house with the summer house; and the houses of ivory shall perish, and the great houses shall come to an end, says the Lord. . . . Hear this, you who trample upon the needy, and bring the poor of the land to an end . . . [who] buy the poor for silver and the needy for a pair of sandals. . . . The Lord has sworn by the pride of Jacob: 'Surely I will never forget any of their deeds. Shall not the land tremble on this account . . . ?'" (3:15; 8:4-6; 7-8)

The prophet Amos was not popular at Grace Church when I first came here. He was associated with a kind of self-righteous, bleeding-heart liberalism that was deemed theologically bankrupt. However, someone said back in the seventies that a sign of Grace Church's theological maturity would be that we would finally add the Old Testament prophets to our repertoire of Romans and Galatians! Sure enough, this began to happen in the eighties, when Ken Swanson, Bobby Massie, Christopher Brown, and others were here, and the ministries of Grace Church began to expand in new directions, as a shelter for homeless men and a ministry to people with HIV-AIDS were added to our long-standing commitment to overseas missions and to biblical education.[4]

Still and all, however, the prophet Amos is an uncomfortable person to

---

4. Kenneth B. Swanson went on to become Dean of Christ Church Cathedral in Nashville. Robert Kinloch Massie is well known for many things, including his acclaimed book about the South African struggle, his commitment to liberation theology, his political activism, and his decades-long survival in spite of hemophilia, hepatitis, and HIV-AIDS. Christopher Brown earned a Ph.D. in theology from Union Theological Seminary and is rector of Trinity Church in Potsdam, New York. Ashley Null, another member of the clergy staff in the 1980s, later earned a Ph.D. from Cambridge and a Guggenheim Fellowship, and is an authority on Thomas Cranmer. Ross Wright earned a master's from Princeton and a doctorate from St. Andrew's, and is now rector of the Church of the Good Shepherd in Richmond, Virginia. These and many other influences in the 1980s, including the work of leading laypeople of all ages — several of whom are now ordained and/ or teaching in divinity schools — powerfully enriched the ministry at Grace Church.

have around. A church that is not experiencing Amos that way has probably become complacently works-righteous and needs to repent. It is Amos who brought the word of the Lord so often quoted and made even more famous by Martin Luther King Jr.:

> "I hate, I despise your feasts, and I take no delight in your solemn assemblies [worship services]. Even though you offer me your burnt offerings.... I will not accept them.... Take away from me the noise of your songs; to the melody of your harps I will not listen. But let justice roll down like waters, and righteousness like an ever-flowing stream." (5:21-24)

This theme recurs throughout the prophetic books; it is prominent in Isaiah and Jeremiah. The Lord loves the poor. The Lord sees the suffering of the poor. The Lord wants justice for the poor. He is not pleased with the affluent, no matter how many prayers they say and no matter how many church services they attend. Believe me, I do not consider myself exempt. On the contrary, I am ready to stand first in line for the judgment. I am asking myself this week what I can do to respond to the Lord's word through his prophet Amos.

I don't need to spell it out, do I? It's a good bet that a lot of sermons are being preached on the prophet Amos today because this week the Congress passed a sweeping bipartisan vote ending "welfare as we know it," and "it is clear that the country's main $23 billion-a-year Federal welfare program, Aid to Families with Dependent Children, is headed toward extinction."[5] It is a week in which legislation to dismantle the Federal Medicare and Medicaid programs advanced in both houses of Congress. Let me hasten to say that this is not going to be a partisan political speech. My elder daughter is an ardent Republican in the HMO business, and she would not allow me to make such a mistake. I am in no position to say what sort of reforms we need in the sphere of health care and public assistance; the more I read about it, the more uncertain I become, and the more I realize how little I know. So please do not construe this sermon as Democratic Party propaganda. For all I know, it may be better to turn these matters back to the states. This is not my area of expertise.

I think I do know something, however, about taking the temperature of American culture, and on that front, I think there is plenty for biblical peo-

---

5. *The New York Times*, 21 November 1995.

ple to be concerned about. There is a mean spirit abroad in the land.[6] There is a spirit of me-first. There is a spirit of untrammeled self-interest and hedonism. I'm a student of print advertising, because it's a quick way of finding out what's going on in the culture without having to watch hours of tasteless television. What I see in print advertising is repeated messages, both liminal and subliminal, that say, You are free to construct your own life as you please without reference to anybody else. As the Ralph Lauren ads say, there are "no boundaries." You should simply "go for it." And the way to do that is to identify with the cool people who are depicted in the ads, which of course ultimately means buying the products that they are selling, and even more pernicious, being swept up into the virtual worlds that the ads portray. I believe that advertising is an almost unstoppable juggernaut today. I don't think Calvin Klein is the least bit chastened by the reaction to his latest ad campaign.[7] Personally, I started boycotting Calvin Klein two years ago; it made me feel better, but you know and I know that the high priest of American sportswear doesn't want me as a customer anyway.

Here we are, then, in a land where untrammeled self-indulgence is recommended on every hand. The "Me Decade" is supposed to be over, the greedy eighties are said to be at an end, but the gap between haves and have-nots in America, almost all observers agree, is growing greater all the time. And the Lord spoke through the prophet Amos and said:

> You have built houses of hewn stone, but you shall not dwell in them; you have planted pleasant vineyards, but you shall not drink their wine. For I know how many are your transgressions, and how great are your sins — you who afflict the righteous, who take a bribe, and turn aside the needy in the gate.... Seek good, and not evil, that you may live; and so the Lord, the God of hosts, will be with you.... Hate evil, and love good, and establish justice.... (5:11-15)

What all of this suggests is that there is a special vocation for a congregation of Christians on lower Broadway in New York City. We are not located in an affluent suburban neighborhood where we can separate ourselves from the poor with gates and walls and security guards and burglar alarms. We are

6. As this book goes to press, it is both striking and sad that these words about health care and political tension seem equally applicable fifteen years later.

7. It is almost forgotten now, but Calvin Klein's advertising, including a large, lavish supplement which had recently been distributed, was pushing the margins of advertising far beyond what many would have thought tolerable.

not even on the Upper East Side, where social discordance is kept to a minimum. This is more like the real world down here. Most of us take subways to get to Grace Church. Most of you are here all summer, toughing it out with the rest of the city who have no second homes to flee to. Some of the seamiest, raunchiest activity in town is going on within eyeshot of our Fourth Avenue entrances, as I can testify. Homeless people sleep on our very doorsteps. Our valued parishioner Hilberto Medina, recently deceased and much mourned, was cared for at Columbia-Presbyterian Hospital for many years without cost under precisely the programs that are now threatened.[8]

Because this is an urban church in a downtown neighborhood, it is not so easy to avoid the presence of the poor. We *see* them. I wonder if that is not part of our vocation, to *see* the poor, to be the Lord's eyes — because the Lord sees the poor, and he loves the poor, and he sends his people to serve the poor. That is a message that pervades the Scriptures from end to end. There is something seriously out of balance in American Christianity. I am personally opposed to abortion, but there is nothing explicit in the Bible about abortion. There is nothing explicit in the Bible about prayer in the public schools; there is nothing explicit in the Bible about the American flag or the right to have a gun. There are, however, thousands of explicit words in the Bible about justice and compassion for the poor. There are thousands of words in the Bible about defending those who are defenseless. It is worth noting at this point that the aforementioned Grace Church warden Whitney North Seymour was one of the founders of the Legal Aid Society, now threatened with cuts like so many other institutions that exist to serve the poor.

There is a harsh spirit in America today, a self-centered and callous spirit that goes against the grain of the gospel that has brought life to this congregation. Grappling with this combination, the combination of the gospel of Jesus Christ and the current mood in America, is surely part of the calling of Grace Church as a Christian community.

As a theologically mature congregation, you will easily recognize the right answer to a little guessing game. Which of these two non-biblical folk sayings is in the spirit of the Christian gospel?

1. God helps those who help themselves.
2. There but for the grace of God go I.

---

8. Hilberto Medina was a resident of the Grace Church shelter for the homeless for about a year. He eventually was rewarded with a Habitat for Humanity apartment where he successfully raised his young son. It was a great work of the Lord through the parishioners.

Can there be any question about which one is biblical and which one is not? "God helps those who help themselves," the great American creed, is definitively contradicted by St. Paul's explicit words: "While we were still *helpless,* Christ died for the *ungodly*" (Rom. 5:6; my emphasis). The entire story of Jesus of Nazareth — his welcoming of sinners and outcasts, his radical undermining of all class distinctions, his ongoing conflicts with the self-satisfied and self-righteous, and his stories about God's love for the poor and needy — teach us to say, always and in every circumstance, not "Thank God I am not as other men," like the Pharisee in the parable, but "There but for the grace of God go I."[9] This is what we have been learning at Grace Church for many years now.

I believe that this theological maturity, if that is what it is, has led to some real results. There are, of course, individual exceptions to everything, but I do not believe, for instance, that racial prejudice would find fertile soil in this congregation. I am not suggesting that we have no racial prejudice among us. I do mean, though, that racism does not have a lot of room and space to grow here. I do not believe that anti-Semitism would find hospitality here; I am not suggesting that we are free from it, but I do not think it would be fertilized and watered here. What we do need to work on, it seems to me, is the pro-active side of our ministry and calling. There is so much more that we could be doing. There are good signs of this already, as we mentioned; a recent example would be the warm welcome that we extended to the nearby Genesis apartment project. Another sign would be the fact that the number of people at Grace who identify themselves as members of minority groups has increased to 20 percent. A strong Christian congregation at Tenth and Broadway means that many people are finding here an opportunity to discover the meaning of being in community and solidarity with others. This is truly a great thing. It is a gift that God has given us. It has been a privilege to watch all this happening.

In the final analysis, though, we can never forget to repeat the story, to tell it to ourselves every day:

> For you know the grace of our Lord Jesus Christ, that though he was rich, yet for your sake he became poor, so that by his poverty you might become rich. (2 Cor. 8:9)

9. This saying, in various forms, has been around for a long time. It is attributed in Bartlett's to John Bradford (1510-1555), the chaplain to Edward VI, who is reported to have made a similar remark upon seeing prisoners led to their executions.

Here is the ultimate reason for caring for the poor: that Jesus himself became poor. And why did he do this? He became poor in order to make us rich. Here is the heartbeat of the gospel, the promise that Jesus makes to all who come to him. "Blessed are the poor in spirit, for theirs is the kingdom of heaven" (Matt. 5:2). Flannery O'Connor put her finger on it when she wrote that "we are all The Poor."[10] That's what it means to sing, "Amazing grace, how sweet the sound that saved a wretch like me."

When are we closest to God? When we see ourselves as we really are: "Just as I am, without one plea, but that Thy blood was shed for me, and that Thou bidd'st me come to Thee, O Lamb of God, I come. . . ."[11] The world of getting and spending does not understand this. The world of intellectual sophistication does not understand this. The world of plastic surgery and high fashion, the world of mergers and acquisitions, the world of clawing and stabbing does not understand this. But as Paul the apostle said to those worlds, "I am not ashamed of the gospel" (Rom. 1:16).

As for me, I know myself. I know that I am self-willed and materialistic and neglectful of others. I know that I need a Savior to turn me from my own concerns to those of his needy people. For he in his infinite plenitude has turned to me in my moral poverty. He loves me in spite of myself. He loves the poor especially, because they have no one to notice them, but what is even more remarkable, *he loves the rich too*. He loves us too much to leave us the way we are — selfish, turned inward, focused on our own wishes all the time. He is at work in the church, at work loosening our grip on our own possessions, softening our hard hearts, helping us and guiding us like a loving father to show us the joy of generosity, the joy of forgiveness, the joy of helping, the joy of empathy, the joy of forgetting one's self, the joy of giving to others, and then the most joyful thing of all, the joy of reaching out our hands like a child at Christmas[12] and receiving from the depth of the Lord's bounty "the unsearchable riches of Christ" as Ephesians says — "the immeasurable riches of his grace which he lavished upon us" (Eph. 1:7-8; 2:7). God is at work. May we all enlist in his work as we find ourselves called, and may we continue in that calling with full and thankful hearts until the Day of the Lord.

AMEN.

---

10. Letter to "A," 9/15/55, in *The Habit of Being: Letters of Flannery O'Connor,* ed. Sally Fitzgerald (New York: Farrar, Straus & Giroux, 1969), p. 103.

11. From the hymn "Just as I Am" by Charlotte Elliott (1789-1871).

12. This image is Karl Barth's.

# Nineveh "R" Us

GRACE CHURCH IN NEW YORK

---

*September 1990*                              Jonah 4:1-11; Daniel 9:3-19

*I do not remember the circumstances in the congregation that
are referred to in this sermon, though it is a typical Wednesday night sermon from Grace Church in its informality. Obviously it was a time of some disturbance. Not remembering
is helpful, however, because it makes the sermon more univer-
sally applicable.*

. . . . . . . . . . . . . . . . .

The book of Jonah is a paradox. In one respect it is probably one of the
best-known books of the Bible, and in other respects it is one of the least
known. People who have never darkened the door of a church have heard
about Jonah and the whale, whereas people who come to church two or
three times a week have no idea what the theological message of the book
of Jonah is. In fact, I think people have been turned off by the whale business, as though such a silly story could not possibly be worth serious attention. Nothing could be further from the truth. In fact, the book of Jonah is quite sophisticated and advanced in its thinking, more so than
some of the other biblical writings of the time, such as Ezra and
Nehemiah. It conveys a message that is similar to our New Testament lesson tonight, the parable Jesus told about the laborers who worked in the
heat all day and then were angry and jealous because they didn't get paid

any better than the lazy bums who were hired last and did hardly any work.

Let's look at the outlines of the Jonah story. It begins like the stories of all the other servants of the Lord, who had no particular distinction until God spoke to them. The word of the Lord came to Jonah: "Arise, go to Nineveh, that great city, and prophesy against her people for their wickedness" (1:2). Nineveh was the capital city of the Assyrians; the Israelites hated and despised the Assyrians as much as the Kuwaitis of 1990 hate and despise the Iraqis. No doubt Jonah would have been delighted to prophesy destruction against these Assyrian heathen if he'd thought God would go through with his threat to destroy them; but Jonah had a sneaking suspicion that God was going to back down, and he couldn't stand it. So he attempted to get as far away as he could by getting aboard a ship set to sail to the opposite end of the Mediterranean. The story says that Jonah was trying to get away from the presence of the Lord. In the context of the story, this is definitely a joke, because the reader of the Hebrew Bible knows that there is nowhere to run away from the presence of the Lord.

The whole story is humorous, which adds to its charm. When Jonah is tossed off the ship and swallowed by the whale (actually it's "a great fish," not a whale), he eventually gets belched up right back in the direction he started out from. We may be permitted also to laugh at the statement that when Jonah finally does go to Nineveh to preach hellfire and damnation against the Assyrians, the Assyrian king repents instantly and orders the whole population, including the cows and horses, to put on sackcloth and ashes.

Then God does exactly what Jonah has feared all along: "He repented of the evil which he said he would do to them, and he did not do it" (3:10). Jonah is beside himself with outrage and disgust because God has pardoned the city. He tells God that he'd just as soon be dead. God asks him, in a rather sly way, "Are you really so angry about Nineveh, Jonah?" By way of answer, Jonah storms out of Nineveh, sits down on the ground, and glares back at the repentant city as though he himself would obliterate it with a murderous look if he could. This is the part of the story which reminds us of the parable of Jesus about the laborers: the good guys can't stand it when the bad guys don't get penalized. We might think also of the prodigal son's older brother, who was furious with their father for giving a party for the younger brother who had behaved so outrageously.

Then God plays another trick on Jonah; again, it's quite amusing. God causes a nice green plant to grow up over Jonah's head to protect him from the ferocious Middle Eastern sun, and "Jonah is exceedingly glad because of the plant" (4:6). God then sends a worm to attack the plant, whereupon it withers and dies. By this time Jonah is understandably stressed out and asks to give up the ghost. God asks Jonah, again in a rather sly way, "Are you really so angry about the plant, Jonah?" "Angry enough to die," Jonah responds. Then God delivers the zinger:

> "You are concerned about the plant, for which you did not labor and which you did not grow; it came into being in a night and perished in a night. And should I not be concerned about Nineveh, that great city, in which there are more than a hundred and twenty thousand people who do not know their right hand from their left, and also much cattle [or "many animals," depending on the translation]?" (4:10-11)

We should experience this as both comforting and encouraging. First of all, it really is funny. God has certainly played a trick on Jonah, but it is an extraordinarily kind and graceful trick; it has the same quality as Karl Barth's favorite story of the man who did not know he was crossing a frozen lake until he was already safe on the other side.[1] God has overwhelmed Jonah with grace and kindness, whether Jonah knows it or not — and in the process of telling this little story, the unknown author has taught a lesson that stands with the greatest of Old Testament prophecies and with the radical message of the apostle Paul, who wrote, "God has consigned all men to disobedience, in order that he may have mercy upon all" (Rom. 11:32). To put the point in Paul's favorite rhetorical style: If Jonah, who was disobedient himself, is so affected by the fate of a plant that he not only didn't create but didn't even grow, *how much more* is God concerned about the creatures that he has made and nurtured, both human and animal, and *how much more* will he turn evil away from them, even when they do not deserve his mercy?

Like the story of the prodigal son and his older brother, like the story of the laborers in the vineyard, this story can be read from two different points of view at any time. We play both the parts at different times in our lives. Sometimes we are Jonah: we can't stand to see people forgiven and reinstated when they haven't worked as hard or been as good as we have. And

---

1. It can be found in *Deliverance to the Captives,* a collection of Barth's warmly approachable, profoundly biblical sermons, which should be better known (New York: Harper & Row [Ministers Paperback Library], 1978), p. 38.

sometimes we are the people of Nineveh, pitiful in our ignorance and stupidity, not knowing our right hand from our left.

I have played both these parts in one day, even in one hour. For instance, I might be meeting with a person whose self-centered behavior is annoying to me, for whom I feel little compassion — and then I remember
what God said to Jonah. Later on that very day or hour, I catch myself in
some egregious mistake or rebellious act, and I know I am like the people of
Nineveh, not knowing my right hand from my left. Then I am filled with
shame for myself and gratitude for my Lord, who is as Jonah remembered
him, "a gracious God and merciful, slow to anger and abounding in steadfast love, repenting of the evil" (Ps. 103:8) that he had every right to bring
down upon my head.

Which of these categories do you think we as a congregation belong in?
Are we the elect, the righteous, the commendable, the exemplary? Or are
we like the people of Nineveh, not knowing our right hand from our left?
Where shall we stand as a people when we come before the Lord with our
prayers and with our lives? My sense of our congregation at the present time
is that we feel rather more like the Ninevites. Isn't it comforting beyond all
expectation to know that the Lord had mercy upon the people of Nineveh?

There is a prayer in the book of Daniel that places all of this in perfect
perspective. It is a prayer uttered by Daniel not as an individual, but as
spokesman for the whole people of God. It is one of the most important
prayers in the Bible; in fact, it has been called the *Kyrie* of the Old Testament. Like any confession of sin, it may sound very negative at first, but it is
actually a very comforting and encouraging prayer when it is understood in
the context of which we speak tonight. As the conclusion to this sermon,
and as a corporate act of worship, I invite you to join me in this prayer of repentance and trust and above all of hope, as a congregation, as a people in
need of God's guiding, directing, and saving hand. I invite you to join with
me by kneeling as I read the prayer of Daniel on behalf of all of us Ninevites:

"O Lord . . . we have sinned and done wrong . . . and rebelled, turning
aside from thy commandments. . . . To thee, O Lord, belongs righteousness, but to us confusion of face . . . because we have sinned
against thee. To the Lord our God belong mercy and forgiveness, because we have rebelled against him. . . .

"Now therefore, O our God, hearken to the prayer of thy servant
and to his supplications, and for thine own sake, O Lord, cause thy
face to shine upon thy sanctuary. . . . We do not present our supplica-

tions before thee on the ground of our righteousness, but on the ground of thy great mercy. . . . ⟩

"O Lord, hear;
O Lord, forgive;
O Lord, listen and act;
For thy own sake, O Lord, do not delay,
    for thy city and thy people are called by thy name." (Dan. 9:3-19)

AMEN.

# The God of Small Things:
## St. Bede and the Evangelical Faith

---

*The Feast Day of the Venerable Bede 2005*          Zechariah 4:1-10

*This sermon was preached for the institution of the Reverend Douglas Holmes as rector of Grace Church, Camden, South Carolina.*

..................

UP WHERE I live in New York, there has been a good deal of conversation this week about a huge front-page article in Sunday's *New York Times* about evangelical Christian groups infiltrating Ivy League campuses. National Public Radio gave this subject a full hour on Monday. The interviewer was trying to be impartial, but you could feel the disdain oozing out of her voice. The media and the culture in general have made it a rule that there is a sharp division between the so-called evangelical churches and the so-called mainline churches (the traditional Protestant denominations). This idea of a clear-cut division between evangelical churches and liberal mainline churches is doing a great deal of damage to the Church of Christ. So this evening, let's reflect together on the meaning of evangelical faith in the context of a new ministry here at your "mainline" Episcopal Church.

An annoying aspect of the current debate is that few seem to be aware that *all* of the Protestant mainline churches were more or less evangelical at one time. It all depends on how you define *evangelical,* of course. The word used to refer to the solidly Protestant theology of such people as George

Herbert, an Anglican, and Martin Luther, whose hymns we are singing to-night — one by Luther and *two* by Herbert — not to mention the hymns of Charles Wesley, which are loved the world over. The theology of these hymns is solidly based in the Reformation, and before that in the theology of St. Augustine and St. Paul. The Prayer Book that all of us "over-sixties" grew up with in the Episcopal Church was, in this sense, thoroughly evangelical. Think, for instance, of the words of Thomas Cranmer from the Communion service, where we throw ourselves upon the mercy of God, who is "not weighing our merits, but pardoning our offenses." That is pure evangelical theology!

Evangelical theology means a primary emphasis on the grace of God. It means a high degree of reverence for the Scripture (which is not the same thing as fundamentalism). It also means classical Christology, the confession of the ancient church that Jesus Christ our Lord is the incarnate Second Person of the Blessed Trinity, the glory of which we celebrated this past Trinity Sunday. Evangelical theology means an emphasis on the victorious work of Christ on the Cross in the overcoming of Sin and Death. And it means a very high concept of the ministry of the Word of God. Preaching, in the Reformation, was fired by the biblical promise that the Lord speaks through human beings. There has never been a greater evangelical preacher in the English language than the Anglican John Donne, who was Dean of St. Paul's in London, and that's about as "mainline" as you can get.[1]

Well, there is no denying that evangelical theology in the mainlines has taken a lot of hits in the twentieth and twenty-first centuries, and a good many of those hits have come from *within* the church. But that is no reason to acquiesce in the idea that evangelical commitments have no place in the Episcopal Church. When you have Anglican liturgy and evangelical preaching together at the same time, you've got the closest thing to ecclesiastical perfection that we're going to see this side of the Last Trumpet.

But we don't have to restrict this subject to Protestantism. Let's take this history back further. Today is the feast day of the Venerable Bede. When I was a young person studying English history, the very name of the Venerable Bede made me giggle. It sounded like a person as far away in time and as lacking in seriousness as Fred Flintstone. However, St. Bede, far from being a joke, was an extraordinary man of vast intellectual capacities who dominated the scholarly world of his time not only in England but also on

---

1. Who got the idea that the Methodists were "mainline" and not "evangelical"? One hates to think what the nineteenth-century Methodists would think about that.

the continent.[2] He was curious about everything, including science and mathematics, yet he spoke and wrote about our Lord and the Scriptures with a passion that any evangelical today would recognize.[3]

One of the many, many books that Bede wrote was a biography of St. Cuthbert which is still considered reliable today. Cuthbert was a greatly beloved bishop when Bede was a young man. "His holiness [and] learning . . . his care for people *and his fervent preaching* were already legendary in his lifetime."[4] Bede writes of Cuthbert's evangelistic passion to bring "the word of salvation" (Bede's phrase) to the people of Northumbria.[5] The words *evangelical* and *evangelism,* as we all know, come from the Greek word *evangel,* meaning "good news." Today, the eagerness of American "evangelicals" to spread the "word of salvation" is regarded with suspicion, but in the time of St. Cuthbert and St. Bede, zeal for evangelism was the hallmark of a true Christian.

Let's turn now to a word of salvation from the fourth chapter of the book of the prophet Zechariah which you heard read a few minutes ago. I hope you noticed a primary verse as it went by: "Not by might, nor by power, but by my Spirit, says the Lord" (4:6). This wonderful utterance has

---

2. A German scholar has called Bede "The Father of the Middle Ages."

3. More about Bede: His reputation in modern times rests upon the excellence of his *Historia Ecclesiastica Gentis Anglorum* ("Ecclesiastical History of the English People"), completed in A.D. 731. He worked like a modern historian by collecting materials from reliable sources, carefully identifying them, and meticulously separating facts from legendary material and hearsay. In Dante's *Paradiso* ("Paradise"), the Venerable Bede is found in the Circle of Twelve Lights (Canto X), the Doctors and Teachers of the Church, along with Thomas Aquinas and others.

4. "Guide to Durham Cathedral," text by Michael Sadgrove, Dean of the Cathedral (Norwich: Jarrold Publishing, 2004).

5. A pectoral cross and a Gospel book were buried in Cuthbert's coffin when he died in A.D. 687, and we can still see these amazing objects today. The oddly proportioned cross is in the Treasury of St. Cuthbert at Durham Cathedral, and the Gospel book is in the British Museum. A recent scholarly paper about Cuthbert and Bede points out that these two articles were "particularly apt, not only in signifying Cuthbert's role as bishop and *as teacher and preacher,* but also *as the ultimate symbols of orthodox faith*" (Michelle P. Brown, "In the Beginning Was the Word: Books and Faith in the Age of Bede," The Jarrow Lecture 2000 [Newcastle-upon-Tyne: J. & P. Bealls Ltd., 2000]; emphasis added). We might equally well say "evangelical faith." Brown's imaginative lecture ends with these stirring words: "The apostolic mission [of the one, holy, catholic and apostolic church] had indeed reached and embraced the far ends of the earth. The material and literary culture of these extremities [Jarrow and Lindisfarne in Northumbria] proclaims that they were no provincial outpost, but a vibrant, integrated part of that universal, eternal communion. The manifestation of Christ Incarnate and the portal to divine revelation which is the Lindisfarne Gospels [the famous illuminated manuscript from Cuthbert's monastery] was, and is, open to all."

long been recognized as a central text of Scripture. It is an evangelical text, because it places the emphasis not on human initiative, but on the *divine* initiative, the active working of *God*.

It's more significant when you know the context. When the Babylonians conquered Israel (Judah) and destroyed the famous Temple of Solomon, the Hebrew people were forced out of their homes into exile in a strange land. This caused the greatest crisis in the history of Israel. It was not just a social, political, and psychological crisis; it was a "theological emergency."[6] Remember, these were the chosen people. God had bound himself to them as their covenant partner for all time — or so they had thought. With the razing of the Temple and the forced deportation of the people to the land of the Babylonian gods, it seemed that the very existence of God's covenant had been permanently undermined.

After two generations of humiliation in the great capital of Mesopotamia, the people of Israel were permitted to straggle back into the Promised Land. There was nothing remaining there to raise their spirits. The legendary days of David and Solomon were gone forever. Meager buildings, poor agriculture, and a depleted population were all that remained. There were no signs of a return to greatness. In the prophet Zechariah's words, the return was, at best, "a day of small things." The leaders were not men of stature. The name of Zerubbabel, who is featured in our text, is hardly one to ring down the ages, even if we could pronounce it. And yet . . . and yet. The prophet brings this word from the Lord: "Whoever has despised the day of small things shall rejoice, and shall see the plummet in the hand of Zerubbabel" (4:10). Now Zerubbabel was an extremely insignificant person, even though he was the governor of Judea [Judah]. It wasn't like being the governor of South Carolina, not even in the years just after the Civil War. The defeated American South at its lowest ebb was not as low as Judea after the Babylonian exile. Yet God has destined his servant to rebuild the Temple. The image is that of Zerubbabel standing over the construction site with a plumb line in his hand, preparing to lay the cornerstone for the new house of worship. It seemed a feeble undertaking, "a day of small things," but the promise of God is the foundation upon which it will be built. Listen again to our great text:

> "This is the word of the Lord to Zerubbabel: Not by might, nor by power, but by my Spirit, says the Lord of hosts."

6. I have borrowed this phrase from the eminent Old Testament scholar John Bright.

If you go to Northumbria, in England, you can still see St. Bede's Anglo-Saxon church at Jarrow, built in the year A.D. 681. Talk about small things! This is the humblest little building you can imagine, put together out of stones left over from the Roman occupation, utterly unornamented and plain. It was a long way from the isolated northeast coast of England to the centers of civilization at Rome and Constantinople, yet a great enterprise was going forward at Jarrow in the power of the gospel of Jesus Christ. Fifteen miles away, four hundred years later in the years 1093-1133, there rose on a promontory above the River Wear one of the greatest cathedrals in Christendom, the Durham Cathedral, where the pilgrim of today who knows church history will stand awestruck before the tombs of St. Cuthbert and St. Bede, both of them buried in that magnificent edifice. Who, looking upon the minuscule stone church at Jarrow, could have imagined such a thing?

> "Whoever has despised the day of small things shall rejoice, and shall see the plummet in the hand of [the builder — but] this is the word of the Lord to [the builder]: not by might, nor by power, but *by my Spirit, says the Lord.*"

Now we shouldn't be overly romantic about cathedrals. The seat of the Bishops of Durham was not always a model of the Christian simplicity and charity that distinguished Cuthbert and Bede. Durham became a center of political and military power as well, not all of it edifying.[7] But one of the great watchwords of the Reformation was *semper reformanda,* always being reformed.[8] There is never a time when the church can stop confessing its sins. Churches — whether large or small — can be overtaken by pride, greed, and lust for power in a heartbeat. The church must always, every day, seek the face of God and ask for a new beginning. But the promise of God to the church is unconditional and unbroken. Listen to this, from tonight's Epistle reading — but be sure to hear it not as a *command,* but as a *promise:*

> We are to grow up in every way into him who is the head, into Christ, from whom the whole body, joined and knit together by ev-

7. Sir Walter Scott famously called the cathedral "half house of God, half castle 'gainst the Scot."

8. There are some things that Latin does better than English. My Latin experts tell me that the Latin *reformanda* is a future passive participle, and the "a" at the end of *reformanda* implies "all things." Therefore, the meaning is that all things are to be continually reformed. The passive voice implies an Actor who keeps this constant reformation in motion.

ery joint with which it is supplied, when each part is working properly, makes bodily growth and upbuilds itself in love. (Eph. 4:15-16)

That is the Church of Christ. It is founded on Christ himself, the cornerstone; therefore it cannot fail. The God of small things will build great things, not because *Christians* are great but because *God* is great. He is "not weighing our merits, but pardoning our offenses."

You have a lovely building here. But my quite extensive travels among the various lovely church buildings of this country teach me that building the church today does not mean building more buildings. We already have a lot of buildings. All over the British Isles there are empty church buildings — redundant churches, they call them (a dreadful term). They have become community centers, art galleries, private residences, even gas stations. Here in America we have to spend a great deal of money taking care of the buildings we already have. Building the church today means something more than buildings. It means building up the family of God, the communion of saints, the Body of Christ.

Lots of rectors and pastors seem to think that their calling is to have capital fund campaigns. For all I know, maybe you will have to have one too, for maintenance or growth or something. But what the church really needs, and what you have in Doug Holmes, is a leader like Zerubbabel — standing up tall like a Rockwell Kent drawing with a plumb line in his hand, getting ready to lay the cornerstone, not of a new *building*, but of a new *ministry*. That may not sound very glamorous. In this day and age we are accustomed to seeing our heroes with laser guns, not plumb lines. But if we believe what the Lord has promised, the *true* building of an *eternal* future is not by capital campaigns, nor by muscle, nor by the vainglorious exercise of human power and self-aggrandizement, *but by my Spirit, says the Lord.*

The best kind of evangelical is theologically grounded in the Scriptures, deeply rooted in historic Christianity, generously liberal in heart and mind.[9] I have never seen your new rector when he was not telling the story

---

9. The NPR interviewer last Monday kept asking why the evangelical churches are outperforming the mainline Protestant churches. All sorts of sociological reasons were given for these trends, from the GI Bill to the aging boomers to the Internet to stuff that I can't even remember, because it was all completely beside the point. What was never said but needed to be said was that the mainline Protestant churches began to lose ground when they started turning away from their biblical, evangelical roots. It can't be demonstrated that this turn was the *cause*, but it most certainly happened *coincident with* the decline.

It is said — and polls have been backing this up for years — that today's young people are not

of our Lord, tending the church, fighting for the right thing — every day, no matter what the discouragements. You are going to be built up by the Spirit here at Grace Church. I can sense it in the way Doug tells me you have welcomed him. You are responding, whether you recognize it yet or not, to a genuine evangelical of the sort that was not created yesterday at the non-denominational megachurch. I am not saying those congregations are not genuine, but the sort of evangelical that we are talking about here tonight is grounded in the tradition that produced the Nicene Creed almost two thousand years ago. God has determined the future of the church. No set-back can halt God's purpose — no obstacle can block it; no opposition can defeat it. *Not by might, nor by power, but by my Spirit, says the Lord of hosts.*

I close by evoking the great hope of St. Bede, in words written by him in his commentary on the book of Revelation, words that appear over his tomb in Durham Cathedral:

Christ is the morning star, who when the night of this world is past, brings to his saints the promise of the light of life and opens everlasting day.

AMEN.

---

interested in orthodox faith, but prefer to pick and choose their own religious beliefs. This is given as a reason for church decline. It could equally well be argued that if the churches had done a better job of presenting the apostolic faith, young people would not be cast adrift to invent their own "spiritual journeys." The remarkable success of the Church of the Redeemer in New York City would support this view.

# The Bottom of the Night

---

*November 14, 2010*        Malachi 3:2-3; 4:1-3; 1 Thessalonians 3:12-13

Poets, at their best, are our truth-tellers. W. H. Auden and W. B. Yeats were two of the greatest. Auden wrote a poem in memory of Yeats. Here are two lines of it:

> Follow, poet, follow right
> To the bottom of the night.

This is the time in the Christian calendar, just before Advent, that takes us to "the bottom of the night." After All Saints' Day, the lectionary readings take a turn toward what is called the Last Things, and we begin that relentless Advent search into the heart of the human predicament which is announced by John the Baptist.

The next-to-last Sunday in the church year brings biblical readings about crisis and judgment. The so-called Synoptic Apocalypse is always read — the chapters in Matthew, Mark, and Luke where Jesus announces the coming judgment of God. It's even in the last verse of today's Psalm: "In righteousness shall God judge the world." And yet the churches today, following the lead of our feel-good culture, have turned away from the theme of judgment. We are determined not to be one of those backwoods hellfire-and-damnation churches. Those kinds of sermons did exist in the nineteenth and early twentieth centuries, but it's been a long, long time since we've heard one anywhere near an Episcopal church.

The main character in Albert Camus's novel *The Fall* says, "Above all,

[ 415 ]

the question is to elude judgment. . . . Each of us insists on being innocent at all costs, even if he has to accuse the whole human race and heaven itself. . . . The essential thing is that [we] should be innocent. . . ."[1] (It's both ironic and significant that his name is Jean-Baptiste Clamence — John the Baptist crying out.)

The book of Malachi is the last book of the Christian Old Testament. The Hebrew Scriptures are arranged differently; they end with the Wisdom writings, whereas our Old Testament ends with the Prophets. That's important. The Bible of the Christian church looks forward to a consummation yet to come. The last section of Malachi is appointed to be read at the end of the church year. Today's reading begins by announcing that all the arrogant and all the evildoers will be burned up on Judgment Day.

Ah, but we don't believe that, do we? That's too primitive for us in our higher stage of enlightenment. Mind you, it's all right for our drones and missiles and Special Ops forces to eliminate evildoers, but we don't believe that *God* is going to burn anybody up. How barbaric would *that* be! The only people who believe *that* are out there somewhere on the fundamentalist right wing!

Now it's quite true that there is a metaphorical element in the Bible. Much of it is not to be taken literally. "Burned up" is an image — an exceptionally powerful image — conveying the power of God to destroy. In the Last Day, God will judge and finally destroy evil. That's the promise of the seven-week season that includes Advent and its preceding Sundays. Advent is not really the season of preparation for Christmas. Properly understood, Advent is the season of the *Second* Coming of Christ.

In Luke's version of the Synoptic Apocalypse, Jesus says:

> "There will be signs in sun and moon and stars, and upon the earth distress of nations . . . , men fainting with fear and with foreboding of what is coming on the world; for the powers of the heavens will be shaken." (Luke 21:25-26)

This doesn't exclude anybody. *All human beings* will be filled "with foreboding of what is coming on the world." There isn't anyone who will be unaffected by the judgment of God. The scene of the Last Judgment in Matthew 25:32 tells us: "Before the Judge will be gathered all the peoples." This refers not only to all the national and ethnic groups, but to all kinds of

1. Albert Camus, *The Fall* (New York: Alfred A. Knopf, 1956), p. 76.

people *within* those groups. The CEOs of the biggest corporations and the lowest workers cutting up chickens will be there. The captains and the kings and the nameless Mexicans stumbling illegally across the border deserts will be there. The educated and the illiterate, the oppressed and the oppressors, the judges and those whom they judge — all will be there. You will be there, and I will be there. And then, as the parable continues, "[The Lord] will separate them one from another as a shepherd separates the sheep from the goats" (Matt. 25:32).

Now it's very interesting that although we are told that modern Christians don't believe in the Last Judgment anymore, no one objects when a judge in a courtroom hands down a judgment. We *believe* in *that* kind of judgment — as long as it's a judgment on someone else, someone who deserves it. So in our minds we are already dividing the righteous from the unrighteous, with ourselves — of course — on the side of the righteous.

But isn't that a rather perilous place to be? How much effort does it take to remain on the right side of that balance sheet? And by what criteria, and by whom, will this determination be made?

I'm going to be referring now to the recent case in Cheshire, Connecticut, where the wife and two daughters of a local doctor were horribly abused and then burned to death in their own home. I need to say, though, that although many Christians believe that the death penalty is wrong and should never be used in any case, that is not the theme of this particular sermon. I want to focus somewhere else.

The twelve jurors in the trial (just concluded) had to descend into the bottom of the night. They had to look at photos and listen to testimony that most people would never want to see or hear. When it was over, Dr. William A. Petit said a remarkable thing about the sentencing of the murderer of his wife and daughters. He said, "This is a verdict for justice, [but] the defendant faces far more serious punishment from the Lord than he can ever face from mankind." This expresses something important — a sense that human justice is never adequate. The jury reached agreement, but the foreman of the jury said, "No one is happy. Nothing is better. Nothing is solved."[2] That's why the doctor was reaching for the idea that there is *another judgment beyond human judgment.*

So there are several major problems here. First, are we to believe in the

---

2. William Glaberson, "For Jurors, a Harrowing Trial, but Unity on the Proper Punishment," *The New York Times,* 9 November 2010. All the quotations from the trial are from this article.

divine judgment, or not? A second problem is the inadequacy of human justice. But the most radical problem of all is raised by the reading from the prophet Malachi. "The day comes, burning like an oven, when all the arrogant and all evildoers will be stubble; the day that comes shall burn them up, says the Lord of hosts." Where does this business about being burnt up begin and where does it end? Who exactly are the arrogant and the evildoers? Malachi goes on:

> "But for you who fear my name the sun of righteousness shall rise, with healing in its wings. . . . And you shall tread down the wicked, for they will be ashes under the soles of your feet, on the day when I act, says the Lord of hosts." (4:1-3)

Hey, that sounds pretty good. Isn't that what we want? Don't we want the Taliban and Osama bin Laden and the suicide bombers to be ashes under the feet of our troops? Don't we want child rapists and murderers to be wiped off the face of the earth? *That* would serve the cause of judgment.[3]

But what about the ordinary garden-variety sinner, the man who cheats on his income tax, the woman who employs and underpays the illegal immigrant, the people who give only a pittance to charity and never give a thought to the poor? What about the unfaithful wife, the neglectful father, the cheating student, the doping ballplayer, the lying politician? What about all the rest of us who by our mere existence are polluting the environment and supporting the exploitation of the planet?

Whenever we are sure that we are among the righteous, we immediately find ourselves among the arrogant. The signs of Advent are humility and repentance in the face of pervasive and indiscriminate sin. Repentance, however, does not come easily to human beings. It's not human nature. As Jean-Baptiste says, "Each of us insists on being innocent at all costs, even if he has to accuse the whole human race and heaven itself. . . . Above all, the question is to elude judgment." The distinctive thing about Advent is that it thrusts the subject of judgment in our faces.

There are two common ways of dealing with the idea of judgment within the church. One is to say there won't be a divine judgment because

---

3. I recognize that there is some confusion here. First I suggest that we don't want to think of God as a Judge burning up people. Then, here, I suggest that we would be OK with God burning up terrorists and child rapists. But then, our thinking on these matters tends to be somewhat irrational.

God loves, forgives, includes, welcomes, and embraces everybody. The other way is to assume that only the undeserving bad guys will be judged, while the deserving rest of us will get a pass. But here is the great truth of the matter: Only God knows who deserves what.

Now *that* is *truly* scary. Only God knows the hit-and-run driver. Only God knows the extent of financial misconduct. Only God knows the secrets of a marriage. Only God knows the times that we have turned away from someone who needed us. Only God knows who has "rebelled against his holy laws." We are very good at covering up these things even from ourselves because "the essential thing is that [we] should be innocent . . . [and] escape judgment." At this time of year, the gospel calls us to abandon our pretensions to being on the right side of the divine judgment and to ponder the possibility that we and all our favorite people might be on the wrong side. That's why we have a general confession, a prayer of repentance that we all say *together,* as if we were all on the same level. When I was a child, we all said, in the general confession, that we were *all* miserable offenders and there was no health in us. Now *that's* radical leveling! We don't say those things anymore, but we've given up a lot in the process. We've given up the freedom that comes with acknowledging that we are all in this Last Judgment thing together.

If we are all in it together, then what is our hope? How can we live without being continually at work to prove to ourselves that we are among the righteous, not among those who are going to be trampled underfoot? Our hope is expressed by St Paul in the last two verses of the reading from 1 Thessalonians:

> May the Lord make you increase and abound in love to one another and to all human beings . . . , so that he may establish your hearts blameless in holiness before our God and Father, at the coming of our Lord Jesus with all his saints. (3:12-13)

Everything depends on how we read this. If we read it as an exhortation to abound in love and to be blameless in holiness, then your goose and my goose are cooked. The Scripture never says, "Just do your best." It never says, "Try to do it within reason." It never says, "Do it up to a point."[5] It says, "Be

---

4. From the Book of Common Prayer.

5. Actually, Paul does say something along these lines in Romans 12:18, but it is heavily qualified by its theocentric trajectory.

ye perfect, as your father in heaven is perfect" (Matt. 5:48). Doesn't that leave us without a place to stand?

In an earlier passage, Malachi states it flatly: "Who may abide the day of his coming, and who shall stand when he appears?" (3:2). The astounding answer to that question is that we are already being prepared to stand before the Judge at the last day by the action of God himself, working in us by the power of the Holy Spirit. Paul is able to express confidence in his congregation — in all their manifold imperfection — not because they are innocent, not because they have never done anything deserving judgment, but because *the Lord is at work* in them. The Lord is at work establishing their hearts "blameless in holiness" at the coming of the Lord Jesus with all the saints. And so the righteous Judge is *the one who is preparing us* to stand *before himself*. Malachi again: the Lord will "purify the sons of Eli." The sons of Eli — that is, the priests of Israel — had become so corrupt that they fully deserved to be trampled underfoot. But that's not going to be their destiny. Remember this the next time you hear Handel's *Messiah:*

> He will purify the sons of Levi and refine them like gold and silver,
> that they may offer unto the Lord an offering of righteousness. (3:3)

One of the jurors in the Cheshire trial was a woman named Diane Keim. During the worst days in the jury box, listening to the gruesome details of the girls' deaths, she said, "I just wanted to hold the girls. I wanted to take whatever they experienced before they died and take it away. *But it wasn't in my power.*"

No. Human beings do not have the power to undo evil. Only God has that power. The promise of the divine judgment is that evil and death will be undone by the only power greater than they — the power of Almighty God. And that means that all the evil within our own hearts, our own guilty hearts, will be undone.

Advent acknowledges that human life is a time of waiting. When we look around us, evil often seems triumphant, and God seems absent. But Advent promises that God will come. The Old Testament ends with the astonishing words of the Lord through the prophet Malachi:

> "Behold, I will send you Elijah the prophet before the great and terrible day of the Lord comes. And he will turn the hearts of parents to their children and the hearts of children to their parents, lest I come and smite the land with a curse." (4:5-6)

The prophet Elijah, you see, will come again in the person of John the Baptist. He will announce the coming of the great and terrible day of the Lord, the day that could have been a curse upon every single one of us but, instead, will be a new day of universal reconciliation that cannot be achieved by human means. Malachi's image of the Day of God is that of broken families brought together, a thing impossible for human beings — but all things are possible with God. May he establish your hearts blameless in holiness before our God and Father, at the coming of our Lord Jesus with all his saints.

AMEN.